EXPANDING TONAL AWARENESS

*A Musical Exploration of the Evolution of Consciousness
—From Ancient Tone Systems to New Tonalities—
Guided by the Monochord*

Heiner Ruland

Translated by John F. Logan

RUDOLF STEINER PRESS

First published in Great Britain in 1992 by Rudolf Steiner Press,
Hillside House, The Square
Forest Row, RH18 5ES

Reprinted 2014

E-mail: office@rudolfsteinerpress.com

www.rudolfsteinerpress.com

© Verlag die Pforte 1981
This translation © Rudolf Steiner Press 1992

Originally published under the title *Ein Weg zur Erwiterung des Tonerlebens* by Verlag die Pforte, Basel, in 1981

A catalogue record for this book is available from the British Library

ISBN 978 1 85584 395 0

Cover by Morgan Creative
Typeset by Emset, London
Printed and bound in the UK by 4edge Limited, Essex

For Renate, Erdmute and Elmar

CONTENTS

Appendices

Foreword

This book began as a series of letters to a group of young people. It was written by a musician for musicians. I only look to the domain of musicology when it can help clarify matters in which the artistic instinct of a contemporary musician would be insufficient on its own. For I am not in the least interested in accumulating scientific facts in support of some thesis. I am interested in tracking down those qualities of musical experience that show promise of deepening today's musical consciousness and of widening its horizon—both when its casts an eye back into the past and when it strives to anticipate the future.

Sometimes my efforts have been misunderstood, and now and again I find that among my colleagues I have acquired the reputation of being a musical theorist. But why must someone be classified as a window cleaner just because he cleans his window from time to time, the better to see out? The cleaning is not what satisfies him. He is interested in the view and harbors no secret ambition to have the cleanest window.

The reader will only encounter discussions of existing theories when this is necessary to clear the way for practical musical exercises. 'Ear training' in today's usual sense of the words is not, however, what is intended here. I want to explore the wakeful inner experience that begins where external hearing ceases. After practicing in this way for a while, you will discover that in the process your external hearing also has acquired an extraordinarily heightened capacity for differentiation. What is really musical can only reveal itself when tone and interval are taken up into an inner experience, a conscious soul experience. This book is concerned with *musical* tone, not just tone. Whether it is a matter of tone relationships, tonal order, or the way certain tones build a scale, the most important question is to find the tones' specific, felt quality—the specific inner location where they can be experienced.

By rights, a study of music's rhythmic, temporal side belongs with the present study. But the inner investigation of harmonic-melodic tonal relationships yielded such a rich harvest that it was necessary to restrict the present work to that field. Otherwise it would not have been possible to arrive at a well-rounded or fruitful picture of the nature of musical tone. Rhythm is a part of musical tone, just as a person's characteristic arm and hand movements are a part of them. Nevertheless, it is justified to dwell on the still countenance when seeking the inner nature of a person—and justified to dwell on the intervalic relationships, the scales, the tonal systems.

Anyone who pursues the path outlined here, following along with active musical practicing, soon realizes that depths are revealed which cannot be expressed adequately in words. On such a path it would be inartistic and unmusical to give more than directed hints. I myself find that certain of the things touched on in this book are at the limits of what can be described sensibly.

It is essential that the reader who wants to follow this path should really make use of the scale of musical-mathematical proportions included with this book. Therefore, a monochord must be acquired or built, be it ever so primitive. For my own use I still have nothing more elaborate than a homemade monochord that is constructed from a single solid board and a length of normal household wire. This instrument fulfils its purpose well enough to have been used at an international musicological congress. A monochord must be used if one is to free oneself from today's rigid piano intonation and become acquainted with more differentiated tonal orders.

As a composer, the central impulse behind my efforts always has been the search for new artistic foundation for contemporary music. Originally I had no intention of investigating ancient tone systems. At a time when I was in the process of practicing hearing intervals that were new to me, I used a monochord to build tone systems that contained nothing but octaves and natural sevenths 7/4, or nothing but octaves and natural sixths 13/8. In this way I stumbled on the *Slendro* system, which is built on natural sevenths, and on the ancient Persian system*

---

* I have written about the rhythmic tendencies of particular scales and interval epochs in my book *Die Neugeburt der Musik aus dem Wesen des Menschen.* (*The rebirth of Music out of the Nature of the Human Being.* Freiburg im Breisgau, 1987. Not Translated).

built on sixths. I was astonished to discover that such tone systems existed in very ancient times—leading us back beyond ancient Persian and Indian cultures to Atlantis. I also was astonished when I first discovered how the results of comparative musicology support Rudolf Steiner's description of how the development of modes of consciousness based on certain intervals relates to the development of particular cultural epochs.[1] Thus did my studies teach me to see the ancient tone systems as priceless, spiritually alive etudes—etudes composed by a developing humanity, and essential study material for the musician in the search for a new, expanded experience of musical intervals.

Some readers may find themselves unsympathetic toward Rudolf Steiner's description of humanity's musical development. Other readers' knowledge of the researches of comparative musicology may incline them to judge the present view of non-European tonal systems as impossibly over-simplified. If you are one of these, I make the following request: for the time being (N.B. "for the time being"!) set the scientist in yourself to one side, ignore all reality, and start by regarding the present account of the development of tone systems as pure utopianism. To begin with, read this as a utopian musical novel. Immerse yourself in it and first judge it only on its own terms. Judge whether the picture it gives of musical development makes artistic sense, whether it is 'symphonically' formed, whether it embodies its own law and can stand artistically without the help of external, inorganic supports. Then you can discover that this 'work of art' was not created by the present author or by any other. For what person created the natural seventh? No one. Nor did anyone create the sixth (13/8) that every fundamental tone produces. Nor did anyone endow these intervals with their specific powers to form scales and tone systems. Once this 'artwork' has been experienced through real musical listening and real music-making—not just theoretically—*then* go back to science. Go back wholeheartedly and see whether its results do not harmonize with what is described here.

Although the author is simply a musician, not a professional comparative musicologist, this is the path he has tried to follow. He has tried, with the means at his disposal, to balance musical practice and listening with careful scientific work. As a result, he discovered that there are clear connections between his artistic discoveries and the researches of the comparative musicologists. The results of this research are described in two papers. The first of these, "On the tonality of an American Indian melody," ("Zur Tonalitaet einer Indianermelodie"), was published by Professor Fritz Bose in the *Jahrbuch fuer musikalische Volks-und Voelkerskunde*, which he edited. It was again Fritz Bose who encouraged the writing of the second paper, "On the genealogy of the gipsy scale and halftone pentatonic" ("Zur Genealogie der Zigeunerskala und Halbtonpentatonik"), for which he also gave critical advice. This article was to have appeared in the eighth volume of his journal. I want to take this opportunity to express my thanks to this undogmatic musicologist who was so open to new points of view. Unfortunately, the second article never was published, although Bose believed it to be the more scientifically convincing of the two and found that it threw light on the general development of music from the standpoint of comparative musicology. When Bose died in 1975, the article had been included in the manuscript for Volume VIII, which was complete and ready for the printer. But Bose's successors withdrew the article without bothering to inform its author. For this reason, certain technical, scientific facts which should long since have been publically available are not yet generally accessible to support the more artistically oriented description of the development of tone systems given in the present book.

As I wrote this foreward, news of the death of Dr. Hans Erhard Lauer reached me. His many wide-ranging, philosophical and anthroposophical writings include a small book called *The Development of Music Though Changing Tone Systems* (*Die Entwicklung der Musik im Wandel der Tonsysteme*). In this little book (p. 18 ff.), Lauer followed the lead given by Rudolf Steiner in his descriptions of musical development. He thus became the first person to connect the interval of the sixth with ancient Persian culture. He did not speak of the natural sixth 13/8, however, and Steiner himself never said outright that the sixth was the dominant interval of ancient Persia. Ernst Bindel, in his book, *The Numerical Foundations of Music* (*Die Zahlengrundlagen der Musik*, Vol.II, p. 115 ff.), investigated the intervalic qualities of seven, eleven and thirteen. Among other things, he built cycles of the intervals produced by 7/4, 11/8 and 13/8. But he proceeded purely mathematically, without drawing any connection between what he discovered, e.g. as a pure mathematical order in 13/8, and a particular stage in the development of human consciousness and interval awareness. Only in the case of the natural seventh does he voice suspicion of a connection with Atlantis. I owe my thanks to both of these writers for their work helped me along the path which led, in 1962, to my discovery of ancient tone systems.

Jean Louis Gaensburger first brought the numerical-harmonic qualities of seven, eleven and thirteen to my attention in 1959, in Paris. I immediately came under the artistic spell of these when he introduced me to the research of Kathleen Schlesinger.

For another decisive impulse I must thank Professor Hermann Pfrogner. At a time when I was totally immersed in Schlesinger's radial tone world, his book, *The Twelvefold Tonal Order* (*Die Zwoelfordnung der Toene*), convinced me of the musical reality of the cyclic principle. In the following years this made it possible for me to form a clear musical idea of the polarity between cyclic and radial systems. Eventually this led me to composing within the framework of a quartertone system and, in 1966, to my having Franz Lengemann of Fischerhude build me a quartertone clavichord. Ever since I first sought him out personally in 1962, it has been my good fortune to be able to count on the fatherly friendship of Hermann Pfrogner. He has always engaged himself in my musical ideas with great warmth and intensity. Although he by no means always agreed with what I wanted to do, his total spiritual energy and the imposing 'mass' of ideas over which his work as a musical researcher gives him command always were there for me. They always have been at the service of attempts to find the right foundations for a modern renewal of tonality through new harmonic-numerical qualities. Two far-reaching and significant articles were born of his commitment to this search. In "Does diatonic music have a future?" he points especially to the radial, second-oriented element in Bartok's work. ("Hat Diatonik Zukunft?", *Musica*, 1963/64) Other aspects of the search were taken up in "Cosmic consonance and ego consonance" ("All-Konsonanz and Ich-Konsonanz", *Blaetter fuer Anthroposophie*, Feb., 1964). It was he who insistently confronted me with the problems posed by the musical side of Arabism, which I at first was too inclined to see as inconsequential. Without Pfrogner's goading, the chapter on Arabism, which contains material I now regard as indispensible for understanding today's third-based consciousness, surely never would have been written.

For other essential assistance I must thank my music therapy patients at Klinik Oeschelbronn. Certain things, such as aspects of the experience of intervals, never could have become so clear to me without my daily work with my patients or without their cooperation. As a simple musician one is not inclined to wrestle with the nature of the elements of music—at least not with the tenacity and thoroughness required by music therapy. For in therapy music must be made accessible to the most varied sorts of people, many of whom, although actually musical, believe that they are not.

But, above all, it is the work of the great teacher, Rudolf Steiner, that stands behind everything contained in this book, even in those passages where he is not explicitly mentioned. Without this background, an attempt like the present one would not be possible in our day and age. I have tried to proceed, however, without assuming any prior understanding of Steiner's anthroposophical concepts on the part of the reader. Rather I have sought to let them develop from out of the context of the discussion. When the context demands it, I have even used terms that differ from the usual anthroposophical ones. I agree with Rudolf Steiner's conviction that every real musician is already at least a latent Anthroposophist—all they need to do is to make themselves conscious of what the real basis of music is:

> "Music's achievements have brought it to a high point in the whole development
> of human culture. Musicality alone, as we have access to it today, should be enough
> to make it inevitable that a person be an Anthroposophist. But today, music must
> hold its own in such a materialistic age, in which everything else that people
> experience corrupts what is musical."[3]

In this passage, the concept of being 'anthroposophical' can be translated as 'being artistically aware of a spiritual reality that can be sensed both in the depths of the human soul and in the cosmos which surrounds us.'

BASIC CONCEPTS AND
BASIC PHENOMENA

I. MUSICAL TONE

We are walking in the mountains. It is windy. Just as day is turning to twilight we hear a long, drawn-out tone. We stop, concentrating on listening. Could it be the wind breaking against a rock ridge or caught in some mountain cavern? "Would the wind really make such a tone?", we ask ourselves, for it also might be a man's raised voice. An uneasiness seizes us. That could be the cry of a man whose life is in danger. Should we search for him and try to help? Once more we hear the tone, this time more strongly, and then it drops: a melodic step, a fifth. Other tones follow. An alphorn sends it restful melody out into the evening.

The differing attitudes and feelings this experience precipitated in us are worth observing. At first, thinking the tone was caused by the wind, we simply listened intensely, trying to sense how the moving air might make such a sound. We would listen in exactly the same way to running water in order to percieve whether it is a wide, smooth current or a brisk, hurrying little brook or a mountain stream tumbling over rocks. If a wood or metal or stone disk were being beaten, we would listen in the same way to hear whether the material is thick or thin, compact or diffuse, hard or soft, under tension or slack, smooth or rough. In these cases, our sense of hearing enables us to listen our way into solid, fluid and airy substances so that they can reveal their inner condition through tones. Our sense of sight cannot penetrate substance in the same way; in contrast to the sense of hearing, it is arrested by the outer surface.

As for the alphorn, in the first stage of listening to the sounding element, the air, we have not yet perceived a truly musical tone. So long as we hear the tone as the howling of the wind, we have recognized only the timbre layer, or physical sound layer of the tone—taking it to be a natural phenomenon, we regard it with an attitude of observation.

But matters changed immediately when we percieved the speechlike character of the alphorn. The imploring summons, the hollow lament, of the alphorn led us to experience it as the anxiety-laden cry of someone in danger. Without being able to hear—let alone understand—a single word in this cry, it gripped us and took hold of our feelings. The appended thought, that perhaps someone's life is in danger, naturally brings in something further. But prior to the thought we already were experiencing something uncanny. It was hardest to free our feelings from the grip of the cry during those moments when we still had no conception of its source. In this fleeting state (we will not stop now to consider whether this state was before or after the mere listening to the sound-layer) we were most aware of the speechlike quality, or the speech-layer of the tone. At this stage we could not remain the objective observers we were when listening to the tone at the level of mere sound. The experience took place on an entirely different level. The speechlike quality of the alphorn tone could only be experienced as an expression of a conscious, ensouled being, an expression which carried our own soul along with it whether we liked it or not. This is how we experience the cries of joy and pain of ensouled beings, whether man or animal. Even when we hear conceptually understandable words, we still experience expression of soul through the varied ways the words are spoken. With how many speech-nuances—i.e. soul-nuances—can words like "good morning" come to meet us? Happy... oppressed... annoyed... masterful... indifferent... aggressive... loving...

Now, returning to the alphorn tone, we must acknowledge that even though the experience of its speechlike character moves us to strong feelings, still it does not lead us to what is specifically musical in that tone. We could not perceive music until the tone had been joined by another tone a fifth below it and then continued with other tones in a melody. The fact is that the physical or speech-like sound of the alphorn tone we first heard must be reshaped by us inwardly in order for it to become a musical tone. And thus, even at this early point in the discussion, we can already sense that a musical tone—or the musical layer of a tone—can only come into being through a creative act of the human spirit.

The physical sound of the alphorn is what we have to start with. It provides us with the outer occasion for this creativity; it is, so to speak, the lump of clay for Adam's creation which we, the creators, still can coolly observe from a distance. The speech-quality of the tone already is of another substance: we feel it within us as our soul vibrates and breathes in unison with another feeling being. A musically perceived tone involves yet another, completely different, situation. Nothing outward communicates itself to us—neither anything bodily or physical, nor anything of a soul nature. In the case of a musical tone we remain entirely within ourselves. We must dive into the tone, finding ourselves reflected in it, finding ourselves at the same time immersed deep in the sources of our own spiritual being. Then we can experience there the musical nature of the tone, i.e. experience the tone's spiritual correlate or its innermost, spiritual nature. What we find there is more than the outer expression of the state of solid, fluid, or gaseous matter in sound, and is also more than just the expression of a state of soul. To be sure, we experience a musical tone deep within our souls, but it belongs to a realm of the most objective and supreme order—of spiritual order—which is not to be found in the flowing subjective world of our feeling life.

II. SOUND, UTTERANCE AND TONE

Sound is the 'body' of tone. It is the aspect of tone that has to be experienced via the physical sense of hearing. It is what tone reveals of itself to hearing. Every tone communicated from one person to another—from singer or performer to a hearer—must clothe itself in sound. But a tone can resound for us inwardly before we produce it outwardly by singing it or playing it on an instrument. Even when someone sings falsely, the true melody probably still resounds for them inwardly, for otherwise they would not be able to recognize familiar melodies or experience them musically. What such a person is unable to do is translate the true inner representation of living musical tones into sound. They cannot produce the sounds with their voice. They do not know how high or low to reach with their voice to find the musically experienced tones. But they happily recognize the desired tone or sequence of tones as soon as it is sung to them.

Utterance, the speechlike aspect of sound could be called the 'soul' of tone. The physical senses can perceive only physical sound, but within this pure sound perception, my soul can empathize with the nuances of feeling of another soul. If I am forced to experience vanity and hypocrisy in the utterance of a singer, the most superb quality of sound production and most perfect intonation are not enough to rescue my musical experience. On the other hand, how strongly can a simple melody grip us—or perhaps even reveal its true nature for the first time—when we hear it sung by children or by simple people whose reverence allows the uttered tones some good fresh air in which to breathe!

Certainly, in both of the cases just described, the 'spirit' of the tones, i.e. their true musical nature, must have been present. Otherwise there would be no question of music. But in the first case, the musical 'spirit' of the tone was falsified by an utterance whose individual life and individual coloration prevented the musical tone from shining through, whereas in the second case it could shine through in its purity as through clear crystal.

Only a human being can perceive the true musical being of tone. This is because, over and beyond a soul nature, humanity also participates in the spirit. Animals, being only ensouled, can attain only utterance. The quality of utterance of animal sounds is highly differentiated: the birds, whose winged forms have been an emblem of the spirit since the times of ancient myth, come close to making musical utterances, but it never quite becomes music. It is just this "almost" that makes a nightingale's song so tantalizing to a musically sensitive person. The sounds of frogs and crickets are at the extreme other end of the spectrum. They are much closer to the realm of (physical) sound.

The question whether a sound is simply physical sound, or is an utterance, or is musical tone, cannot be answered by a physical-acoustic sound analysis. Information about harmonic and non-harmonic partials, frequency phenomena, and so on, can only give us *indications* as to what kind of sound is encountered, and we should never lose sight of this fact. The ultimate criterion is whether the listener remains at the level of sounds that are conveyed entirely through the physical sense of hearing, or whether he lets himself—can let himself—be lifted beyond this to the soul experience of utterance or to the spiritual experience of music itself. Naturally, a listener can be mistaken, as our initial example of the alphorn showed: the sound which clothes a musical tone can be mistakenly perceived as nothing but physical sound or as utterance. Conversely, an accidentally 'musical' physical sound or utterance can yield a fleeting musical experience. And during the last hundred years people have even shown an extraordinary inclination to encourage a confusion between (physical) sound, utterance and (musical) tone. Ever more exact sound-producing machines have been developed to satisfy the modern desire for experiencing speech or music. The machines imitate the physical vehicle of utterance or music so well that the expectations of our senses are met, even without the direct participation of any ensouled being. No one is expressing himself in the utterance or music. In due course, the immense proliferation of sound machines has made such an unquestioned habit of the confusion between sound, utterance and tone, that this very confusion has become the foundation and first premise of a modern 'art of tone'—of composition. These days this is a stubborn knot to try to untangle.

Two things can lead to confusing physical tone, speech tone and musical tone: either a too-inaccurate and insensitive perception of the physical sound, or else an overhasty judgement as to which of the three is being perceived before what is there to hear has been thoroughly heard. Today's musical culture would be completely transformed if two things were cultivated—sensitivity and awareness of sense perception on the one hand, and, on the other, careful, intuitive judgement of what is heard and felt within this finely differentiated sense experience. Then, for example, none would imagine they could hear a song out of loudspeaker. Inevitably the loudspeaker would be perceived as an electromagnetically driven tympanum that produces an extraordinarily differentiated range of physical sound.

The drawing of clear-cut distinctions between what is purely sound as against the utterance or tone clothed in it would be only one of the results of the cultivation and schooling of this kind of hearing. It would lead to more besides: people would learn to take a further step and feel something utterance-like in the pure sound of a lifeless thing like water or wind—the *transcendent , soul-like aspect* of the elements water and air—just as one quite naturally experiences the immament soul life in the utterance of an animal. Such experiences are by no means unusual among poetic-artistic natures, and among aboriginal people who have not participated in the intellectual Fall of the civilized world, it is simply taken for granted that an object's soul, or 'demon', speaks in the sounds the object makes. This is no mere sign of primitiveness, but rather of a more sensitive perception and a heightened capacity for experience. Nature has only become soulless since we began to allow intellectual concepts to overshadow sensibility of perception.

Further training in this direction would at last lead to our perceiving not just the transcendent soul aspect, but also the *transcendent spiritual* —the transcendent musical, the 'tone-spirit'—in the sound of lifeless things. Here is the dawning of a realization of what Pythagoras and the ancients called the music of spheres, or *musica mundana*—the music in which lives the spirit that created and ordered the universe, right down to the very chemical structure of the smallest material object. Every musical tone reveals something of the immanent spirit and of the spirit immanent in all people. It is this alone that can make a musical tone out of a physical sound. Similarly, if I make this further step, I will begin to experience in each sounding object something of the spirit which created and ordered it, but which no longer can live in the sounds it makes. This spirit dwells above it in a higher sphere as transcendent musical tone.

III. MUSICAL INSTRUMENTS

When an instrument is played, music clothes itself in tones and makes its appearance in the arena of our hearing. We can listen to how physical sound and utterance participate in a quite specific way in each and every tone. Furthermore, the way sound and utterance participate in the musical tone differs characteristically from one instrument to another.

Compared with the other sorts of instruments, the harp-like string instruments that are plucked or struck have least to do with physical sound. When the string is struck, the distinctive timbre of string and instrument body is slightly discernable, but it should only play a slight role. Accordingly, these are the instruments that can present spiritual-musical reality most strongly. Their tensed strings are tuned exactly according to the objective, numerical-harmonic order of this spiritual-harmonic reality. (Later, the objective, numerical-harmonic order will be considered in detail.) It is another story with the percussion instruments, especially the ideophones (chimes, xylophones, lithophones.)[3] With these, the physical properties of the sound are the most pronounced—the timbre of the particular material. The material is only adapted to the numerical-harmonic order up to a certain point. It still is allowed to make its distinctive contribution to the sound.

On the one hand, the individual timbre or sound of matter, on the other, the spiritual, numerical-harmonic order, the comprehension of which we recognize as belonging to the sphere of the human spirit—these mark out a polarity that is crucial when music is played. Indeed, it is only in the field of tension between them that a person can have a living experience of what music is. The one, the numerical-harmonic ordering of the tone, has its source in the musical experience of the human spirit, which participates in the living, spiritual-musical source of things, in the Harmony of the Spheres. The other, the individual timbre of a particular material, reveals the last dying away of the creative Harmony of the Spheres. Matter is the music of the spheres reduced to silence. Sounding music reunites what has fallen asunder— the eternally living and that which is mute and dead.

Musical hearing demands an ever more exact and pure intonation. This indicates that the objective spiritual, the spiritual order originating in the Harmony of the Spheres, strives to be ever more immanent in the physical sound of the tones and to be ever more clearly heard in the musically experienced tones. If we look at the instruments from this point of view, we will see that they are treated differently in this regard.

A much more exact intonation is required of the harp, lyre, zither, harpsichord or piano, than is expected of other instruments. On the one hand, this has to do with these instruments' predetermined, unchangable tone, which makes an impurity especially disturbing. On the other hand, it lies in the nature of these particular instruments to be specially representative of the spiritual Harmony of the Spheres in which the harmonic order of their tones has its origin. Accordingly, the soul-utterance aspect and the sound-timbre aspect tend to be relatively ignored.

With wind instruments one is more tolerant about matters of intonation. They embody more the element of living, ensouled utterance; intonation is left much more to the personal expression of the player. Of course, this can only be said of all wind instruments in a very general way; each particular wind instrument—recorder, flute, oboe, trombone, etc.—has its own characteristic balance between tone and utterance. The human voice is unquestionably the most prominent instrument of ensouled utterance. Perhaps it is consideration for the voice's ability to express the movements of the human soul that makes us especially tolerant in matters of vocal intonation. Singing that achieves the right expressive utterance, but lacks absolutely pure intonation, is preferable by far to a soulless singing with perfect intonation. Obviously, a certain degree of accuracy in the intonation is essential, but measurement with modern electronic instruments has demonstrated how much tolerance there is here.

The bowed string instruments take a middle position between the wind instruments and the instruments related to the harp. They require active participation of hand and ear from beginning to end of tone production. It is a question of whether more emphasis is placed on the purity of the tone or on the ensouling of the tone. On the one hand, there is the clear, crystalline tone of older music, on the other, the 'sobbing' vibrato of the cafe fiddler. The right tone on a string instrument achieves a balance between these two extremes in a fashion appropriate to the piece being played.

Characteristics of the harp family and the wind instruments are brought together in a different fashion by the organ. One could call the organ a sort of 'flute-harp'. It is a wind instrument capable of a rich variety of sounds with utterance-like tone color—from the flute to the reed pipes. And yet, because it has been freed from the human breath and because its tones have a fixed pitch, the organ also has characteristics of the harp family. It therefore demands the greatest purity of intonation.

To summarize: the tone of the wind instruments has more the quality of utterance, of being alive and ensouled, whereas the tone produced by the harp family has more of the tone itself in its objective-spiritual, mathematical-harmonic reality. It is significant that both the organ and the bowed string instruments only began to be developed in and around the first centuries Anno Domini. They share characteristics of both of the other sorts of instrument. With its ebb and flow, the bow of our stringed instruments bestows the movement of breathing on the older string instrument, giving it something typical of all ensouled beings, thus ensouling and subjectivizing its tone. The organ liberates the wind instrument from the breath and thereby objectivizes its utterance-like tone.

We already have observed that the percussion instruments introduce, above all else, physical sound and noise into music. Indeed, in the case of drums, cymbals, castanets and their ilk, this is so pronounced that the instrument has no definite intonation of its own and only supports the music's rhythmic flow with darker or brighter noises. But also with the tuned percussion instruments—from tympani to bells, metalophones, lithophones, xylophones—what speaks is above all the material sound of the stretched hide, the metal, the stone, the wood, and not the harmonically tuned pitch. When a chorale is rung from a bell tower, the chief delight is in the sounds of the different bells. No matter how perfectly they have been tuned, the various dictinguishing partial-tones of the bells always produce false harmonics, so that the harmonic relationships of the music cannot be enjoyed as fully as we can enjoy the sound of the bells themselves.

IV. THE NATURE OF TONE AND THE NATURE OF NUMBER

At early stages of musical development, the *physical sound* is simply elicited from various objects in a rhythmic play with things like rattles, sticks, rasps and drums. Certain aspects of this stage are reflected in the play of a small child: the most beloved playthings often are those with which sounds can be made. At this stage, there still is a lively instinct for that transcendent musical connection with the Music of the Spheres that lives enchanted in every physical sound. There is a related and equally strong feeling for the transcendent soul world. In the sough of a whirligig, for example, one enters into a magical relationship with the transcendent soul and spirit worlds, i.e. with the 'Wind God'. Comparative musicologists call this the stage of sound magic.

At a subsequent musical stage one finds the imitation of *animal sounds* in a singing or speaking of "animal-like emotional utterance" (Curt Sachs).[4] As soon as the human voice makes its appearance, this stage mixes with the first in many ways. It is the earliest musical emergence of the universal soul world from out of the earlier music of physical sound. Here, characteristically, man allies himself with the animal kingdom, where one finds the pure embodiment of soul. In this music, the expression of the human soul, not to mention the personal soul, still is out of the question.

The spiritual aspect of tone—tone as related to the Music of the Spheres—appears at a third stage, although with a certain earthly shading, as the old teachings concerning *musica mundana* and *musica instrumentalis* always pointed out. Here is where true *musical tone* makes its first appearance. How does this come about?

That *number* is one of the most essential manifestations of the creative spirit and, indeed, is its most spiritual manifestation on earth, is a wisdom that has been passed on to us from various antique cultures, especially from the Greek Pythagoreans. But the sense of this is difficult to grasp because, for us, a number is at first nothing more significant than a colorless value of measure or a stastical cipher. Number is the most abstract, the deadliest, thing we can imagine. And yet in its very abstractness, number can reveal its unmediated spiritual nature.

Just consider: if we are confined to our senses we can perceive... an apple, and then, with the same sort of sense experience...another apple, and finally...yet another apple. Purely as perceiving beings—and also as soul beings who can enjoy the scent and taste of an apple—all we can say is: an apple...another apple...and yet another apple. Only as bearers of a spiritual center can we say: *three* apples. The three is nowhere to be found, neither in the outer world that meets the senses nor in the stirrings of our soul—here is merely: apple, apple, apple. The sense experience is merely a stimulus, the nature of the three has to be grasped spiritually. Once grasped, the 'three' lives independently of apples, pears, or any other sense objects. In other words, it is 'abstract.' It resides in our spirit, in the spiritual capacities we possess: in our thinking. No experience of soul, no matter how intense, no matter whether of aversion or pleasure, can make me uncertain that there are *three* apples (unless pathological growths in the soul choke my thinking). And this shows that to comprehend number, my personal, subjective soul-life must be transcended so I can attain an objective, eternally valid realm—in other words, a spiritual realm. When we are occupied with the laws of number, with arithmetic laws, we move in spiritual realms with the power of our spirit. These realms are untouched by the soul-world or the sense-world. Naturally we can apply mathematical laws to the sense-world, but these laws can only be comprehended in a realm beyond the senses, in the spirit.

When physical sound or utterance becomes musical tone, an immanent spirituality is experienced in tone. To the extent that this happens it becomes important how the nature of number enters into the nature of tone. For the perception of merely physical sound or of utterance, number is insignificant, at least as regards the relationship of various sounds or utterances to one another. But with musically experienced tones, number creates out of its own nature a relationship that can be directly perceived between them. The wavelengths of the sound-body of one tone are harmonized with those of another in accordance with definitely structured numerical relationships.

To be sure, these numerical relationships elude the normal wakeful thinking of a mathematician. They must be apprehended by dreamlike feeling. Experiencing musical harmonies is like the not uncommon experience of awakening after a dream with the happy feeling, ''This was just *the* right solution for the problem,'' without knowing what the solution—or even the problem—was. We *know* nothing about the sounding numerical proportions and so feel their harmonic quality all the more strongly. In this very fact lies the secret of musical experience: that a spiritual capacity remains submerged in half-conscious, dreaming life of feeling instead of awakening into thoughts or images through the mediation of the brain. If this were not so, music could never take hold of our whole emotional life so deeply and intensely, instantaneously reshaping it from within. No abstract mathematical ideation could ever achieve this effect.

The other side of the coin is that, because the very thing that has spiritual objectivity remains in the realm of feeling, it is possible for music to work within the emotions, ordering and objectifying feelings so as to establish the inner centeredness necessary for clear, objective thinking. Such results can be observed in educational and therapeutic practice and are of inestimable worth. The influence of music is also to be seen within the course of humanity's development, ordering and clarifying the life of feeling in accordance with spiritual laws and inplanting the original seeds of a spiritual, objective power of thought. The 'taming of the wild animals' by Orpheus and other mythical singers paints us a picture of the spiritual ordering and harmonizing of soul-life. In itself, without musical-spiritual tempering, the soul is like an animal.

Listening musically, we apply the criteria of harmony-disharmony, purity-impurity, directly to the tone heard: musical hearing feels these with exactitude, because the objective spirituality in us corresponds directly with the objective, spiritual-numerical nature of the tones. Applied to our initial alphorn example, this means: my musical hearing can be convinced or satisfied only if the pitch of the horn actually falls a pure fifth so that the frequency of the initial higher tone and that of the lower, strived-for tone stand in a proportion to one another which very closely approximate 3:2. To the extent that we hear only physical sound or utterance our hearing does not search for any harmonic proportion between the frequencies of the tones; even if there does happen to be a harmonic proportion between them, it is not significant.

At the third of the three previously mentioned stages in the development of human music-making—following the stages of making music with physical sounds or with animal-like utterance—an objective spiritual order enters into music in the form of numerical-harmonic proportions between the tones. Mathematical-harmonic relationships between tones introduce an objective spiritual order into music for the first time and thus does musical tone as we know it today emerge for the first time. This stage is not by any means to be seen as isolated from the preceding two stages, but rather as standing behind them and gradually penetrating the physical sounds and animal-like utterances. Our epoch is the first to demand absolute harmonic purity of musical tone; the more we look to the past the more tolerance we find in this respect. Certain non-Eruopean musical systems tolerate an extraordinarily varying intonation, even though a fundamental form implying an objective, numerical-harmonic source can be recognized in their scales.

In the past, harmony was experienced more as something behind the tones than as something in them—it was still more then half-way to being a transcendent Harmony of the Spheres. Today one can still experience how certain native non-European singers find their tones with a dreamlike certainty, but also with a dreamlike fluctuation of pitch. They do this without the slightest hint of a need to listen to their own physically hearable tones in the fashion of any cultivated European singer. And if one considers the ancient theorists, one feels they are more concerned to acknowledge and meditate upon the numerical background, which is understood in a mysterious symbolic relationship with the Harmony of the Spheres, than to guide musical practice directly. Often enough they emphasize the contradiction between musical practice—a superficial activity they often disdain—and the inward spiritual vision of their theory. The knowledge of the numerical secrets of tone (as also of other things) was, after all, originally the affair of the temple priests—initiates like Orpheus, who were concerned to implant spiritual capacities in the people of their day.

In modern times, if not before, the last remnants of this sort of guidance fall away. Humanity has learned to use thinking as a spiritual capacity. We have taken possession of an inner 'I' which grows ever more independent. Our musical experience has thereby wakened to the physical qualities of outwardly sounding tones. But we have become correspondingly deaf and blind to those harbingers of the Music of the Spheres that once were perceived weaving in physical sound. Technology's horrible, spiritually-estranged world of noise bears testimony to this—a world which humanity has erected around itself. In the future, people will be able, and must be able, to enter so deeply into physical sound with their own inner musicality that their immanent musical nature once more communes with the Music of the Spheres (See p. 155). This implies a much more intense and perceptive musical consciousness than has ever before been brought to bear on sound.

The transition from the level of utterance to that of musical tone can be detected in the singing of so-called primitive peoples. C. Sachs makes a clear distinction between two types of melody. He describes one type as "short-breathed, restricted to two or three tones and narrow intervals, lacking any determinate rhythmic order, endlessly repetitious in their tonal cadence, *resembling speech*." Then he continues, "Yet, existing side by side with these one finds people who are no more culturally advanced who sing 'plunging melodies' of wide range, which contain properly intoned octaves, frequent octave leaps (Sach's musical example indicates that he means rapid descent to the lower octave tone), and rich rhythmic structures."[5] (See the example, p. 65.)

The first type of melody remains entirely in the domain of speech and utterance. A tonal-melodic element, in which mathematical, harmonic realities first reveal themselves has not yet developed; the narrow, fluctuating seconds still can be interpreted as variations of a single speaking-singing tone. It sounds as though the musical tone is still being sought for in speech. In contrast to this melody that still is bound up with speech and utterance, the second type of melody already has musical tone and the strength of mathematical-harmonic law that it brings with it. Hence it can develop strongly and freely in itself, with astonishingly certain melodic leaps and fluctuations—like a bird which, flying at last, lifts itself free of the earth to discover the element in which it is truly at home. These melodies are free and, in a sense, they are at home in the heavens. They are almost always pentatonic. In contrast, the first type of melody is monotone, narrow, heavy, earthbound, and has no ordered scale through which mathematical-harmonic elements can reveal themselves.

A fundamental distinction between two principles of musical harmonic relationships must be mentioned at this point: the distinction between what here will be called the *radial* and the *cyclic* principles of scale structure. Later this distinction will be considered at length (see Ch.XIX), but it seems to me that the present discussion points toward the original source of the two principles.

The first, narrow-ranging, monotone type of melody seeks out the mathematical-harmonic nature of the tone from within, in the movement of the tone utterance itself. The tendency can be recognized even though it could hardly be realized with its original, primitive intensity. The earliest forms of wind instrument belong to this stage of music when sound is experienced foremost as utterance. They are instruments particularly bound up with utterance. For example, consider the shell trumpet, a forerunner of the horns. Originally it was not blown—rather one called or howled into it. Or consider the mirliton (a leaf held within a pipe), which certainly prefigures the reed instruments, but which originally was used to alter and augment speech or cries with a buzzing sound. Zoltán Kodály was able to report of folk musicians who still staunchly clung to the ancient custom of humming into their reed pipes while playing, thus producing clear accompanying voices to their melodies out of the resultant combination-tones.[6] What we have called the *radial* musical principle underlies combination-tones, overblown tones and, in general, the overtone and undertone series. This principle comes most strongly into its own with the wind instruments. It is a mathematical-harmonic principle which is at the same time both a physical-acoustic principle and a musical principle. It arises from within, out of the movement of the tone utterance itself: thus tone-utterance first acquires musical tones.

Not so with the second, wide-ranging type of melody. In this case, the mathematical-harmonic

9

element is not derived from the tone utterance itself. Rather the reverse is the case: the spiritual, mathematical-harmonic source draws the tone utterance up into itself, having already affected the human response and penetrated it with its own spiritual being. The harp family is more allied with this second kind of music. In the former kind, the utterance-like melodies of narrow compass give rise to musical tone in such a way that human, spiritual-musical nature comes into correspondence with the Music of the Spheres that sleeps enchanted in physical sound and utterance i.e. with physical, acoustic laws—it is a kind of awakening of music within the earthly sphere. In the second case, the musical tone arises when the living Music of the Spheres itself descends, as a quality of spiritual individuality, and unites with the human soul, only clothing itself in sound and utterance in so far as people sing and make music. Here, the heavenly music sounds forth out of the human soul. Here, the principle underlying the scale structure is always the opposite to that earthly, radial principle of overtones or undertones; it is the principle of *cyclic* generation of tones out of the octave and one single other repeated interval as in the case of the circle of fifths. A scale structure clearly embodying this arithmetic-harmonic principle crystallized very early. This is precisely the type of melody intended in subsequent chapters when we speak of the Altantean and Old Indian system of sevenths. The other, monotone type, is merely the germ of a radial tonal structure. The tone system of the Greek aulos was the first to begin to give this germ its proper arithmetic-harmonic expressions. As we shall see, it has real significance in modern times.

These days, as one would expect, there are attempts enough to derive the arithmetic-harmonic laws of tones from the physiology of the ear or else from outer acoustic phenomena, e.g. from the resonance phenomena arising between two harmonically tuned tones, from the 'equalization' of two almost purely tuned organ pipes located beside one another, or from the phenomena of the overtone series, and so on. All of this is exceedingly interesting to a musician, but it leaves the real nature of musical experience untouched. And indeed, we have already observed that neither the ear as sense organ nor the external sound phenomena can determine whether we experience music or not; for it is the *same* ear which, under varying circumstances, hears exactly the *same* sound phenomena as physical sound or utterance one time and as music the next time. It is our own inner experience which inattentively passes over the harmonic relationships immanent in the sound in the first case (the alphorn example), but then understands them and feels them artistically.

EXPLORING THE MUSICAL MATERIALS

V. THE MONOCHORD, ITS CONSTRUCTION AND ITS USE

Pythagoras used the monochord (Greek: 'one-string') to study the spiritual and mathematical foundations of musical tone. This instrument is ideally suited for making clear and visible the mathematics of what is heard musically. In this respect, the monochord is a true offspring of the Greek spirit with its striving to make invisible experience manifest in space.

A string is stretched along a long, narrow resonating body (a). Its vibrating length (b-c) is determined by two immovable bridges (b and c). With a third movable bridge (d), the vibrating length can be divided into various proportions.

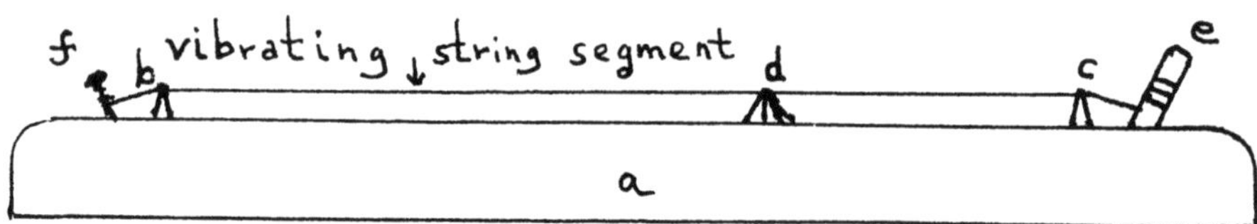

If we take away the movable bridge d and pluck the string length b-c, a deeper tone results than when the bridge d stops off a part of the string so that only the length b-d sounds. The nearer the bridge d is moved towards b, the shorter the length b-d becomes and the higher its tone. If the length of b-d is increased by sliding the bridge d towards c, the tone produced by the string length b-d becomes correspondingly deeper. Unlike other string instruments which achieve tones of different pitch by means of difference in string length or string tension or string thickness, the monochord obtains different pitches by altering only the vibrating length of a string whose tension and thickness remain unchanged. Only with such an instrument could Pythagoras use the spatial relationships of string length to study the connection between non-spatial pitch relationships.

For our proposes we need a small monochord whose string has a vibrating length (b-c) of 50 cm. A simple board, 58 cm. x 7 cm. x 2 cm., is sufficient as a sounding board. At e, about 1.5cm. from the end of the board, a tuning pin (from a zither, lyre, psaltery or harpsichord) should be set in at an angle in a previously drilled hole. The hole should be of a smaller gauge than the pin so that it fits tightly. Similarly, the fastening pin (a nail with the head filed off) should be set in at an angle at f. Both pins should be equidistant from the sides of the sounding board—3.5cm. Two roof-shaped blocks of hardwood (blocks with a triangular cross-section) 3cm. to 4cm. long and 1cm. thick serve as the fixed bridges, b and c. The 7.5cm long movable bridge should also have a triangular cross section and be of hardwood. The following diagram indicates its proper shape and size.

The edge (i) of the affixed rectangular block must lie at a 90° angle to the upper edge of the bridge and to edge h, so that it is exactly parallel with the measuring lines. The notch (g), which should not be too small, makes it possible to sound the full string length b-c, which is the fundamental tone of the monochord. To do this, the movable bridge is pulled away from the sounding body so that the notch g frees the string. A section is taken out of the movable bridge, cutting along g at right angle to the base, so that the scale can be read.

Any string—from a lyre, a zither, a harpsichord, a piano, or a psaltery —will do, so long as it is unwound. If necessary, even the household wire obtainable in a hardware store will

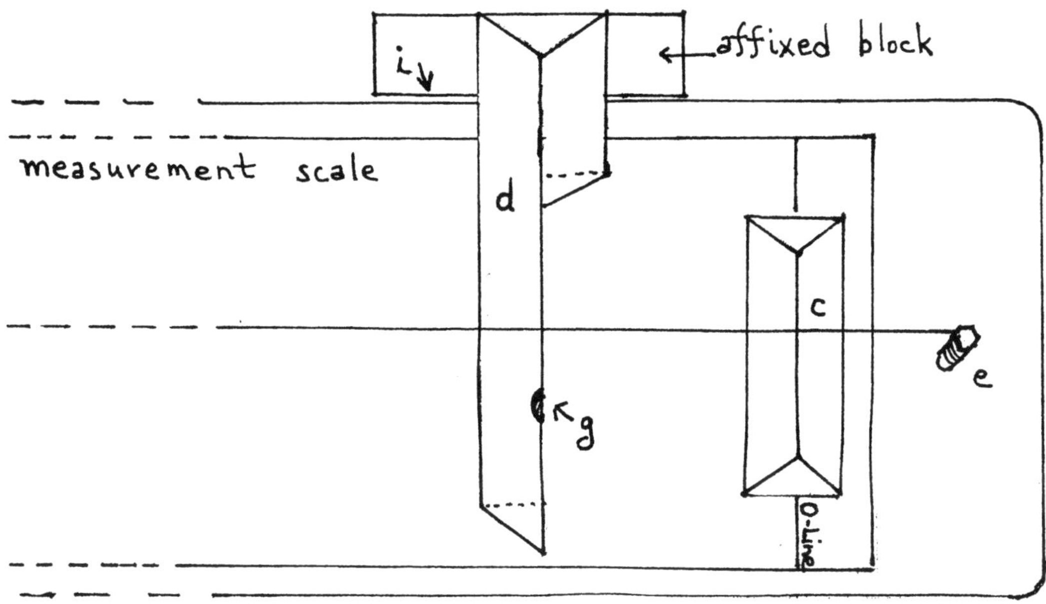

do. The string should be fastened to the fastening pin, f, with a loop and then wound on to the tuning pin with an appropriately sized tuning wrench, at first with only moderate tension.

Now the linear scale included with this book should be glued to the board so that the line marked "Arith.—Sequence/Harm.-Sequence" lies under the string and exactly parallel to it. The 0-point of the linear scale should be 2.5cm. from the tuning pin. In order to prevent the marks of the scale from eventually being rubbed away, it should be covered with a protective coat of transparent film or with clear varnish. The fixed bridge c should be positioned so that its edge is exactly over the 0-mark. Since conditions of printing, of temperature or humidity or the like, may have altered the absolute length of the scale so that it no longer is exactly 25cm. long, the fixed bridge b should not be positioned by measuring 50cm. from bridge c. Instead, the distance between the edges of bridges b and c should be exactly double the 25cm. as it appears on the scale between the 0-mark (the prime C) and the octave mark (octave c). In this way the measurements will preserve the right proportions.

This done, we tune the string to c' ('middle c' as nearly as possible 256 c.p.s.) and check to see that bridges b and c remain in their proper places. The movable bridge is pushed under the string so that its long side is flush with the rear long side of the board. This side (i) must remain flush with the side of the board in playing, so that the upper side and the edge of the movable bridge are at right a angle to the measurement line. To obtain a particular intonation, one brings the edge (h) of the movable bridge exactly over the desired point on the measuring line. The right hand moves the bridge d and at the same time lightly damps the segment of the string that should not be sounding, but without pressing down on it. The left hand plucks the string.

In the following text, indications for the monochord will be written with the abbreviation "Mch".

VI. THE OCTAVE

If we slide the movable bridge d to the middle position which divides all the scales on the measuring line (at 25cm). and pluck the string segment b-c, we obtain the tone c an octave higher. Thus we disclose the first and most important mathematical relationship in the world of musical tone: the proportion 2:1 of the octave. The upper tone of an octave is generated by a string one-half the length of the string of the lower tone. Since the half-length string segment must vibrate twice as fast as the entire string, the string segment producing the higher tone vibrates twice as fast as that of the lower octave tone.

c' has a string length of 50cm. and a frequency of 256 c.p.s.   (vibrations per second)

c''has a string length of 25cm. and a frequency of 512 c.p.s.

The proportions of string lengths and of frequencies of vibration between c' and c'' are exactly reciprocal, i.e. in the one case, 50:25 = 2:1, and in the other, 256:512 = 1:2.

We can reflect on the fact that the ratio 2:1 lies behind every musical octave that ever sounds, not only behind c'—c'', but also c—c' , d'—d'', etc, (only with different frequencies of vibration). We can reflect further, that the octave is the closest of all tonal relationships, a relationship which already has led man instinctively for thousands of years to give these tones the same name and value (C—c—c'—c'' and soon.). These reflections can lead us in Pythagorean manner, to unite the mathematical ratio and the musical interval in a unifying meditation on a cosmic principle. It is an experience which can grow ever stronger. What would our musical space be like if we could not order it with the help of the octave's identity principle, and if we did not encounter the same tones, c,d, and so on., in each of their various higher and lower octaves? Without the octave to order our musical cosmos, our tonal space would be a labyrinth, a gaping chaos.

Every scale is contained within the space of an octave; the space of an octave is sufficient for the presentation of every tone system, whether it be diatonic, chromatic, twelve-tone, or quarter-tone. All other tonal space is only a reflection of this one octave. It seems to us that the wonder of the octave is musically and philosophically inexhaustible so we do not intend to attempt to be exhaustive here. But perhaps one more thought might be mentioned: if a man and woman sing in "unison", then their voices are normally bound by the span of the creative octave, the interval which, like a microcosmos, can contain within itself or produce out of itself all of tonal space.

If we divide the string segment (25cm) for c'' once more, the length 12.5cm gives us the second octave, c'''. In similar manner every relationship of string segments which has the ratio 2:1 appears musically as the interval of the octave.

VII. THE FIFTH

If we use the movable bridge to stop the monochord string so that exactly 2/3 of the string sounds, we obtain the pure fifth. The prime and the fifth stand in the ratio 3:2 to one another as regards string length, or in the ratio 2:3 as regards frequency of vibration (c' = 256 vibrations per second; g' = 256 x 3/2 vibrations per second). If this ratio is not achieved exactly, then one obtains beats when the prime and fifth are sounded together, and this happens with all the harmonic intervals when the mathematical ratio is not absolutely pure. Divide the 50cm. string length by 2/3:

$$\frac{50 \times 2 \text{ cm.}}{3} = 33.3 \text{cm.}$$

The bridge lies exactly over the point g on the line marked "Pythagorean Scale" when it is at 33.3cm. When we pluck the string we hear the pure fifth g'.

The octave (1:2) presents us with the repetition... or the mirroring, or the rediscovery... of the same tone at a higher level. But the ascending fifth gives us something else to contemplate: it opens a door which allows us to move away from ourself. The reverse happens with the descending fifth: it is a coming to oneself, it closes the door. Whoever finds it difficult to experience this in two bare tones is advised to try once to experience intensely how a piece like Mozart's "Minuet" from the *Kleine Nachtmusik* (here transposed to the key of c)—

lifts itself into the key of the upper fifth in the trio—

With this modulation the piece becomes more lively, happier, more unrestrained. Only after the change does one really get outside of oneself: through the ascending fifth, c to g. When the minuet comes again and the piece modulates back to the tonic, one comes to oneself again, more self-collected and somewhat more serious: the descending fifth, g to c. We shall soon see that this can not be fully accounted for as the effect of the contrasting rhythmic flow of the trio.

What is true of the descending fifth is also essentially valid for the ascending pure fourth, for the modulation from minuet to trio can equally well be seen as descending by a pure fourth (c down to g), and from the trio back to minuet as ascending a pure fourth (g up to c). Thus, the pure fourth is an *inversion* of the fifth: descending, it opens out like the ascending fifth, moving away from itself; ascending, it closes like the descending fifth and comes to itself.

This much we can say provisionally, even though the opening and closing of the fourth has a somewhat different quality from that of the fifth—a matter which will require more exacting attention later. The two intervals, fourth and fifth, supplement one another to build the octave: they are complimentary intervals. In frequency ratios:

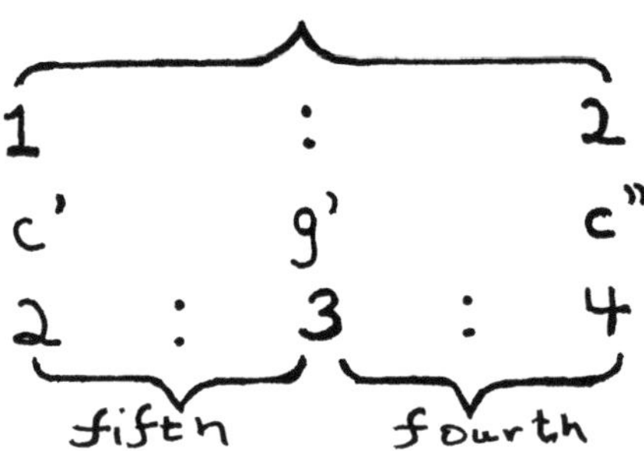

The ascending fifth moves out from its source, c; the ascending fourth finds this source again at a higher level. On the other hand, the descending fourth moves away from the source, c, to which the descending fifth then returns.

A brief side-excursion into the subject of meter is permissable here, since it allows us to approach the nature of the 2 and the 3, which underlie the fourth and fifth, in a still livelier musical fashion. If I change from a 4/4 meter (2/2, 2/4, 4/8, etc.) to a 3/4 meter (3/2, 3/8, 6/4, 6/8, etc.), in other words, from the prime number 2 to the prime number 3, the change is experienced similarly to the way one experiences the melodic step or the key change of a rising fifth (or descending fourth) : I go out of myself and becomes more buoyant. The famous 'joy-triplets' of Schütz's period are a fine example of this, as are the 'Hop-Dances' which the 16th century listener expected to follow more sedate dances in even, duple meter. They were an enhancement, buoyant finales in a triple meter. (e.g., Pavane—Galliard, Allemande—Courante.) The return from a triple to a duple meter—and also from triplets to duplets—is experienced as a coming to oneself, a solidifying, a return to earth, to the ground. The advent carol, "Es kommt ein Schiff' geladen " ("There comes a ship all laden"), is a wonderful example of this.[7]

The next tone we want to obtain on the monochord is f', the tone a fifth down from the octave c''. To do this, we divide the string by 3/4. With the bridge at 50 x 3/4 cm. = 37.5cm., it is on the point marked F (Mch: Pythagorean Scale).

As the fifth below c, f has a still more pronounced musical quality of closure or of turning into itself. Returning to our Mozart minuet, we transpose the trio from the fifth above, g, to the fifth below, f, by changing the key signature to one flat and by starting the melody on a. We will discover that, as compared with the minuet, the trio now has acquired a remarkable seriousness, sedateness and respectability which contrasts extraordinarily with its rhythmical liveliness but cannot be overridden by it. What a difference when the trio comes a fifth higher! One feels that only so can the dancing really come to life! In order to sense this contrast strongly it is best to sing the exercise—the experience is more intense than when it is played.

The three tones that we have obtained up to now form a triumvirate around c:

Fifth above (fourth below)	g	Movement out of oneself (brightening)
Middle	c	Coming to oneself
Fifth below (fourth above)	f	Movement into oneself (darkening)

We will encounter this triumvirate again—as the dominant, tonic, and subdominant of the classical cadence.

16

VIII. FROM THE SCALE OF FIFTHS TO THE CHURCH MODES

We can go further in our quest for the fifth by using it to produce still more tones.
G , the fifth above our fundamental tone (c'), was produced by 2/3 (33.33...cm.) of the entire string (c'). If we take 2/3 of this 33.33...cm., the resulting 22.22...cm. segment produces the tone d'', which is a fifth above g'. (Mch: See, in each case, the line for the Pythagorean Scale.) By doubling this length—to 44.44...cm—we obtain d', an octave lower. Taking 2/3 of 44.4...cm we obtain, at 29.629...cm., the a' a fifth above d'. Going further, 2/3 of 29.629...cm yields the next fifth, e'', at 19.753...cm., and 2/3 of 19.753...cm., the following fifth, b'' at 13.169...cm. Then we double the string lengths of e'' and b'' to obtain their lower octaves: e' = 39.506...cm.; b' = 26.338...cm.

Now we can play a complete and pure scale, c' d' e' f' g' a' b' c'', whose tones all, without exception, arise from an unbroken succession of fifths (naturally, with the necessary octave transpositions):

$$f \leftarrow c \rightarrow g \rightarrow d \rightarrow a \rightarrow e \rightarrow b$$

This intonation of the scale, generated by pure fifths, is called '*Pythagorean*' (Mch :Pythagorean Scale).

The chain of fifths upon which the pythagorean scale is based is a scale of brightness with seven degrees, ranging from the darkest, most inward pole, f, to the outermost and brightest pole, b. In order to clarify this we need the higher octaves of our original tones: c'', d'', e'', f'', g'', a'', b'', c'', are obtained by halving the string segments of c', d', etc.

Then, starting from f'—the darkest tone of the chain of fifths—we play an ascending scale: f' g' a' b' c'' d'' e'' f'' (Lydian mode). This scale differs from the usual major scale in that the fourth tone, b', produces an augmented fourth, a tritone, instead of a perfect fourth. If we begin a scale on the next higher tone (c')of the chain of fifths then f', the fourth tone of this scale (Ionian mode), is a perfect fourth from the starting tone c', while all the other intervals correspond to those of the f-mode: the second, third, sixth and seventh are major intervals, the fifth and octave are perfect. If we start from the next tone of the chain of fifths, g', we once more obtain a scale (Mixolydian mode) which differs from the proceeding one (on c'—Ionian) in only one interval, namely the seventh which, as f, is lowered to a minor seventh. In the next mode (Dorian) on d, it is once more the f through which the new interval—a minor third instead of a major third—appears. In the succeeding modes the f lowers the sixth (in the a-mode—Aeolian), the second (e-mode—Phrygian), and finally, in the b-mode (Locrian), it presses the perfect fifth down to a diminished fifth.

Thus it always is f, the deepest tone of the chain of fifths, which introduces the new, darkened degree in each succeeding mode. Going from the f-mode to the c-mode, to the g-mode, and so on, we watch the scales acquire progressively more minor character. If we then go back in the other direction, starting with the darker-than-minor b-mode, moving left on the diagram to the modes on e, a, d, and so on, we will discover that it is now the tone b, the highest tone of our chain of fifths, through which the darkened intervals are made bright again. One comes at last to the brighter-than-major mode on f, in which even the pure fourth has been pushed upward to an augmented fourth.

The mode with f as starting tone is brightest because all the tones which follow f (except its octave repetition) are brighter tones in the chain of fifths. Being itself based on the darkest tone, this scale is unable to express darkness—all the dark intervals have disappeared. By contrast, the c-mode, our c major, allows a clear experience of the dark quality of the pure fourth, f, which terminates the upward impulse borne by the second and third. We can hear clearly that f is the only tone in the mode which is lower in the chain of fifths than the starting tone, c. Now it is also easy to see why the b-mode is the darkest: all the other tones of this mode stand below b in the chain of fifths. So when we experience the other tones from the perspective

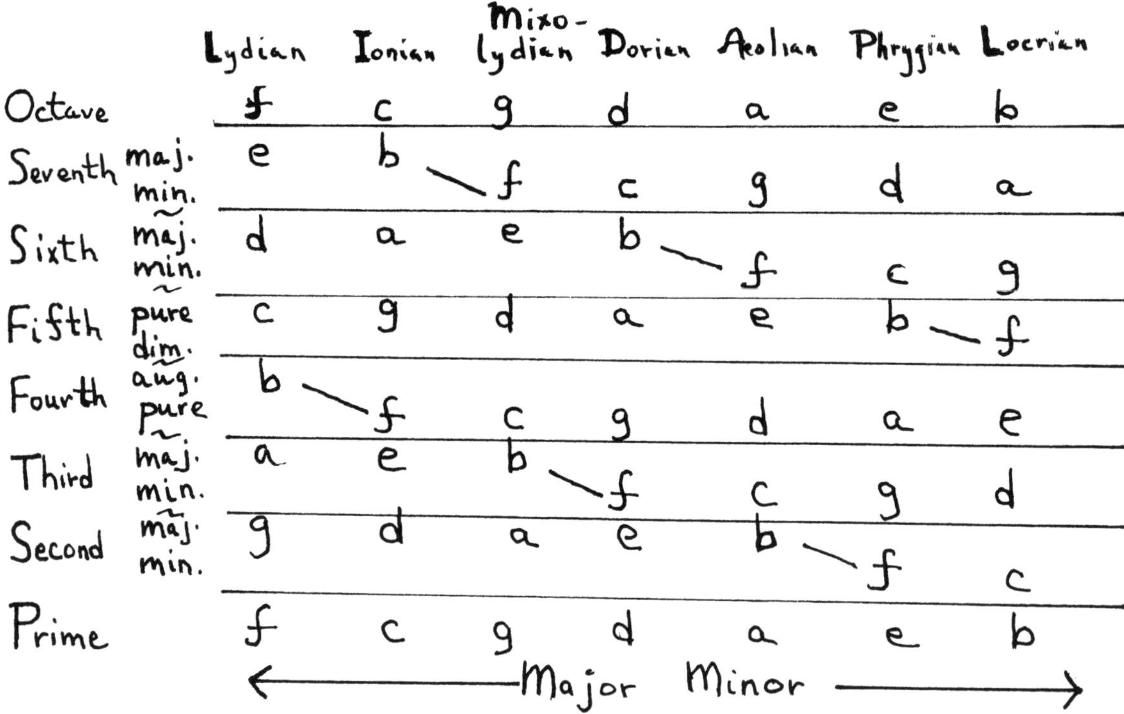

of the starting tone b, not one has a brightening effect. All are darker than b. If only the fifth above the starting tone of this mode were not diminished, the perfect fifth would provide us with a single open window and at least one opportunity to get outside of ourselves.

These seven scales are commonly called the 'church modes'. They are the fundamental tonal system of the European Middle Ages. Their names, taken from various Greek tribes, indicate an origin in antique times. But, in the course of time, the significance of the names has altered, and they were used in several senses during the Middle Ages. [8] Our usage follows the common practice of today.

IX. PENTATONIC MUSIC BASED ON FIFTHS

When f and c, the two darkest tones, are left out of the the chain of fifths, there arises a five-toned scale with a remarkable, fluctuating, weightless character:

d   e   g   a   b

The pentatonic scale is found in the musical prehistory of every continent (although, admitedly, the fifth-based pentatonic just mentioned is not the oldest form). It is among the oldest scales one can find. In the oldest form, which we will learn to know as a pentatonic of sevenths, there is no discoverable variation in the brightness of the tones such as one already finds in the pentatonic of fifths thanks to the chain of fifths. For with the pentatonic of fifths one also finds that the pentatonic mode based on the deepest tone of the chain of fifths is the brightest, most nearly major. The modes based on d and a are progressively darker, the modes on e and b are the most minor in character.

After a longer acquaintance with the pentatonic, one will notice that there is little tendency in it to fix upon one tone as a tonic—in contrast to the seven-toned scales, especially the major. At no place does it really stand on the ground. Its two 'feet', c and f, have been taken away or, better said, are not yet there. As soon as c and f are added, the semi-tone relationship brings b and e into leading tone relationships with c and f. Now the attraction between tones and the different weight of the tones with respect to one another weakens the weightless, fluctuating character of the pentatonic and one is on the way to experiencing a tonic, a 'ground-tone'.

C d e g a and c d f g a are also possible pentatonic scales within the limits of our seven original tones. But one will always arrive at d e g a b as the classic pentatonic, and also be inclined to experience it as such, since it lacks those two tones of the chain of fifths which are at once the darkest and which serve as the center points, or points of attraction, towards which the leading tones they have brought into being are striving.

X. MAJOR AND MINOR SCALES WITH PURE TRIADS

The tuning we found for the scale c d e f g a b c was based on a chain of fifths. It will satisfy us so long as we play melodic lines, especially those in the style of older, monophonic music. This tuning is also ideal for the early medieval polyphony, which restricts itself to consonances of octave, fifth and fourth.

But it is a different matter when we tune an instrument capable of playing chords (a lyre or a spinet) in this Pythagorean manner and then play the sort of piece, based on triads, to which we have become accustomed in the last 500 years. The third of the triad on c will sound too high in pitch and will not form an agreeable harmony with c. When c and e are played together, an unpleasant vibration accompanies them. If we check the relationships of the string-lengths upon which the Pythagorean third is based, we will no longer be surprised that it does not sound very harmonically pure: the string-length for e is exactly 39.506172839...cm. and has a complicated relationship to c' (50 cm), expressed in the ratio 64:81. If one lengthens the string-length for e' by only approximately 0.5cm, we have a 40 cm. string-length for e' and a simple relationship to c' (50 cm.), expressable in the ratio 4:5. Only when it is built upon this simple relationship does the third sound completely pure and harmonic to us. But this pure third relationship is not to be found in the chain of fifths, which is built entirely of the prime numbers up to 3. In the pure third, we must employ the further prime number 5. In antique times, Didymos noticed the difference between the impure, Pythagorean third and the harmonious, perfect third. He described it as the ratio 80:81 (the Didymic, or syntonic comma), for:

$$4:5 = 64:80 \text{ (pure third); } 64:81 \text{ (Pythagorean third).}$$

The pure third 4:5 only acquired true musical significance when the fourth and fifth-based experience, typical of ancient times and the Middle Ages, begins to change to the third and triad-based experience of modern times, in the 14th to 15th centuries. In harmony based on thirds, the Pythagorean third, which is born of fifths, sounds impure.

If we want to tune our scale c d e f g a b c so that we can play pure thirds and triads, we have to introduce pure thirds with the ratio 4:5 into the fifths of the chain of fifths (f c g d).

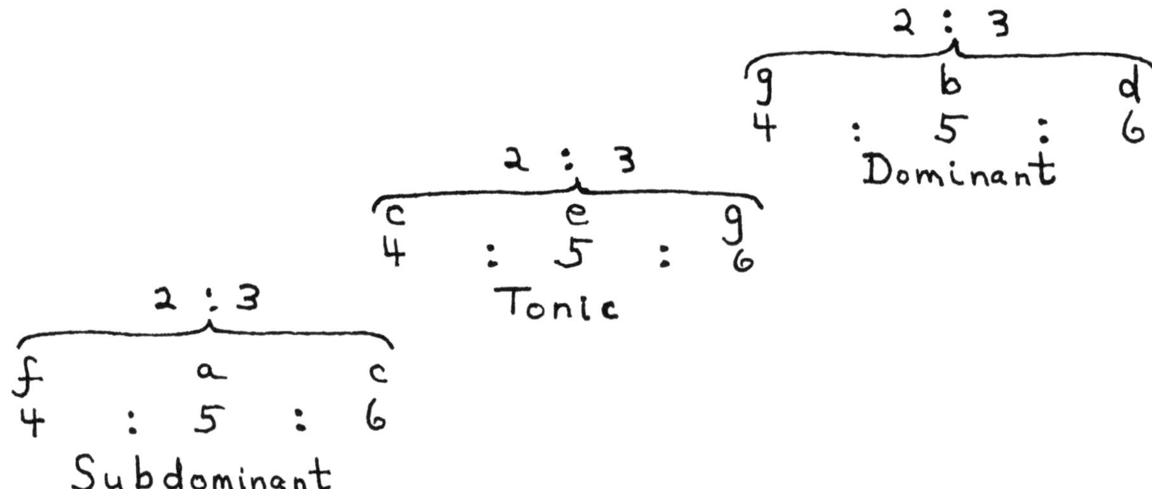

(The numbers above indicate the relationship between the frequencies of vibration. The relationships of the corresponding string segments are reciprocal.)

All seven tones of the C major scale are represented in the three major triads, f a c, c e g, g b d. These three triads appear again in the classic cadence as subdominant, tonic and dominant chords. The three triads of the cadence have replaced the seven tones that compose the links of the chain of fifths and embodied the structural principle upon which the scale was built. (See fig. p.46.) Every pure major scale is built on this same principle; they differ only in that the sequence of thirds begins on different tones. For example, D major is built as follows:

$$\begin{array}{ccc} & & a \quad\quad c\# \quad\quad e \\ & & 4 \;:\; 5 \;:\; 6 \\ & d \quad\quad f\# \quad\quad a & \text{Dominant} \\ & 4 \;:\; 5 \;:\; 6 & \\ g \quad\quad b \quad\quad d & \text{Tonic} & \\ 4 \;:\; 5 \;:\; 6 & & \\ \text{Subdominant} & & \end{array}$$

On the Mch line for "Scale with pure triads" we find the measurements for a C major scale with pure thirds. (Naturally, the sequence thirds of f a c e g b d has been brought together in one octave to form the sequence of seconds c d e f g a b c.) Comparing the measurement points on the two lines, "Pythagorean scale" and "Scale with pure Triads", we can clearly see the differences as regards e, a and b (the comma of Didymus), whereas all the other tones remain with the old measure. In contrast to the Pythagorean scale whose five wholetones are all of the same size (8:9), the scale with pure thirds has two distinct wholetones, the "large wholetones" (8:9) c—d, f—g, a—b, and the "small wholetones" (9:10) d—e, g —a.

Playing these two versions of the tone sequence c d e and letting their differences speak for themselves, it will be found that the third, e, strives toward the fourth, f, in the Pythagorean tuning, whereas in the tuning with pure thirds the e is more at rest in itself. The semitone, e—f, is now much larger and sounds less like a leading tone striving toward f. The individual character of the third only comes to full expression in the new tuning: an inward, warm experience which one can carry *within oneself*, but also with the danger that it can become all too full of feeling. By contrast, the fifth is chaste, inapproachable and objective, with the danger of becoming all too cool and empty.

An old symbolism acquires a new life when put alongside our observations concerning the third and the fifth: the symbolism of the rose and the lily, whose blossoms present us with the same numbers as these two intervals. The rose radiates in five directions, and out of the number five arises the third (4:5). The lily radiates in three or in six directions, and 2:3, or 4:6, is the ratio of the perfect fifth.[9] The ideal human mood of soul, the ideal of inner beauty, is expressed in the symbolism of our sagas and fairy tales as the marriage of the rose and the lily, of red and white, of blood and snow. The triad built of third and fifth has embodied this ideal in music since the fourteenth and fifteenth centuries.

Just as we built the pure C major scale out of the three major triads on f, c, and g, a corresponding minor with pure thirds may be built upon the three minor triads on d, a, and e. In order to do this, all we have to do is extend the structure of thirds of C major downwards by one third to d.

C MAJOR

$$\text{Subdom.} \quad \overset{\text{Tonic}}{4 : 5 : 6} \quad \overset{\text{Dominant}}{\underset{4 : 5 : 6}{4 : 5 : 6}} \quad \left.\right\} \text{Relative frequency of vibration}$$

$$\begin{array}{ccccccc} d & f & a & c & e & g & b \;\;(d) \\ 6 : 5 : 4 & & & & 6 : 5 : 4 & & \end{array}$$

$$\underset{\text{Subdom.}}{} \qquad \underset{\text{Dominant}}{} \qquad \left.\right\} \text{Relative string length}$$

$$\underset{\text{Tonic}}{6 : 5 : 4}$$

a minor

The numerical ratios in the minor triad are the exact reverse of those in the major triad. In a major triad, the major third is below, with a minor third above it; in a minor triad, the minor third is below, with a major third above it. Because of this, the relationship—

major third		minor third	
4	:	5	:	6
c		e		g

which expresses the ratio of *tone frequencies* for major, expresses the (reciprocal) ratios of the *string lengths* for minor:

minor third		major third	
6	:	5	:	4
a		c		e

(With ratios for string length, the *larger* number always applies to the *lower* tone, because a lower tone requires a *longer* string. With ratios for tone frequencies, the *smaller* number always applies to the *lower* tone, because its string vibrates more *slowly*, i.e. it vibrates less times over a given time span than the higher tone.)

If we try to realize this tuning for a minor scale on a chordal instrument, we are led to a discovery that is both surprising and disagreeable. The d of the major scale with pure thirds (Mch: see the measurement line for the scale with pure thirds: d' = 44.4...cm., d'' = 22.2...cm.) turns out to be totally unusable in a minor with pure thirds. For this d, upon which the minor subdominant must be built, does not yield the perfect fifth below a but, instead, a 'false' fifth that is too narrow. A perfect fifth below a' = 30cm. must be tuned at d' = (30x3/2)cm. = 45cm. (Mch: see the short stroke next to d on the measurement line). Only then will the subdominant be built of the right proportions, 6:5:4 = 45:37.5:30. Therefore, pure intonation demands a different d in the minor from the one we used in the parallel major. But a tuning that leads us to a scale with two d's that differ from one another by ⅛ of a tone is an artistic impossibility. This is clear as soon as we reflect on the musical fact that parallel major and minor almost always appear together—that few movements in major fail to employ the parallel minor, and few minor movements get by without using the parallel major. Anyone skeptical of these observations should find a Renaissance piece without accidentals in the key signature and play it for themselves in this tuning.

All those who believe that *every* musical tone relationship must be derived from a pure mathematical relationship are emphatically advised to dwell on this problem—here their program must fail no matter how they twist and turn. Here appears the first true dilemma in the relationship between tone and number, a dilemma not to be evaded or covered up. Here, in the most simple, innocent C major with pure thirds, is the germ of that musical 'tempering' which so many have despised!

XI. TEMPERAMENT AND THE MEANING OF MUSICAL DISTANCE

The word 'temperature' comes from the Latin for 'correct mixture, right ordering, moderation.' Within a musical tone system it has to do with the finding of a compromise between the demands of two diametrically opposed tonal laws or structuring forces, each of which has a full claim to realization. Without tempering, only one of the laws can be purely realized—and only at the expense of the other, which then either is not realized at all or else is forced into a badly distorted, musically unpleasing form. In the case of the scale with pure thirds, it is the major and minor with their respective triads—each with a rightful claim, each musically necessary—which stand in polar opposition to one another and require us to use tempering for the first time in order to find a compromise.

The pitch of each tone is not exactly predetermined for the wind instruments and the strings, so in their case it is possible to allow the two poles to function together in a living play of forces. That is the really ideal 'temperature.' But for instruments of fixed pitch one must proceed differently: one must decide on an outer compromise by finding pitches equidistant from the diverging pitches demanded by the pure tuning according to one or the other pole. The play of forces between these poles is objectively realized in the playing of wind instruments, with their living, fluctuating intonation. But in the case of keyboard instruments, harps, and so on, this play of forces has to be entrusted to our subjective musical experience.

When we use tempering to find a compromise between two pitches demanded by different mathematical-harmonic considerations—e.g. between the two distinct d's needed for the scale with pure triads—we are forced to abandon mathematical-harmonic thinking and, instead, consider how far the conflicting tones are from one another *in tonal space*. Thinking about distances in tonal space it becomes necessary to find out the exact size relationships of the harmonic intervals. For this we have to have an exact way of measuring the distance between tones.[10] The (spatial) size of the octave is taken as the fundamental interval. Then the octave space is divided into 12 equal spatial distances. Mathematically, this means that one determines the twelfth root of the frequency ratio of the octave: $\sqrt[12]{2/1} = \sqrt[12]{2}$. This figure corresponds to the size of the semitone in tempered piano tuning, in which twelve equal semitones fill out the space of the octave, therefore, it is often referred to simply as the semitone, or halftone (abbreviated "ht"). The size of an interval in ht can be determined by putting its frequency ratio—or string length ratio—into the following formula, where 'a' must be the larger value, 'b', the smaller:

$$\frac{\log a - \log b}{0.0250858} = \text{Ht (a decadian logarithm!)}$$

In this way the intervals thus far considered turn out to have the following 'spatial' sizes, i.e., the distance between the higher and lower tone is as follows:

Octave	2/1	12.0000 ht
Fifth	3/2	7.0196
Fourth	4/3	4.9805
Pythag. Third	81/64	4.0782
Pure large Third	5/4	3.8631
Pure small Third	6/5	3.1564
Large Wholetone	9/8	2.0391
Small Wholetone	10/9	1.8240

We should remain steadfastly clear that the ht value of an interval does not express anything about the quality or harmony of that interval, but only its size in tonal space. Ht values are purely and simply values of measurement, comparative sizes. On the other hand, the numbers corresponding to frequency and string length are numbers which themselves express the quality of an interval creatively and essentially. The very simple numbers always yield a harmony when they come to expression as a ratio of frequencies or of string lengths; with these same simple numbers as ht values that is not at all the case.

Let us review the distances in *the chain of pure triads* (rounded off to three decimal places):

$$5 : 6 \qquad\qquad 4 : 5 : 6$$
$$4 : 5 : 6 \qquad\qquad 4 : 5 : 6$$

(d)	f	a	c	e	g	b	d	
1.824	4.980	8.844	0	3.863	7.020	10.883	2.039	ht

Thirds: 3.156   3.863   3.156   3.863   3.156   3.863   3.156   ht

The same transposed into the space of one octave (Mch: Scale with pure triads):

c	d	e	f	g	a	b	c	
0	2.039	3.863	4.890	7.020	8.844	10.883	12	ht

Seconds: 2.039   1.824   1.117   2.039   1.824   2.039   1.117   ht
         Wt   wt   Wt   wt   Wt

In the scale with pure triads, the two sizes of wholetone are clear to see: the large wholetone (Wt) and the small wholetone (wt).

Now, by way of comparison, the Pythagorean scale of fifths with only one size of wholetone (Mch: Pythag. scale):

c	d	e	f	g	a	b	c	
0	2.039	4.078	4.980	7.020	9.059	11.098	12	ht

Seconds: 2.039   2.039   0.902   2.039   2.039   2.039   0.902   ht
         Wt   Wt   Wt   Wt   Wt

XII. MEAN TONE TEMPERAMENT

Mean tone temperament developed out of various 15th and 16th century attempts at tempering. It establishes a compromise between the demands of pure fifths and the demands of pure thirds, and was the tuning most used in the 17th century. Characteristic of this temperament is the absolutely pure intonation it achieves for the major third, which is the newly discovered and newly experienced interval of modern times. Here, the major third is the authoritative interval, whereas the fifth is less well tempered than on today's normal piano.

Mean tone temperament proceeds from the necessity of making a closed circle out of the chain of thirds, or triads, upon which C major is based, so that the tone d does not disintergrate (as earlier described) when the parallel minor is used. In the tuning with pure triads, a closed circle is not obtained:

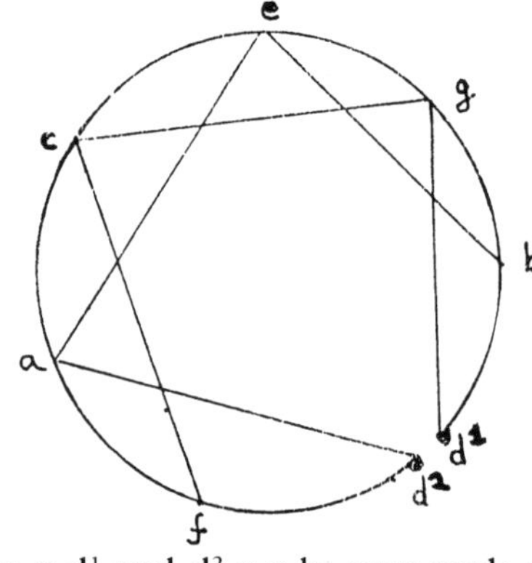

The two chains of fifths, f c g d^1 and d^2 a e b, pass each other by without their being able to meet in the tone d. Mean tone temperament achieves this meeting by doing away with the syntonic comma which separates d^1 from d^2. So it becomes necessary to narrow the four fifths so that they yield a pure third rather than a Pythagorean third. E.g., starting from C:

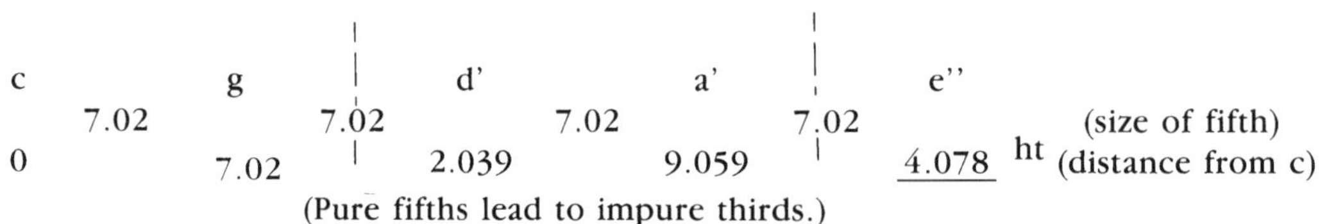

c		g		d'		a'		e''	
	7.02		7.02		7.02		7.02		(size of fifth)
0		7.02		2.039		9.059		4.078 ht	(distance from c)

(Pure fifths lead to impure thirds.)

c		g		d'	a'		e''	
	6.966		6.966		6.966		6.966	(size of fifth)
0		6.966		1.932	8.897		3.836 ht	(distance from C)

(Compressed fifths yield pure thirds.)

The latter size of fifth rounds off the chain of thirds for C major into a closed circle, while at the same time allowing an uninterrupted chain of fifths, f c g d a e b:

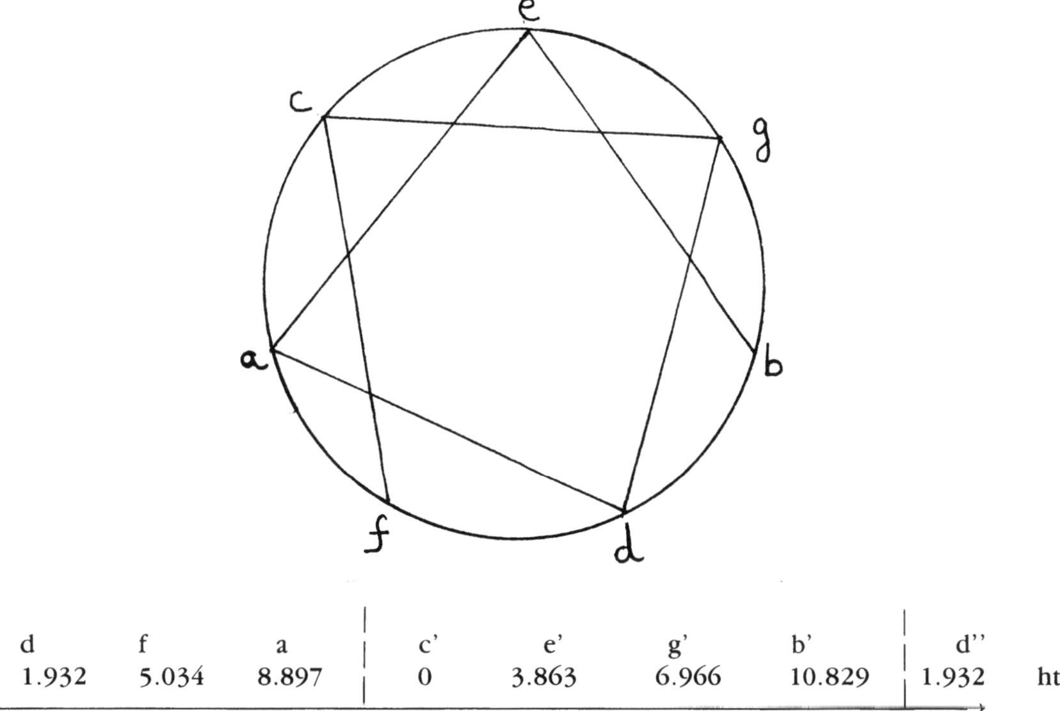

d	f	a		c'	e'	g'	b'		d''	
1.932	5.034	8.897		0	3.863	6.966	10.829		1.932	ht

The d from the parallel subdominant and the d of the dominant are now identical.
As a series of seconds, the C major scale now looks like this:

	c	d	e	f	g	a	b	c	
	0	1.932	3.863	5.034	6.966	8.897	10.829	12	
Size of seconds		1.932	1.932	1.171	1.932	1.932	1.932	1.171	ht

(Mch: Mean tone temperament)

The large diatonic halftones are characteristic of this temperament; the distinction between large and small wholetones, which we encountered in the tuning with pure thirds, has disappeared.

Mean tone temperament is primarily concerned with making a circle out of the diatonic scale's seven-tone chain of thirds. But it was extended to twelve tones by proceeding in tempered fifths of 6.966 ht from f to b^b and e^b, and from b to f#c# and g#. In this way one obtained closed circles for B, F, C, G, D and A major; i.e., these keys are playable in this tuning. In order to play in E major, one must retune e^b to d#. In other words, the chain of fifths remains a chain with a beginning and an end. It does not close into a circle of twelve fifths as if does in modern piano tuning.

Among the twelve half tones that arise when these fifths are transposed into the space of an octave there is a clear distinction between the size of the diatonic halftones which can occur in a particular key (e.g., f# —g), and the chromatic, or non-diatonic, half tones (e.g., f—f#); the diatonic half tones are well over twice as large as the chromatic half tones:

c	c#	d	e^b	e	f	f#	g	g#	a	b^b	b	c	
0.76	1.171	1.171	0.76	1.171	0.76	1.171	0.76	1.171	1.171	0.76	1.171		ht

XIII. MODERN EQUAL TEMPERAMENT (THE CYCLE OF TWELVE)

Just as mean tone tempering brings the major scale's and minor scale's seven tone chain of triads into a circle, modern equal temperament binds together the twelve tone chain of fifths in a circle. Implicitly, this temperament also contains the closed circle of the seven tone chain of major or minor triads as well. Just as there are six diatonic cycles, each containing seven thirds, contained within the twelve tones of mean tone temperament, so there are twelve cycles of seven thirds each, contained in the twelve tones of the modern temperament (Mch: 12-division).

Modern equal temperament arises when the twelve fifths of the chain of fifths are narrowed just enough so that an exact octave of the first tone is obtained after the twelfth fifth. Twelve pure fifths overreach the (seventh) octave of the initial tone by a small amount:

$$7.0195 \times 12 = 84.234 \text{ ht}$$

If we deduct seven octaves (= 84 ht) from this, we obtain the remainder, 0.234 ht, the so called *Pythagorean Comma*. Thus, in order to obtain a closed circle of twelve fifths, each fifth must be diminished by one twelfth of this amount. The resulting narrow fifth is substantially nearer to the ideal fifth of pure tuning than is the fifth of mean tone tuning, whose divergence of 0.0537 ht makes it almost three times as out of tune as the modern fifth.

The closed circle of twelve fifths did not establish itself as the tone system of Europe until the 18th century, when it succeeded the mean tone and other, non-equal temperaments of Bach's time. But the idea is much older, reaching far back before the era of the experience of the third. Thousands of years earlier, China had put this system into practice and, later, had calculated it exactly.[11] The division of the octave space into twelve equal half tones—a result of this tuning—is an idea the rudiments of which also are to be found in Greece in the thought of Aristoxenos of Tarent (born between 375 and 360 BC).[12]

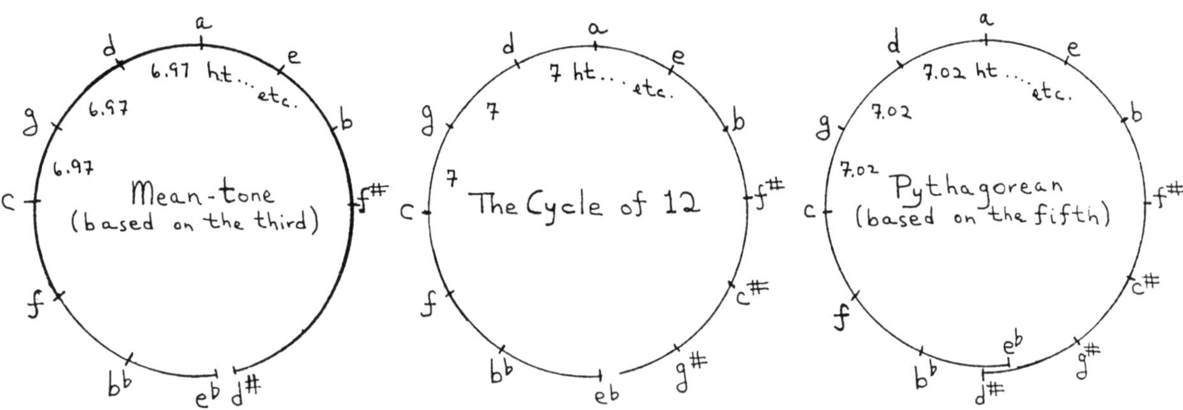

That the great cycle of twelve already was present in the era dominated by experience of the fourth and the fifth, when the third still was not considered to be a consonance, should not cause us great wonder. In this tuning, the large third diverges from a large third with pure intonation approximately seven times as much as its fifth diverges from a purely intoned fifth:

the large third is 0.1369 ht too large, whereas the fifth is only 0.0195 ht too small. In other words, the fifth is much purer here than the third. Actually, the modern temperament leads away from a tuning with pure thirds and goes halfway back to the old Pythagorean tuning. It can also be understood (see the following diagram) as a middle way between the chain of fifths of mean tone temperament, where the tuning is dominated by the *pure large third*, and the Pythagorean *chain of pure fifths*: the one does not quite reach the goal of the seventh octave, the other overshoots the mark.

The question, often asked and debated by musicians, whether a pure d # (g #, c # ...) is higher or lower than a pure e♭ (a♭, d♭...), can be answered from our newly won perspective. In mean tone intonation with pure thirds, the tones d #, g #, c #,... are *lower* than e♭, a♭, d♭... because the chain of fifths determined by the third *falls short* of the seventh octave. In intonation with pure fifths, or Pythagorean tuning, d #, g #, c #... are *higher* than e♭, a♭, d♭...because the chain of pure fifths *overreaches* the seventh octave. In the modern cycle of twelve, the pitch of d #, g #, c # ...) is *the same as* that of e♭, a♭, d♭..., because this chain of fifths *leads precisely to* the seventh octave.

As regards the size of the halftone, modern temperament presents an extraordinarily simple picture, because the octave is divided into twelve equal halftones. Indeed, the halftone unit is defined as one twelfth of an octave.

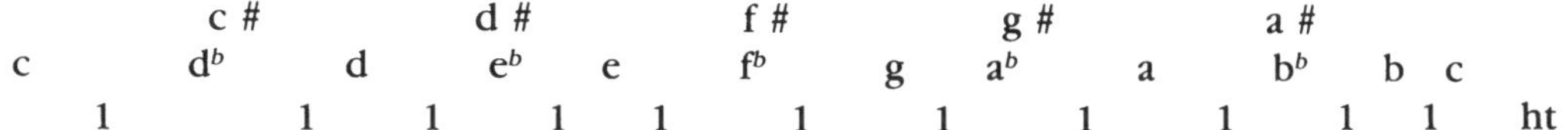

In C major/a minor, the cycle of triads is measured in half tones as follows:

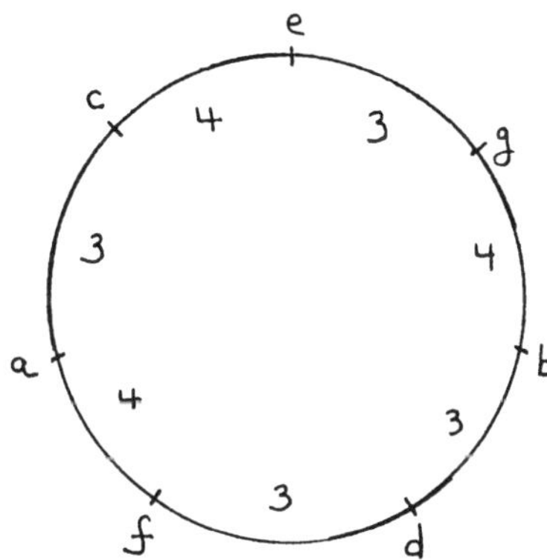

Naturally, in the modern tuning these distances apply to all twelve cycles of the diatonic keys.

Here, with the exception of the octave, all of the intervals which the classic harmonic sensibility hears as consonant— all pure fifths and fourths, all major thirds and minor sixths, all minor thirds and major sixths—all are equally out of tune. Therefore all produce the same 'beat' ...if one discounts the normal variations of actual tuning practice. [13] Thus, in contrast with all other temperaments, none of which permit of such a thing, modern equal temperament can be described as *having equal beats* (German: "gleichschwebend").

XIV. CONCERNING THE CHARACTER OF THE KEYS

The modern closed circle of twelve tones, which has become the usual temperament since the time of J. S. Bach, is more than merely an artifice of the piano tuners. It is the result of an inner musical reality that reflects the constitution and consciousness of modern humanity. This fact can perhaps be most clearly felt in the spectrum of moods typical of the twelve keys. Bach was the first to use these in their totality. Thereafter they were assimilated by classical and romantic music.

First, let us recall how, in the era of the third, the scale was built up of three triads related to one another through the interval of the fifth. The major triad on c stands in the middle of the key of C major, with the subdominant F major triad and the dominant G major triad swinging pendulum-like from either side, and with the full cadence being the archetypal harmonic sequence. Modulating to G major, the old dominant becomes the new center for a tonic around which C and D orbit as the dominant and subdominant of its cadence.

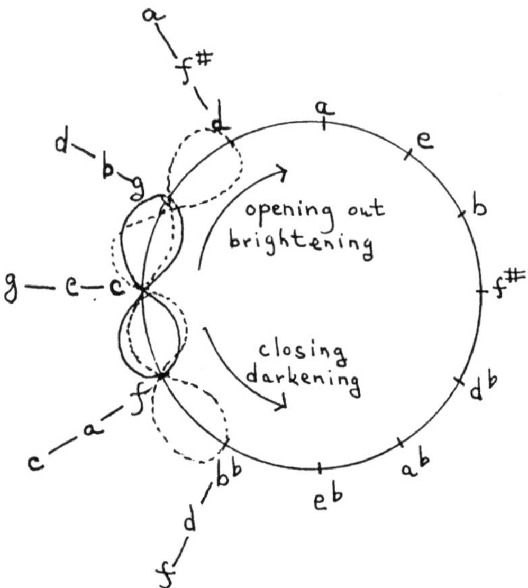

By transforming the next dominant into a tonic one arrives in D major, and one can proceed further in this fashion to the following sharp keys, A major, E major, and so on. From G major to E major these keys become progressively more diffuse, brighter, higher—in other words, they increasingly assume the characteristics that the *dominant* has in the cadence: opening out, widening, leading one outward.

Modulating from C major to F major by transforming its *subdominant* into the new tonic, and proceeding in the same fashion to B^b major and E^b major, etc., the character of these flat keys becomes ever more inward, darker, deeper—in other words, the whole key takes on more and more of the character of the *subdominant:* closing off, encompassing, leading one into oneself. Thus the cadence of the original 'parent key', C major, contains the germ of the entire circle of keys: in its dominant reside all the potential sharp keys, in its subdominant, all the potential flat keys.

There has been much controversy over whether the keys have specific qualities, since in the course of time the absolute pitch of the tones has undergone frequent changes, e.g., a baroque D major would sound physically more like today's D^b major. In reality, as soon as we develop a feeling for the original key C major, be it ever so tentative a feeling, then the other keys fall into place—D major as D major, E^b as E^b major—no matter what the absolute pitch is. Naturally there are individual limitations: what a person with absolute pitch finds difficult or even impossible is accomplished by someone with relative pitch without a second thought.

The qualities of the keys result from the fact that the entire human tone system grows out of its one root, which is the original tone, c. The root tone is an archetype lying deep in our musical subscious; by no means can it be dismissed as merely the result of the familiar conventions about how to notate the various sharp and flat keys—a notation that requires no accidentals for C major. Our musical notation is simply an accurate reflection of a musical reality that is grounded in our nature. If the character of the keys really were dictated by the musical notation, someone who cannot read music would not be able to experience the character of the keys. But this is by no means the case.

If we proceed, say on the piano, in triads from C major to G major, to D major, and so on , it is noticeable how the keys become more and more radiant and outward-streaming. Then something remarkable happens: although we proceed always in fifths with ever more sharps, there comes a point, at the latest at B major, when the radiance ceases to increase and the keys become more damped-down and reticent instead. If one investigates this inward turning phenomenon, one discovers that in E Major the full radiance of A major already has begun to go over into something more like warmth, or ripeness, than brightness—as if the brightness had turned inward. The opposite phenomenon confronts us on the side of the flat keys: going from C major to F major, to B^b major, the character becomes darker and more inward. But, at the latest with D^b major it is noticeable how the character is definitely brighter than A^b major, although tonally one has continued to descend in steps of a fifth, adding more and more flat tones.

This extraordinary restraining and damping of the sharp keys' brightness in E major and B major on the one side, and on the other, the brighter character of D^b major as against A^b major—this shows that the sharp keys do not ascend into ever brighter regions, nor do the flat keys descend ever further into darkness. It could easily be assumed that such would be the case, but our inner musical experience teaches otherwise. Instead, the two sides really join in a circle, a true *'coincidentia oppositorum'*. B major is dampened by intimations of the flat stream approaching from the other side; D^b is brighter because somehow we sense the sharp stream approaching. B major and D^b major also happen to be keys that can be notated from the other side: B major as C^b major, D^b major as C♯ major .

In the pre-Bach tonal system, before the closed circle of twelve was brought into play, it is clear that only the progressive brightening of the sharp keys was experienced, and only the progressive darkening of the flat keys. A contemporary description of the two most extreme sharp keys of that time make this especially clear. Of the keys of E major and B major Johann Mattheson said (1713): "A sadness, despairing even to the point of death, is incomparably well expressed by E major, which is the most comfortable key for those beloved matters in which one is helpless and hopeless, and which, in some circumstances are so cutting, separating, suffering and penetrating that they can only be compared with a fatal separation of body and soul."[14] Here we see how the inward-turning flat stream does not yet flow into E major from the other side, bringing its summery ripeness and warmth to help balance the extreme striving that carries the soul outward in E major. For the earlier sensibility, E major drew the listener's soul 'helplessly and hopelessly' out of him so that he experienced a separation of soul and body. For the older musicians this was 'incomparably well' expressed by E major. In those days, B major only was used in very extreme situations, and Mattheson characterized its mood as 'hard and unpleasant,' i.e. he could not enter artistically into the real musical character of the key in spite of the availability of some skillful solutions to the problem of temperament.

The closed circle of twelve tone temperament is the outer expression of the inner, musical closure of the circle of keys. It bears within itself a special secret of humanity's inner nature: just as, in the macrocosm, rays streaming in opposite directions meet at infinity, so in the microcosm of the human being a striving outward into the boundless and a striving into inner boundlessness meet at last and close in a circle. The secret of the closed circle of keys first became musically experienceable in Bach'time —"was *again* musically experienced" we must rather say, for it was already present on the musical scene in ancient times. (See p. 72f.)

> *C major:* I feel myself wholly in myself, completely wakeful, completely present. Neither am I sunk in myself, nor am I out of myself. Without reflection, without

enthusiasm, fully impartial, with a holy sobriety and prosaicness. Feeling and deed are one.

G major: The first bright opening out of oneself; there is contact with the surroundings, still restrained, but rich in experiential content, like a scent; springlike; flowerlike.

D major: I step forcefully out of myself, enjoy the world and take fresh possession of it. Conquering clarity.

A major: The greatest height and brightness is achieved; in so far as I try to go further out of myself, the counterstream from the flat side already makes itself felt here and builds something like an inner mirror that reflects the brilliant light into which I have come.

E major: As I proceed further into light, it transforms itself into warmth which presses in on me and penetrates my feelings.

B major: On the one hand, I am still further out of myself—I no longer experience myself—and yet that which I receive completely outside of myself touches my inmost being. Meditatively listening to evening bells. The 'most musical' key, so seldom used because its inward musical location corresponds exactly to the blind spot in the eye.

If we go from C major in the other direction:

F major: A first approach to what lives *in* me, without my diving too deeply into self experience. The joyous life of a child of nature. Humor, lightness, movement, dance.

B♭ major: Consciously I enter more deeply into what lives in me and enjoy it; the snugness of half darkness where the inner world can speak more strongly than the outer. Here F major's childlike lightness often becomes self-enjoyment. But if the self-enjoyment of B♭ major is overcome, it acquires cosmic breadth and radiance and becomes the 'key of the stars' (H. Beckh.)

E♭ major: The night key. The profoundest depths are reached. I am sunk in my own corporeality, yet filled with a festive mood. I feel my surroundings only as 'a holy something' which is to be but lightly touched. Around me, darkness; in me, the beginnings of a warm light. Like the radiant gold interior of a mountain in a fairy tale.

A♭ major: Although it becomes ever darker around me, yet the sinking into myself takes on a greater intensity and is transformed into longing, dedication, love and a deep acknowledgment of other beings,. Just as in E major (four sharps) the outer brightness began to enter into me as warmth, so in A♭ major inner experience radiates outward. The key of love.

D♭ major: Just as on the sharp side, in B major, I found myself led directly from the greatest heights into my innermost nature, here I discover the eagle heights of the world within my inmost being: soaring flights of thought experienced musically. If music fails to achieve these heights, D♭ major becomes sentimentally reflective, for what is sentimentality but an experience of what is thought, rather than what is real!

G♭/F♯ major: The bridging, enharmonic key. An irridescent dance on a tightrope stretched between two worlds. Spanning the gap between the 'listening' of B major and the 'thinking' of D♭ major, this key is best characterized by what they have in common: the Word. In most elevated form, the word of ritual and prayer, F♯ and G♭ major can become gossipy, just as D♭ major can become sentimental. Both keys conceal something of the romantic magician or tempter.

Actually, the characterization of a major tonality in the circle of fifths should include an account of its parallel minor key. The two mutually illuminate one another. The minor key is a counterpicture—a shadow—cast by the parallel major.

A minor: Counters the sobriety and balanced clarity of C major with passion, defiance and rebellious exuberance.

E minor: Is cool and crystalline, in contrast to G major's springlike sprouting and blossoming. Often it has a twilight mood, elfin and ghostlike, as against the May morning mood of G.

B minor: Demands reverence and contrition in the mood of the ascetic or the monk, instead of the fresh enjoyment and engagement of D major. It can be warning, judging—even damning.

F♯ minor: The blackest darkness, the abyss, in opposition to the light-filled heights of A major.

C♯ minor : Cool, subdued moonlight in contrast to the sunlike fire and warmth of E major.

G♯ (A♭) minor: The inconsolable monotony of the dead; the element of death in contrast to the 'listening' of B major, which brings inner refreshment and revelation.

On the flat side:

D minor: In contrast to the lively, natural, humor-loving F major there is an lapidary, monumental rigidity; seriousness; the inwardness of stone arches.

G minor: An heroic pain, strength, categoric necessity, as against the ease and glory of B♭ major.

C minor: Whereas E♭ major is a festive repose in the depths: one's own and those of the world, C minor is an heroic rebellion against imprisonment in matter; a soft touch becomes a fighting counterblow.

F minor: A dragonlike imprisonment in oneself and in one's own darkness, as against an inward turning toward another self.

B♭ minor: Instead of an inner experience of the eagle-heights of thought (D♭ major), the ruling mood is that of facing what is ungraspable, incomprehensible and can only be encountered with the power of a deep-seated belief. This often is the mood of death.

E♭ (D♯) minor: Contrasting to the light, floating eloquence of G♭/F♯ major, E♭ minor introduces the mood of an unutterable mystery. Hermann Beckh points to a connection between E♭ minor and the godlike words of Christ.

Obviously, these brief characterizations can only serve as bare indications. Each person must expand them from out of his own experience of the tonalities, for musical experience teaches how capable the tonalities are of assuming varied nuances according to composition and composer. A Beethoven C minor is different from a Bach C minor. In this respect, the recently republished book of Hermann Beckh must be mentioned.[15] In Beckh's book the individual characteristics are discussed and demonstrated much more extensively. Here, the character of the keys has been discussed in order to show how the circle of fifths gives us *a closed circle of tonalities* which corresponds to a deep inner musical experience—the experience that there is not an endless chain of sharp tonalities on one side and of flat tonalities on the other. The modern equal temperament which first made it possible to realize this circle is a reflection, albeit in a rigid form, of this real musical experience. It is not just an artificial solution born of necessity, as one so often hears it described.

Some musicians believe that the various key characters only can come to expression in a tuning in which the 12 tones are tempered, but not equally tempered—so that each key would have its own somewhat distinctive and characteristic intonation of the intervals. (If this view were true, by the way, the usable keys within mean tone tempering would have no character differences!) For various reasons one can sympathize with a tempering of the cycle of twelve in which the tones are treated in a more alive and individual fashion, instead of being tuned to produce the same beat. In Bach's time an instrument so tuned was called 'well tempered.' But such a tuning is not necessary for establishing the characters of the keys. This variety is grounded in realities which exist on a plane entirely independent from that on which the variations of intonation exist.

XV. MAJOR AND MINOR STREAMS IN THE CHAIN OF FIFTHS

((*Translator's Note*: Two facets of the German language make this chapter easier going in the original than in English. In the first place, the German for major and minor, 'dur' and 'moll', preserves the early Latin 'durum' and 'molle' which mean 'hard' and 'soft', respectively. Thus the German language preserves a stage of musical development that no longer is discernable in English. The German words are a constant reminder that the concepts of major and minor originally were applied to two intonations of a single tone, not, in the first place, to the character of intervals, chords or keys. Furthermore the tone called 'b' in English is called 'h' in German. In German, 'b' refers to our b♭—a reminder that this tone is the ancestor of all flat tones. And the 'h' meant that Bach could spell his name melodically, a fact which he and subsequent composers took musical advantage of in various works.))

The birth of the Latin names, 'durum' and 'molle', came when the rigid, closed, sevenfold system of root tones, which is the basis of the seven medieval church modes, was thrown open by the introduction of additional halftones. This event marked the early stages of the development of the later twelvefold system, already encountered in the previous chapter, out of the medieval system of seven tones and modes.

The old seven tones were named, in succession, by the names of the first seven letters of the alphabet. For reasons not to be discussed at this point, the outbreak of new halftones began on the old tone b (which now is called 'h' in German). According to the requirements of the music of that time, the old b was intoned in two different ways: either higher, like today's b (German h), or lower, like today's b♭. The former nuance not only was experienced as a halftone higher, but also as having a harder, more crystalline, brighter character. So it was called '*b durum*', '*hard b*'. To indicate this in the musical notation, the tone b was preceeded by the 'b *quadratum*': b, the 'square b' out of which, in the course of time, the signs # and ♭ developed, and perhaps the german 'h' as well. The deeper intonation of the old b was experienced as softer and more rounded, and so was named '*b molle*' ('soft b'). In the musical notation it was preceeded by the '*b rotundum*': b, the round b, which later became the all-purpose sign for indicating the lowering of any scale tone by a half-step. At this place where a tone first was split into two halftones the German language has erected a memorial. It has preserved the name 'b' for the lower of these tones, instead of calling it 'h flat', which consistency requires.

Superficially seen, one tone has been split into two spatially separate tones, 'b durum' and 'b molle'. But what real effect does this have on the inner forcefield of the tone system? Earlier we saw that the basis of the seven tones of the church modes is the Pythagorean chain of fifths, f c g d a e b , in which b is the tone with the brightest characteer. If we lower this tone, b('b durum'), to b♭ ('b molle'), we have introduced into the chain of fifths a tone of still darker character than that of the former darkest tone, f. In other words, the foundation of the old sevenfold system is burst asunder by the tone *b molle*, which descends to new depths. Between the tones *b molle* and *b durum* —b♭ and b —is the entire span of the old system, from its brightest tone (b♮) to its darkest (f).

The result of further splitting of tones into half tones—f into f—f# e into e—e♭, and so on.—was that the entire old system of seven tones appeared once more, reflected in the heights above b   and again, a third time, below f in the depths:

<pre>
                                    f#   c#   g#   d#   a#   e#   b#
                        f   c   g   d   a   e   b
f♭   c♭   g♭   d♭   a♭   e♭   b♭
</pre>

An unbroken chain of 21 fifths results when the reflection below in the seven flat tones is added to the seven root tones and the reflection above in the sharp tones. If we proceed further with the chain of fifths, further reflections connect with it above (f^x c^x g^x d^x a^x e^x b^x)

and below (f^{bb} c^{bb} g^{bb} d^{bb} a^{bb} e^{bb} b^{bb}). As far as abstract possibility goes, the chain of fifths can proceed infinitely in both directions, building more and more reflections of the original seven tones. The limited range of human hearing sets no limit to this process, since we always can transpose the tones by octaves.

Whatever tone we select out of this endless chain, then with respect to it, all the lower tones in the chain are minor ('molle') tones and all the higher tones are major ('durum') tones. For example, starting upward from a, e is the *open* fifth, b the *major* second, f# the *major* sixth, c# the *major* third, g# the *major* seventh, d# the *augmented* fourth, a# the *augmented* octave, etc. Proceeding downwards from a, d is a *closed*(perfect)fourth or the subdominant, g is the *minor* seventh, c the *minor* third, f the *minor* sixth, b^b the *minor* second, e^b the *diminished* fifth, a^b the *diminished* octave, etc. Whatever tone one choses from the chain of fifths, precisely these intervals will be found above and below it.

Thus one sees how the splitting of tones into halftones gives each tone a potentially *infinite* major stream above itself and a potentially *infinite* minor stream below. In the nature of these two streams dwells the prospect of a limitless darkening or brightening, limitless introspection or extroversion. Integration of the two endless streams in the finitude of the circle requires an entirely new and higher principle—the principle of the twelve which we met in the pervious chapter. Even so, the higher principle does not cancel the potential infinity of the two streams, it only integrates them, as is shown by the appearance of 'x' and '$_{bb}$' in our musical practice.

If we glance back at the church tones, we see that there is no question of there being an unlimited major or minor stream for a tone. Starting from d (Dorian), the two streams run dry after three fifths, either upward (a e b) or downward (g c f). There is no major stream at all for b (Locrian), which has six fifths in its minor stream. The remaining church modes fall somewhere in between with varied, but always limited, major and minor potential. Just like the individual within the medieval class structure, each single tone has precisely limited possibilities of inner and outer development according to its place in the system. The splitting of the tones into halftones began an expansion of each individual tone's possibilities of development—in the major stream or the minor, inwardly or outwardly.

The middle tone system's twelve tone chain of fifths was actually only an extension of the earlier caste system. The minor stream played out at the tone e^b, the major stream at g#. But musical development pressed irresistably for ward, demanding in the one direction the tones a^b, d^b, g^b, c^b, f^b and the double-flat tones, and the tones d# a# e# b# and the double-sharp tones in the other. At last it was necessary to call in the intervention of the principle of the twelve to give our musical culture a limited form in which to contain this drive toward limitless unfolding.

Following the late Romantics, the early atonality of the 20th century took matters so far that the major and minor streams of each single tone seemed to have dissolved in endlessness, to have 'burnt out.' All that remained were the twelve, single, naked keyboard tones of the even tempered piano. Once these had encompassed infinity. Now they were left behind, burnt out slag from which no further sparks of major or minor could be obtained. For this reason it is commonly assumed today that major and minor are dead streams. The question whether a Phoenix can be born out of these ashes is reserved for later chapters.

XVI. MAJOR AND MINOR TRIADS

How can the major and minor streams in the circle of fifths be related to the classical major and minor, which are harmonically grounded in the major and minor triad? Significantly, major and minor were first spoken of in the Middle Ages after the third had joined the fifth of the old Pythagorean system. They appearance of the third was what first created the polarity between the upward and outward striving major stream and the downward and inward striving minor stream.

Within the chain of fifths, we still are free to proceed a fifth up or a fifth down from a given tone; the choice of starting point, and whether we go from there in major or minor direction is left open. In this case, major and minor first occur through the temporal course of a melodic sequence. As a simple example: from a c we can go upward to the nearest g, proceeding by a fifth in the major direction; if we exchange the beginning and end of this sequence going down from the g to the c, we go a descending fifth in the minor direction. Similarly, if f—c—g is in the major direction, g—c—f would be in the minor direction—simply through reversing the temporal order. If these tones are sounded simultaneously, the result is neither major nor minor.

It is different in the case of the triad: c—e—g can only be experienced as belonging to the major direction, no matter whether the tones sound at the same time, or after one another, or even in the reverse order (g—c—c). These tones remain major. And for our experience it is just as clear that c—e^b—g belong to the minor direction, no matter whether they are played at once, after one another, or in reverse order.

The reason for this is to be sought in the numerical relationships of the tones: c—e—g has the frequency relationship 4:5: 6, ie. an *upwards* proceeding arithmetical sequence with the lowest value as 4 (c') and the highest 6 (g)[16] The first member of this sequence is *below*, in the c. The frequency relationship expressed in c—e^b—g is 10:12:15, which corresponds to the segment, ⅙ : ⅕ : ¼, of the harmonic sequence, which by its nature proceeds *downwards*. Member one of this series (1/1) lies *above* in the g'''. (With string lengths, these relationships are reversed: major arises out of the harmonic sequence, minor out of the arithmetical, i.e., c : e : g = 1/4 : 1/5 : 1/6 of the string: c : e^b: g = 6 : 5 : 4 equal parts of the string.)

Thus we can say, according to the principle which the minor triad c'—e^b'—g' embodies, the fifth (as g''' or g') *strives downward to the root tone c'* : the minor direction. The major triad, c'-e'-g', *strives upward from the root tone* (C or c') to the fifth: the major direction. Because the triad contains three tones progressively less separated from one another either in the sense of the airthmetic or of the harmonic sequence, the major or the minor direction of the triad is determined unequivocally.

WIth fifths, or the circle of fifths, the situation is entirely different, for, in the sense of the geometric sequence, the successive tones are always equidistant from one another. Therefore such tone sequences remain ambivalent as regards direction up or down, major or minor.

<table>
<tr><td>

```
 ↑  6  g'
 |  5  e'
 |  4  c'
 ⋮
 1 (1  C)
```

</td><td>

```
 ↑  9/4  g'    1
 |  3/2  c'   2/3
 |   1   f'   4/9 ↓
```

</td><td>

```
   (g'''  1/7) ↑
         g'   1/4  ⋮
         e♭'  1/5  |
         c'   1/6  ↓
```

</td></tr>
<tr><td>

Direction upward
from the root tone
in major (arithmetic
sequence)

</td><td>

Ambivalence of the
sequence of fifths
(geometrical sequence)

</td><td>

Direction downward
towards the root tone in
minor (harmonic
sequence)

</td></tr>
</table>

Accordingly, in the major triad we can recognize the movement of the ascending fifth whose temporal-melodic nature has been frozen into a spatial chord by the appearance of the major third. In the minor triad we can recognize the movement of a fifth downward to the root tone whose temporal-melodic nature likewise has been frozen into a spatial chord by the appearance of the minor third. Whether a melody ascends or descends in a broken triad, be it major or minor, changes nothing with respect to the principle of major and minor direction. This principle shows that the root tone is the starting point of movement in major and the goal of movement in minor. Those readers familiar with the history of music will know of the connection between the appearance of triadic music and of music with a solidly established tonal location.

Let us look at the classical cadence. It unites the temporal principle of fifths with the chordal principle of the triad. The temporal sequence of chords on the root tones C F G C stands as follows in the major-minor tensions of the chain of fifths:

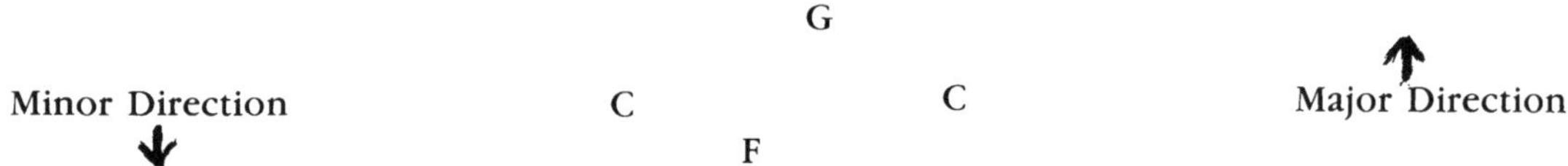

The triads of the cadence, which determine whether the key is major or minor, embody either the upward striving principle of the arithmetic series (major) or the downward oriented principle at the harmonic series:

Classical Major Cadence   Classical Minor Cadence

XVII. MONISTIC AND DUALISTIC CONCEPTIONS OF MINOR

The preceeding chapters point toward a dualistic view of major and minor: the polarity between the ascending arithmetic order and the descending harmonic order is embodied in their tones' frequencies. The following chapter will further clarify this. But first we will pause to cast a glance at the monistic conception of minor as it is represented by Paul Hindemith, among others.[17] He sees major and minor as proceeding out of one and the same principle, namely out of the overtone series.

The fourth, fifth and sixth tones of the physical overtone series, whose musical significance is yet to be considered, produce a major traid. According to Hindemith, this is the only natural triad; the minor triad is supposed to be merely a clouding of this triad. By 'clouding' Hindemith means varying the major third in a way that is understood purely in terms of distance. Thus Hindemith totally ignores the numerical-harmonic principle of the arithmetic series—which he had taken to be the original source of the major triad. In our opinion, the numerical-harmonic form of the minor triad is much too unequivocal, clear and independent a musical experience for it to be written off as the result of a mere clouding (i.e., a making unclear) or deformation of the major triad.

It seems equally indefensible to derive the minor triad from the partials 10 : 12 : 15 of the arithmetic, or overtone, series. This derivation is forced. It takes an arbitrary selection from the tones of the ascending arithmetic series, tones which actually express a numerical relationship of the descending harmonic series:

$$10 : 12 : 15 \ = \ 1/6 : 1/5 : 1/4 \quad \text{(Mch: Arith. Series 10,12,15)}$$

With equal right the major triad can be explained as members 10, 12 and 15 of the descending harmonic series:

$$1/10 : 1/12 : 1/15 \ = \ 6: 5 : 4 \quad \text{(Mch: Harm. Series 10, 12, 15)}$$

What is clearly lacking here is an eye for the archetypal polarity of ascending, arithmetic order versus descending, harmonic order.[18] Humanity experiences this polarity *within* itself in the musical-artistic experience of major and minor. *Outside* of the human realm it appears in natural acoustic laws—the tendency toward lightness and the tendency toward weight in the vibration of matter. (See p. 51f.)

The same holds for trying to derive the minor triad from a selection of tones still higher in the arithmetic series such as 16 : 19 : 24. This particular intonation of the minor is even said to sound more harmonious than 1/6 : 1/5 : 1/4 , presumably because better difference-tones [19] result when the tones sound together, which is something especially discernable in recorders. For these same reasons, even the Pythagorean intonation of the minor triad is supposed to be better than that with pure thirds.

If one investigates the circumstances more exactly, it turns out that all three intonations of the minor triad result in similarly dissonant difference-tones—the tuning by thirds, the aforementioned selective arithmetic, and the Pythagorean. A dissonant *A* results from the original harmonic intonation, a dissonant E from the selective arithmetic and also from the Pythagorean. And in the latter case the E falls exactly where it would in the modern, equal tempered 12 cycle (4 half tones), namely higher than the pure large third. *G*, which appears pure as a difference tone of the series 24:19:16, is too low in the Pythagorean intonation by the amount of a syntonic comma (0.215 ht). Thus the Pythagorean minor triad by no means wins the laurels, even though it happily stands as the representative of minor in practice.

XVIII. OLD EUROPEAN SCALES BASED ON THE ARITHMETIC SERIES AND ON THE HARMONIC SERIES

In order to understand the nature of the major triad, we must see it as governed by the law of the arithmetic numerical series. We discovered the nature of the minor triad in the harmonic series. Although polar with respect to one another, both of these numerical series embody a principle which transforms the temporal melodic movement of tones into something spatial and chordal. The interval structure alone is enough to give us an experience of upward oriented major movement or of downward oriented minor movement, without our needing a melodic description of this movement in time. We called this effect a frozen intervalic movement.

The arithmetic series from 1 to 6, which produces the major triad, was known in older music theory under the name 'senarius,' i.e. "the space if the six." It was held that all tonal relationships had to originate in this "space of the six". Basically, that is still the view today. In *The Craft of Musical Composition*, Paul Hindemith voiced the opinion that the number 7 marks the beginning of a "holy territory" where the musician does not belong.[20] In so far as they are not repetitions of the tones obtained from the *senarius*, what distinguishes the tones obtained from 7 and above is that they do not belong to our tonal system at all. For our ears, the tones obtained from the prime numbers 7, 11 and 13 sound either too high or too low, whereas the tones of the *senarius* and their multiples all sound pure.

The Arithmetic Series of Frequencies (from C):

1   2   3   4   5   6   7   8   9   10   11   12   13   14   15   16   etc.

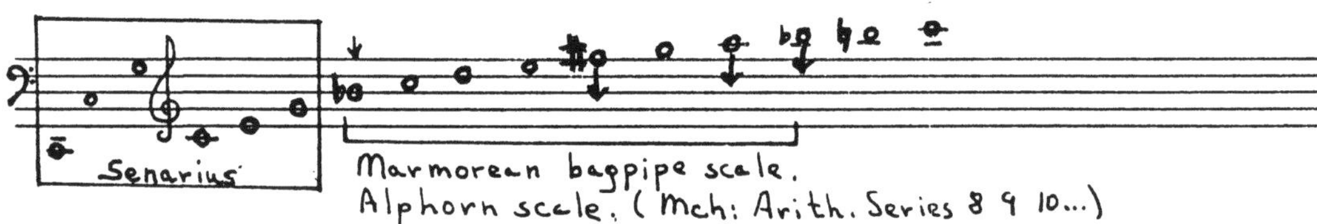

Nevertheless, in the older music of shepherds and peasants one sometimes encounters a scale which corresponds to the frequencies from 7 to 14—with 8 as the tonic. For example, it occurs as the scale of the Marmorean[21] bagpipe, which was recorded by Béla Bartók. And around 1800, in Swabia[22], Justin Heinrich Knecht and Friedrich Chladni heard handworkers and farmgirls singing in these scales, taking special care to achieve an intonation corresponding to the tones 11 and 13.[23] Also the alphorn—like all the deeper wind instruments without keyholes—produces this scale naturally. Everything speaks for the 'falsely' intoned tones, 7, 11 and 13, having originally been experienced as musical tones with no special need to justify their existence in the way that later was felt necessary. For the musical culture of the city, which in the Middle Ages had evolved through the Pythagorean church modes to an experience of the triad, such tones were experienced as rural and false, and were regarded with suspicion.

The earlier Alpine yodelers surely must have sung with the same intonation as that of the Swabian folk tunes mentioned by Knecht and Chladni, for their notation often points unequivocally to the scale of the alphorn, as does this 'Ruguser' from Appenzell (taken down in 1798[24])

Clearly, it was only in the 18th and 19th centuries that the triadic cadence function and the dominant seventh chord so typical of that time were smuggled into yodling. (See p. 157) They took from it its old, almost magically effective bond with nature and replaced it with a lovely, human warmth of heart which can degenerate into kitsch.

As we already saw in the last chapter, the harmonic series of frequencies produces the minor triad within the bounds of the *senarius*. There, as a 'frozen' descending movement, it is the mirror image of the major triad.

Harmonic Series of Frequencies (from c'''):

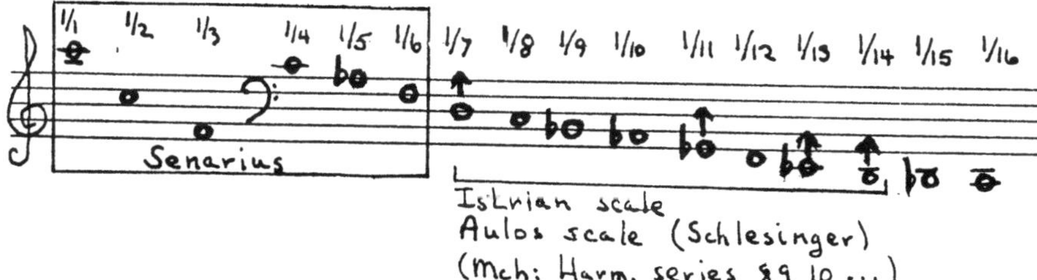

The shifted tones of the arithmetic series, those which correspond to the prime numbers 7, 11 and 13, and which do not occur in our tone system, appear reflected here as a matter of course. Moreover, the tones 7 to 14 of this series also are to be found as an ancient scale in rural folk music —in the 'Istrian scale'[25] noted by Béla Bartók.[26] This same scale, with varying starting tone and with occasional use of the 15th tone, was discovered by Kathleen Schlesinger[27] on the ancient Greek *aulos*, a form of oboe. Allusions to this scale also can be found in Scandanavian folk music and in music of the Scottish bagpipes. Historically, the scale based on the descending harmonic series seems to be older than its polar counterpart based on the ascending arithmetic series. The presence of these scales even earlier is indicated by ancient Egyptian pipes with bored holes, as well as wind instruments from Mesopotamia, east Asia and even from Peru.[28]

As we tried to show on page 9, an archetypal principle underlies scales that embody either the arithmetic or the harmonic series. This same principle is implicit in the nature of wind instruments—instruments whose originals probably produced an utterance-like expression that only approximated musical tones. This scale-building principle, which is the *'radial'* principle examined in the following chapter,[29] can be found at least incipiently on all parts of the earth. But, whereas these scales remained in more-or-less rudimentary stages outside of Europe and clearly never made the full transition from sound and utterance to true musical tone, the radial principle has been at work in European musical development, imbuing it with inner musicality, ever since the development of the Greek *aulos*. Later it will be shown how, with the emergence of the triad, the radial principle has become the real principle of the future for European musical development. The ancient Greek *aulos* scales and their early European descendants, the radial scales of shepherds and country folk, are preludes to our modern development. They anticipate it. The developments in Greek and Latin musical culture first were aimed at overcoming and surpressing this sort of scale structure, so that by the Middle Ages only the Pythagorean system of fifths remained to provide a starting basis for the unfolding of polyphony and, later, for the classical triadic harmony.

XIX. CYCLIC AND RADIAL SYSTEMS

The two systems encountered in the last chapter differ fundamentally from one another: the Pythagorean system on the one hand, on the other the scales of the shepherds and farmers and of the Greek *aulos*. They indicate that we must look for two completely different means by which musical scales or musical systems can be formed:

1.) *One* single interval, based on a relationship expressable in simple whole numbers, eg., the fifth 3/2, is repeated in a chain until an octave of the initial tone is reached (the mathematical geometric series). Such a *closing of the circle* in the nth octave never comes about naturally, but only through tempering, which is a deed by which the human spirit creates culture. If the entire, wide-spanning chain of intervals is transposed to one octave, one obtains a *spatial* division of the octave into *equal steps*. We will call such a system a closed circle system, or a *cyclic system*. Up to now, only the circle of fifths has been mentioned. Later, however, other cyclic systems will be encountered.

2.) In principle, the tones of the arithmetical or the harmonic series stream from one tone-point (the tone 1, or 1/1) out *into infinity*, unfolding *in ever smaller steps*. Out of this series is extracted the octave (tones 7 to 14) that is filled out with seven tones and thus corresponds to our own human inner musical structure, which also unfolds in seven intervals. We will call such a formation a radiant system, or a *radial system*. In this case, the octave is filled out *naturally*, without any need of tempering . The only act requiring the intervention of the human spirit is the repetition of the seven-membered octave in higher and lower positions. It is true that this octave repetition, which allows repetition of particular tones in the musical space, is a cyclic element and is not born out of the pure arithmetic or harmonic series. But a truly cyclic system like the system of fifths has first to draw its tones out of its far flung chain of intervals and then transpose them into one octave in order to build a scale. Not so the radial system, which finds its tones already ordered in seconds within the space of a single octave to begin with, and then reflects this filled-out octave into further octaves.

Thus, in the formation of radial systems we find a *centrifugal*, expanding tendency, and in the formation of the cyclic systems, a contracting, *centrepetal* tendency. In contrast to the *equal steps* of the octave drawn together in a cyclic system (the half tones in the system of fifths), the octave of the radial system is filled out with *seven different seconds*, which become narrower as one ascends in the arithmetic series, and narrower descending in the harmonic.

If we listen to the radial scales, we will discover that they *have more life* than the scales of a cyclic system, be it the Pythagorean or the modern, equal-tempered one. Assisted by the monochord one can gradually become familiar with these scales, natural for the *aulos* and the alphorn, until their initially strange intonation becomes accessible to our inner musical sensibility. On the other hand, by comparison with an *aulos* or alphorn scale there is *greater clarity* in a scale taken from a cyclic system. The clarity is largely due to the unity of the interval distances in the tonal space. It proceeds from one tone to the next with *intervals that are always the same*, and in the way each tone relates to the others it is always the same intervals and consonance relationships which feature again and again, eg. every tone (except b) has a tone a pure fifth above it and every tone (except f) has a tone a pure fifth below, tones that are a second apart form either a large or a small second,all thirds are either major or minor thirds. Not so for the intervals arising from the various tones of the alphorn or *aulos* scales. These give rise to *always differing intervals*— seven different seconds, seven different thirds, and so on.

In Greece, the Pythagorean system, with its striving towards cyclic completeness, stands opposed to the *aulos* scales, which embody a radial system. The former is connected with the Apollonian string instruments, the lyre or the cithera, the latter,with the Dionysian aulos. If we follow the Greeks' clarification of the name Apollo, "a-polys", as Plutarch gives it[30], we can concretely identify the work of the "un-many", the god of unity or individuation, in the cyclic system of fifths. The tonal system of the *aulos*, which Plato called "panharmonic"

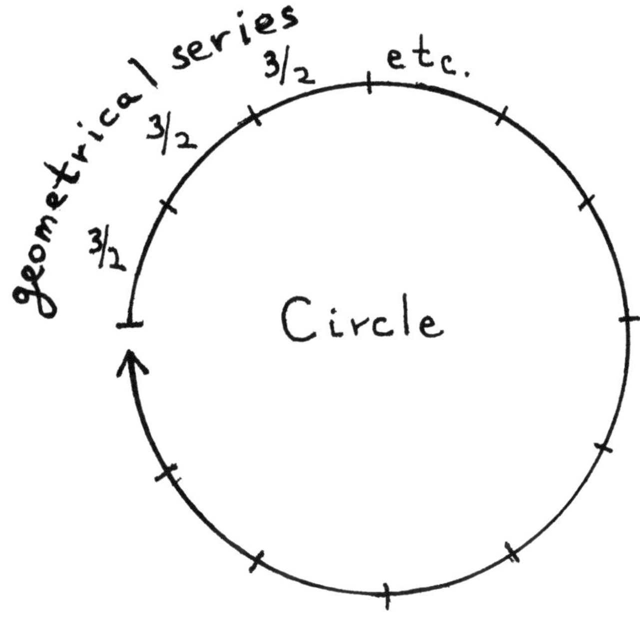

Ray

Arithmet. series (ascending: major)

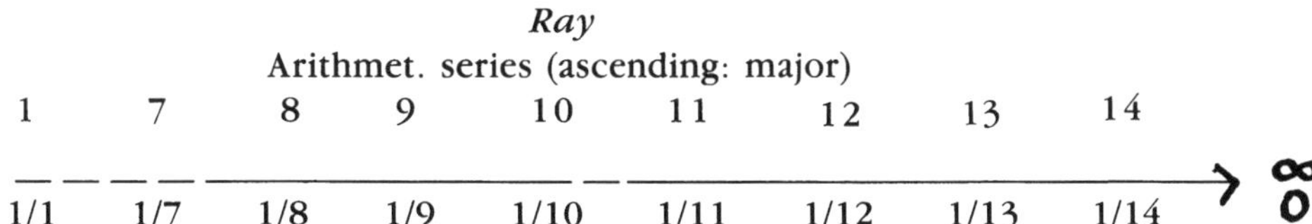

(all-harmonic, containing all harmonies)[31], reveals, by contrast, the work of Dionysos, the apprentice of nature and of Pan, the god of multiplicity. Just as Apollo, the god of light, wants to bring us to ourselves by means of the clear mirror of day-time wakefulness and clear, conscious thinking, so does Dionysos, the god of the mysteries, strive to unite us with totality through the feeling and experience of our own, night-like inner world. This contradiction can be experienced musically by comparing the old Greek Dorian mode (the Phrygian church mode), which descends through the tones e d c a g f e (in Pythagorean intonation), with the *aulos* scale (based on the harmonic series 7 8 9 10 11 12 13 14) ! These two sorts of scale construction, polar opposites by nature, are to be found in various combinations in Greek music. Later, in the chapter on Greece, the matter will be considered in more detail.

Ultimately, the Pythagorean system, associated up with the lyre and cithera, triumphed. It was carried over into the medieval church modes while the radial system of the *aulos* was driven to the periphery of western cultural development. We rediscover the radial system in the long ignored music of shepherds, in the music of rural cultures, the music of 'backwoods' people who live close to nature.

Later, in the 14th century, this radial, pan-harmonic 'natural reservoir' began to flow back into the mainstream of western music. One knows that the old European, rural folk music stood by as godfather as the experience of the third began to take hold and transform the empty Pythagorean fifth into a triad. The triad originates in the radial principle, as the segment 4:5:6 of either the arithmetic (major) or the harmonic (minor) series. The *classical cadence*, which contains the real inner structure of our triadic scale, unites the cyclic and radial principles in a marvelous way that surely was not dreamed of in antique times.

The Classical cadence:

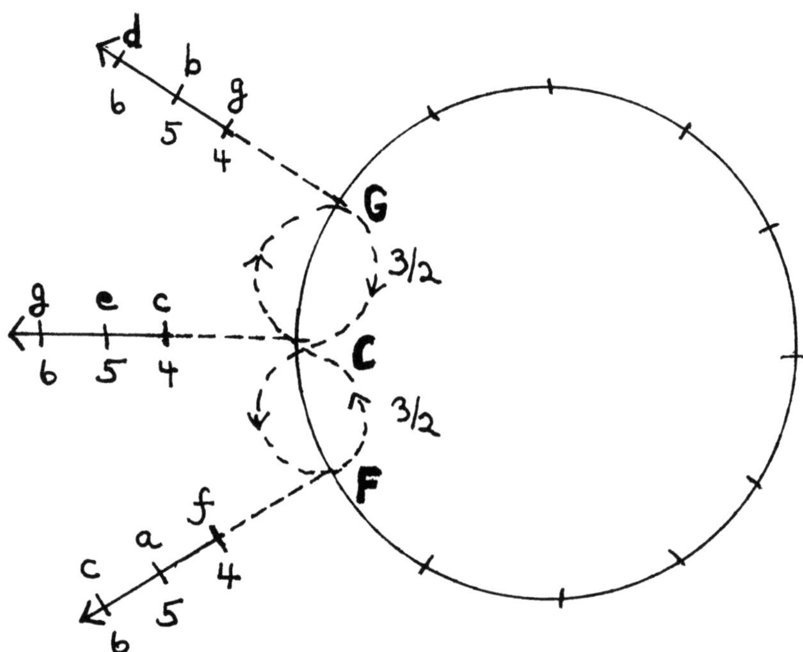
d
b
g
6
5
4
G
3/2
g
e
c
6
5
4
C
3/2
F
f
a
4
c
5
6

XX. THE PHYSICAL OVERTONE SERIES

As we spoke of the scale based on the arithmetic series— the bagpipe and alphorn scale in old European folk music—the knowing reader perhaps has long since thought, "But this is simply the overtone series!" Insofar as the form of the scale goes, the observation is partially justified. The seven tones of this scale correspond to tones 7 to 14 of the overtone series. Yet, when it is a matter of how this scale came into being, of its inward musical birth, it has no fundamental connection with the physical overtone series, for there was music using this scale long before the natural scientists discovered the overtone series.

What is the overtone series? When one tone sounds, then a series of higher tones, whose frequencies stand in a pure arithmetic relationship to the frequency of the fundamental tone, sound softly at the same time. But musical perception does not distinguish these secondary tones as tones or chords at all—for the listener, they merge entirely with the fundamental tone and determine the timbre of this tone. Sometimes secondary tones not belonging to the arithmetic order of the overtone series also affect the characteristic timbre of an instrument: undertones (which will be discussed later), or completely strange, non-harmonic secondary tones which can color the sound to the point of its becoming noise. The overtone series remains, however, the basic law of pure sound.

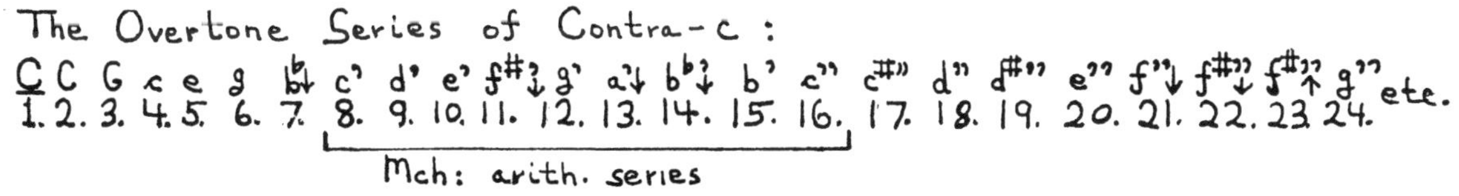

The Overtone Series of Contra-c :

C C G c e g b♭ c' d' e' f♯↓ g' a↓ b♭↓ b' c'' c♯'' d'' d♯'' e'' f'' f♯'' f♯↑'' g'' etc.
1. 2. 3. 4. 5. 6. 7. 8. 9. 10. 11. 12. 13. 14. 15. 16. 17. 18. 19. 20. 21. 22. 23. 24.

Mch: arith. series

For practical reasons, one designates the fundamental tone as '1', although the so-called second overtone is really the first. In this way, each overtone is designated by the number which expresses its frequency relationship to the fundamental tone. For example, the fifth overtone vibrates 5 times faster than the fundamental tone. Thus, the numerical formative principle of the overtone series—and also of the series of natural tones on a wind instrument—really is identical with this radial mathematical principle. We first met it in the chapter on major and minor triads as the principle behind the harmony of the major triad. There we looked only as far as the sixth partial.

We can practice hearing the overtone series in the following fashion: we set the entire length of the monochord string in vibration (c') and then tap quickly and lightly on the exact mid-point if the string. This point is a node.[32] After touching, it all we hear is a soft c''. With a little practice, listening concentratedly to this tone we can learn to hear it as the second over-tone when c' itself sounds, without having to tap the string. Similarly, by touching the string at g (Pythagorean scale) we produce a string vibrating in thirds, with two nodes, and hear a soft g''. Again, we can learn to hear this as the third overtone when the string vibrates as a whole. Then we proceed further to the fourth overtone which sounds when we touch the string at one quarter of its length, and so on. For the more distant overtones, it is a help to begin with a longer string (eg. one metre long). with patient experiment and practice, one can learn to hear more or less up to overtone 20. One only has to learn to concentrate on one particular overtone in order to be able to isolate it consciously from the general sound. For the higher overtones, it is a further help if one plucks the string with a fingernail and near the bridge.

As a rule, the overtones which sound with the fundamental tone become weaker as one proceeds upwards, but they are physically demonstrable far beyond the tones mentioned here. If I sing the vowel E on a given tone, its higher overtones are brought out, the deeper ones weakened; with the vowel U, the upper overtones are weakened while the lower ones become more prominent—always in the context of a progressive weakening as one goes higher. With A ("ah"), one obtains a balanced overtone spectrum. From this it is clear that the overtone series has not the slightest thing to do with what is really musical in a tone, but rather with the sound in which it is clothed, with its *sound-shell* which we now see has its own order, and with its character as *speech-sound*. It would be clearer to call it the 'oversound' series.

Nevertheless, we do not want to be unduly pedantic about the name of the overtone series before we have gone more thoroughly into some of its real mysteries. How could it come about that, one fine day, people were able to discover the overtone series? What had to happen to them? Only when one ceases to view the overtone series as a physical acoustic problem and recognizes it as a problem of musical consciousness does it become musically interesting.

XXI. AWAKENING TO THE OVERTONES

It is extraordinary that people concerned themselves with tones for thousands of years without ever discovering the overtone series, even though it is more or less to be heard in every naturally sounding tone. Of course, in musical practice, one knew of the natural tones obtainable by overblowing a wind instrument—the same series of tones as the acoustic overtone series. Similarly, at the latest by the time of Pythagoras, one knew of the mathematical ratios of the pure intervals, something also to be found in the overtone series. Nevertheless, it was reserved for the beginning of the age of the natural sciences, the 17th century, to discover this marvellous numerical order in the cloak of overtones which clothes every tone. It seems that this order had to be implanted first in the human spirit through thousands of years of musical development and then, finally, scientifically, through the Greek Pythagoreans, before it could be physically rediscovered in the sound in which a tone is clothed. There it is the last remnant of the harmony of the spheres, the *musica mundana*, which has died into matter.

Of course, modern humanity, who was accompanying the natural sciences in their descent into materialism, made a disastrous mistake (as with so many of those grandiose discoveries of natural science which abound in mystery): they began to treat the frozen order of the physical overtone series, the "*end* of the path of God," as the *origin* of music. They began to seek the origin of music in the dead order of their material surroundings instead of looking for the source in themselves as participant in the living, spiritual Music of the Spheres. Thus, from the 18th and 19th centuries on, the harmonic theories ever and again attempted to explain pure, inner musical phenomena by means of the physical overtone series. Some teachings even go so far as to dismiss all musical phenomena not derivable from the overtone series—tempering, minor, etc.—as false developments or as traditional nonsense, instead of taking advantage of these "absurdities" to wake up to the fact that, in spite of their mysterious agreement, the overtone series and music are not the same thing.

This materialistic development is largely responsible for the dichotomy between scientific music theory and the inspired creativity of the real musicians. The further one looks into the past, the more one finds 'theories' which are still inspired and spiritually aware and under whose aegis the artists could create. They did not have to disclaim them as the artists must do with today's theories in order to be creative. Given the state of today's musical and scientific awareness, this is a goal yet to be achieved. Today it should be one of our highest goals. To achieve it, both musical and scientific consciousness must be transformed.

Only when people began to fall away from music, did they discover the overtone series. The French musical amateur who, as the story goes, was one of the first to do so was listening to the low C of his cello. But he certainly was not paying complete inner attention to his playing when he made the discovery. He was more awake at the periphery of musical experience—more awake to the sound which clothed the tone than to the piece he happened to be playing or practicing. In order to become conscious of the overtone series, I must disregard the musical aspect of c as tone and turn my attention to analysis of the sound which clothes it. For this reason, the phenomenon only could be discovered after people had learned to observe the world—in this case, the world of tones—in a purely materialistic-analytic fashion, i.e. after people had learned to hear *unmusically*. For when I attend to the sound-like or speech-like garment of tone and let that affect me, this can hardly be called musical hearing. Musical hearing requires that I directly perceive what I hear as a gesture which refers me to my deepest inner being, my spiritual centre, which is the only place where music can live. Humanity of earlier times could hear in *no other* way; an encounter with tone transported them immediately to a spiritual, immaterial life, and the earlier the period, the more ecstatic the experience. The interest in an analytic understanding of sound—and equally, the interest in exact intonation—first arose when an analytic hearing based on the purely physical senses began to take its place beside musical hearing. The fact that tonal color only began to be considered in the composition of a melody in the 18th and 19th centuries testifies to this process of development. In

Baroque and Renaissance music tone color was treated freely and varying realizations of a piece were expected.

Schoenberg's efforts with "*Klangfarbenmelodie*", melody of tone color, took music to the very end of this path. Afterwards, all that remained of music was its sound-shell, which no longer was distinguishable from the sounds of the everyday world—auto horns, motor noise, the hum of generators.

Today, we have lost our connection with music. It is no exaggeration when Herman Pfrogner, in his book *Lebendige Tonwelt*, speaks of "the zero hour of music" in the 20th century. Musical people of our century often reach back into the paradise of Renaissance and Baroque music, times before "the tones fall from grace", in order to preserve their musical experience. This simply shows how our own time tends to drive us out of the realm of music. Often one is driven to think that the marvellous music and the lively, spirited musical practices of the 15th 16th, 17th and even the 18th centuries are expressly there to help the 20th century through this null point. They are a sign of the spiritual heights of which music is capable...and which it will be able to achieve in the future.

Nevertheless, we must also say that the discovery of the overtone series has granted to music a wholly new beginning. Something fundamentally unprecedented has happened: those pure intervals of octave, fifth, fourth, third, etc. which previously had a musical life only in our own spirit and could not be experienced through any living, ensouled being outside of ourselves—those intervals now are heard in the vibration of dead matter and that, moreover, with a purity beyond the accomplishment of the best musician. When we link our own inner musicality, which is a quality of our spirituality, with the overtone series, we release them from the world of sound and utterance in which they have lain dormant up to now, sleeping an enchanted sleep. For we can do no other than to hear the overtones 1 and 2 as a *musical* octave, 2 and 3 as a *musical* fifth—not as a relationship of physical vibrations! Once we have discovered it, the "over-*sound* series" is transformed into the over-*tone* series. It is a child born of the marriage of the human spirit with the Harmony of the Spheres, the 'harmony' out of which worlds are born, but which just now seems to lie in a death-like sleep.

Just as the wine of the spirit is given to humanity as a gift, one must say that our music up to now, with its tones and intervals, has been a God-given gift. Music was brought to us through 'geniuses', i.e. through higher beings working through an especially gifted person. But with the awakening to the overtone series, matters are entirely changed. This, with its tones and intervals, has been engendered by us ourselves out of the earthly world of sound, thanks to the power of our own 'drop of spirit'. It is our *child* and, as such, stands entirely under our protection and is our responsibility. The divine guardianship that inspired older music no longer exists. The only guardianship remaining is a human one. The time of geniuses is past. Now it is up to us alone to nurse this delicate child who still has to grow up to become   "human music"— to nurse it with heart's warmth and with a knowing awe, so that it can take its place beside the inheritance of thousands of years of noble, God-given music and also beside the inheritance of its last inspired masters, our great classicists who, living in times of spiritual downfall, often broke under the weight of their genius. Now it will become apparent whether we are worthy of the grandiose inspirations of the past—whether we will have anything more to offer this child than a chilling, scientific-materialistic intellectualism. If not, we will have to escort it to its grave almost as soon as it has been born.

XXII. THE PHYSICAL UNDERTONE SERIES

Often one encounters the view that the undertone series is nothing more than a theoretical reflection of the overtone series and that there really is no such thing. This view arises because the undertone series does not occur with every sounding tone in the same fashion and with the same absoluteness as the overtone does. It is manifest only under certain circumstances.

Hold one prong of a vibrating tuning-fork against a piece of paper. You will hear a succession of tones in the humming of the paper, according to whether the tuning-fork touches the paper nearer the edge or nearer the centre. After a bit of practicing and experimenting with an a'-fork, one can discern the tones a' a d A F D. This is the harmonic series of frequencies which we met on page 43 and which, in this case, descends from a'. It comes about in the following way: with a', the paper reverberates with every impulse of the prong of the tuning fork and thus achieves the same frequency. In the case of a, the paper—for example an edge—is too sluggish to have completed one reverberation in time to be ready for the succeeding impulse. For this reason, the impulses 2, 4, 6, 8,.... of the prong are lost into the surrounding space, and only impulses 1, 3, 5, 7, ... make contact with the paper. This means that the frequency of the paper is one-half that of the tuning fork: the tone appears an octave lower. If the paper is still more sluggish, it takes up only every third impulse and the paper vibrates with 1/3 the frequency: the d, a fifth below the octave (the twelfth), appears. With still more sluggishness, the paper vibrates with only 1/4(A), 1/5(F), 1/6(D) .... of the frequency of the tuning fork.

Undertones come about whenever one has a resonating membrane which is too sluggish to accompany each vibration of the main tone. In that case, it can only accompany with 1/2, 1/3, 1/4, ... of the frequency. Whereas the whole series of overtones of a main tone sounds along with it *as a matter of fact*, the undertone series of that tone only indicates the *possible* places at which one of its undertones might occur. As with the overtone series, the main tone of the undertone series is already designated as the first tone. Thus, the second undertone is the tone whose frequency is 1/2 that of the fundamental tone, the third undertone 1/3, the fourth undertone 1/4.

The undertone series originates in a higher generating tone and manifests itself through the progressively increasing weight and sluggishness of matter. It leads us from lightness into heaviness. Conversely, the overtone series arises through the progressively increasing lightness and quickness of vibrating substance. It leads us out of weight into lightness. If I search in my musical experience for the same order as underlies the natural phenomenon of the undertone series—mathematically, the harmonic series of frequencies—I find the experience of minor. If I seek in myself the order underlying the overtone series, I find the experience of major. The undertone quality, minor, displays 'before my very ears' how the Harmony of the Spheres sinks, dying, into the heaviness of matter. The overtone quality, major, displays the contrasting resurrection of matter out of weight into lightness and light. Minor guides me musically into a past in which I can divine the mysteries of the heavenly, spiritual, primeval sources of the world, but along with which I must feel the tragedy of the dying of all spirit into matter. I experience minor remembering, reflecting. Major is much more on the surface; it is of this world, 'concrete', but it points confidently from the here-and-now to the future. We do not experience major reflectively—at most it conveys a dream of paradise, and not a lost one, but one which lies ahead of us as a hope and expectation for which we whole-heartedly and joyously strive.

As we indicated earlier, the scales based on the harmonic series of frequencies, the order of the undertone series, are clearly older than those based on its reflection, the overtone/major order. Not only does minor lead us to experience the past musically, by reason of its very principle it belongs to the past. It corresponds to an old, pre-Christian feeling for life, which experienced the spiritual more in what had been created and was finished than in the process of becoming. It was out of an unbelievably clear and penetrating insight into the development of music that Rudolph Steiner found it necessary to allude to elements of "primal music"

("Urmusik") in speaking of the *aulos* scales discovered by K. Schlesinger which are based on the undertone series.[33] Albeit that details of Schlesinger's researcher are subject to criticism, one thing is certain: the undertone-based, radial principle of scale-formation which she discovered is the true maternal source of interval and scale formation (see p. 60). To us it seems no accident that it was a woman who rediscovered this sort of scale formation in the 20th century for, indeed, it originates in ancient chthonic-maternal inspiration.

From music history one knows that in pre-Christian times the scales were experienced as descending. The *aulos* scale, as expounded by Schlesinger, is the scale which, more consequently than any other, embodies this orientation downwards. It inner harmonic order and principle of formation work downwards. The radial, overtone scales—such as the Alphorn scale and the Marmorian bagpipe scale—must be viewed as the post-Christian descendants of the undertone scale. These ascending scales come about as a mirroring of the undertonal 'mother scale'. From out of the old chthomic-Dionysian primal source they produce an anticipation of a future in which the human spirit, immersed in the earthly world of sounds, freshly creates its own inner music—a creating which, to be sure, also signifies a rediscovery.

As with the undertonal mother-scale, the overtonal scales of the old shepherds and rural people finally had to be forgotten. In myth, we are told that Dionysos no longer is to be seen: dismembered, he resides in all the world of nature. He can be resurrected from out of the inner being of nature when he is released by a spiritually creative humanity. As we shall see, the radial principle clearly has great significance for the future.

XXIII. THE SEVEN INTERVALS

Having deepened our understanding of the nature of the overtone and undertone series with respect to the formation of scales, the question inescapably arises: "But what is the source of the sevenfoldness of the scale?" The overtone and undertone series give us no basis for the division of the octave into seven steps in the way that corresponds to the inner, musical scale experience of the last few thousand years. Both series begin with the empty octave, which then is followed by octaves divided into two, four, eight, sixteen, etc., parts. In order to obtain a sevenfold division of the octave out of this, the listener, out of herself, has to add something to the order of the undertone or overtone series which it does not itself contain. She has to select out of it the seventh to the fourteenth overtones or undertones, and this means she does not even take the fundamental tone, or one of its octaves, as her starting point.

We see that the sevenfold principle of the scale is diametrically opposed to the principle of the overtone or undertone series, which is given by nature. The sevenfoldness of the scale only can arise out of our own inner musical experience. Of course, it can ally itself with the overtone or undertone principle, but this has nothing essential to do with it. (Incidentally, exactly the same is the case with the three-foldness of the triad.)

We have met the sevenfold scale in church modes with their Pythagorean fifth orientation, and as the triad-oriented major and minor scale, and also as a radial scale with seven different nuances of the interval of the second. Ancient, non-European musical cultures provide us with still further ways of shaping a sevenfold scale. We can even find traces of sevenfold order behind the fifth-based pentatonic, without subscribing to the view (of Handschin)[34] that pentatonic is merely a deficient heptatonic. Obviously, we cannot here examine exhaustively the nature of this sevenfold order of the scale, which allows transformation into all imaginable tonal species and tone-systems. All we will do is try to come a bit closer to it in its most familiar guise, in the ascending intervals of the simple major scale.

Prime: A centered resting-in-oneself; self and world correspond. Total trust in oneself and the world. Sleep.

Major second: A first, dreamlike movement; tension; expectation. Murmuring; the incessant movement of water with no set point of reference. Vegetative. Deep dreaming.

Major third: Experience; soul; a smile beams at me. A harbor of friendliness and devotion. Between dream and waking. Soft.

Fourth: Hard and clear; wide awake; gathered together; challenging. Concentrated intensity, ego, awakening to oneself.

Fifth: Going out of oneself; opening oneself; loving self-relinquishment. The feeling of the wide, clear arcs above and below us which both expand and hold us fast.

Major sixth: The arc of the fifth is broken through. Soul experience expands joyously into the widths. Euphoric.

Major seventh: It tears at me in order to entirely draw me out of myself. Scintillating; the highest degree of tension and movement.

Octave: The rediscovery of oneself at a higher stage. Achievement of a goal. The eighth interval is at the same time the establishment of a new prime, and so the scale remains sevenfold.

It is not our intention to give a total description of the nature of an interval, but rather to give indications which make clear the general dynamic of the (major) scale as a series of intervals leading to the goal of the octave. Up to the fourth we experience ourselves within ourselves: asleep in the prime, dreaming in second and third, and wide awake and ready for action in the fourth. The fifth opens the door on the outside world and our view becomes expansive.

In the sixth and seventh we fly out... to find our goal in the octave. This general dynamic which we have described for the major scale is to be found again in every seven-stepped scale— but naturally, with very different points of emphasis and with variations according to the structure of the scale.

HISTORICAL CHANGES
IN THE
EXPERIENCE OF INTERVALS

XXIV. FROM THE PAST TO THE PRESENT: SEVENTH, SIXTH, FIFTH, FOURTH, THIRD

The further we trace back musical development, the more those authentic remains of ancient musical experience—those that we still can discover among surviving folk groups—indicate an ecstatic musical experience. Music once transported us to an enraptured, trance-like state. At this stage, an exact intonation is less necessary for musical experience, since those making the music are "out of themselves." What we have called the spiritual aspect of tone, which is especially expressed in its kinship with number, is not yet fully immanent in the sounding tone. It is experienced as something transcendent, approachable through an ecstasy engendered by a kind of sound-magic or magical form of utterance. (See p. 7 where we have described this). Nevertheless, this music exhibits the outlines of tonal structures which are based on the form and dynamic of certain definite intervals. Someone who experiences music in the primal, ecstatic way, could never become analytically conscious of these intervals, but they would be living in them and be carried unconsciously by their specific dynamic.

Rudolf Steiner was the first to indicate that the ecstatic musical experience of earlier humanity was especially related to one interval—that which today we would call the *seventh*.[35] Our characterization of the intervals shows that no interval can be experienced more ecstatically than the seventh although, of course, the tension of our seventh in a major scale has a particular orientation as the leading-tone to the octave. We have to assume that the primal experience was of a different seventh, one possessing the tension particular to the seventh without its being that of a leading-tone—in other words, a seventh of which one can have a sustained experience without falling into atonality or into a yearning for the octave.

We find such an interval in what today is called the natural seventh, an interval based on the numerical relationship 7/4. It is to be found in the arithmetic sequence of the overtone series (partials 4 and 7), and also in the harmonic sequence, or undertone series (Mch: Arithmetic Series, or Harmonic Series, 8-14). Anyone who plays a brass instrument or an alphorn knows this seventh well as the unwanted interval which appears above the triad when the attack is not skillful. It is a tone which sounds false within our tone system and consequently the player has to repress it constantly. But as soon as we free ourselves from our habitual hearing and listen to this interval in its own right, it sounds ever more consonant and displays a lively, naturalistic charm all its own. In contrast to the major seventh, which pulls us and threatens to tear us asunder, we feel immersed in the natural seventh as in a soap bubble. It lifts us up; we swim in it.

The next interval to be taken up in the course of our developing musical experience was the *sixth*. Here again, the relevant interval is not the familiar major or minor sixth of today (5/3 or 8/5), both of which are derivations of the modern third experience. The participation of the prime number 5, which is characteristic of the third (5/4 = major third; 6/5 = minor third) is in itself an indication of this. Today we are all too accustomed to the folksong-like accompanying voices in which parallel thirds and parallel sixths are harmonically identical, so that where parallel thirds do not fit in they are replaced by parallel sixths.

For earlier times, we have to turn to a sixth unrelated to our contemporary thirds-sixths-ecstasy: the sixth 13/8 (Mch: Arithmet. Series 8-13). This sixth is built over the fundamental tone of the arithmetical series, or over its octave, whereas our sixths either hang downward from the fundamental tone (8/5), or are independent of it (5/3). In span, the ancient sixth 13/8 lies between the major and the minor sixth, somewhat nearer the minor sixth.

Major sixth	Ancient Sixth	Minor sixth
5/3	13/8	8/5
8.844 ht	8.405 ht	8.137 ht

56

This at first unfamiliar interval only reveals its character after some extensive listening and practicing, when one finally ceases to gauge it by the normal minor or major sixth and can hear and experience 13/8 as a harmony in its own right. The impression is difficult to describe. The nearest characterization is "golden". It has neither the flaming enthusiasm of the major sixth, with its euphoric flight of blissful fancy, nor does it have the feeling of rejectedness, of inner burning or of passion, which one finds in the minor sixth. From the point of view of musical experience, as well as from that of distance, the old sixth 13/8 stands in the middle between the major and the minor sixth; the dazzling, cascading glow of the major sixth receives from the side of the minor sixth a weight, a reddening, a depth, an inner glow. It is the red gleam of heavy gold—more objective and raised above the human and more super-earthly than the major sixth's bright jubilation or the minor sixth's dark glow. Both of these latter sprang out of third experience and thus are of much more human origin. Something uncanny is to be sensed behind this ancient interval. The seventh 7/4 which was strange enough to us to begin with, seems natural and familiar in comparison with the sixth 13/8.

The nature of this interval becomes still clearer if we set the bridge of our monochord so that the string segments stand in that ratio which since ancient times has been called the 'golden section' (*sectio aurea*) or the 'divine ratio' (*sectio divina*)—i.e. so that the ratio of the entire string to the larger segment is the same as the ratio of the larger segment to the smaller segment. Thus divided, the whole string (c') and its larger segment of 30.9 cm ($a^b{\downarrow}($ or $a{\downarrow})$ yield an interval of 8.330 ht (the larger segment and the smaller (f''$\downarrow$) yield the same interval). This interval differs from our 13/8 by only 0.075 ht, a difference that carries little weight for musical experience.[36] For practical purposes, the sixth 13/8 is the musical golden section.

In the following period, musical experience began to orient itself by the interval of the pure fifth 3/2, the neighboring interval in the arithmetical series. Here lies the origin of our present-day tone system, which is still based on the fifth (as is shown by its basic framework, the circle of fifths). We already have become acquainted with fundamental characteristics of the fifth in earlier chapters. Approaching it by way of the ecstatic seventh 7/4 and the still totally unearthly sixth 13/8, the fifth makes us feel we are at home in an earthly frame for the first time. Although the fifth always has the feeling of wide spaces—like a broad arching sky—still it is here that we first breathe the air of the earth and stand on firm ground. Its simple numerical relationship gives the interval something extraordinarily logical and conclusive...downright geometrical. The ascending fifth (say, c-g) is like the question of a child, completely open to the world in its astonishment, selflessness, wonder and trust. It voices a question asked in complete assurance of an answer. A falling fifth is the answer (say, c-f), an answer which states no opinions, but rather issues so out of the matter itself that it resolves all doubts.

If I take the same three tones as a sequence of fourths, the falling fourth c-g is also a question—no longer a child-like open one, but rather a question I put to myself, inwardly weighing the matter and genuinely wondering whether there is an answer. The ascending fourth c-f is an answer, but not out of the outer facts—rather it is as if a decisive inner voice speaks: "So be it! Should everything stand against it, still I will do what is necessary to resolve this question." In other words, it is my own deliberate, moral answer—the result of an inner awakening, watchfulness, and self discovery. Thus, we come to discover that the musical border between external and internal experience is precisely that between fifth and fourth. (Naturally, this is only possible if we awaken ourselves, with careful, penetrating practice and testing, to the quality of the intervals.) If I invert a fifth to make a fourth, a revelation of the world— or of the spiritual in the world—becomes a revelation of my own inner nature. Here we arrive musically at that stage of development where, in the Greek world, the old, naively received mystery wisdom was transformed into philosophy and into independent thought. In Greece came the real age of the fourth—in Greece and in the succeeding period of the Roman culture and the early and high Medieval periods. The fourth expresses the human spiritual situation of those times.

The next step beyond the fifth-and-fourth-dominated consciousness of antiquity and the Middle Ages brings us to the third experience of the era in which we are still living. We have already seen the effects that this revolution in musical hearing, which occurred in the late Middle Ages, had on the intonation of the scale and the structure of the tone system. As regards musical experience, the third brings the personal, inner side of human experience to expression for the first time. Even though today the third can seem to us all too personal, all too human, and all too akin to sentimentality, we must nevertheless recognize it as the fruit of the inner ripening of humanity in Europe during the Middle Ages. Experience of the third is unthinkable without the Christian mysticism of the Middle Ages. The person of antiquity still experienced the divine outside of himself, in the world and in nature. Not so in the Middle Ages, when Meister Eckhart's "small spark of the soul" was experienced entirely in the inwardly-directed devotion of folded hands and in the innermost chambers of the individual soul. The fourth provided the bridge to this inner shrine of the third. None of the great masters of western music is imaginable without this inner temple of the third, which provides shelter for both a communion with the highest spirituality, which is the origin of all music, and also for inner personal experience. With the third, music is completely human for the first time. Therefore, in the 20th century the third has become global—the natural musical expression of practically all humanity whatever their race or people.

Not least because of the major-minor duality introduced by this interval, a completely personal, subjective musical expression of mood has become possible to a degree not previously attainable. In major I can reveal my inner nature to the world with joyful affirmation; in minor I can mournfully withdraw into my own inner world or I can pass by the illusory world with inner strength and resolution. Morever, both thirds can round themselves out to a triad by taking on the pure, unmodified fifth, which has come over to us out of the interval consciousness of an earlier time as the embodiment of objective spirituality. Third and fifth relate to one another as *soul* and *spirit* : soul which with inner warmth experiences everything in hope and despair, rejoicing and mourning, laughing and crying, love and hate—and spirit which stands coolly above all that, participating in a clear, objective and unchangeable order.

At the beginning of the 20th century, the subjectivity of third experience had degenerated to sentimentality and to the kitsch of mood music or entertainment—something that hardly could have happened to any other interval. Because of this, there were schools of composition that tried to bring spirituality and objectivity back into music by turning back to the use of the fourth and the fifth: the 'open' fifth, parallel fifths and fourths, also church modes and pentatonic (both sprung from the fifth)—all of these were once more 'modern' and for a while even modish. Their unique, archaic charm revived intimations of the old objective power of the fifth. Priceless sources of life were thereby recovered for music-education, even though the real musical expression of our time was not to be found in this direction.

The will to fight one's way free of the subjectivity of the third is the most persistent single tendency of 20th century music; out of it arise the most diverse attempts, which at times totally contradict one another, at times intermingle. Thus, we have on the one side the search into the past for objective musical experience: one tries to relate today's music to the old, medieval, fourth-dominated experience or to the experience of the early modern age, the Renaissance, or the Baroque times when the third, pure and fresh as dew, still was objective and carried a spiritual life of its own. On the other hand, the 20th century has seen the attempt to achieve musical objectivity by conscious separation from history and tradition: a 'serial', mathematical order was forced upon the twelve tempered tones (which, of course, are borrowed from tradition), upon rhythm, dynamics and tone color. Soon one discovered with disappointment that, although these laws indeed have the objectivity of all mathematical laws, their connection to music is largely accidental and that, for musical experience, most of these laws of objective order remain artistically imperceptible. Thereupon yet another new movement arose, one which simply set up the personal unconscious and the accidental as musical objectivity itself. In the search for musical objectivity, the tone system was reduced to tatters, until one actually believed one had at last discovered musical objectivity in externally producible sound—in noise and vibration. But this did away with the very distinction between music and non-music. Music itself—i.e. the specifically musical inner experience as we characterised it on p. 2ff came in this fashion to be repudiated as subjective and the mere product of tradition.

In the last analysis this musical crisis within which we stand today was precipitated by the experience of the third. Though consciousness of the third, music ceased to be a more-than-human, Godly concern and became a purely human concern; our music today reflects our daily existence. It is no wonder that in a culture of passive consumers' music has become a

58

cosy 'central heating' for souls chilled by the grey of daily life; or that for commercial, political and religious agents it is a mere propaganda tool; or for the self-consciously educated, an object of conversations about proper interpretation; or for rowdys, a decibel-hullabaloo; or for the snob, a matter of pretence; or for the pure intellectuals, an abstract computability; or for the intellectual anti-intellectuals, an 'action' with sounds, on so on.

If we contemplate the beginnings of third experience in the late Middle Ages, we learn to really love the third. Contemplating the present, we are tempted to hate it. But this would be self-hatred for, from now on, it is we who must learn to fulfill the third, anew and from out of ourselves, just as in the past the third filled the inner experience of personal lives with its musical substance. To do this, we must establish a new humanity, painstakingly built up through a new mode of thought, a new awareness, and most directly through a new understanding of art and music.

*　*　*

The musical consciousness of ancient humanity was embodied by the wide interval of the seventh. This is how the Atlantean and earliest post-Atlantean (old Indian) ages are described by Rudolf Steiner[37] on the basis of his spiritual researches. We tried to pursue this in musical experience and discovered in the natural seventh 7/4 a musical expression answering to that age. Rudolph Steiner describes how music developed as succeessive ages took up successively narrower intervals, step by step. We discovered in the sixth 13/8 an interval answering to the following stage of development (old Persia) and, for the next stages, the pure fifth 3/2 (Egypt, Chaldea), the fourth (Greece, Rome) and at last, in modern times, the third. If we gather together these stages of development musically, the result is a scale which comes out of the arithmetic series or out of the overtone series. It descends from the seventh. Only the fourth 11/8 seems at first not to belong to the sequence.

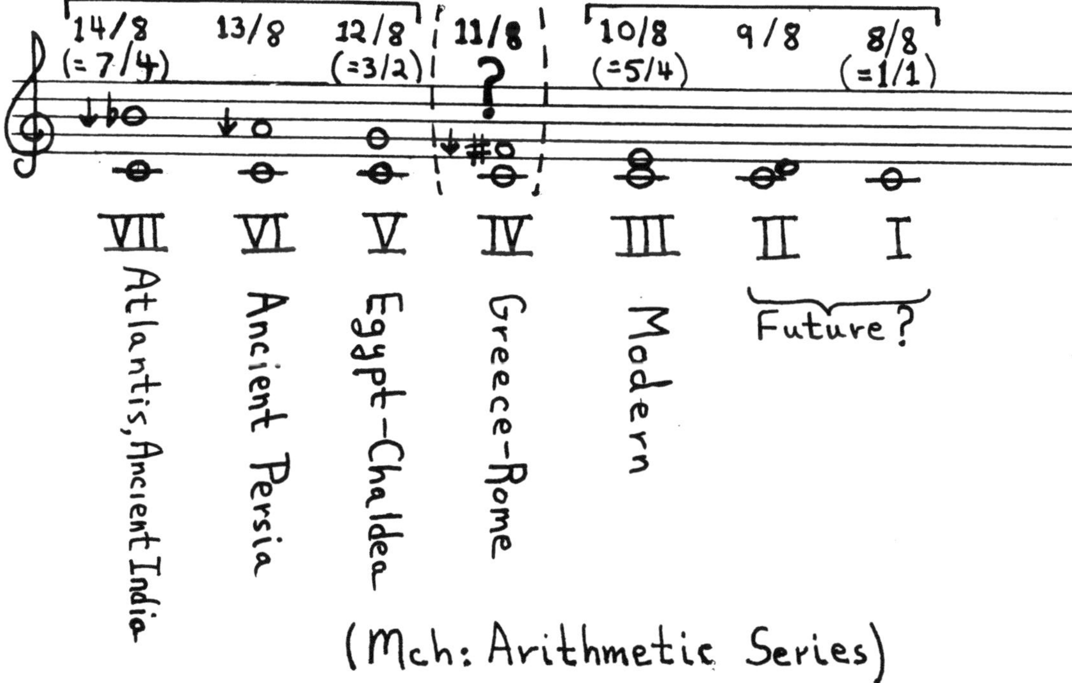

The three uppermost intervals of the scale belong to the old oriental cultures and to Atlantis before them. The three lowest intervals—now that scale has been completed with 9/8 and 8/8—correspond to the third, second and prime of the modern, major scale. The large third 5/4 is the one we must address as the archetypal third; a small third only arises when the large third has been filled out with a fifth, or else through the inversion of the thirds in the minor triad.

Similarly, 7/4, 13/8 and 3/2 are the archetypal seventh, sixth and fifth, for they all stand over the fundamental tone of the arithmetic series or over one of its octaves. For musical experience, these fundamental-based intervals rest on solid ground, whereas the intervals not based on the fundamental tone—eg. the fourth 4/3, and the major and minor sixths (5/3, 8/5)— have a less stable charater in spite of their being consonant. This is because their lower tone is not a fundamental or an octave of the fundamental tone whose overtone series would produce that interval. The scale arising out of the arithmetical series contains all seven intervals in their archetypal form—all based on the fundamental. For this reason, we will call this scale the *fundamental scale* .

This fundamental scale, which nature herself has woven secretly into the earthly overtone series—could it also be the law of the development of human consciousness? Precisely the striking simplicity of the law makes one sceptical. But that should not prevent our testing it, as we shall do in the following chapters. Then we shall see whether the great tree bearing humanity's musical past and future can have grow out of this tiny seed.

Since the Middle Ages, modern, post-Christian people have oriented themselves musically through the experience of a tonic or ground-tone, and so have experienced scales and intervals primarily as ascending. Thus it is most natural for us to picture the development of interval consciousness in terms of the correspondingly ascending fundamental scale of the overtone series. In order to present this same series of post-Atlantean intervals in its older, pre-Christian aspect, it would have to be the inverted, undertone 'mother scale' (compare p. 51f.), in which every interval hangs downward from the octave 8 of the higher generating tone.

The two aspects are equally important for the overall development, and each leads to the same result: the old, undertone-based, minor aspect shows how the intervals of our development have their common root 'in heaven'; the overtone-based, major aspect shows how they stand 'on earth' today, on the ground-tone.

XXV. EXPERIENCE OF THE ANCIENT TONE SYSTEMS: SECOND AND THE PRIME—FUTURE IMPULSES AT WORK IN THE PRESENT

Just once we must dare to try to build a sensitive, lively imagination of how our musical experience would be transformed if we could make the step from our present day experience based on thirds to a future mode of experience *based on seconds*!

Let us start from the wide-awake, clear fourth 4/3, which still belongs to the objective, spiritual forcefield of the fifth and which allows us to take hold of ourselves as if from outside. Proceeding to the third, we are brought into a realm of more dream-like feeling, a realm of inner, personal self-experience. If this realm is spiritually illuminated, then love, reverence, strength of belief and inner divine fulfillment are at home there. Without such light, it is a realm of personal wishes, egoistic longings and illusionary hopes for a hazily-pictured good fortune.

Our characterisation of the intervals shows that the second would take us deeper still into the realm of dreams—namely, to that border where soul experience strikes into the forces of our bodily life. It is the area which today is generally called the unsconscious, an area around which science has been prowling curiously for decades. It is a charateristic of this realm that within it one no longer meets anything personally subjective that has been shaped by our individual life-experience, but rather with something super-individual, objective, archetypal. The objectivity of this realm of the second contrasts strongly with that of the fifth and fourth realm: fifth and fourth experience transpose me into an outer objective world order that I can grasp as a waking human being, beholding and thinking; it leads to the spiritual that lies behind my surrounding sense world. The experience of the second, by contrast, leads to an objective spiritual world which is the hidden basis of my own life forces. In the experience of the second I have to turn so deeply inward that I begin to have artistic musical experiences in the deeply dreaming realm of my own life forces.[38]

Some music of recent times is already rattling the door to the second. But it has not yet been able to open it. The clash of seconds remains more an outer acoustic stimulation than something leading to real inner musical experience. For our normal musical awareness, the second is still a dissonance, an interval of passage, i.e. musical experience cannot yet approach it. One has to go by it and enter at the 'neighbor's door', at the third. Why must the door of the second remain closed? It is because we cannot yet be given free access to our own life forces—not in our present state as citizens of the 20th century, full of egoistic, materialistic, intellectualistic banality and subjectivity. In this state, we would completely shake to pieces the basis of our own physical and psychic health. The disquieting wave of neurotic and psychotic illness which now sweeps over us is a sign that, unintentionally—pathologically— or willfully through such means as drugs, we are advancing into this realm. We are not ripe for it yet, so it works destructively on soul and body.

The ripeness for this further step in consciousness, which would lead to a true musical grasp of the second, can only be achieved by working through our present crisis over the nature of the experience of the third, so that the positive fruits of this crisis can ripen. Our problem and our test is to spiritualise and objectify the realm of the third, working in complete freedom, independent of the past, out of our own inner being. Spiritual laws must become part and parcel of our inmost nature, the most intimate component of our soul experience. Then we can grow naturally into the world of our archetypal unconscious. This no longer would be destructive. Rather the contrary. The world within us which lies hidden behind the musical experience of the second would come to meet us like a stream of unbelievably colorful, differentiated life and strength.

It must be *absolutely clearly* understood that we are not interested here in formulating a programme for the future of musical development. This development goes its own way without paying any heed to clever reflections. What we can do though, if we immerse ourselves deeply enough in the nature of the intervals, is to make ourselves more clearly aware of what already has begun—to sense through purely artistic perception the paths which the music of the present already has begun to forge, albeit as a sleepwalker. In this way, we can discover yet another path alongside that leading towards the interval of the second (which we have tried to clarify by referring to the inner nature of the second). We will try to throw light on this other path in what follows by looking at the development of music in modern times. Both tendencies spring directly out of the status of the third in the present, and each path now and then enlivens the other, although they are of a fundamentally different nature.

When mankind first entered the realm of the third, during the waning of the Middle Ages, it brought with it out of the world of the fourth and fifth the capacity for an objective, spatial musical perception . This tide flowing out of the past on into the period of the third led to the marriage of third and fifth in the triad and carried the third, still living, up to the very gates of the 20th century. Then it subsided. The third experience ceased to be carried on the tide of fifth experience. It was left alone (the most expressive example of the third abandoned and alone: Schoenberg's early atonal piano piece Op. 19, No.2, written in 1911.)

Due to this development, the triad became an empty cliché and, ultimately, disintegrated. With the collapse of the triad, the structure of the major and minor scales which, in the last analysis, are founded on the triad, also fell to pieces. And the process went yet further: when the stream of the fifth ran dry, the circle of fifths, which was the foundation of our tonal cosmos, no longer had a viable musical basis. Before, there had been a living course of upward and downward flowing fifths leading into light or into darkness, opening out or turning inward—all manifest in the colourful life of the church modes, cadential harmonies, and the wonderfully differentiated twelve-fold circle of tonalities. Now, all that was left of this was twelve unrelated tones standing in space, divested of all tonal interval relationships, divested of all possibility of functional or enharmonic clarification. Twelve paralyzed, absolute *primes* stand like uncanny, speechless, stony riddling sphinxes in a desert whose dead and endless stretches of sand give no hint of the blossoming life which lies buried beneath it.

The development towards atonal music must be seen as a path whose goal is the experience of the absolute prime. In 1915 Rudolf Steiner was already describing such an experience as coming in the future.[39] What he described then is by no means fully contained in our present experience of the prime. Atonal tone experience is only a very first beginning out of which this future prime experience can eventually be achieved.

Transformed into music, the sort of experience which recently befell Mihailov and his friends would appear as the real experience of the prime. Into the dark horrors of their years of imprisonment flooded the truth of Solzhenitsyn's sentence, in all its mystical depth: "The centre of the cosmos is within us." The resurrection of the inner spiritual self in the midst of death, destruction and horror, the perfect capacity to maintain our spiritual integrity when the world no longer gives us any hold at all—that is the absolute experience of the prime which we can see coming in the future. It will come at last as the fruit of a development over thousands of years, but it is a development whose beginnings are well known to us: it began in the Middle Ages when we won our way through to the experience of the tonic (prime) tone in the scale.

ANCIENT TONE SYSTEMS

XXVI. THE SYSTEM OF SEVENTHS (ATLANTIS AND ANCIENT INDIA)

We can build a chain out of the seventh 7/4, analogous to the chain of fifths which makes up the system of fifths. If we do, we discover that we already have come full circle after the fifth seventh, for this fifth seventh overreaches the fourth octave of the first tone by a mere 0.442 ht. In order to make this an equal-tempered system, each of the five sevenths has to be shrunk by 0.088 ht: instead of the 9.688 ht of the pure intonation, its new span is 9.6 ht. Experience shows this to be an eminently acceptable intonation for the natural seventh. It is far purer, for example, than the intonation of the large third in our circle of fifths.

The Circle of Sevenths:

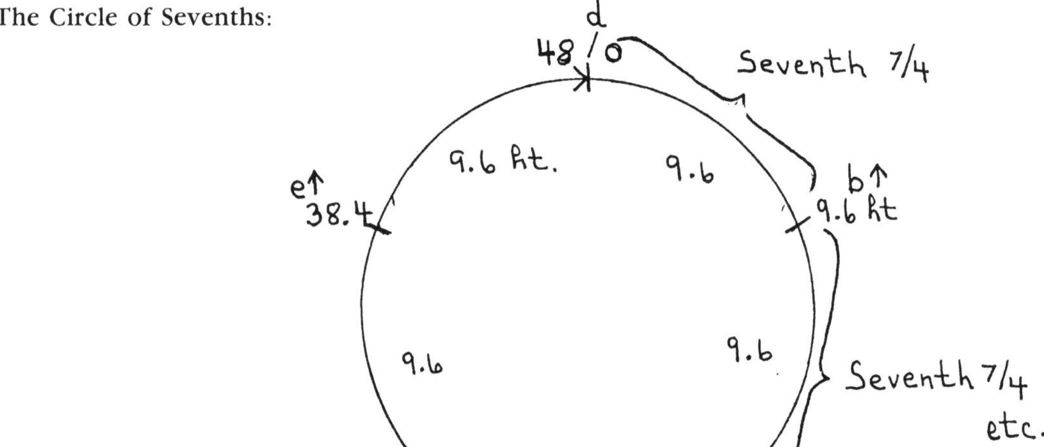

If we once more proceed analogously as with the system of fifths and use octave transposition to bring this tower of sevenths into the space of a single octave, we obtain a scale with five equal steps of a second which, being 2.4ht. in span, lie between our large second and our minor third. Thus, we uncover a pentatonic which seems to level out the difference between large second and minor third found in our familiar pentatonic based on pure fifths. Instead of these two intervals, there is one interval throughout, a quasi-second.

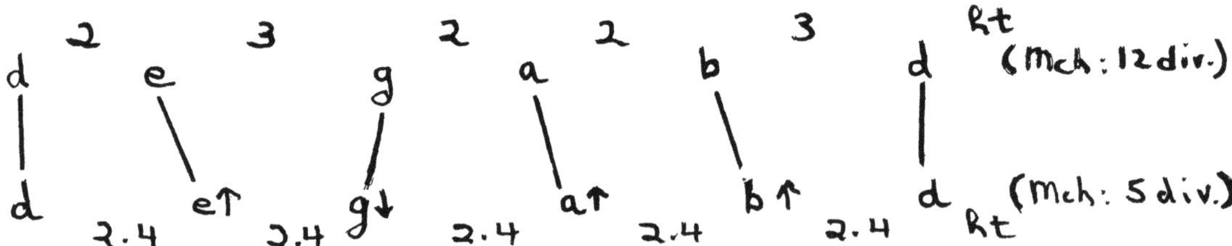

But what has actually happened here is that the seventh 7/4 has brought about the crystallization of a first cyclic system. Anyone who has taught himself to hear and experience this seventh can hear it in all the tonal relationships of this system, just as the fifth can be heard in all the tonal relationships of the Pythagorean system.

Such a pentatonic of equal steps is still to be found in our century in Indonesia's Slendro Scale, as well as scattered over Africa in culturally isolated areas where it clearly is the oldest tonal system (see H. Husemann). It was possible for the this author to show how it also is the real tonal background of certain North American Indian songs. Heinrich Husmann, who is not himself interested in any connections with the natural seventh, believes that the Slendro Scale must be of "ancient Indian" (i.e. India) origins. And, for various reasons, he comes to the conclusion that "the music of the pre-Arian culture, large portions of which have survived in southern India to this day, must have employed the Slendro Scale." [40]

According to Rudolf Steiner, the ancient Atlanteans, who lived on the now sunken continent between America and Africa-Europe, lived musically in the seventh. In those times "...everything was tuned in successions of sevenths. One was not yet even acquainted with fifths."[41] Because the fifth was not yet experienced, it remained an interval which only appeared accidentally in the system of sevenths. Just as the Pythagorean third is not intoned purely in the system of fifths where it is an accidental interval, (i.e. it is not yet really experienced as the interval of the third,) the fifth is impure in the system of sevenths. Rudolf Steiner described how the seventh continued to be experienced on into the early post-Atlantean epochs—the first post-Atlantean epoch is the ancient Indian—until it began to be experienced as unpleasant.

One can see how Rudolf Steiner's description is borne out by musical ethnology: the existence of a system of sevenths in both America and in Africa can be explained by a common place of origin, namely Atlantis, which once lay between the two. The founders of the Old Indian culture, which Steiner pointed to as the first post-Atlantean culture, took this tone system, inherited from Atlantis, with them as they wandered east. Then the system must have spread to Indonesia, where it still is to be found, having meantime fallen out of use in India itself. Naturally, this system built on sevenths also would have used in other lands, for example in South America, where we believe it almost certainly could still be found by someone who has an ear for it. As subsequent post-Atlantean cultures developed in Europe and Asia this system would have been transformed into later systems. Legend has it that the system of fifths was introduced into China during the third millenium B.C. when the twelve *Liu* were introduced. Before the twelve *Liu* there must have been some other tone system, probably the system of sevenths as in India.

For the sake of tonal orientation we have allowed ourselves to refer to the tones of this system with the designations used for the classical pentatonic based on fifths—d e g a b— which actually only developed much later out of the archetypal pentatonic based on sevenths. Nothing regarding the absolute pitch of the tones is thereby intended. It simply would go against the grain to weigh down this tone system, which still is experienced as floating, with today's c, which, as a dark tone among the established basic tones of our system, is much too earthy for the pentatonic. (See p. 19.) Thus, for the Slendro Scale one can either retune the monochord to d, or else one can—"ad libitum"—experience the c' as d'. Furthermore, one must not be misled by our nomenclature, which makes the intervals d-b↑ and g↓-e↑ look like major sixths. In reality, they are natural sevenths just as , for example, e↓-d is. Just as the distinction between the large second and the small third disappears in Slendro, so also does the distinction between their complementary intervals, the small seventh and the large sixth. Similarly the pairs major-third/fourth and small-sixth/fifth each merge in a single interval.

A snake song of the Hopi Indians

One of the most extraordinary aspects of this first cyclic system is that the entire circle of sevenths is present in the single scale. Here, tone system and scale are identical, in contrast to the circle of fifths where a single scale—pentatonic or heptatonic—is only one segment

of the whole. We must even assume that the original system of sevenths consisted of a tower
of consecutive sevenths spanning three to four octaves—a compass over which members of
present day primitive cultures still have practical command. The compression of the sevenths
into the space of a single octave seems to be a later development. The framework of consecutive
fourths found in songs of the Melanesians, North American Indians, African Bushmen and
Laplanders points to such a structure. Walter Wiora[42] believes it might be of paleolithic
origins and in the case of Indian melodies it can be shown to have connections with
Slendro.[43]

This apparent structure of fourths seems to be none other than an early stage in the compression of the tower of sevenths. It arises when the two extreme members of a five-tone chain
of sevenths are transposed two octaves into the midst of the chain. The result is a chain of
small fourths.

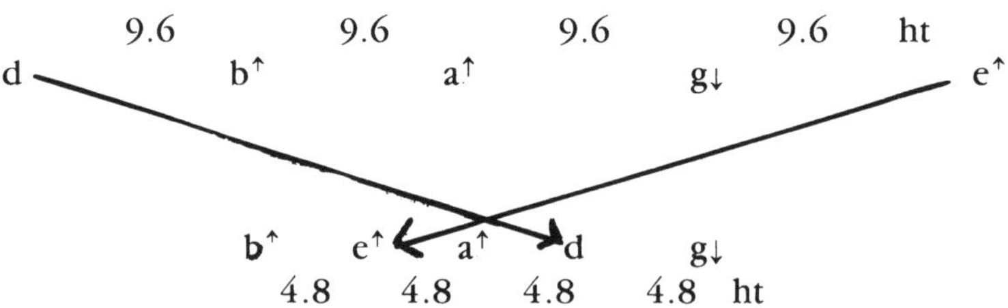

In the second stage of compression the two extreme tones again are transposed into the chain,
the result being the Slendro Scale, a series of large seconds within the compass of one octave
(or seventh).

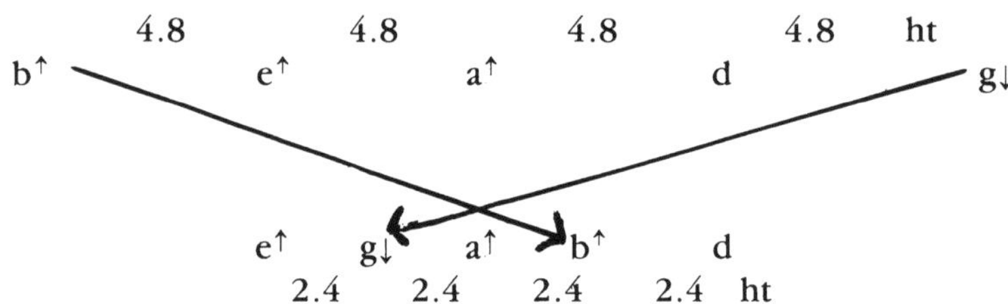

The Indian song just cited points to an early phase in the compression of the chain of fourths—
just the sort of interpenetration of the two stages one would expect to find in practice.

The following provides a picture of the stages of compression of the cycle of five:

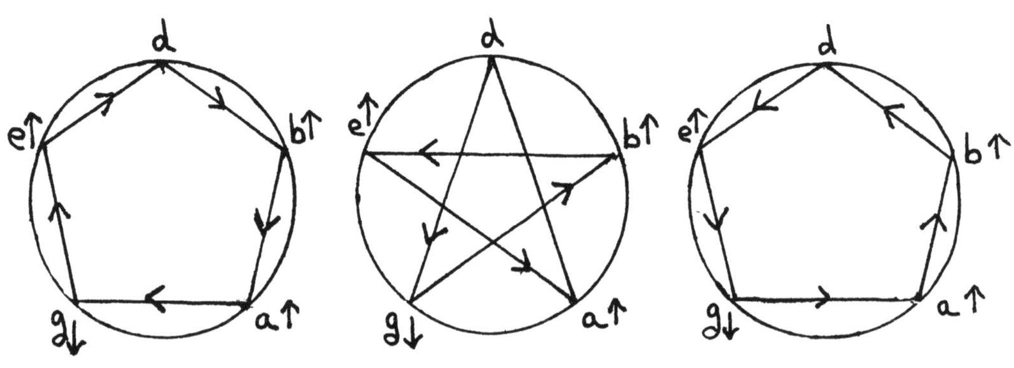

Stage of Sevenths   Stage of Fourths   Stage of Seconds

In the case of the cycle built on sevenths, the centripetal tendency we described as characteristic of a cyclic system is clearly manifested in the actual historical development, whereas the compression of the circle of fifths remains a theoretical supposition. In general, the cycle of sevenths stands out as *the archetypal cyclic system*. By comparison with later systems, it manifests the characteristics of cyclic systems with a unique clarity: the centripetal compression out of a more widely spaced sequence of intervals and the *unified*, symmetrical articulation of the scale. There are only two sorts of second in the scale built on fifths, but the scale built on sevenths has only one, because the entire cycle is contained in the scale. A greater degree of unity in the structure of a scale cannot be imagined.

If one searches music history for something comparable with this system, one is amazed to discover that the only parallel is our own, modern, twelve-tone music. For here, also, an entire cycle—the cycle of twelve—is conceived as a scale, a quasi-scale of small seconds. Thus, at the beginning of cyclic development we find the Slendro, a system which, without developing it, lays the basis for differentiating intervals. (Thus the problem of enharmonic change, which is bound to arise in a cyclic system, does not yet emerge.)[44] At the end of cyclic development we find a system containing a method of differentiating intervals which, in principle, could go on infinitely (See p. 36.) But then atonality leaps over this possibility and makes enharmonic transformation into a hidden factor of every single tone.[45]

If we form the system of sevenths out of pure natural sevenths (9.688 ht) without tempering and close the circle on d, then the first stage of compression would yield a chain of fourths of 4.623 ht. The second stage would yield the following scale of seconds (Mch: Pure 7/4, $f_\downarrow$ is located at the long mark above and to the left of $e^\uparrow$):

(d		$f_\downarrow$		g		$a^\uparrow$		$c_\downarrow$		d)	
0		2.753		5.065		7.377		9.688		12	ht
Size of the second:	2.753		2.312		2.312		2.312		2.312		

The first step $d\text{-}f_\downarrow$, would be larger than the rest. Thus the ambivalence between a large second and a small third might first arise at this point. For the rest, this ambivalence is shared alike by all the oversized seconds of the Slendro Scale. But in this form the first step of the scale would tend to be heard as a small third. The resulting scale is highly agreeable. One should try it on the monochord. The first two steps closely approximate the arithmetical relationship 6:7:8. They take on a radial character when one listens carefully to them.

It is extraordinary that among the recorded and measured Slendro Scales of primitive peoples there is no detectable sign of a tendency to enlarge one of the seconds, although this tendency would follow from a pure intonation. In spite of all the variations in size of second, the measurements of Slendro instruments of Africa and Indonesia give an overall picture of equal steps.[46] It lies in the nature of the system of sevenths to be experienced as a closed cycle, so that the need for tempering never enters consciousness at this stage of musical experience.

XXVII. THE SYSTEM OF SIXTHS (ANCIENT PERSIA)

As post-Atlantean musical consciousness developed further, the sixth 13/8 came within its grasp. This sixth is another interval out of which a cycle, analogous to the circle of fifths, can be built and, indeed, with amazing exactness. Ten such sixths, set over one another in a tower, overreach the seventh octave of the initial tone by a mere 0.05 ht. In order to make a perfect closed circle, each of the ten sixths must be reduced by 0.005 ht , from 8.405 to 8.400 ht. This is one-fourth the degree of tempering (0.02 ht) the perfect fifth must undergo to form our familiar circle of twelve tones—for practical purposes it is an inaudible change.

The circle of sixths:

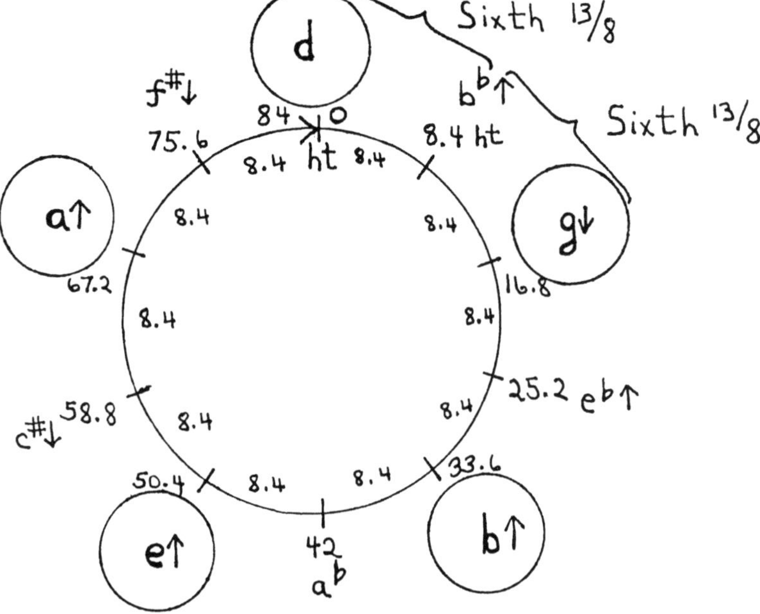

If all ten tones of this tower of sixths are transposed into the space of one octave, the result is a sequence of ten oversized half tones (1.2 ht) which divide the octave into ten equal parts. Thus, in terms of distance, the system of sixths yields a further subdivision of Slendro. The old tones of the system of sevenths—the encircled tones in the following diagram —remain.

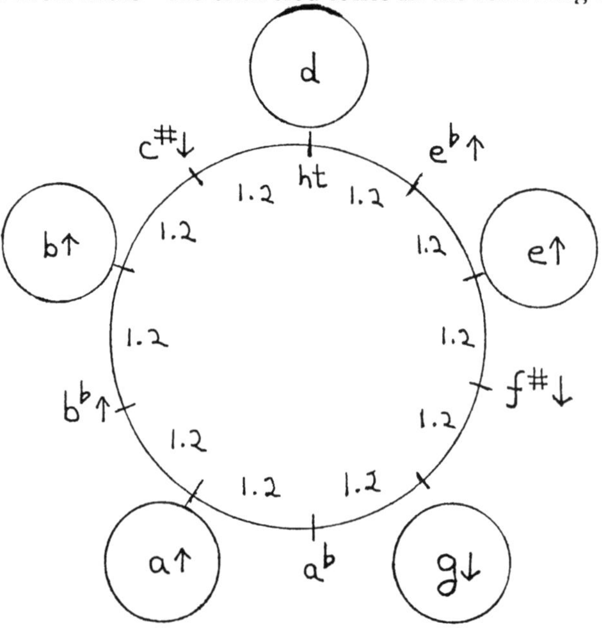

(Mch: 10-division: long and short marks)

Jaap Kunst[47] has reported that Javanese musicians subdivide the Slendro and form two distinct pentatonic scales out of the resulting tenfold division: Madenda and Degung.[48]

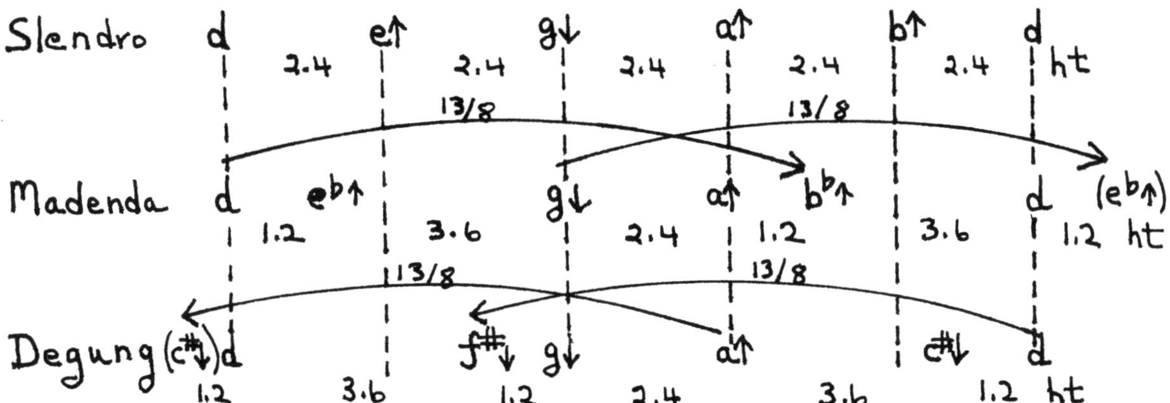

In this so-called halftone pentatonic, the old Slendro acquires, in both cases, two 13/8 sixths: ascending sixths from d and g↓ in Madenda, descending ones from d and a↓ in Degung. The framework of fourths and fifths remains as in the Slendro.

Xylophones tuned to a Slendro scale in which a single sixth has been inserted in a similar manner are to be found in Africa, especially among the Azande.[48)]

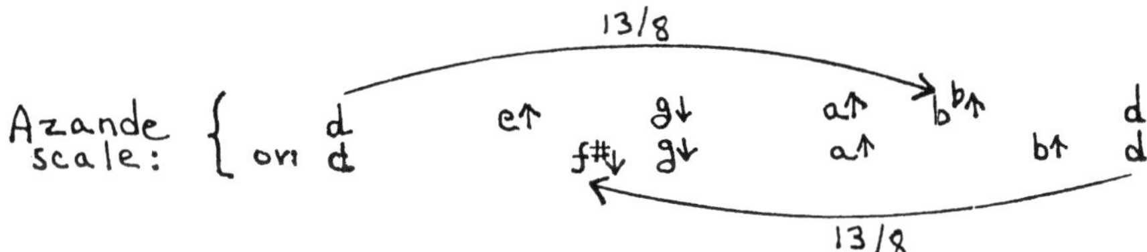

These clearly are stages of transition from the system based on sevenths to that based on sixths—such stages as would be expected for the period of cultural change between Old India and Old Persia. The question whether the Slendro with a single sixth came about as a native African development or as the result of foreign influence is a question which cannot be debated here. Nevertheless, it is interesting to note that, so far as we know, the so-called halftone pentatonic never has been found on the American continent, but only in those parts of the world which lie east of Old Atlantis—places where there was a post-Atlantean cultural development.

A scale built up consequently out of nothing but the sixth leads us—how could it be otherwise?—into the realm of the second post-Atlantean culture, the ancient Persian culture. If we take six sixths, with d as the central tone, out of the circle of sixths:

c# ↓		a↑		f# ↓		d		b♭↑		g↓		e♭↑
	8.4		8.4		8.4		8.4		8.4		8.4		ht

—then we obtain the following scale by bringing these tones into the compass of one octave using octave transposition:

The Persian scale:

d		e♭↑		f# ↓		g↓		a↑		b♭↑		c# ↓		d	
O		1.2		3.6		4.8		7.2		8.4		10.8		12	ht
	1.2		2.4		1.2		2.4		1.2		2.4		1.2		ht

When this scale is played on the monochord (Mch: 10-division), the typical scale of the Near East greets our ears, the scale which, up to now, has had the somewhat misleading name, 'gypsy scale', imposed on it. H. Husmann calls it "the ideal scale of the Persians." Here it will be referred to as *the Persian scale*. Above, the symmetrical form of this scale is shown, built of two matching tetrachords, but this is only one of its forms. As with the church modes, six other forms are possible, and all of these are to be found in the music of Persia, Arabia, the India subcontinent, Israel, North Africa and Southeast Europe.

This scale's over-sized seconds still are widely used. Only with these is it possible to get a genuine impression of the scale—played on the piano with normal halftones it sounds like a mere imitation and is prone to fall into sentimentality. The reason for this is that the objective sixth 13/8 no longer can appear, but is replaced by the subjective sixth 8/5, which has its origins in the third.

But what one does note is that in its present-day form, the framework of fourths and fifths—d g a d—no longer is as it would be if it were derived from the chain of pure sixths, which would be Slendro intonation. Instead, the framework has pure fourths and fifths. Indeed, if we contrast the Persian scale with Slendro, we can hear how the former calls out to have the relationship of the pure fifth incorporated into it, for the fifth relationship occurs no less than four times between the tones of the lower tetrachord, d e^b f# g, and the upper tetrachord, a b^b c# d. Although this structure is exclusively the result of the sixth, it is as though made to order for announcing the experience of the fifth which, for Old Persia, was an experience that still lay in the future. Ultimately, these four fifths are bound to be experienced and intoned as pure fifths of 7.02 ht with the relationship 3/2, instead of the 7.2 ht intonation of the Slendro system.[50]

(Mch: Pers. scale with pure fifths)

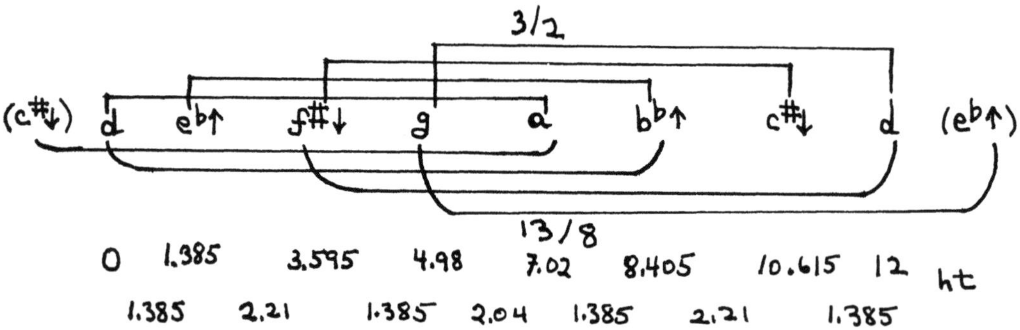

Once the step to pure fifths has been taken, the system of sixths reveals itself as the ideal bridge for carrying over musical development from the Atlantean system of sevenths to the system based on fifths, which is the truly central system of post-Atlantean development.

The same tendency already is to be found in the halftone pentatonic of Madenda and Degung. They consist of two similar trichords which stand in a fifth relationship: d e^b g/ a b^b d, or d f# g / a c# d. Consequently, when halftone pentatonic appears today, it usually is with a framework of pure fourths and fifths—but almost always with over-sized halftones: as, for example, Nyorog and Melog in the Renteng intonation on Java, or as the typical Japanese pentatonic in the Madenda-Nyorog form. The Degung, or Melog, form with its characteristic large halftones, has even been found in Europe. Zoltán Kodály discovered it as the typical scale of the Transdanubian death laments. (Mch: Pers. scale with pure fifths)

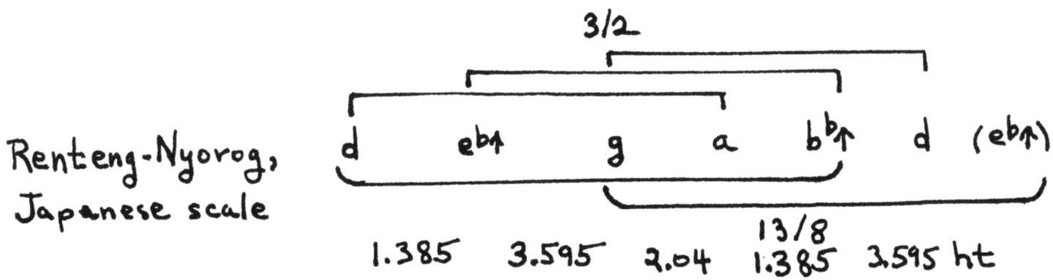

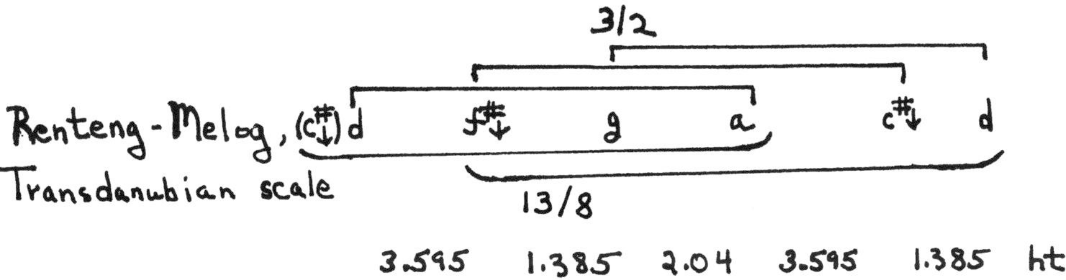

And, as an example to top all the others, a form of the Azande scale with pure fourths and fifths occurs in Rhodesia/Zimbabwe: (Mch: Pers. scale with pure fifths, using the shorter lines for e↑ and b↑)

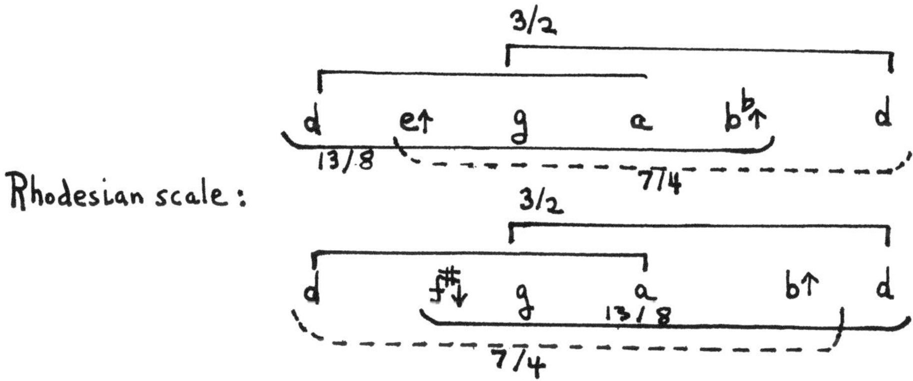

All three intervals —seventh, sixth and fifth—play a role in these scales.

The manner in which the sixth paves the way for an awareness of the fifth is made especially clear by a complex of Javanese scales which are called 'Pelog'. Pelog is a system of seven tones of varying intonation. From these, different pentatonic scales are formed by the omission of two tones. They generally have a halftone pentatonic structure like that of Nyorog and Melog, but with the possibility that the already overlarge halftones can grow to almost wholetone size so that the scale closely approaches the form of a pentatonic with pure fifths and wholetones. Elsewhere the present author has shown more exactly what lies behind this extraordinary phenomenon, a tug-of-war between the sixth 13/8 and the pure fifth.[51] It is a complicated story and would lead us too far afield to go into it here. For now, it is sufficient to indicate essential stages of the transition so that one can play them on the monochord and experience this development from Madenda to a pentatonic of fifths. In reality, the measurements taken indicate points singled out of a continuous transition in which individual stages scarely can be distinguished. Furthermore, the thirds and seconds are not always the same size even on a single given instrument.

$$
\begin{array}{lcccccl}
 & d & e^\flat\uparrow & g\downarrow & a\uparrow & b^\flat\downarrow & d \\
\text{Madenda} & 1.2 & 3.6 & 2.4 & 1.2 & 3.6 & \text{ht (Mch: 10-div.)} \\
\text{Nyorog} & 1.385 & 3.595 & 2.04 & 1.385 & 3.595 & \text{ht (Mch: Pers. scale w/ pure 5}^{\text{ths}}\text{)} \\
\text{Siamese scale} & 1.71 & 3.43 & 1.71 & 1.71 & 3.43 & \text{ht (Mch: 7-div.)} \\
\text{Pentatonic of fifths} & 2 & 3 & 2 & 2 & 3 & \text{ht (Mch: 12-div. or Pyth. scale)} \\
 & d & e & g & a & b & d
\end{array}
$$

The same thing can be demonstrated for Degung, where the structure of the scale has been stood on its head.

At the third stage of transition one encounters a tuning not met before, a system that divides the octave into seven equal steps of 1.714 ht. This sevenfold division of the octave is typical of Siam/Thailand and Burma. In Indonesia it is to be found as one of the possibilities within the Pelog complex, and in Africa the use of a sevenfold division as the basis for pentatonic is widespread. Clearly, this system is an extraordinary sort of arrangement. The sixth 13/8 and the fifth meet, each interval approaching the other by virtually the same distance (sixth: + 0.166 ht; fifth: − 0.162 ht).

When musical consciousness of the sixth 13/8 begins to make itself felt, a confusing multiplicity of scale structures flourishes in its sphere of influence. Connections with the old system of sevenths continue to be maintained after connections with the new interval, the pure fifth, already have been established. There is no longer any question of finding the virtually paradisical simplicity, wholeness and completeness found in the system of sevenths. Already with the Azande scale, in which only one sixth appears, there is a dualistic split: depending on whether the sixth is ascending or descending one finds something which is already akin to our minor and major experience. This distinction becomes more outspoken in the case of Madenda and Degung, or of Nyorog and Melog, which all have two sixths. Consider the authentic scale of sixths, the Persian scale which occurs in the cycle of ten. It has the strongest minor character—at least for our experience—in that mode whose starting tone has the most tones above it in the chain of sixths. The mode with the most tones under it in the chain of sixths has the strongest major character.[52] In other words, there is a remarkable reversal of the relationships found in our scales built on a system of fifths where ascending fifths are allied with major character, descending with minor. Nevertheless, in both the system of fifths and the system of sixths, ascending or descending in the system results in one of two clearly distinguishable qualities. Both are a complete contrast with the system of sevenths, where all sevenths, ascending or descending, lead to the same scale structure and the same single quality. No differentiation between major and minor can arise in Slendro.

We are looking at a musical expression of the fundamental transformation involved in moving from the ancient Indian's feeling for the world to that of the ancient Persian. For the Persian, India's unified world was split into the fundamental polarity of light and darkness. In Old India, whether one pursued the path which led through the *maya* of sense experience or whether one pursued the path through the depths of ones own soul, the pursuit led to experience of the same unified spiritual world. The Persian, however, encountered the upper gods on one of these paths through the mysteries and the lower gods on the other. There was an immeasurable abyss dividing the two.[53] The same secret lies at the heart of the contrast between the ascending and descending streams of fifths and, furthermore, is what is behind the contrast between our sharp keys and flat keys. From such a vantage point one begins to suspect what immensities lie hidden behind the possibility of enharmonically transforming a sharp tone into a flat tone.

The ascending path and the descending path first separate musically in the tone system of ancient Persia. This entails the separation of scale and tone system. The two no longer are identical as in Slendro. The scale becomes one-sided—it can only embody one path, one aspect. The tone system contains the entire world, but it cannot be grasped from one direction alone, or from a single aspect. The scale is subject to the laws of time, is changeable, has a beginning and an end. The tone system exists in an enduring space, changeless, encompassing infinity within itself.

This perspective shows how this most unique, sevenfold division of the octave in the Siamese scale might have come about. It very nearly manages to unify scale and tone system again, for in this pentatonic the sixth and seventh tones can appear casually as passing tones, or secondary tones (like the Chinese *pien*). The contrast between the major and minor forms of the halftone pentatonic is thereby neutralized because the distinction between halftone and wholetone disappears—that distinction between halftone and wholetone being the only thing distinguishing *nyorog* from *melog* . On the other hand, the sevenfold division stops short of a tuning with pure fifths and true wholetones and so avoids being affected by the fifth stream's twofold path into the unlimited. Does the form of this tone system perhaps reveal the efforts of a cultural movement to cover up by force the abyss which was beginning to open out before the human soul? —and thus to preserve a paradisical world unity at the post-Atlantean stages of sixth and fifth experience?

XXVIII. THE SYSTEM OF FIFTHS (EGYPT-CHALDEA, CHINA)

The interval of the third post-Alantean cultural epoch is the pure fifth 3/2, an interval which is especially prominent in ancient Egypt, Chaldea, and in ancient Hebrew culture. This epoch begins approximately with the third millenium before Christ. Rudolf Steiner described a major turning in the history of humanity at this time: from this point on there was a progressive loss of the capacity for having direct spiritual experience except when it was kept awake through special schooling in the mystery centers. Naturally, isolated cases of clairvoyance also occurred, atavistic relics of earlier times. This clouding over of ancient clairvoyance is what is meant when Indian texts speak of the beginning of the 'Kali Yuga',the 'dark age'. At this time cultural development begins to be based on outer things, things experienced through the senses. That is why historical accounts of outer facts go back no further than this period. Before it, we have almost nothing but mythical accounts, i.e. descriptions of supersensible events clairvoyantly observed. Anything before 3000 B.C. is 'prehistoric'.

Advent of the Kali Yuga left its mark in the course of musical development: tone systems which antedate 3000 B.C. were based on intervals involving the high prime numbers 7 and 13; they were superceded by the simple relationship 3/2 of the pure fifth. Perceptually and acoustically the relation of the pure fifth is easy to grasp. With the Kali Yuga the fifth becomes the fixed horizon by which musical hearing orients itself. Anyone who pays close attention will notice that it is necessary to get a little bit outside of oneself in order to experience the seventh 7/4 or the sixth 13/8 musically. Then, when one comes to the fifth, one sets one's feet on the earth for the first time. Earlier music theory was very clear about the fact that the musicality of earthly humanity reaches only as far as the number six, the *Senarius* , in the relations of the arithmetic and harmonic series. Well into the 20th century we find Paul Hindemith remarking that beyond this boundary, from seven on, is the beginning of a 'holy region' which is 'inaccessible to our tonal experience'[54] — in other words, for the tonal experience of earthbound humanity. It is only because we now are in the beginning of an age after the end of the Kali Yuga that it is possible for us to begin to hear intervals like 7/4 and 13/8 musically and understand the wonderful tone systems based on them.

In the past, we Westerners have been so entirely under the influence of the Kali Yuga —i.e., under the musical influence of the Egyptian system of fifths — that we could only register the ancient exotic systems as curiosities. Such systems were closed off from our musical experience because the guiding-line of the fifth was missing. The first half of the 20th century witnessed a scientific tragicomedy which, to this day, has not been understood. Clarification lies in seeing that someone was trying to deal with these ancient systems while he still was a complete captive of the system of fifths. Erich von Hornbostel[55] discovered that a too-narrow fifth could be produced by unskilled overblowing of a panpipe segment. Having thoroughly misled his own musical sensibilities concerning this "blown fifth" ("Blasenquint"), he proceeds to try to force the ancient tone systems into the fictive framework of a 23-tone "circle of blown fifths"("Blasenquintzirkel"). If he had been able to start from the old intervals he would not have had to do such violence to his own musical hearing or to the ancient tone systems. He would have been able to enter into the exotic systems in a completely natural way. (For justice's sake, we must mention here that Hornbostel's students reported that his early death prevented his retracting his theories, in which he no longer believed.)

As these connections begin to dawn on us, we can only acknowledge with astonished gratitude the guidance of our world, which has preserved the last remnants of those intervals from the 'holy region', 7/4 and 13/8, in the exotic musical systems—preserved them, moreover, into the time when a new musical consciousness begins to make itself felt and before the global influence of western music totally blots out more ancient music. One would expect to find these intervals used in the Syrian and Egyptian predecessors of the *aulos* . Certainly, they are prominent in the 'mother scale' of the ancient Greek *aulos* , which flows as through subterranean channels down the thousands of years of the Kali Yuga into the music of peasant and

74

shepherd of the early 20th century. Bartók found it there a few years before the channel ran dry, at precisely the same time as the circle of fifths inherited from Egypt arrived at its final station in Europe, atonal twelve-tone music. Here, also, the current of the ancient, 'holy' intervals was just strong enough to carry them to a point from which they could be taken up in a new, inward way at the dawning of a new age.

To be sure, today it is not possible to enliven these ancient intervals by simply drawing on their prehistoric past—by reviving Slendro or halftone pentatonic or the Persian scale. This must be acknowledged with all possible clarity. These intervals can never become really artistically fruitful for today's music by way of superficial attempts at imitation. First, we need to follow the path of musical intensification as far as the third (the path we described on p. 57f). Then, having objectified the experience of the third, we can press foreward toward the second and the prime. Only then can the ancient intervals be reborn—out of an entirely new musical consciousness. Then they can be taken up artistically.

The earliest steps on this path inwards must be set at about 3000 B.C., at the beginning of the dark time of the Kali Yuga. It was only through humanity's loss of supersensible experience and its consequent isolation as a solitary spiritual dweller in the desert of mere sense experience that the inward path became possible. Thus, the loss of the old sixth and seventh also was necessary for the interiorization of musical experience, for these led people out of themselves rather than to themselves. The pure fifth, a descending fifth, gave humanity its first opportunity to find itself in musical experience. As we more than once have observed (p. 15ff., 31, 35f., 57.) the ascending fifth once more carries us outside ourselves. Thus the fifth is the only interval in which we can weave back and forth between experiencing ourselves from within and from without. We remain *outside* of ourselves in the sixth and seventh. In fourth, third and second we remain *in* ourselves. In the fifth there is a breathing between within and without.

For the sake of a better understanding, let us return to the listening example described on p. 57. There we made the following observations: the ascending fifth (such as c-g) is like a question and opens itself to the world; the descending fifth (such as c-f) is an answer, a returning to oneself in which one receives and assimilates the clarifying and resolving answer that approaches. Now, let us make the same experiment with the sixth 13/8 (Mch: 10-division f# ↓d—b^b↑)! Very quickly we experience that we have lost the feeling of alternately breathing ourselves in and out, now open, now closed, swinging about a central point. The movement upwards detaches itself from the movement downwards. The ascending sixth and the descending sixth throw us into entirely different worlds. We lose the middle that binds the two spheres together, i.e. we lose our center within ourselves. With the fifth, I myself am that which opens itself out or closes itself off. With the sixth, two contrasting spaces are revealed, spaces which no longer can unite in me. Thus the fifth with its breathlike alternation between going out of oneself and drawing into oneself, is the earliest interval of musical self-discovery.

Once this is grasped it becomes clearer in retrospect why—in contrast with the fifth—the *ascending* Persian sixth results in a scale which is experienced as similar to *minor* and the *falling* sixth results in a sort of *major* scale (see p. 72.) I *raise myself* into the heights with an ascending fifth—thus major; I *myself sink* into the depths with a descending fifth—thus minor. In contrast, what is below *raises itself* into the heights with the ascending sixth 13/8—the darkness of the depths wells up: minor. With the falling sixth 13/8, what is above, the light of the heights, descends: major.

Having repeatedly met the fifth as the bearer of the earliest musical self-discovery, it should not surprise us that a tone system containing the laws of the ego is based on the fifth. Just as the seventh led to a cycle of five tones and the sixth to a cycle of ten, the fifth leads to a cycle of twelve, a twelvefold division of the space of the octave. Rudolf Steiner explained how the laws of human selfhood are bound up with twelvefoldness. The twelvefold organization of the human senses is one of the most fundamental prerequisites of earthly self-consciousness. Long after it was known that the traditional five were an incomplete picture of our senses, Rudolf Steiner described how twelve different senses connect us with our earthly surroundings or, differently expressed, how there are twelve senses which enable us to live in earthly surroundings.[56] Anyone who carefully studies Steiner's teaching about the senses can discover how the nature of the individual senses is to be found again in the characteristics of the twelve keys of the circle of fifths, as we briefly sketched them in the chapter on the character of the keys. This is no subject, for nearsighted speculation. It requires a reflection on real musical experience. (See Appendix I).

It is an accomplishment of the third post-Atlantean cultural epoch, the age of the fifth, to have taken the specific laws of humanity that have to do with our nature as ego-bearing beings with senses, and to have made this order the inner structural principle of a tone system. In this age, the Kali Yuga having begun, humanity became much more dependent on the activity of the senses; people had to unfold their individual beings within the restrictions of this sense activity, cut off from clairvoyant experiences. The senses became the means by which humanity had to come to terms with its earthly surroundings.

Unlike the ancient Persian or the ancient Indian, the people of this third epoch were not able to penetrate consciously to what lies *behind* sense appearances. But the Egyptians, and especially the Chaldeans, were able to arrive at imaginative forms accessible to sense experience which captured the spiritual laws on which matter is grounded. Thereby the logic which rules the world of the senses was revealed to humanity. In this fashion there arose in those times something which we today would call geometry and astronomy—not, however in the form of a rational science, but rather as an imaginative wisdom drawn from the world of the senses. The pure fifth is bound to be at home in such a culture, as one can easily feel on the artistic and musical level. For one thing, the fifth is accessible to the senses. In every sounding tone, the fifth is present as the third and most prominent overtone. For another, there is its clarity and spirituality. It gives one the feel of an absolute logic which, lying clearly spread out before the senses, does not need to be pondered or puzzled over. The world of the fifth is musical geometry.

The Egyptians and Babylonians experienced the laws of the sun's path through the heavens in the same manner: in terms of the zodiac with its twelve grandiose pictures, a cosmic circle of fifths which marked the limit of the world the senses could reach. Behind the sphere of the stars begins a spiritual world not accessible to the senses, even as the supersensible, spiritual being of a person begins behind the circle of the twelve senses. The sense world unfolds between these two, and the people of the Kali Yuga had to learn to deal with it. In the macrocosm, the twelve signs of the zodiac are both the limit of the sense world and the gate to the spiritual world... which is just what the twelve senses are in the human microcosm.

In music these two are one and the same thing: the twelve-membered circle of fifths. Hermann Beckh has described this circle (understood as the circle of keys) more from the point of view of the Zodiac.[57] We tried, at least in sketch form, to show how the keys might be characterized from the other side, showing how music reflects the twelve inner qualities, or attitudes, by which the self connects itself with the world through the twelve senses. We believe that both approaches give direct access to the musical realities and are in agreement musically.

What a contrast greets one when one turns from the twelve to the ten of the ancient Persian system! It is engendered by the ratio of the golden section (*sectio aurea*), see p. 56f. which qualitatively expresses a superhuman endlessness. The longing for the endless also is characteristic of the Persian scale taken from the cycle of ten. In Egypt, the divine ratio became the simple proportion 3/2, which was so important to the Egyptians that they even had a special hieroglyph for it. Out of 3/2 grew a musical twelvefoldness which was more than a 'mere' endlessness: it is an infinity that is graspable by finite means (See p. 35f.)

In order to give the infinite temporal stream a finite character, the Egyptians ordered time in twelve: the twelve months of the year which arise through the sun's yearly circuit of the Zodiac and, further, the twelve hours of day and night. Even the Seven, that great counterpart of the Twelve—both cosmically, as the old number of the planets, and musically—has to make its way through the twelve or the twentyfour before it can participate in the temporal ordering of the week. Dio Cassius (ca. 155-299 A.D.) give the following account of how the Egyptians alloted the various days of the week to particular planetary gods: "One numbers the hours of the day and night, beginning with one, and allots the first to Saturn, the second to Jupiter, the third to Mars, the fourth to the Sun, the fifth to Venus, the sixth to Mercury, and the seventh to the Moon. This accords with the spatial order of their spheres as the Egyptians reckoned them. Continuing in this way until one has counted all twentyfour hours, one finds that the first hour of the following days falls to the Sun. Continuing through the next twentyfour hours, the Moon receives the first hour of the next day, and each of the succeeding days receives its alloted god by further reckoning. So say the records."[58] Thus, Saturday gets Saturn, Sunday the Sun, Monday the Moon (lundi = Lunae dies), Tuesday Mars (mardi = Martis dies), Wednesday Mercury (mercredi = Mercurii dies), Thursday Jupiter (jeudi = Jovis dies), Friday Venus (vendredi = Veneris dies).

Seven and twelve are interwoven in this fashion in the calendar, just as they are interwoven musically in the system of fifths. The seven always is a path from a beginning to a goal. Musically, it is the scale with its dynamic of seven intervals. All temporal evolution is governed by sevenfoldness. But when time is absorbed by twelvefoldness, it is seen from the point of view of eternity ... as revolving. Twelve turns time into something spatial and static. The seven classical planets are the macrocosmic symbol of temporal change and development. The twelvefold Zodiac of the fixed stars is the macrocosmic symbol of eternal duration and immutability. And in the microcosmos, in the human being, it is the spiritual center which we call the "I" which is immutable and eternal. The Self. By shaping the tone system into a twelvefoldness, the third post-Atlantean culture made it possible for the "I" to have a musical life for the first time. Now the Self could resound in harmony with the macrocosmic Zodiac, the source of duration to which its immutable nature makes it related.

The counterpart of the human "I" and spirit, the soul, is older than both. Its element is the mutable. The soul intimately experiences everything that is changed by time. Thus, in music, the seven—as a seven-membered scale —is correspondingly older than the twelve. It first appears in the Persian scale. But one already can sense the germinal presence of the seven in Madenda and Degung, which are pentatonic scales containing two sixths. If these two scales are combined, the result is the seven tones of the Persian scale. (See p. 69.) A less direct path leads from Madenda-Degung by way of Nyorog-Melog to a sevenfold division of the octave in the Siamese pentatonic with its two *pien* . In comparison with the old, archetypal Slendro pentatonic, what is new in Madenda-Degung and the other halftone pentatonic, inclusive of the Persian scale, is the appearance of a *mutability* of feeling which is somewhat akin to our major and minor. This mutability is the result of seconds of *varying* size, which make a variety of scale structures possible. With this in mind, we should remind ourselves of the sevenfold major and minor differentiation of the church modes (p. 18), and of the sevenfold differentiation of seconds in the *aulos* scale (p. 44f)! Such mutability of experience makes it possible for the *soul* to experience itself in music for the first time, feeling in the music how it reverberates with the dynamic of the planets as they call forth continuous mutation in the macrocosm. To have been the first to have made this possible in music is the great accomplishment of the second post-Atlantean culture, the Old Persian.

Pausing here for an overview of the development of scale and tone-system, we can say: The static quality of space and the dynamic quality of time are not yet separated from one another in the ancient, five-membered cycle of sevenths. Cosmic wisdom and unchanging law and the living soul experience which accompanies them in the stream of time are still held together in one whole. All subsequent pentatonic contains an echo of this state of being: for example, the pentatonic based on fifths which is so natural to younger children. The sixth, which makes a places for itself in the Slendro scale and ultimately transforms it into the seven-membered Persian scale, separates off the soul from the cosmic order and makes it independent of that order. At last, with the system of fifths, both of these find expression and are brought into relation with one another— the static, spiritual, cosmic order of the Twelve and the dynamic soul-mutability of the Seven. Thereby the soul's development, which is presented in the seven intervals of the scale, receives a truly human imprint for the first time, the imprint of the human "I" which is lacking in the Persian scale.

Many contemporaries are bound to object to our description of how a static twelve and a dynamic seven is perfectly reflected in the musical system of fifths. They will object to both the macrocosmic and the microcosmic descriptions on the grounds that this only applies to the old Ptolemaic picture of the cosmos with its seven planets, but no longer to our modern picture of nine planets, exclusive of Sun and Moon (Mercury, Venus, Earth, Mars, Jupiter, Saturn, Uranus, Neptune, Pluto). So the question arises whether our presentation of the musical and cosmic significance of these things is not founded on an old error?

If it is understood in the right sense, there is a comparison that can help us at this point: when one wants to experience a drama fully and take in what its author expressed in dramatic, poetic form, then one gives one's full attention to the persons and actions presented on the stage,. But peering through a slit in the curtain and trying to integrate the activity of the stagehands into the impression of the drama would hardly help to understand the work of art. This latter approach, however, is analogous to what today's natural scientist does, peering at the heavens through his instruments, whereas the Egyptians and Babylonians gazed directly at what the heavens opened out before their eyes. In a process that could almost be called 'artistic', their totally human gaze brought them directly to imagination of the beings who stand behind the planets. But the limits of our senses, of our 'sight', are the limits of our humanity. Only within these bounds are we fully human and in complete and balanced possession of the conscious and unconscious powers in us. Only our calculating and comparing powers of reason are able to go beyond these limits with the help of instruments. Restricted to instruments alone, we will never uncover more than a soulless, inhuman, cosmic machinery, for the full powers of the human soul cannot participate in such research. The ancient Egyptians and Babylonians did not need instruments to witness the drama of the starry heavens as its creator had meant it—it revealed itself to their senses and to their souls. Therefore, please note that we here maintain, flatly contradicting the common opinion of our age, which is estranged from humanity, that the visible world is made, above all else, for humanity.

Someone who wants to use instruments to sharpen their perceptions for research into nature needs to balance this heightening of their empirical perceptions with correspondingly intensified efforts from another side. They need also to intensify their capacity for artistic perception, to clarify and deepen their capacity for a beholding that is informed by a wakeful spirit and soul. Such effort is required, for example, by the schooling of modern, anthroposophical spiritual science.[59] It is necessary for maintaining the state of inner balance appropriate to humanity. By developing such faculties one can discover, for example, how deeply significant it is when our modern science reveals that the Sun, which first appears to our eyes as a planet, actually is a fixed star, and that the Moon, in contrast, is a satellite of the Earth. The modern view makes the nature of these two 'planets' even clearer than it was for the ancients from their perspective. From time immemorial the Sun has been seen as connected with the human ego, and thus with what in humanity is immutable and akin to the fixed stars. The course of the Sun is the Zodiac. The Sun enkindles the sense of sight, the brightest and most awake of the human senses. The Sun rules over the rhythm of waking and sleeping, of day and night, which is a rhythm of the ego. The Moon, on the other hand, is the 'planet' which brings the metamorphosing powers of the planets most radically into the sphere of the Earth—in the changes of the tides and of the weather, in the rhythms of the life forces and reproductive forces, which are also reflected in the soul. The Moon has always been known as the star of changeability and inconstancy. The German word 'Laune' (= mood, temper, humour) is known to have the same root as 'luna'.

Our description of the Egypto-Chaldean system of fifths has been less of an historical description than those of the two preceeding chapters. Instead, we have tried to comprehend the force of this system in terms of the way it works from out of the third post-Atlantean epoch over into our own time. Because the time of the fifth diverges much less from today's musicality than does the wholly contrasting interval consciousnesses of Old India or Old Persia, it is not possible to characterize it with such sharp contours as we did for the times of the seventh or the sixth. The principle of the fifth which was attained in those times is still actively at work in our own music—in the circle of fifths.

It was precisely during the Egypto-Chaldean cultural epoch that the ancient Chinese also began to connect themselves with the fifth as a system-building interval. Indeed, they leapt *immediately* to the closed cycle of twelve. This is recounted in a legend telling how the mythical emperor Huang-ti (3000 B.C.) established the twelve guiding tones, the twelve holy *Liu* . Hermann Pfrogner has pointed out the extremely significant fact that China's system of fifths has its beginning in the archetypal circle of twelve, whereas the western tonal system only comes to the circle of twelve as its goal and fulfillment, having first followed a path of development through the Egypto-Chaldean and then the Greek and Roman cultures.[60] In this, China shows itself to be culturally dedicated to that which is static and archetypally cyclic in nature. China's pentatonic, entirely lacking in halftones and tied to the cycle of twelve, is nothing other than an imitation of the archetypal Atlantean cycle of we encountered in the pentatonic cycle of sevenths.   (See Appendix I.)

78

This primal 'egg', the ancient Atlantean cycle of five, was broken into more and more pieces by the succeeding post-Atlantean cultures, under which it acquired a more temporal nature and developed towards the seven membered scale. This was a musical journey, and only through development it engendered in the human "I" was the totality to be discovered again ... in the cycle of twelve. China circumvented this painful, dangerous path in which the all-encompassing circle is fragmented, i.e. the path through the Age of Darkness. This was accomplished, in the third pre-Christian millenium, by fleeing into the future when it ceased to be possible to preserve a living experience of the Atlantean seventh. Huang-ti replaced the old cycle of five, which still bore within itself the seeds of a temporal development, with the cycle of twelve, which already transcended the temporal and was a musical reflection of eternity. With this cycle and with a pentatonic scale which lacks halftones and which, unlike the seventone scales, cannot be experienced as a 'path', China was able in a certain sense to keep itself musically in the condition of Atlantean primordial wholeness.

It is significant that the Chinese cycle of twelve is not primarily understood as a cycle of fifths, a cycle in which each ascending fifth expresses an opening oneself outward, and each descending fifth a closing oneself off—just that very thing is missing which we discovered as the seed of self discovery in the experience of the fifth.

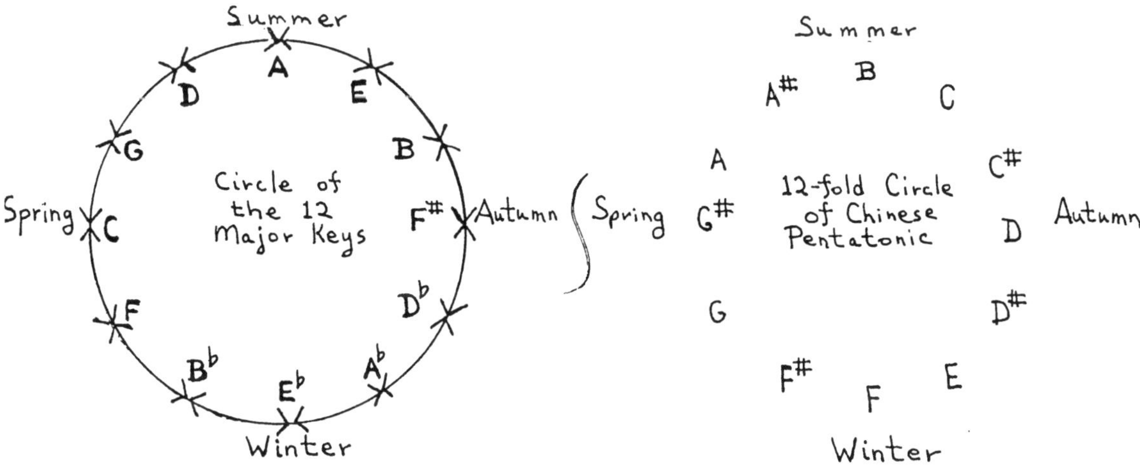

E ^{b} major is experienced by us as akin to midwinter. From there the soul opens itself in a succession of ascending fifths, month by month, coming to a springlike experience in F major and C major, and to a May experience in G major, proceeding on toward summer, autumn and again to winter. Beginning with E major and B major, we proceed from the outward, visible world to the invisible world we enter in autumn and winter. For the Chinese, the prescribed scale for winter is that based on the first *Liu* , the Chinese 'concert tone', *'Huang tschung'* (approximately our f):

f g a   c d

The following months are not alloted so that spring is approached through a series that open out in steps of a fifth from this f. Instead, they follow in a simple succession of half tones:

f$^\#$ g$^\#$ a$^\#$ c$^\#$ d$^\#$

g a b   d e

Thus, the human soul, with its capacity for self experience, for ego experience, is not engaged in such a way that it can experience the course of the year as a rhythmic inner swinging between within and without. The cycle of the year has been projected into the static sphere of eternity—at least, that is how it looks to us today.

To be sure, the Chinese understood how the ascending fifth opens out and how the falling fifth draws together, but they did not understand them as embodying polar capacities of the soul, capacities that can be found in one individual and that manifest in a swinging toward and away from the individual's center. They understood them simply as two distinct entities, one embodying each tendency. With their fine sense for giving things appropriate names, the Chinese called the lower tone of a fifth the 'man'. This is the tone emphasized by the falling fifth with its characteristic conclusive, concentrating forcefulness—rooted, as it were, in the soil. The upper tone of a fifth they called the 'woman', for the rising fifth expresses receptiveness, openness, a going out of oneself, devotion. For the Chinese, a being rooted to the earth clearly had nothing to do with the nature of womanhood: they even saw to it that their women's feet remained small.

We are aware that today's musical research is still uncertain whether the tones of the Egyptian and Mesopotamian scales already were determined by fifths, but much speaks for the view that they were and nothing contradicts it. The more deeply the fifth is experienced, the clearer it becomes how perfectly it expresses the bearing of soul achieved by the Egypto-Mesopotamian—and also the Hebraic—cultures. And the musical problems of our present age still are unmistakably influenced by that third cultural epoch, the epoch of the fifth.

More than once, Rudolf Steiner described the materialism of the modern age as the "shadow of Egypt", as an element of Egyptian culture which had progressed no further. In the Egypto-Chaldean cultures those forces which wholly bound humanity to the realm of the material senses first began to come into play. When the effectiveness of these forces extends beyond their own period they hold humanity imprisoned in the realm of the material. That is what is happening today...in a time when we again should free ourselves from this realm.

Thus today the system of fifths has two faces. One of its aspects is that it brings to music that maximal clarity without which self-consciousness could never come to musical expression. No other tonal system has the crystalline logic and inner stability of the system based on fifths. Seen from another side, this very same strength is capable of imprisoning music in a straitjacket which prevents any further development. Today's tonal system still is dominated by the fifth. It has about it a kind of complusiveness against which many of today's musicians rebel—instinctively, if not out of a thorough understanding. Unfortunately, this rejection frequently spends itself in bitter theoretical complaints about our twelvetone temperament. After the complaints, when things get serious and something practical must be done, the old system is wheeled back on to the field.

There is no doubt that modern tempering involves a further descent into the imprisoning laws of the fifth as compared with the middletone temperament or Baroque unequal temperament. (See p. 28) From this one aspect, the 'shadow of Egypt' really is to be seen in the tempered cycle of twelve, from its early beginnings to its rigidification in twelvetone atonality and twelvetone technique. But a superficial repeal of the tempered cycle of twelve does not achieve much for the further development of music. It can only be overcome from within, when a new interval consciousness, expressive of newly won regions in the human soul, begins to shine through our music.

XXIX. THE SYSTEM OF FOURTHS (GREECE AND ROME): THE APOLLONIAN CYCLIC SYSTEM BASED ON THE PURE FOURTH

At the dawning of the next epoch, the fourth post-Atlantean epoch, we encounter three fundamentally distinct scale systems: a cyclic system based on the pure fourth, a radial system in the *aulos* scales and a chromatic, or enharmonic, system.

* * *

The first of these systems is the Pythagorean system mentioned in earlier chapters. It is nothing other than the fifth-based system just described, whose origin is in the interval consciousness of the Egypto-Chaldean epoch. The only difference is that the Greeks base this system on the interval of the fourth rather than that of the fifth. In an earlier chapter we saw how the fourth, as complementary interval of the fifth, leads to the same tonal system: proceeding in the contrary direction to the fifth, the fourth also generates a cycle of twelve.

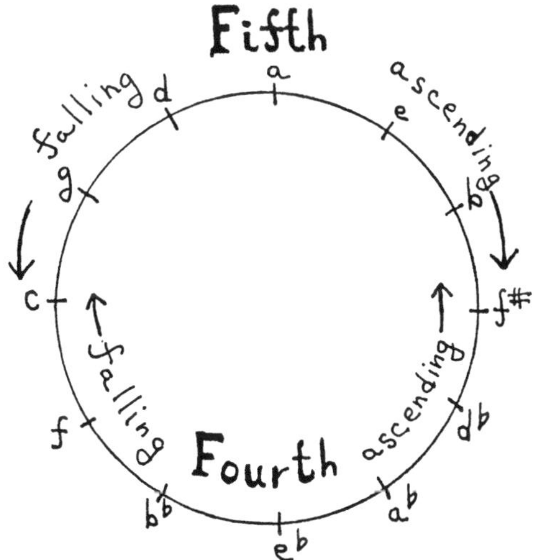

In a listening exercise (p. 58) we heard how the fifth is inverted and made more inward in the experience of the pure fourth. The question that the ascending fifth asked of the world became, in the falling fourth, an inner question that one put to oneself. The answer which the facts give me in the descending fifth becomes in the ascending fourth an answer I must produce out of myself.

The Greek philosopher-thinkers found it necessary to search more and more within themselves for the imaginations which an Egyptian or Chaldean found in his immediate sense experience. This change marks the point in evolution where the macrocosm first can arise anew in human thought as microcosm. In Greek philosophical thought the Logos of the macrocosm is reborn, stage by stage, as the Logos of the microcosm. The transition from Platonic to Aristotlean thinking was a significant step in this development: whereas for Plato the "Ideas" were understood imaginatively as being that in the Macrocosm which produces the things of the senses, Aristotle connects ideas with the microcosmic nature of human thinking.

In Plato's *Timaeus* we witness how the creator god builds up the macrocosmic World Soul entirely out of musical-mathematical relationships. The groundplan is laid out in accordance with two mathematical sequences based on two and three—in other words, on the prime numbers which build the fifth. The conception still is very much in the spirit of the Egypto-Chaldean epoch.

Sequence 1:	1(C)	2(c)	4(c')	8(c'')
Sequence 2:	1(C)	3(g)	9(d'')	27(a''')

(The tones embody frequency relationships)

The first members of the two sequences stand in the relationship of the prime to one another (1:1); the second members in the relationship of the fifth (2:3); the third pair builds a double fifth, or ninth(4:9); the fourth pair a triple fifth, or thirteenth (8:27). If the sequences were pursued further, the thirteenth pair would yield the twelvefold fifth ($4096:531441 = 2^{12}:3^{12}$), which also is the sevenfold octave (plus the Pythagorean Comma) and thus would close the twelve-membered cycle of fifths. Earlier we saw the connection between geometrical sequences and the structure of cyclic systems. Here, we encounter this principle in the fundamental structure of the Platonic World Soul, although only the first four members—a Pythagorean *tetrakys*, tetrachord—are mentioned. According to the *Timaeus* , a second principle participates in the further building up of the World Soul, namely the principle of arithmetic and harmonic division which we have encountered already in the principle of major and minor. The result of that principle here is that 'inner fourth spaces' appear between members of the two sequences:

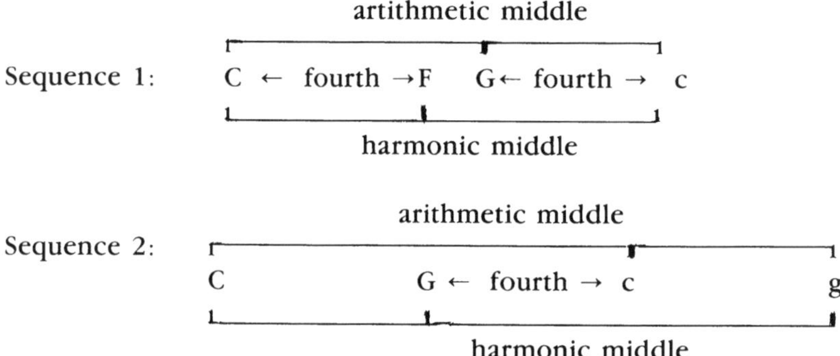

When the World Soul has revealed its structure to this extent—so that the fourth has appeared as the first inner interval—then matters are far enough (for Plato, or Timaeus) so that the state of the world can light up as an idea in the human soul. For the fourth is the constituitive interval of the Greek soul. It is significant that the further activity of the creator god is not described as construction, but only a filling-out of the empty fourth-spaces with the wholetone 9/8 (the '*tonos*'). For the Greek sensibility, the wholetones and the small seconds that appear in the leftover spaces (*leimma* = remainder) are musical filler, more or less accidental matter that could not yet be fully grasped by musical consciousness. (Since the 'Timaeus Scale' is fully examined elsewhere, this account dwells only upon its most essential features. For a fuller discussion, see, e.g., E.Bindel, *Zahlengrundlagen der Musik* , I, p.53ff., and H.Pfogner, *Lebendige Tonwelt* , p. 107 ff.)

If the fourth is filled out with the '*kinumenoi* ' so that the remaining halftone is below, the result is the Greek Dorian (medieval Phrygian) tetrachord:

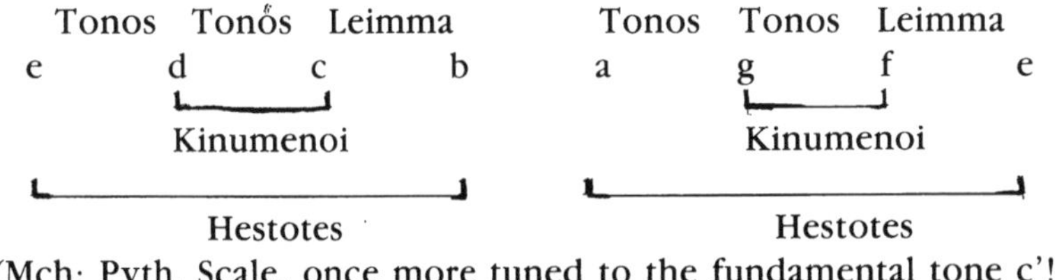

(Mch: Pyth. Scale, once more tuned to the fundamental tone c'!)

This is the fundamental diatonic scale of Greece; all the other diatonic scales are derived from it as modes. Like all other Greek scales, it is experienced as primarily descending, and thus is the exact inversion of our major scale in regard to the succession of seconds. When the fourth is filled out from below, so that the leftover interval (*leimma*) appears above, the Greek Lydian (medieval Ionian) scale appears:

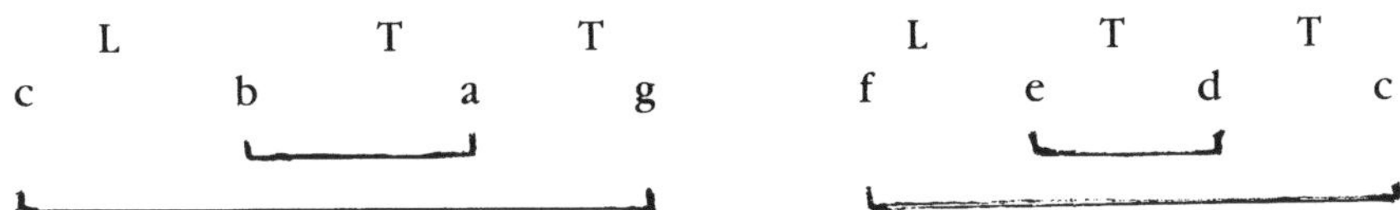

Or, if the *leimma* arises between the two *tonoi*, the result is the Greek Phrygian scale (medieval Dorian) :

All three ways of filling out the fourth also can be used to build up a scale by connecting the two tetrachords with a common tone, e.g., to form the Hypodorian:

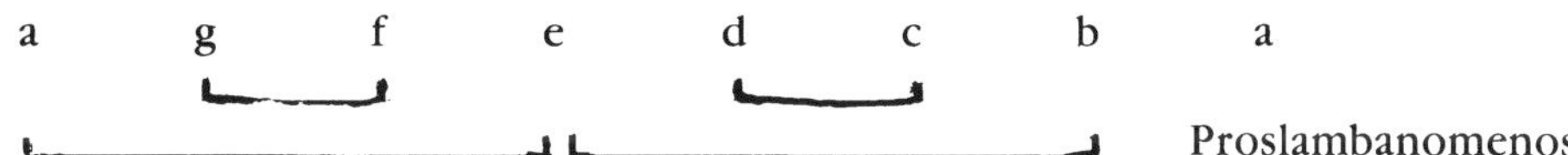

Here, the octave is added on below, since the scale descends, and is called *proslambanomenos*, 'the addition'.

So long as the fourth is filled out with the wholetone (*tonos*)9/8 plus what is left over (*leimma*), the tones of these scales correspond to the chain of pure fifths, f c g d a e b, transposed into the compass of a single octave. Thus the Pythagorean system is both a system of fifths and a system of fourths. Pythagoras, who was initiated in Egypt, brought it to Greece and established it there as the Appollonian tonal system. Later, it became the foundation for the music of Christian Europe.

But antique music theory has recorded that, in addition to the Pythagorean way of filling out the tetrachord with a *tonos* and *leimma* produced by perfect fifths, other diatonic, Dorian tetrachords also were used—tetrachords which retained the Pythagorean framework of perfect fourths, but introduced radial elements in filling out these fourths. In these cases, the prime numbers two and three, to which the Pythagorean system limits itself, were far exceeded.

Didymos (c. 100 B.C.) introduced an intonation of the Dorian tetrachord which be named *diatonon*, which employed the following relationships of stringlength:

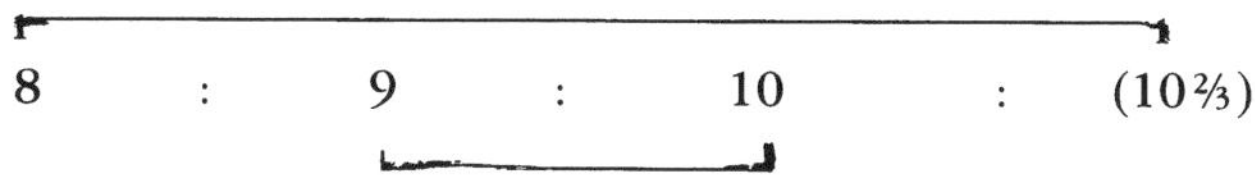

(Mch: Harmon. Series; 10⅔ = Pythag. Scale's g)

Here, the prime number 5 (as 10 = 2 x 5) has been introduced. Instead of 11, 10⅔ appears in order to obtain the pure fourth to 8 (8:10⅔ = 3:4).

The *diatonon homalon* of Ptolemy (c. 100A.D.) also employs radial elements to fill out the Dorian tetrachord insofar as it uses the prime numbers five and eleven:

$$9 \quad : \quad 10 \quad : \quad 11 \quad : \quad 12$$

(Mch: Harmon. Series).

With respect to the frequency relationships, both of these tetrachords are portions of the harmonic series, or undertone series.

In the following intonations one encounters portions of the arithmetic series as far as the prime number seven:

Ptolemy (*Diatonon Syntonon*):

$$10 \quad : \quad 9 \quad : \quad 8 \quad : \quad (7\tfrac{1}{2})$$

(Mch: Arith. Series; 7½ = b in the pure triad scale)

Archytas (4th century B.C.) and Ptolemy (*Diatonon toniation*):

$$9 \quad : \quad 8 \quad : \quad 7 \quad : \quad (6\tfrac{3}{4})$$

(Mch: Arith, Series; 6¾ = a in the Pythag. scale)

If we remember that these tetrachords always are used in pairs to build up a scale, we will see that the resulting scales are of double origin—the *hestotes* originates in the cyclic, Pythagorean system, the *kinumenoi* originate in a radial impulse. For example, the Dorian scale built on the *Diatonon homalon* would be as follows:

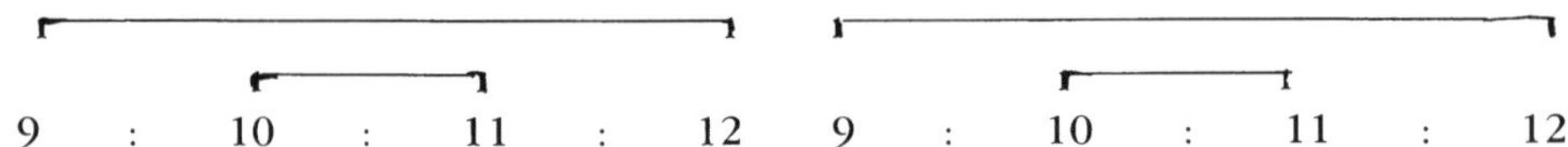

$$9 \quad : \quad 10 \quad : \quad 11 \quad : \quad 12 \quad\quad 9 \quad : \quad 10 \quad : \quad 11 \quad : \quad 12$$

(Mch: 24 division with quartertone alterations upward↑:
e   d   c↑   b   a   g   f↑   e   )

We already have noticed how the fundamental constructive principles of the World Soul in Plato's *Timaeus* only lead as far as to the building of perfect fourths, whereas the manner in which the fourths are filled out appears to be a more or less improvised solution. The *tonos* 9/8, which appears somewhat accidentally between the arithmetic and harmonic divisions of the octave as the smallest interval, has to enter the field and patch up the fourths by a purely additive process. The impossible numerical relationship of what is left over, the *leimma* 256/243, already indicates its accidental nature. It really is just a leftover piece. The other four intonations of the tetrachord just described clearly are the attempts of Archytas, Didymos and Ptolemy to replace a rather accidental and abstract sequence of seconds with a more concrete and essential way of filling out the fourth.

All this may appear to be only a mathematical problem ...until one has really practised hearing the differences in question and so begun to have intimations of what sort of musical powers lie behind them. When this has been achieved, one catches a glimpse of a turning point in the musical development of humanity and in world history: the whole picture of the development of tonal systems needs to be kept in view.

Proceeding beyond the system based on sevenths and sixths, Egypt and Chaldea developed cyclic systems which were the beginnings of a cyclic system based on fifths. While investigating this stage we could hear for the first time a basis for the musical expression of self-awareness, albeit with the qualification that it was a self-conscious experience that was entirely sustained from without through the self's being mirrored in the cosmic world order. In the outer world the "I" confronted itself and became aware of itself. We discovered that the musical boundary between experiencing oneself outside of oneself and experiencing oneself within onself is the boundary between the fifth and the fourth. Thus, when Pythagoras took the Egyptian system of fifths and inverted it producing a system of fourths, he made inward and internalized the interval experience through which the "I" discovers itself in the outer world order. He replaced that experience with an interval experience which enabled the "I" to freely rebuild the cosmic order in the isolation of its own inner being. One should remember how the question asked by the fourth differs from the question asked by the fifth (see p. 58): in contrast to the fifth, the fourth puts its question in a mood which contains an element of doubt as to whether the world can provide an answer!

Nevertheless, experience of the perfect fourth still is concerned with an *outer world—* including the spiritual outer world—albeit one which is built up through inner struggle. This is not yet the experience the "I" requires in order to experience itself. Experience of the fourth does not allow one to leave the outer world behind. Rather, one places oneself in it, measures oneself against it, asserts oneself in the face of it, is awakened by it—even though this originates in an entirely inner impulse. The perfect fourth is like a person whose inner strengths and qualities only emerge when they confront the outer world. But as to a self awareness which remains certain in spite of being free from any support from an outer world order—this experience begins first with the third and will have ripened only when we achieve a full experience of the prime, something that, at most, is only hinted at in the experience of today. (See p. 62) In consciousness of the third, the outer world only plays a role in so far as we shut ourselves off from it in the minor third or joyfully affirm it in the major third. But in both cases *it is we ourselves* who determine these attitudes to the outer world; the outer world has ceased to imprint them on us. Self-experience is the exclusive domain of the third.

Now to return to the Greek fourth and how it was filled out with seconds! The Pythagorean intonation led to an apparently arbitrary method, the fourth being merely filled out with intervals left over from the division into fourths and fifths. If we want to free ourselves from this abstract, additive patchwork of seconds and devise a more concrete way of filling out the fourth with seconds, then we must turn to another sort of principle, one which allows a really organic approach to producing a stream of seconds. Such is the radial principle of the arithmetic or harmonic series for example, as it appears in *diatonon homalon* as 9: 10: 11: 12. Here, the seconds no longer are added together abstractly, rather they are produced in a flowing stream out of a single principle. In the other three tetrachords just described, however, only the two larger seconds are formed in this way, while the small second must remain 'accidental' in order to preserve the perfect fourth.

What is the nature of the radial principle which, so to speak, emerges from these Greek scale intonations—out of the inner realm of the second and third, intervals which were beyond the comprehension of the fourth-dominated consciousness of that time? Where in our previous observations did we first encounter principles embodied in the harmonic and arithmetic series? When third-oriented consciousness transformed the medieval system based on fourths and fifths into the triadic system of modern times, the arithmetic and harmonic radial principles reentered 'official' musical development in the major triad, 4 : 5 : 6, and the minor triad, 1/6 : 1/5 : 1/4, respectively. As shall become increasingly clear, it is the radial principle which enables experience of the *inward intervals* , the second and the third, to build scales. This is the principle we characterized as centrifugal, outward striving (see p. 44). Experience of the *outer intervals*, the seventh, sixth and fifth (Atlantis-Old India, Old Persia, Egypt), led to the formation of scales and tonal systems out of the cyclic principle, a centripetal, contracting principle which draws things together from out of the widths.

Here, in the Greek experience of the fourth, we stand exactly at the midpoint between these two fields of force. The power which engenders human self-awareness is a representative of the cyclic, centripetal principle. It allows the immensity of the cosmos to enter a person through the sense and nerve system centered in their head so that the cosmos can be concentrated and reflected in the microcosm of their thinking. For the Greeks this is the work of the upper gods, especially of Apollo. To Dionysus and the lower gods was attributed the opposing power, the power that is manifested in the radial, centrifugal impulse. It works especially in the lower being—in the pole concentrated in the metabolic and limb system. Instead of leading to an awareness of an outer world that is mirrored within oneself, this power leads to an inward experience of oneself as created of divine substance. It is out of this normally subconscious realm that the centrifugal power of human will radiates into the world.

Remember how—in describing the ancient Persian tonal system (p. 72f)—we already were led to speak of the upper and lower gods. There they appeared as the contrary directions, above and below, of a cyclic system which encompassed both. The tone system reflected the circumstances of a humanity which still experienced itself 'from outside itself.' As an inward experience of the soul arose with the Greeks' consciousness of the fourth, the old 'below' became 'within', and manifested itself in a radial, centrifugal tendency, outward streaming as from a center. The ancient 'above' became 'without' and manifested itself in the cyclic tendency, working inward centripetally from the cosmic circumference.

For the Greeks the path to the lower, or inner, gods was the path of esoteric schooling cultivated in the Dionysian mysteries. It was the counterpole to the more exoteric, Apollonian domain which became increasingly public as Greek culture developed. It finally gave birth to Greek philosophy and art. The Dionysian path was closed to all but those especially qualified and prepared for it, for without rigorous training the experience of one's own godhood leads to uncontainable subjectivism and destructive egoism. Nero's 'false initiation' during the period of decline is a case in point.

Nevertheless, the course of its development has brought humanity step by step to the inner, Dionysian realm. The Greek initiates were only the forerunners. When people began to be able to enter into the consciousness of the third in the late Middle Ages, it was their first step into the inner realm of Dionysus. They never could have done this if the way had not been prepared by a millenium of Christian spiritual development in Europe—if medieval people had not brought to life Paul's "Not I, but Christ in me." Today we can see how the blessing of third-oriented experience only lasted so long as the Christian faith remained the common heritage of western humanity. As the materialistic, scientific skepticism of the 19th century took hold, the all-too-human, or even subhuman, side of the third came more and more to light, leading to the sort of thing that now bawls and groans at us, day in day out, from the loudspeakers. The way human whim, elevated to the status of an absolute principle, is destroying today's music (compare p. 58f.) is traceable to the problem of experiencing the third. What earlier would have been a crisis for an individual Greek aspirant on the Dionysian path is today a crisis in the culture of mankind.

But the path leading into the inner Dionysian realms, the way to experiencing ones own godhead, will be pursued until we have made the intervals of the second and the prime our own—a tendency we already have observed coming into contemporary music (see p. 59f.) Meister Eckhart's "small spark in the soul" will become that "center of the cosmos" which Solzhenitsyn, in anticipation of what is to come, has described glowing within himself. This goal is not attainable until Christianity has been fundamentally spiritualized. Until then egoism and subjectivism will continue to evoke new crises. And there will always be those who long to return to the old universal order and do not perceive that a much mightier and more real objective order is revealing itself within humanity itself.

Before the Greeks could set out upon the path of initiation, they had to orient themselves in the cosmic order described in Plato's *Timaeus*. They first achieved individuation through the offices of Apollo—Apollo, whose colossally harmonizing power to shape things with clarity and unity is musically revealed in the tone system based on fourths and fifths. This had to be the first goal of Greek and of western culture: an individual self-consciousness and a clear world-consciousness which could provide, in the depths of the soul, a foundation for the subsequent developments. Without the effects of this Apollonian schooling, the Greeks and all other post-Atlanteans would have had to remain in the state of dull, instinctive clairvoyance that was natural for the early post-Atlanteans. A consciousness that continued to be ruled by a 'mystical participation' of individual life forces in the life of nature—a consciousness whose last traces still are found among primitive peoples—would have prevented an awakening to true self-consciousness. Humanity would have continued to feel itself just a small piece of the macrocosm so that the microcosm that lives in each person would have remained undetected. Once more we see the centripetal tendency of the Apollonian forces. Out of the ancient, macrocosmic, dreamlike clairvoyance they helped create a point-oriented, individual, waking consciousness. This latter has only taken a form comparable to our centered consciousness since the Greek era. At the same time the old mythical clairvoyance has sunk below the level of consciousness. Thus, everywhere they look, the psychoanalysts find correspondences between ancient myths and the content of our subconscious.

Clearly, the activity we have named 'Apollonian', giving it its Greco-Latin name, begins long before the time of Greek or Latin culture. Musically it is to be found in the development of the cyclic, centripetal systems—from the earliest based on sevenths to those based on fifths or fourths, which were the fruits of the earlier development.

XXX. THE SYSTEM OF FOURTHS (GREECE AND ROME): THE DIONYSIAN RADIAL SYSTEM OF THE *AULOS*

Even though it is primarily a thing of the future, the Dionysian power of the radial musical systems already was active prior to the Greek epoch. There are ancient pipes—we mentioned them earlier—whose holes are bored in a way that indicates the use of radial scales in ancient Egypt. But the Dionysian principle first came into its own during the Greek epoch when consciousness of the fourth finally broke open the door to the inner, Dionysian realms.

The ancient Greek *aulos* scales discovered by Kathleen Schlesinger show how a consistent Dionysian system can be built on the radial principle. As previously explained, the frequencies of the tones of this system are related in accordance with the harmonic, or undertone, series. (See p. 43) Such a series of tones is the result of boring the fingerholes of a pipe equidistant from one another—thus the harmonic-radial principle comes to be realized on a wind instrument in an extremely simple and natural way, What could be more natural for someone lacking any special knowledge or preconceptions than to bore the holes of a flute equidistant from one another? Furthermore, Schlesinger's research shows that the tones of the *aulos,* correspond to a definite section of the harmonic series, namely the undertones 7 to 14, or 8 to 16 (with 15), not a random section. Seven modes were formed from these tones. Schlesinger independently came to an exceptionally happy characterization of these in terms of the seven planets of ancient tradition. Later, Rudolf Steiner confirmed it. Here we give these modes both with the names used by Schlesinger in her book, *The Greek Aulos,* names she borrowed from the other Greek system, and also the names that refer to their planetary character, since this will be of interest to us later in other connections. (See p. 172ff)

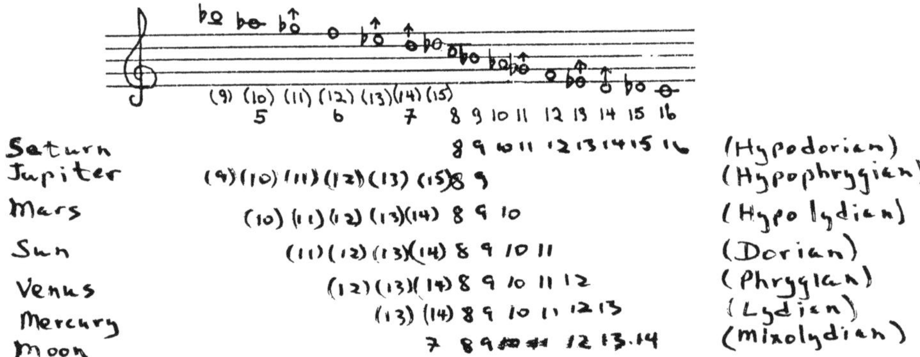

As can be seen on the monochord, the numbers also give the relationship between the various string lengths, e.g., the two lowest tones of the Saturn mode are built by 15 sixteenths (d^b) and 16 sixteenths of the whole string (c'); thus the ratio of the string lengths of d^b : c is 15 : 16. To build the other modes. it is necessary to transpose tones 9 to 15 one octave upward. The transposed tones are indicated in parentheses: '(9)', '(10)', etc; in each case, the string length is one half that of their lower octave; e.g., with '(9)', 9/32 of the string sounds, with '9', 9/16.

According to Schlesinger, each mode begins on the same tone and is distinguished from the other modes only by differences in its interval structure. Here we began with the Saturn mode, whose deepest tone, 16, also is an octave of the generating tone, 1, of the undertone series. We produced the other modes out of the Saturn mode's division into sixteenths by beginning those modes on different tones of this same series—the church modes are similarly produced. While acquainting oneself with this system through meditative listening exercises it is advisable to set the monochord bridge at 11 and then to tune the resulting g^{b}1 to c = 256 Hz. Then all the other scales will appear as modes of the Sun scale.

A unique feature of these scales is that the second has seven different nuances within the octave. Simply learning to hear these is a valuable exercise for every musician. It helps awaken

a more differentiated hearing. The course of differentiated seconds develops most clearly in
the Moon scale, where the straightforward, unbroken procession from 7 to 14 results in a series
of seconds that become progressively narrower as they descend: beginning with 7 : 8, the over-
sized second of the Slendro, it proceeds over a large and a small wholetone and three progressively smaller three-quarter-tones to what is nearly a halftone.

$$7 : 8 : 9 : 10 : 11 : 12 : 13 : 14$$

Wholetone — Large Whole-t. — Small Whole-t. — Three-quarter tones — Half-tone

2.31 — 2.04 — 1.82 — 1.65 — 1.51 — 1.39 — 1.29 — ht

For this reason, the Moon mode is the prototype of these radial scale structures—all the
other modes begin somewhere in the midst of the stream of diminishing seconds, making a
sudden wide step necessary somewhere in their course, namely where the tones transposed
by an octave ((13), (14), etc.) cease. As we already mentioned (p. 44), the octave transposition
of tones of the radial scale introduces a cyclic element which actually contradicts the strictly
radial principle—in this case, that of the undertone series. The sudden unexpected jump with
which one leaves the octave-transposed tones behind elicits an experience like that of waking
up. In the mode of the Moon, the lowest of the subsolar planets, we are spared this experience.
In the Sun mode the jump comes in the middle, between two quasi-tetrachords. In the modes
belonging to the two uppermost of the suprasolar planets, Saturn and Jupiter, the wide step
comes one stage too soon because 15 is used instead of 14. Then it is followed by the smallest
second, the pure halftone 15 : 16. This gives the structure an inconsistency which is clearly
felt by artiscally wakeful listening. For example, its brings the four lowest tones of the Saturn
mode suspiciously close to the Persian scale, which is of cyclic origin. (See p. 69) For the time
being we must allow Schlesinger this anomaly, but with the strong suspicion that we are here
dealing with what we have been calling a mixed structure, one that combines radial and cyclic
elements. (See p. 99!)

The musicologists greeted Schlesinger's research with much skepticism. And in some instances
she had left herself open to criticism, for in her enthusiasm for her discoveries she lost all
sense for the significance of the Pythagorean system and for the cyclic principle in general.
The result was that she allowed herself to be misled more than a few times into trying to derive
cyclic structures from the radial principle. But the most frequently voiced objection to Schlesinger's *aulos* scales does not hold up—namely that these scales could not have existed, since
they never were described clearly by the music theorists of antiquity. Jacques Handschin conceded that such scales "certainly must have been in use,"[61] although he thoroughly rejected
Schlesinger's onesidedness. And, furthermore, we have just seen how the musical consciousness
articulated by scales originating in the radial principle is by and large an anticipation of the
future development of the human soul. Thus, this sort of scale was something which Greeks
must have found difficult to lay hold of with their own theoretical tools. There were sound
reasons why the great Greek music theorist, Aristoxenos of Tarent (ca. 350-300 B.C.), rejected
trying to deal with the *aulos* system rationally (see p. 123f.)

Today's music confronts us with things whose significance we can sense, even though we
cannot explain them theoretically out of what the past has taught us up to now. That is how
these scales must have confronted the Greeks. Their musical consciousness, which was founded
on the fourth, gave them no practical way of approaching such scales. Such scales confronted
them with a fascinating but insoluble riddle. Hearing them, they must have experienced
artistically something of what a soul embarked on the hidden path of the Dionysian mysteries
had to go through. Indeed, Plato testifies to a direct connection between the experience of
aulos music and the experiences of initiation (see p. 100).

Not without good reason was the *aulos* the chosen instrument of the Dionysian realm. It
was used to accompany the tragedies, which were performed in connection with the cult of
Dionysus, and which were capable of uprooting and shaking the innermost depths of the Greek
soul. Here, also, the Greeks' inner soul space—the realm of Dionysus—was burst open as they

experienced in such figures as Oedipus or Antigone how the outer cosmic order disintegrated and how intense pain accompanies entrance into the inner world where we confront our own being. The sharp, mournful, almost painful tones of the *aulos* were part of this experience. There is hardly any other instrument with a tone which can so strongly express the lament—or ecstatic cry of joy—of a god who must live the life of a natural creature. Apollo's instruments, the lyre and the cithera, can neither lament nor can they rejoice; their tones sound as though streaming in from the widths of space, forming things from without, creating order and harmony. They ring out of themselves, liberated from the human beings who bring them into being at their body's very periphery with their merest finger-tips or with a plectrum. Not so the tones of the *aulos* which sound from out of the warm, moist, life-stream of the breath itself as it issues forth from within the player.

But there is a second side to the Dionysian realm. No Greek tragedy was complete without a satyr play. The inner shock of the tragedy needed to be followed by a satyr play in which the '*kômos*' of Dionysus came to light. The 'comic', nature-bound folk who peopled these plays—satyr, faun, silenus—were the way the Greeks pictured a person who still is entirely a creature of nature, untouched by the problems of self-awareness. When I experience myself as such a being, living in happy innocence and without need of second thoughts, given over to natural forces and desires without trace of scruple or remorse—then I certainly experience something godlike in myself, but this is a divinity that fans the first sparks of self consciousness into the flames of a destructive egoism as soon as they begin to glow. Those on the path of Dionysian initiation had to withstand the awareness of the divinity inherent in their own natural existence without losing themselves in egoistic desires. Then they were able to experience the power of the 'lower gods', which were the most ancient most powerful and most real of the gods; these are the ancient, chthonic powers of the 'Mother', which include the life forces of outer nature. It was felt how all humanity—and, indeed, all life—is equal before these chthonic gods, since all life is sustained and permeated by them equally. That was why the whole problemmatic of human self-development and all the struggles and inhibitions brought on by self-awareness were laughable when seen in the light of the wisdom of a satyr or faun—for what further could someone achieve who already is divine through being giving over to the divine natural powers that live in them? Someone drunk with wine can show moments of such wisdom even though they have not rightfully earned it; thus Dionysus is given the somewhat dubious honor of being known exoterically as the god of wine. Nevertheless, this really is a divine wisdom, this "divine laughter" at humanity with its pretenses of selfhood.

For the Greeks to come to a real inner feeling of identity, the Dionysian festivals had to lead them to both experiences: through the tragedy, the extreme pain of feeling their isolation from the gods, and through the comedy, the satyr-play, the divine laughter of being inwardly sustained by the gods. Evidently the popular education by means of the drama was inagurated by individuals who had achieved an awareness of these matters by way of initiation in the Dionysian mysteries. Music played on the *aulos* accompanied both the tragedy and the comedy, or satyr-play. In the soil of the Greeks' familiar musical ground, the fourth, this music secretly was sowing the seeds of inner experience, of consciousness of the third...and, most especially, of the second.

Auletic and drama declined in the late antique period. Then, with the advent of Christianity, this musical stream seems to have disappeared entirely from the arena of western cultural development. In *The Republic* Plato already had rejected "the panharmonic *aulos* " as unsuitable for participation in further Greek cultural development. It could not be confined within the bounds of a unified, clear, Apollonian system. Only the Apollonian instruments, the lyre and the cithera, and only their appropriate scales, were to be retained. Plato's opinion was that the shepherds in the countryside, who were bound by destiny and profession to remain connected with the chthonic powers, could be permitted to continue playing their flutes and panpipes.[62] We already have mentioned how the history of the radial system actually did proceed along these lines: after the antique period it led a scarcely noticed, increasingly disregarded, existence in the music of shepherds and rustics on the outermost borders of western culture. And yet, whenever cultural development called for a musical excursion into the domain of the inward intervals, i.e. for a new development in the musical experience of the Dionysian inner realm of the soul, then this nature-bound, chthonic 'native soil' cultivated

90

in the music of bagpipe and shawm, of alphorn and yodeling, provided a fertile ground in which the radial scales could influence the growth of musical culture. This was the case as music came to terms with the third, and again, in our century, as it grappled with experience of the second—something that shows especially clearly in Bartók's music. We already have observed that the scales of shepherds and rustics underwent the same change of direction as the scales of 'cultured' music, changing from downwards to upwards at more or less the same time as the turning point in our reckoning of time. Thereafter, the radial scales tended to be based on the overtone series rather than the undertone series.

XXXI. THE SYSTEM OF FOURTHS (GREECE AND ROME): THE CHROMATIC AND ENHARMONIC SYSTEMS OF THE GREEKS. THE HIDDEN FOURTH 11/8.

In the Greek chromatic and enharmonic systems we find yet a third, completely different sort of scale. It belongs to a scale system that presents many riddles. Many an admirer of Greek culture would be happier if it never had existed, for our present day hearing finds it much too strange and unenjoyable. And yet the ancient authors recount how chromatic and enharmonic music played an important role precisely at the time when Greek culture was at its height.

These Greek scales have little to do with chromatic and enharmonic in the sense of these words with which we are familiar. It is only because the Greek chromatic involves accumulations of halftones that it has acquired the same name as our modern chromaticism. Today we call the relationship between f$^\#$ and g$^\flat$, c$^\#$ and d$^\flat$, and so on, 'enharmonic' because these tones lie a short distance from one another in the pure or in the middle-tone intonation, and thus involve an interval which, if only very roughly, is comparable to the quartertones encountered in Greek enharmonic. The essential difference between modern and Greek enharmonic lies in the fact that modern enharmonic relationships arise between tones belonging to *different* keys, whereas the quartertone steps of Greek enharmonic arose as a form of second within *one* , seven-membered scale. Similarly, the accumulation of halftone steps in Greek chromatic occurs in a single scale, whereas today's chromatic sequences are not part of any scale or established tonality, but merely belong to the collection of all halftones within the octave.

In the theoretical forms in which they have been handed down to us, both the chromatic and the enharmonic Greek scales retain the framework of pure fourths which we know as the *hestotes* of Pythagorean diatonic. Thus, only the *kinumenoi* , the moveable tones, distinguish this system from the Pythagorean with its scales built on fifths and fourths. The basic form of the chromatic scale resembles that of the Dorian, but with its terrachords altered so that two semitones instead of one lead to their lower tone.

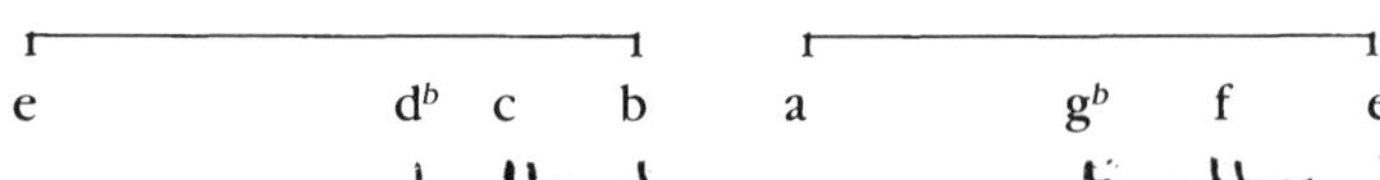

(Mch: 12-division. Note that the tones further to the right are *lower* in pitch).

In the enharmonic scale these halftones are pressed still closer together, downwards, to form quartertones, so that the two compressed quartertones—whose Greek name, '*pyknon*', means 'closely packed'—fit within the space of a halftone.

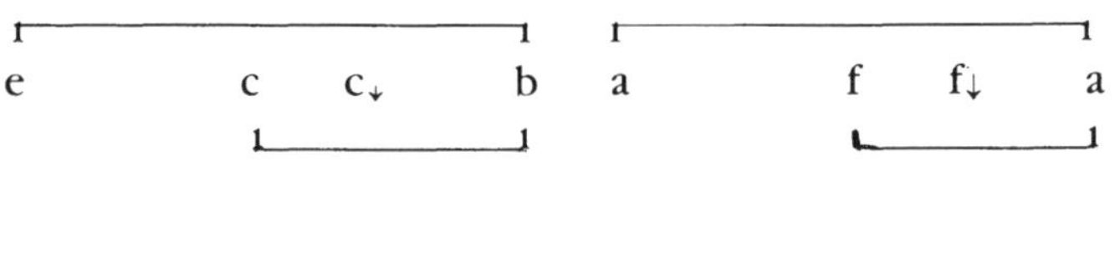

(Mch; 24-division)

Aristoxenos informs us of intonations of the chromatic and enharmonic tetrachords which exactly correspond to our 12-fold and 24-fold divisions on the monochord. But he and other Greek theorists also record a whole series of possible variations in intonation, showing that

92

in practice there was a fluid transition between chromatic and enharmonic. This already is clear from the four chromatic-enharmonic intonations given by Aristoxenos himself:

			Pyknon			
		e	d^b	c	b	
	toniaion (with wholetone)	3	1	1	ht (12-div)
Chroma	*hemiolion* (with tone-and-a-half)	3.5	0.75	0.75	ht
	malakon ('soft' intonation)	3.67	0.67	0.67	ht
Enharmonion		4	0.5	0.5	ht (24-div)
		e	c	c↓	b	

From this it is clear that chromatic and enharmonic refer to various intonations of what is fundamentally one and the same scale. And so the question arises, why did the Greeks distinguish two sorts of tonality?

It is significant that Aristoxenos, in agreement with all the other Greek writers who concerned themselves with music, calls the tetrachord structure chromatic ('chroma' = coloring) so long as the *pyknon* (i.e., the sum of the two lower, narrow intervals in the tetrachord) is noticeably larger than a halftone. The *pyknon* can be compressed from the size of an overlarge wholetone (2.31 ht, as in Ptolemy) to the size of a small three-quarter-tone (1.33 ht) without its taking on the character of another sort of tonality. But as soon as the *pyknon* falls within the compass of a halftone, 'chromatic' becomes 'enharmonic'.

Thus, the Greek distinction between chromatic and enharmonic arises because the variable chromatic-enharmonic complex is gauged by the standard of a diatonic in which the smallest possible step is a halftone. So long as the *pyknon* itself does not demand to be experienced as a halftone, it can be divided into two steps, each being a second (d^b-c, c-b, and so on.) This is still just possible with the *chroma* Aristoxenos calls *malakon* . So long as I can experience the seconds of a tetrachord diatonically, I can experience it as a variant, or 'coloring', of a diatonic tetrachord. Thus, 'chroma' indicates nothing else than a coloring of the seven-stepped, diatonic scale.

But as soon as the *pyknon* is so compressed that it can be heard as a *single* halftone step, as *one* minimal second in itself, then it ceases to harmonize with diatonic hearing and cannot be felt as a particular coloration of one of the seven diatonic steps. At this point, for example, the quartertone c↓ that divides the *pyknon* is heard as something new inserted into the (diatonic) scale's sequence of seconds.[63]

These considerations first begin to make the word 'enharmonic' understandable: *harmottein* means join together; *enharmottein* means 'join together inside of'; so '*enharmonia*' = 'that which has been placed inside of. ' The Greeks called a particular scale structure—understood as a tonality—a 'joining together' (*harmonia*). Thus 'enharmonic' is most accurately translated as indicating the placing of something inside of the steps that have been joined together (the *harmonia*). The usual translation of enharmonic as 'standing in harmony' (M. Vogel) makes it impossible to understand why the Greeks did not also call their diatonic scales enharmonic since, for them, these were the scales that really 'stood in harmony' and, therefore, were called '*harmonia*.' Here, it seems to me, our modern concept of harmony has been projected too much onto that of the Greeks.

In any case, this philological clarification does nothing to solve the riddle of how the Greeks came to 'color' their diatonic by introducing alien tones into it in the first place. And matters actually were still richer and more complicated than we have yet described, for this process was not restricted merely to the chromatization and enharmonization of the Dorian scale. Other modes were built from this scale, so that one had chromatic and enharmonic Phrygian, Lydian, and so on—such scales as would bring today's listener into total confusion.

Up to this time the form of a scale always had been the result of one interval—or occas-

93

sionally of two—which particularly determined the musical consciousness of an epoch. Thus, the equally spaced pentatonic originated in the natural seventh, the Persian scale was based on the natural sixth, the Pythagorean pentatonic and heptatonic were based on the fifth, the major and minor scales were based on the third and the fifth. The only exceptions to this are the pure radial scales, which have a 'panharmonic', asymmetrical structure. The clear, symmetrical structure of Greek chromatic and enharmonic music points so strongly to a cyclic origin based on a single interval—so why should there be an exception to this rule? Could it not be that the diatonic nature of these scales has been distorted for the sake of expressiveness by an arbitrary melodic will? Most of today's musicologists are satisfied by such thinking. But such an explanation is bound to be highly unsatisfactory for anyone who has learned to draw a clear distinction between what has musical character and what has the character of utterance, in the sense that we distinguished these in our initial chapters. For, in contrast to experience which remains merely at the level of soul-utterance, musical experience implies a spirituality that is bound up with the nature of number.

Let us look once more at that remarkable inconsistency we met up with in the Greeks and the epoch of the fourth as we were describing the historical changes in interval consciousness. The succession of intervals characteristic of the post-Atlantean epochs was found to be identical with the descending (arithmetic) radial scale, starting with the seventh:

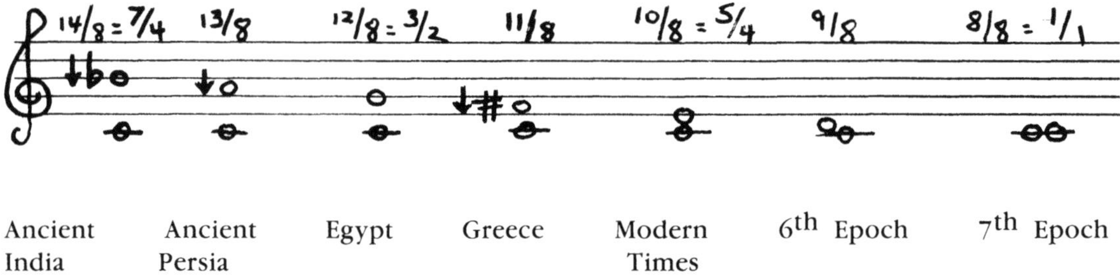

Ancient India   Ancient Persia   Egypt   Greece   Modern Times   6th Epoch   7th Epoch

(Mch: Arith. series)

Only Greece seemed to be an exception to the rule. It clearly connected itself with the fourth 4/3, which is the inversion of the fifth...instead of the fourth 11/8. Thus Greece and Rome seemed merely to have carried on with their Egyptian inheritance and made it more inward.

Now it is time to follow the mysterious trail of the fourth 11/8 and see what kind of tone system and scales result when a cycle is built from it, analogous to those built on fifth, sixth and seventh. A tower of twenty-four fourths 11/8 (i.e. 5.513 ht) leads us, almost exactly, to the eleventh octave of the starting tone; it overshoots the mark by only 0.314 ht. If this difference is distributed over all twenty-four fourths, each fourth would have to be tempered by 0.013 ht, which is only 2/3 as much tempering as the fifths require in the circle of twelve (i.e. 0.0195 ht).

The circle of fourths 11/8 gives an ideal system of twenty-four quartertones when it is projected into a single octave. Exactly in the same way as the ancient Indian cycle of five (which was based on the seventh) was subdivided into a cycle of ten by the succeeding interval 13/8 (the Persian sixth), the interval 11/8 subdivided Egypt's cycle of twelve into a cycle of twenty-four. A remarkable pattern!

The chain of seven fourths from $a^\uparrow$ to $d^b_\downarrow$, as indicated in the circle of twenty-four, yields the following scale when the tones are transposed into a single octave:

	11/8				11/8			
	e	$d^b_\downarrow$	$c_\downarrow$	$b_\downarrow$	$a^\uparrow$	g^b	f	c	
	12	8.5	7.5	6.5	5.5	2	1	0	ht
tempered series of seconds	3.5	1	1	1		3.5	1	1	ht
(Mch: 24-division)									
pure	12	8.435	7.461	6.487	5.513	1.948	0.974	0	ht
series of seconds	3.565	0.974	0.974		0.974	3.565	0.974	0.974	ht

The structure is that of the Greek chromatic scale, but within a framework of 11/8 fourths instead of 4/3 fourths—which reduces the second b-a between the tetrachords to only a halftone.

We could write off this astonishing similarity to Greek chromatic as an accident, and do so in good faith, had the systems built on the natural seventh and the sixth 13/8 not already taught us so forcefully that a characteristic, symmetrically-formed scale can always be traced back to a particular interval consciousness and, furthermore, that one such fundamental form can persist while another, newer interval consciousness modifies it. Here, however, it is not a new interval consciousness that is the prime modifier, but rather the tenaciously preserved interval of the preceeding Egyptian epoch that modifies the truly basic form—the modifying influence is the fifth/fourth consciousness which has remained almost all-powerful from the Egypyian epoch up to the present day. We saw how this consciousness worked into the radial scale structure of Greece, producing the cyclic-radial mixed tetrachords of Archytas, Didymos and Ptolemy (p. 83). In thc same way it seems to have insinuated itself into the structure of a chromatic system based on the fourth 11/8, modifying the framework, e b a e , so that it consisted of perfect fourths and fifths. But, contrary to the information the theorists have passed down to us, Kathleen Schlesinger has demonstrated the existence of a radial scale that lacks these framing pure fourths and fifths. As to whether a scale built entirely on the interval 11/8 also existed?—this can hardly be proven in the same fashion, unless one has learned to understand spiritual-historical and artistic-musical consequence as a form of proof.

To this end it is important to find a way of listening oneself into the truly mysterious fourth 11/8. Being an interval that involves a prime number beyond the *senarius*, it is a total stranger to the time of the Kali Yuga and yet it clearly emerges exactly in the middle of that period at the time of the flourishing of Greek culture. Thus we can understand why the interval led a veiled existence, overlayered by other intervals which were more strongly in the foreground of consciousness. Only the inconsistencies in these other elements leads one to notice what they conceal. It must be conceded, further, that even today the nature of this interval, the so-called 'alphorn fa', only is approachable through long and intimate practice. Then it becomes clear that today's usual name for it, 'natural tritone', is as superficial as it is misleading. The tritone is an interval that only arises secondarily out of a cyclic process; either it is the extremest tension within a cyclic system or it shifts over to a tonal ambivalence that gives a feeling of absolute freedom, of being 'beyond good and evil'. The fourth 11/8 has nothing in common with this, even though it only differs outwardly from the tempered tritone by a mere quartertone.

Let us revive the listening exercise of p. 57 and try to come at least a little nearer to an experience of the fourth 11/8! We begin with the falling perfect fourth 4/3 (c down to g), the 'question put to oneself.' Listening to it, we try to feel as we would feel sitting across from a ruined man sunk deep in guilt and gruesome depravity. Here the questioning of the fourth can take on the mood of a "How can he be like he is ?," which can intensify itself from a burning questioning to an utterance of indignation, of judgement, of rejection. In the falling perfect fourth's mood I draw more and more into myself until finally it is as though I am looking over my shoulder at the other man, having completely dismissed him. I experience this rejection as inner strength, given me for my protection.

Proceeding then to the falling tritone (Mch: 12 division), I find more the feeling of shock that this man evokes in me. But this feeling is connected with a kind of secret loosening up, as if I harbored the thought that I might use the evil in him to serve the evil hidden in me: I feel this possibility, this freedom in myself. What makes the tritone a *diabolus*, which is how J.S.Bach experienced it, is that it dissolves the threshold between inner world and outer world and permits the untransformed inner world to work into the outer world. Earlier (p. 57f.) we drew the boundary between inner world and outer exactly there, between fourth and fifth. The impulse of my untempered inner nature to realize itself in the outer world arrogantly and without undergoing transformation is one side of the devil, the Luciferic side. The other side is in the tendency of the realities of the outer world to pour untransformed into my inner world where they can "pulverize" (Rudolf Steiner's expression) my soul, working deeply into the anxieties and compulsions of my subconscious where they establish themselves as the sole ruler—this is the Satanic ('Ahrimanic') side. Naturally, today we can also begin to sense dimly in the tritone how two worlds that are diametrically opposed as regards time, the inner world and the outer world, resolve themselves into a unity when they are experienced from the aspect of eternity—and this is the truly atonal experience of the tritone which the 20th century has begun to find within the sphere of the twelve.

The fourth 11/8 has nothing to do with any of this. Unlike the atonal tritone, it does not elevate itself to a more than human realm outside the bounds of time. It remains wholly human. But, remaining within the bounds of the purely human—perhaps more so than any other interval—it glows with the experience of the divine, of kinship with the divine. Seeking to live more and more deeply into this fourth, living with its inner gesture—first as a falling fourth—one can come to experience the situation described somewhat as follows: with my whole heart I feel my way into the existence of that morally corrupt, guilt-laden man before me and experience his guilt as my own. Neither the pure fourth nor the tritone allows me to participate inwardly to this degree. This experience cannot be named, simply, compassion (German: *Mitleid*); that would be more accurate for describing the falling large third. It embodies an extraordinary feeling, filled both with colossal earnestness and with unbounded love, and with a presentiment of a luminous, upholding strength. The character of the rising fourth 11/8 is more active, but it lacks the pure fourth's uninhibited, aggressive joy in activity that is unleashed by the outer world. It gives more the feel of action in which the consequences of a deed flow immediately back to the doer while he is still acting. Immediate though this living sense of responsibility is, it does not restrict my activity in the least, rather it makes it selfless, so that what I do happens like an act of nature, that is, like an act of God, although its source lies in my own innermost being.

This is the merest sketch of the character of the fourth 11/8. In reality this interval possesses far more extensive, still wholly unplumbed depths. Anyone who somehow succeeds in approaching the character of this interval will understand that, if it was to be found at all in Greek culture, then, given its particular musical nature, it must have been within the precincts of the higher mysteries.

None of the preceding is spoken of lightly, nor is it given as a convenient explanation. So far as the present writer knows, the bearing of soul that can be sensed in this fourth is nowhere to be found in what the Greek spirit handed on to us outwardly, not even in the 'divine Plato' or his teacher, Socrates. But such writers as Plato point unmistakably to the existence of mystery centers which were active in Greek culture from behind the scenes. The teachers in these mystery centers were men who had achieved a deeper insight into the course of cultural development and a different inner bearing than was possible for a Greek involved in the outer life of his time. It always was the task of these centers to maintain channels uninvolved in the normal exoteric life. Through these, as much as possible was allowed to flow into the culture from the supersensible life of the ages preceeding the *Kali Yuga* before the darkening of supersensible knowledge. Thereby a continuity was maintained with the powers which eventually would lead humanity out of this darkness again. The powers leading into the future met humanity in Palestine with the coming of Christianity at the turning point of time. As the foliage of some plants dies when the fruit appears, so the ancient mysteries died out with the appearance of Christianity—there was only a brief period in which a kind of marriage between the two was able to live in the Christian Gnosis.

As far as music goes, we must imagine that the antique mysteries guarded and cultivated just that domain which Hindemith calls the "holy domain of mystic intervals"[64]—the interval 7/4, and others involving the still higher prime numbers 11 and 13, as well as (probably) to some degree the third 5/4. It was to become the approaching era's principal interval, although in the Greek era it already had emerged halfway into the outer world. But the fourth 11/8, the real interval of the fourth post-Atlantean epoch, had to be confined to the mysteries, for, as we already said, it was an interval beyond the limits of the *senarius* and thus was bound to be a stranger in the Kali Yuga. From the very beginnings of the world it had been destined to rule the fourth epoch, yet it remained an unrecognized regent. One must have gone on beyond it to experience the succeeding intervals of the Dionysian inner space, the third, second and prime, before one can really understand and experience the fourth 11/8. Later chapters will make this clearer. The mystery of the number eleven is connected with the being of the Christ, as already was set down in the Gnosis of the Egyptian, Valentinian (circa 135—160 A.D.)[65]

So there undoubtedly were *two* different scale system cultivated in the Greek mysteries, each of which included intervals from the holy domain: the radial *aulos* scale and the scales of the chromatic-enharmonic system. The *aulos* scale is an exact inversion of the radial scale generated by a groundtone (see p. 59f.) It is panharmonic, embracing *all* the intervals through which humanity has been able—or will be able—to develop during the whole course of Earth evolution, the intervals of pre-*Kali Yuga* eras as well as the intervals belonging to the *Kali Yuga* and the ages after it. It is the archetypal, chthonic, mother-scale of the earth and earthly humanity. Rudolf Steiner heard something archetypally musical in it.[66] The fundamental scale of chromatic and enharmonic music is based on that one interval, the fourth 11/8, which forms *the center and turning point* of the primal scale. This interval not only reflects the outer cosmos inwardly like the pure fourth, it also is the first interval to really lead into the Dionysian inner space of the human soul and it does this without yet making the formation of a radial scale necessary. It is a true *mediator* between outer world and inner world, above and below, macrocosm and microcosm, divine and human, past and future.

Within the limitations of our present stage of listening experience, let us try to compare the two Greek 'mystery scales'. They stand in clear polar contrast to one another, one being a radial structure, the other cyclic.

First we play the following melodic fragment based on the *aulos* scale:

c''   d''↑   c''   b^b'   a^b'   g'↓
8   7   8   9   10   11
(Mch: Harm, series)

The more we listen ourselves into this, the more we feel our lives at one with nature. The oversized second 8 : 7 is especially expressive; one can sense that it is the inversion of the naturebound seventh 7/4 of the Atlantean and ancient Indian periods. The course of seconds streams downward from this second in lively nuance. It is the series of progressively smaller seconds of the Moon mode, the proto-typal *aulos* scale.

If we add an f below and above, as 12 and 6, we obtain the scale of the Norwegian *langeleik*, which Erik Eggen has reported.[67]

(Mch: Harm. series)

Our contemporary sense for thirds makes it easier to feel our way into this series of tones—all the more so when the tones ascend—because it contains a minor triad. If we improvise with it simply, somewhat as follows:

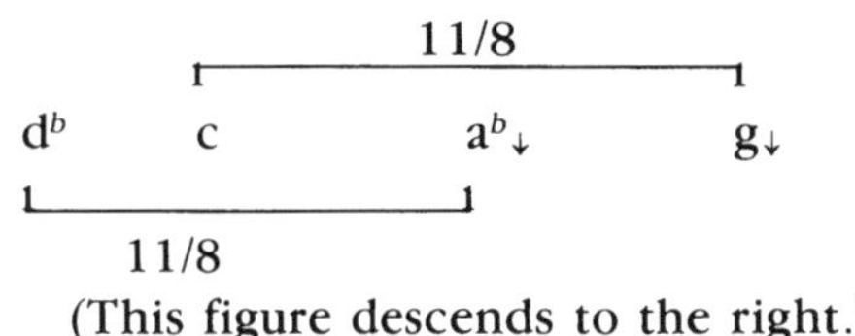

(For interpretation of the unusual accidental symbols, see p. 170.)

We capture the whole magical, haunting quality of Norwegian troll and elf legends. The impression becomes even more penetrating if we substitute (13) = e↓ for 6 = f, producing Schlesinger's Venus mode, or Phrygian mode, in its entirety.

We deliberately have taken the radial scale out of its Greek context for a moment. Thirds and triads help to intensify our experience of it, for third consciousness had its home in radial structures and therefore allows a closer approach to a scale with a radial sequence of seconds. A Greek, not yet having our inner experience of thirds, would have experienced such a scale less as inward, heart-centered, or fairy-tale-like, and more as the awakening of a real natural power in himself. The rousing sound of the *aulos* would have contributed to the effect.

Returning from our northern intermezzo, let us play the sequence of tones once more in its original version, as c d↑ c b♭ a♭ g↓. Then we extract from it enharmonic's fundamental interval 11/8: c down to g↓. With this, we revive the experiences of the preceeding exercise (p. 96). Next, we proceed by annexing a further descending fourth 11/8 (g↓-d♭), having located it in the 24-fold division of the monochord. Then transpose d♭ up an octave and build another 11/8 fourth on it to form the descending interval d♭—a♭↓.

(This figure descends to the right.)

Thus we have woven a pattern that contains the fourth 11/8 two times (as well as its inversion d♭—g↓ = 16/11), a structure that mediates in a double fashion the extraordinary mood we have described as a "loving earnestness". This is a mood wholly contrary to the nature-bound, radial *aulos* scale—although possessed of strong inner concentration, it can nevertheless express complete loving devotion as well. One should allow this structure to affect one for a long while, preferably on other instruments (the lyre) which can be tuned to it.

If we annex yet a fourth fourth a♭↓-d, we arrive at a form of pentatonic which has been

98

passed down—naturally without the quarter-tone accidentals—as an ancient form of enharmonic scale. It is said to be the creation of the mythical *aulos* players Hyagnis, Marsyas and Olympos, and is called *spondeionmelos*, i.e., the *melos* for the festive offering of wine to the gods. Therefore it was a scale played on the *aulos*.

A comparison of the radial *aulos* scale and the *spondeion* scale built on 11/8 makes the cross-references between the two scales apparent and shows that this archetypal enharmonic was performable on the *aulos*.

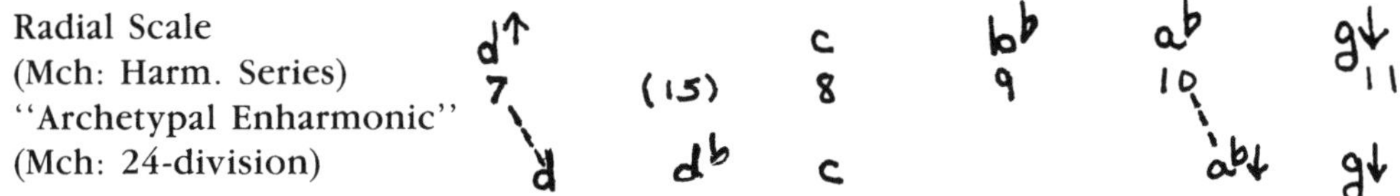

To obtain a mathematically exact archetypal enharmonic scale built on 11/8 from the radial scale Schlesinger has shown to be the natural scale of the *aulos*, one merely has to add the tone d$^{b''}$, which corresponds to (15), and lower the tones d''$^{\uparrow}$ and a$^{b''}$ by a sixth of a tone (0.364 Ht.) and a third of a tone (0.676 Ht.) respectively. As Schlesinger herself concedes, this degree of tone alteration is easily accomplished on the *aulos*. And, as to the 15, which simply does not belong in a seven-membered scale whose course of seconds is radially ordered, its presence is unequivocally indicated by Schlesinger's research. Perhaps its use in an ancient enharmonic is, indeed, the very reason it is to be found on the *aulos*. (See p. 88f.)

Fortunately, there is an antique report verifying that it was possible, and usual, for a single instrument to change from an *aulos* scale to the *spondeion melos*. The report also shows that this change affected the Greeks in a way we might anticipate on the basis of our own experience of its fundamental interval. Iamblichus and Sextus Empiricus report two different encounters in which Pythagoras was able to save a situation by having the *aulos* player modulate into *spondeion melos*. In the one case, a crowd of young persons caught up in a wild Dionysian frenzy immediately changed their mood and came to themselves. In the other, a jealous lover, whipped into a still more extreme rage by a Phrygian *aulos* melody, is calmed just as he is about to set a house on fire. In both cases, hearing the changed tones startles the youths intensely and completely changes their mood.

To our knowledge, such a powerful moral effect is attributed to no other antique scale. One senses that Hyagnis or his contemporaries must have been guided by instruction from priests of the Dionysian mysteries so that they could establish the archetypal enharmonic, the spondeion scale, as a counterbalance to the 'normal' scales natural to the *aulos*. Whereas these latter led the Greeks to experience the activity of the lower gods in the power of the chthonic motherly forces that sustained their life, the ancient enharmonic scale—an Apollonian-cyclic creation, but containing the first true Dionysian inner interval 11/8—must have brought something like a sudden ray of light from the realm of the upper gods into this dark, numbing world of desires. Through the portal of the fourth 11/8 this experience must have struck like a lightning stroke into the Greek inner life with a resounding "I am"—a stroke of lightning which contracted the sultry natural world with a shock and whose accompanying thunder brought untransformed human egoistic desires to their knees in a resounding prelude to the Johannine "Metanoeite!" = "Change your ways!"

The polar tension between these scales must have led the Greeks to a genuine experience of Dionysus, the bringer of egohood. It is the same fundamental polarity that we discovered between the Greek tragedy and the satyr play, only in reverse order. Thus it is no surprise that a fragment of *aulody* (i.e., Dionysian music sung to the *aulos*) that has survived from a Euripidean tragedy is an enharmonic melody. This antithesis in the Greeks' dramatic and musical experience which is capable of rousing them to a genuine self consciousness is obviously an artistic reflection of the real soul experiences one had to undergo on the inner path of the Dionysian mysteries. The experience of the primal power residing in our life forces had to be counterbalanced with the concentrated, wakeful consciousness of an unconditional., all-encompassing love and responsibility before Dionysus could reveal himself in his true, divine form to the hierophant. Behind Dionysus a yet greater figure could be discerned, a figure towards whom the first part of the fourth post-Atlantean culture moved.

Thus our intimitations of the depths hidden behind these two kinds of *aulos* scale! According to Greek tradition both scales, the radial, diatonic[68] *aulos* scale, and the *spondeion* scale, are the creation of mythical Phrygian *aulos* players, Hyagnis and Marsyas. The latter was thought of as a satyr, or a silene. The most highly inflamatory of the diatonic scales, the Phrygian, is especially associated with these two Phrygians. Marsyas' student, Olympos, is supposed to have continued their work and added the Lydian scale, a scale which Plato says is appropriate for drinking parties. Taken together, the myths indicate that the real accomplishment of Greece's three most highly prized auletists lay neither in the radial *aulos* scale, which almost certainly existed still earlier in some form or other, nor in the ancient enharmonic scale, but in the tension-laden marriage of these two polar elements.

The following two passages, one from Plato's *Symposium*, the other from the dialogue *Minos* which also is attributed to him, testify to the relationship which the Greeks felt between the experiences of initiation in the mysteries and the music of the *aulos*, which was oriented towards producing the extremest possible tensions and purifying shocks:

> "*Alcibiades*: For I attribute what Olympos accomplished on the *aulos* to his teacher, Marsyas. Thus, whether they are played by a skilled or by a poor *aulos* player, his works enchant only those who seek the gods and their rites, and they reveal who these men are, for these works are divine." (*Symposium*, 215 c)

> "*Socrates*: Now, can you tell me, which of the ancients are outstanding for laying down musical laws for the *aulos*? Perhaps you don't remember and would like me to remind you?
> *Friend*: Yes, by all means.
> *Socrates*: Are not Marsyas and his favorite, Olympos, known for this?
> *Friend*: You speak the truth.
> *Socrates*: And, furthermore, their musical compositions are thus the most divinely inspired, and they arouse and reveal those who seek the gods." (*Minos*, 318 b)

The knowledgeable reader will be asking why the *spondeion* scale, which we contrasted to the radial scale on p. 99, is written in such an unusual way that at first it seems to bear little resemblance to itself as usually notated. The reason is that the *aulos* tuning, out of which it can so logically be developed, leads to this notation. As one can verify for oneself on the circle of fourths on p.94, this version of the *spondeion* scale is consistently based on a chain of five fourths—c g↓ d♭ a♭↓ d . If, instead of this group of tones, we take from the circle the chain a↑ e b↓ f c↓ (which are the first five of the fourth-generated tones of heptatonic chromatic) and place these in the e octave, we obtain the clear, symmetrical form of the ancient pentatonic enharmonic. The scale d c a♭↓ g↓ is merely a modal transposition of this scale.

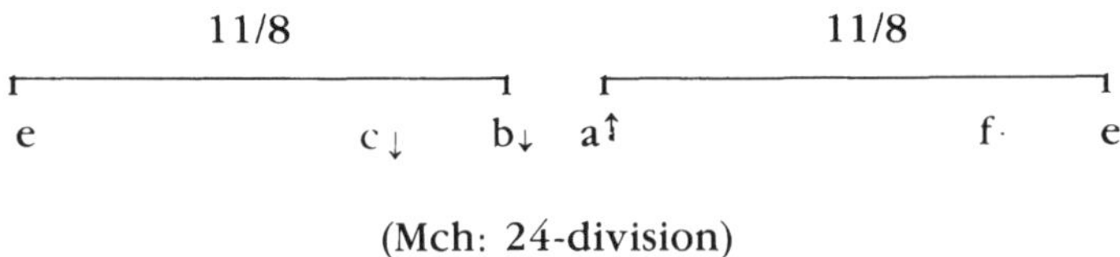

(Mch: 24-division)

From this scale one can develop the seven-toned chromatic-enharmonic scale in a completely consistent manner by adding the neighboring tones, g♭—d♭↓, to it.

Although this thoroughgoing consistency, as well as the character of this fourth 11/8 (at least for those who can experience it) speak for themselves, we cannot forget that neither the *spondeion* scale nor the greek chromatic and enharmonic were ever written down in this form in the greek musical treatises. They were notated within the framework of the fourth 4/3 in the following manner:

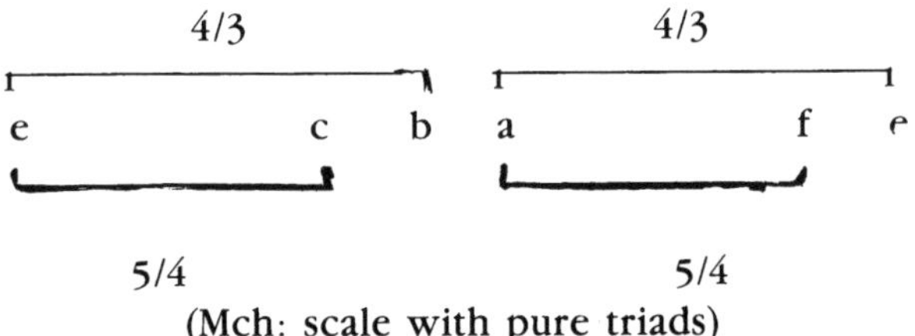

(Mch: scale with pure triads)

In the older form, with interlocking tetrachords, it was:

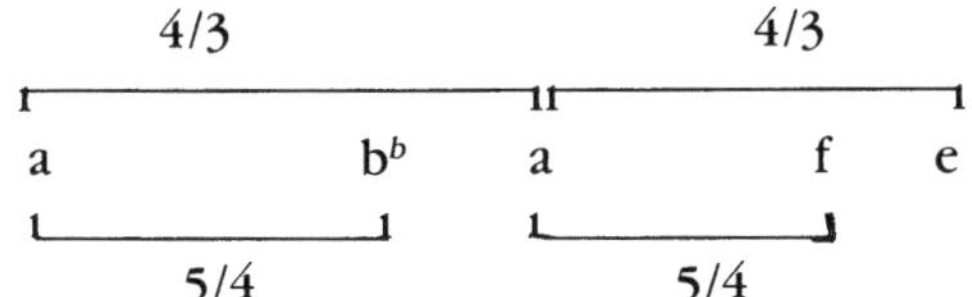

Thus, as Martin Vogel has shown, both the *spondeion* scale and the seven-tone enharmonic scale tend toward an intonation in which the large thirds are not in Pythagorean tuning but rather are already in the modern tuning—5/4—for thirds (e—c, a—f, or d—b^b).[69] According to the accounts, it is just this pure third that is characteristic of these two scales, whereas the recorded forms of chromatic hold closer to a Pythagorean tuning.

Since the Greeks did not view the *spondeion* scale as being so intimately connected with the fluctuating complex of chromatic and enharmonic, nothing would have been more reasonable than for them to have viewed it as a framework of fourth or fifth-based *hestotes* into which two pure thirds had been introduced. From the standpoint of what we can grasp of the exoteric Greek musical life, there could be no objection to this interpretation; the scale certainly existed in this form. And this intonation is easily obtainable from the *aulos* by altering tone 11 by a quartertone:

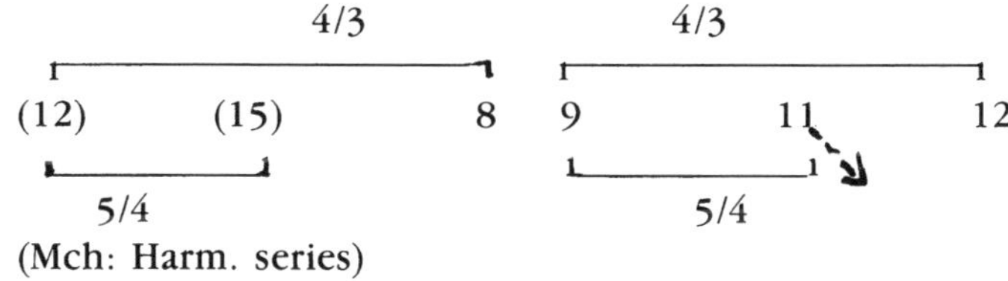

(Mch: Harm. series)

Keeping the whole course of development in view, this recorded form of the *spondeion* scale is the exact counterpart of Renteng-Nyorog, described on p.71. In that case, two sixths 13/8 originally had found their way into the ancient Slendro which was based on sevenths (see Madenda, p. 69), and this, in turn, had led to a new intonation of Slendro's framework of fourth so that it corresponded to tuning based on pure fifths.

Renteng-Nyorog:
(Mch: Pers. scale
with pure fifths)

Recorded form of
Spondeion scale:
(Mch: Scale with
pure triads)

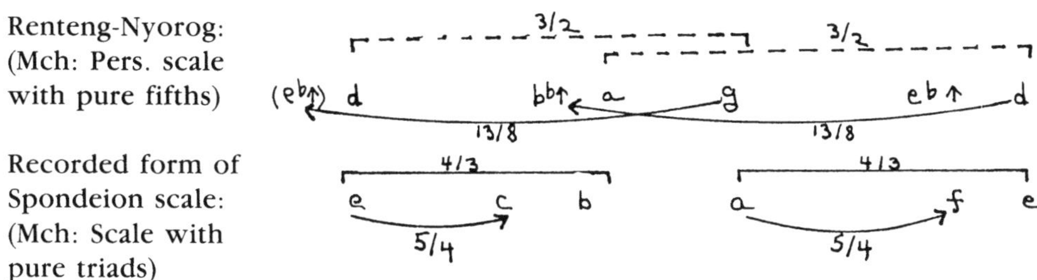

In Nyorog it was the sixths, which led to the quasi-halftones, which were old; the new element was contained in the framing fourths which were tuned to match pure fifths. In the case of the *spondeion* scale, the framework of fourths is an old element inherited from the era of fifth consciousness, whereas the thirds which form the halftones are what belong to the future.

Musicologists (eg. Curt Sachs) have long suspected that the greek *spondeion* scale might have been inspired from abroad—by Asian halftone pentatonic. That the three discoverers of the *spondeion-melos* came from Phrygia, which in antique times bridged Asian and Greco-European cultures, further supports the supposition. But when the Greeks took up the Asiatic halftone pentatonic in which the old ecstatic sixth consciousness was still alive, they transformed it completely. They brought to it a wholly different musical perception, one that was at home in the inner intervals. The Greeks imbued the old scale with the fourth consciousness native to their own soul, and they thereby made something entirely new of it.

At some time this must have led to the Greeks' developing two different ways of experiencing halftone pentatonic—whether at the time of the three great Phrygians or later can be left open. If one persisted with the fifth-derived, Pythagorean-Apollonian *bestotes,* then the new interval relationship had to be obtained by entering into the future's realm of the inner intervals to find the pure third. For pure fourths and fifths are not sufficient for building a halftone pentatonic. Spanned thus between past and future, one still could remain in the realm of intervals belonging to the *Kali Yuga* . But from the side of the antique mystery schools it must have been sensed that the halftone pentatonic has its real home in the holy region of the old mystic intervals from beyond the *senarius* and outside the bounds of the Egypto-Chaldean circle of twelve: alongside the ecstatic seventh of the Atlanteans and the golden sixth from the time of the ancient Zarathustra. Now one has to search for them once more, going beyond the bounds of the *senarius* and beyond the limits of the twelvefold circle which carries the stamp of the world of the senses. And behold how the halftone pentatonic, the archetypal enharmonic form, arises—much more powerfully and consequently than could be grasped in ancient times—out of that single interval which was the hidden signature of the Greek epoch, the first truly inner interval, the fourth 11/8 ! This requires neither that one support oneself by holding to the past nor that one anticipate the future by taking up something still beyond the limits of one's feeling. All that is required is to plumb the depths of the present in a full experience of the fourth 11/8. From what we have learned of this fourth's character, it is obvious that it would not have been accessible to every Greek who was involved in the exoteric life of their time.

It must be admitted that our method of observation is only permissable to us as musicians. As theoreticians and pure scientists—in today's sense of these pursuits—such an approach would lead us into the realms of hopeless speculation. Only musical practice, only a progressively more intense musical listening, can determine which soul region is evoked by one version of a scale and which region by some other version.

The whole strength of the trichord

11/8

e   c↓   b↓

(Mch: 24-division)

with its astonishing, concentrated seriousness and its intimate devotion is lost when its intonation is altered to

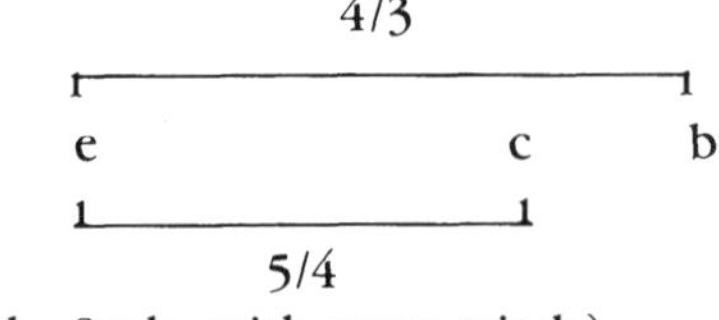

4/3

e   c   b

5/4

(Mch: Scale with pure triads)

In the second version the falling third is like a mournful lament with a personal, subjective melancholy. It has overtones of self-indulgence—all the more so for its being followed by the descending perfect fourth. This fourth is the 'question put to oneself.' It tends to turn the focus of experience inward and enclose a person in himself. The first trichord is capable of expressing love and compassion in a personal way. Its role in exoteric Greek culture was to implant these experiences in the people. The viewer of a Greek tragedy experienced a catharsis. Aristotle described the process that leads the soul to catharsis as involving "compassion and fear." Transposed into the mood a student in the mystery schools had to develop, this would become "a concentrated, reverent seriousness, a loving responsibility, a total personal devotion." The intonation based on 11/8 captures this mood musically.

In the heptatonic scale built on 11/8, $d^{b\uparrow}$, the sixth tone in the chain of fourths, takes its place in the upper *spondeion* trichord. The seventh tone, g^b, is part of the lower trichord. With an eye to enharmonic notation, we can also name these tones c♯↓ and f♯.

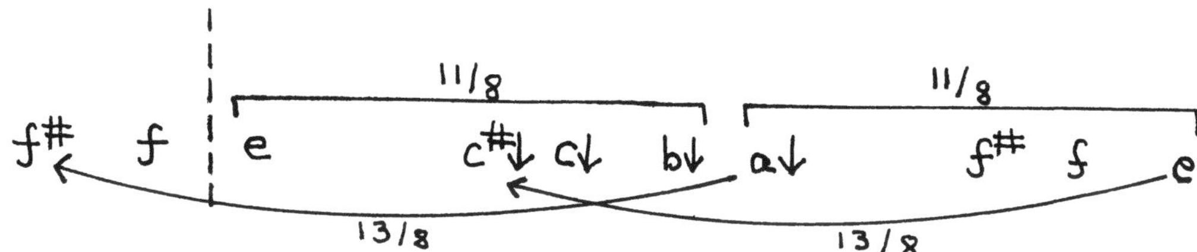

(13/8, pure intonation, = 8.405 ht; here it is 8.435 ht.)

Here we can see how the sixth and seventh tones of the chain of fourths introduce a very close approximation of the golden sixth 13/8 of the ancient Persian culture, that boundless interval which is a practical musical realization of the golden (divine) section. This is yet another reason why the ancient form of enharmonic had to remain within the confines of the mysteries. The ancient, ecstatic sixth could not be allowed to reenter the general musical culture at a time when all needed to be concentrated on inner awakening, on the inner intervals.

Hermann Pfrogner has noted the extraordinary fact that Greek music theory never allowed a tonal relationship involving the number thirteen, even though it often goes far beyond the bounds of the Pythagorean relationships.[70] It only appeared as the sixth 13/8 of the strictly radial *aulos* scale, a scale which never was theoretically understood. There the sixth is so embedded in the radially generated course of seconds that it hardly can be experienced as an outer interval. Furthermore, we sensed a mystery in the *aulos* scale which could only enter conditionally into the Greek exoteric musical life. It seems almost as though the Greeks had to protect their musical soul life from incursions of ancient Persian culture, just as they had to defend themselves territorially and politically against the Persians. As we shall see, the Persian-inspired Arabic culture unerringly identifies itself with the ancient Persian thirteen, even though its music theory initially was entirely derived from the Greeks'.

Thus there are two clear reasons why the guardians of Greek culture would not have allowed a form of heptatonic chromatic and enharmonic based purely on 11/8 to be taken outside the confines of the mysteries. In the first place, the nature of this fourth 11/8 was *not yet* within the compass of the souls of those not initiated in the mysteries. Secondly, the old sixth (which it reintroduced) *no longer* had a rightful place, for it threw people out of themselves in an atavistic fashion.

The solution that was found for this problem was ingenious. The heptatonic scale entered exoteric Greek culture bearing a double aspect: on the one hand as chromatic with halftones, on the other as enharmonic with quartertones. The almost fluid transition from one to the other points to their common origin.

The chromatic scale retains more the outer, spatial, 'melodic' form of the original scale. Both Aristoxenos and Plutarch more than once attest to the greater age of the chromatic scale as against the enharmonic with its quartertones. Thus it is clear that chromatic halftones are a characteristic part of the original scale. Consequently we must see the chromatic scale as a form of the original scale which simply has been adjusted to fit a framework of perfect fourths and fifths. Today, anyone unfamiliar with the fourth 11/8 would hear the matter conversely. They would hear the original scale as a somewhat out-of-tune version of the Greek chromatic that has been handed down to us.

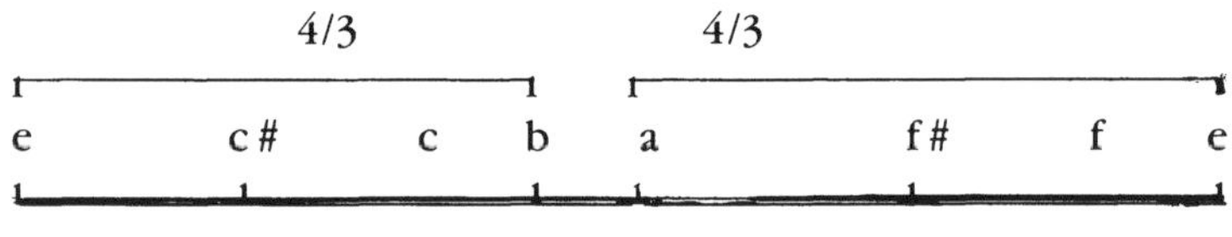

Pentatonic based on fifths
(Mch: Pythag. scale or 12-division)

This scale leans heavily on the support of the Egypto-Pythagorean cycle of twelve, which reflects the outer cosmic order. But it only adheres to the cycle of twelve's organic formative principle as far as a series of five fifths, a e b f#c#—in other words, as far as pentatonic. Then it is built further through accumulations of halftones. These latter derive from the abstract, external, spatially-ordered distances of the circle of twelve when it is taken as a sequence of halftones. In consequence the scale has an extraordinary musical character: while giving the effect of inner experience, its outer smoothness and its quality of striking a pose make it more like a marble object standing in the outer world. Comparing it to the heptatonic built on 11/8, it is immediately clear that the 11/8 scale has an essentially deeper and more direct effect on the soul.

The foregoing characterization of the chromatic scale, which contrasts it with the original scale, is , however, not to be taken negatively. On the contrary, it seems to us that it embodies a fundamental principle of classical Greek culture, namely that the soul of one beholding a work of art is not to be moved directly, that emotional involvement should not be direct, but that the feelings should be objectified, Apollonian fashion, in a beautiful outer appearance. The chromatic tuning for lyre and cithera that has been handed down to us obviously represents the more Apollonian side of what developed in Greece out of the mysterious complex of chromatic-enharmonic music.Its form reveals the transforming activity of the Apollonian fifth and its cycle of twelve.

We must observe how the Apollonian power of the fifth and the circle of twelve can objectify a tonal structure so that it almost seems to exist in external space. There it can draw the sheen of beauty over itself like a skin; there it can exist like a visible object. This observation can give us insight into why the antique myth speaks of the flaying of Marsyas. The satyr had challenged Apollo to a musical duel. Marsyas played the *aulos* , Apollo the cithera. The ear of the judge of the contest, the Phrygian king, Midas, was more inclined toward the tones of the satyr than toward those of the god. Nevertheless, so the myth goes, the satyr is flayed alive in punishment for his sacriligious challenge. Rudolf Steiner observed that Marsyas really did not have to be flayed since he was skinless by nature. Marsyas' music entirely dispenses with the Apollonian elements which would distance it from the hearer and allow it to be apprehended in an outer space, covered over with a 'skin' of beauty. The *aulos* scale and the scale built on 11/8 are 'skinless', their appearance really is not beautiful...no more than a satyr is truly beautiful in comparison with an Apollonian form. But for all their lack of beauty these have something that moves our soul directly. They go deep beneath the skin and if we make ourselves accessible to them they can reveal a different, inward beauty to us—one which has less to do with the radiance of beautiful outer appearance and more to do with the life of a powerful, inner, wholly concrete energy. In Greece this only would have been experienceable to those who were "inclined towards the gods and their initiations," the students of the Dionysian mysteries. For those Greeks who lived in the exoteric culture it must have been painfully apparent that, in contrast to Apollo, Marsyas was musically skinless, as if he had been flayed alive. The myth of the flaying of Marsyas is a conscious formulation of this perception. Simultaneously it gives a picture of Apollo's victory, signaling his dominant role in subsequent cultural development.

Insofar as we see the chromatic scale as an Apollonian reshaping of the original scale, we cannot doubt that the enharmonic form with quartertones is the scale more akin to a Dionysian experience. True, it also is a scale that was played upon the lyre and cithera. True, it is not a radial structure, being built on a framework of pure fourths and fifths. And yet its very first step—which almost always is given as the pure third 5/4—leads so strongly into the Dionysian inner space that this outweighs all the other elements. Furthermore, it contains quartertone structures which we can feel to conceal their own specific mystery...provided that we, as modern westerners, are able to experience them at all. How contrastingly open and clear are the halftone structures of the chromatic scale!

The veil of mystery surrounding the enharmonic quartertones lifts somewhat when we contrast the enharmonic scale handed down to us with that built on 11/8.

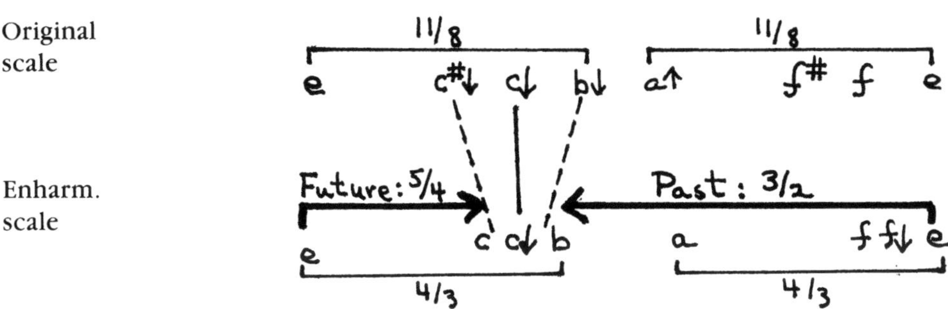

(Mch: 24-division)

The diagram shows how, on the one hand, the tone b↓ is modified upwards a quartertone when it is taken into a stream from the past bearing the impulse of the interval of the fifth 3/2. This outer interval lives on in the Pythagorean framework of fourths. On the other hand, it shows how a stream from the future bearing the inner interval of the third 5/4 alters the tone c#↓ downward by a quartertone. Today the tone c ↓ lying precisely between b and c would be called an irrational tone. In the enharmonic system it is *mesopyknos* and the one and only tone carried over from the original scale is this tone. The Greeks' enharmonic clearly was bound up with this tone. Neither in the *spondeion* scale nor in the chromatic scale did they abandon it. Rather than do so they developed the scale into a highly complicated structure—even to the point of using otherwise unheard-of quartertones—for its sake. So narrowly wedged in between the Scylla and Charybdis of past and future is this tone that it almost escapes the musical grasp. Yet it was only through this tone that what really stood behind Greek enharmonic and, indeed, behind the Greek era of the fourth, could now and again flash up: the experience of the fourth 11/8. The same structural principles governed the series of quartertones in the lower tetrachord with the *mesopyknos* f↓.

Let us place chromatic and enharmonic beside one another, this time in their Mixolydian form. We can see how the interval 11/8 appears, thanks to the quartertones c↓ and f↓ which are introduced into the halftones. And we can see the fourth 11/8 appears in the enharmonic at the step where the tritone appears in the chromatic scale.

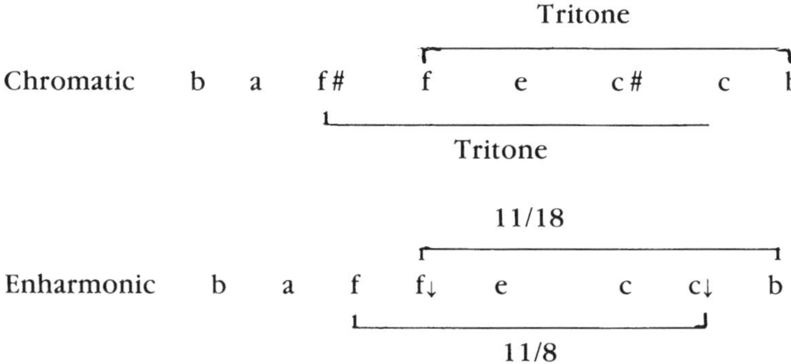

There is a surprising remark of Plutarch about chromatic and enharmonic that becomes clearer in this context. He is describing the musical theories of Aristoxenos and, like him, he frequently attributes the greater age to chromatic. But in one passage he points out that "of course it is only with regard to the accidents of human nature and its needs that one can speak of an older sort of tonality, since as regards the nature and origin of the (two) tonalities (κατὰ γὰρ αὐτὴν τὴν τῶν γενῶν φύσιῷ), neither is older than the other." (*De Musica*, c. 20.)[71] If one takes Plutarch's statement seriously, he basically is implying that the nature of chromatic and enharmonic and their origin lay beyond the scope of the subjective human nature of his time. The chromatic genus *seemed* to be the older, more original, form—so we would say today—only because the hearer could clearly perceive its external, accidentally occurring structure of halftones. As regards the real musical origin and archetypal form of the two, the enharmonic is in no way less primary, notwithstanding the quartertone structure which it later developed.

* * *

Of the members of the trio—Pythagorean system, *aulos* scale, and chromatic-enharmonic—it is the latter which appears as a highly mysterious, tension-wrought culmination in the musical experience of the Greek epoch. It stands between the impulse borne by the fifth and that borne by the second, between the impulse to hold fast to the past and the impulse to jump into the future. Furthermore, the interval 11/8 in which it has its origin is a kind of mediator between Apollonian outer experience and Dionysian inner experience. Later we shall see that an extension of the system of fourths 11/8 to a full circle of twentyfour quartertones makes it possible to achieve an organic interworking of the polar opposites, the cyclic Pythagorean structures and the radial, panharmonic scale (see p. 167ff.)

In other words, a quartertone system is not necessarily the artificial spatial structure obtained by an abstract subdivision of the circle of twelve that Hindemith and others take it to be. The interval 11/8 is its harmonic basis. In addition to this interval it reintroduces the natural intervals of the 'holy domain', joining them with the intervals of the *Kali Yuga* that are contained in the circle of twelve. The natural seventh 7/4 and the golden sixth 13/8 are intervals connected with ancient, selfless, clairvoyant modes of experience. In this quartertone system they find a place within the laws of the twelve, which express the laws of the ego. These latter could only be comprehended in an 'age of darkness.' Joining them, the ancient intervals with their special powers are thereby transformed into something that leads us beyond the musical boundaries of the *Kali Yuga*. When speaking of the fourth 11/8 and the twentyfour tone system which it generates, it seems to us to be no exaggeration to speak of the musical deeds of Him who said, "Behold, I make all things new!"

One must ask, "How is it then that the Greek enharmonic disappears without a trace in late antiquity, in Roman times? Why do the enharmonic scales and the *aulos* scale entirely give way to the Pythagorean system in the music of Rome and of early Christianity? Is this not a sign that human culture and the corresponding state of human souls had regressed to something comparable with the ancient Egyptians?" If one observes the forms of rule since late antique times one can as a matter of fact see such a regression. The ideals of Greek democracy and of the Roman republic were abandoned for a thoroughly Egyptian sort of theocracy or 'emperorship by the grace of God', not only in antique times starting with Caesar and Octavian, but through the Middle ages and right into the 20th Century. And the external Christian church itself, with its hierarchical structure culminating in the Pope, still bears the stamp of Egypt today, just as it did in the Middle Ages.

We have no desire to practice shortsighted historical criticism. Certainly it was necessary for the Christian church music to begin by once more coming thoroughly to terms with the experience of the fifth. The fact that the ancient Hebraic music such as the Davidic psalmody was taken up by the Christian church was especially instrumental in bringing this about, for the elements of ancient Hebraic music really came from the era of the fifth. A.Z. Idelsohn[72] has been able to show that not only the text of the Catholic psalmody, but also the way it was sung, was entirely of ancient Hebrew origin. Clearly, medieval Europe—unlike Greece— was more closely related to the fifth than to the fourth. But the fifth was what made possible the development of western polyphony and, ultimately, of the triadic harmony and the circle of keys of our modern third-oriented consciousness.

106

FROM
MEDIEVAL AND MODERN TONE SYSTEMS
TO
TONE SYSTEMS OF THE FUTURE

XXXII. THE SYSTEM OF THIRDS:
THE GREAT TURNING POINT IN MUSICAL CONSCIOUSNESS

We have come to know ancient Persia, the epoch of the sixth, as a dramatic transitional period in which a consciousness based on the seventh gradually gave way to one based on the fifth. The epoch of the fourth, the Greek epoch, was perhaps even more dramatic. It was a time of unprecedented, widespread tensions, a time when mankind had to create the transformations and transitions necessary for building a bridge from the fifth-oriented consciousness in which one is still outside of oneself to third-oriented experience in which there is a full awakening within one's own earthly individuality. When the consciousness of thirds finally emerged toward the end of the Middle Ages, it was actually the result of an immense musical process of incarnation. Through the course of the entire pre-Christian development, the music of humanity gradually had ceased to be that of an excarnate, ecstatic cosmic being, until at last it became the music of an incarnate citizen of Earth.

What went on within humanity during this development is vividly illustrated by the accompanying changes in the scales and tone systems. We have seen how scales and tone systems built on the cyclic principle were created out of the powers residing in the earliest intervals to be taken up...until the fourth begins to emerge. The cyclic systems built on seventh, sixth and fifth are pictures of how humanity experienced itself musically as a spheric-cosmic being of the periphery. The cyclic system of fourths no longer places us at the periphery, but we still experience ourself as having been brought into being from out of that periphery. The greatest change of all comes with the third, for the third no longer generates a new cycle of tones. Instead, it brings an entirely new principle into play.

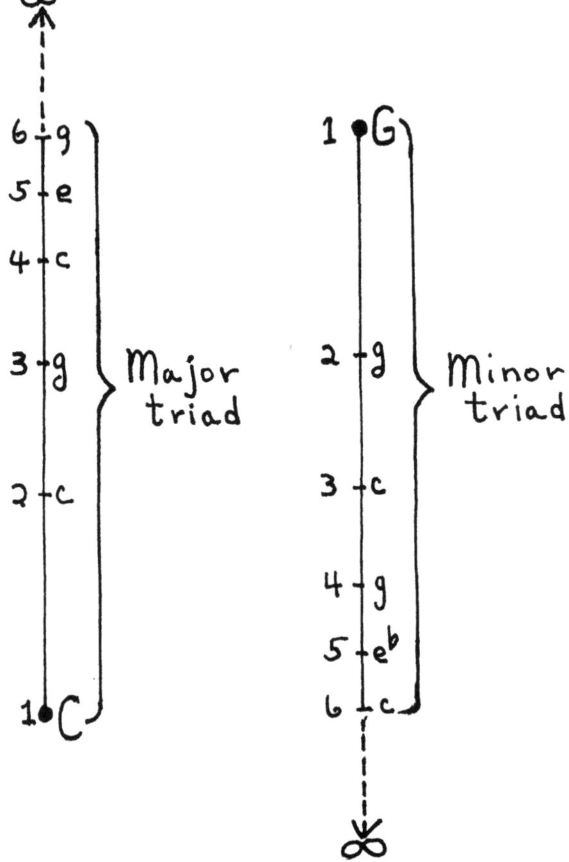

One could, in theory, build a cycle of thirds. Three identical large thirds arrive at the octave
with the help of tempering: c e g # b # (= c). But such a structure only has musical significance
as a dissonant chord within a system of twelve tones, not as a comprehensive tone system
in itself. Furthermore, it lacks an integral characteristic of cyclic systems, namely that they
compress a much more widely spaced chain into the compass of an octave. In other words,
it lacks the characteristic centripetal tendency of cyclic systems. The chain of thirds does not
reach beyond the space of one octave, hence it cannot be compressed through octave transposition. It can only be extended into higher or lower octaves. Thus its tendency is *centrifugal*
rather than centripetal.

In fact, the emergence of third-oriented experience did not lead to such an augmented triad,
a structure which belongs to late Romantic music that already is half atonal. The emergence
of experience of the third led to the pure triad. But, as we already know, the triad embodies
an entirely new structural tendency—the linear, radial principle. The major triad is a segment
of the sequence of tones corresponding to the arithmetic series. The sequence begins in one
tone, the fundamental or groundtone, and radiates upward into infinity. The minor triad is
the corresponding segment of the harmonic series, and radiates infinitely downward from its
fundamental tone.

Leaving the ancient Dionysian scales to one side, we would have to say that third consciousness introduces the linear principle into scale structure for the first time. (The ancient
Dionysian scales were more the forerunners of what was to come and thus were eleminated
from the main stream of development and forgotten.) The radial principle gives us another
clear musical picture of how humanity no longer experiences itself as being solely determined
from out of the cosmic periphery, but rather as a self-sufficient being with its own center,
capable itself of deliberately radiating into the cosmos. To be sure, the circle of fifths preserves
the power of a cyclic-spheric structure for the tone system. But through the third experience
and through the triad the groundtone of the scale has become an inwardly experienced,
radiating center. During the epoch of the fourth, the Greek scales had nothing comparable:

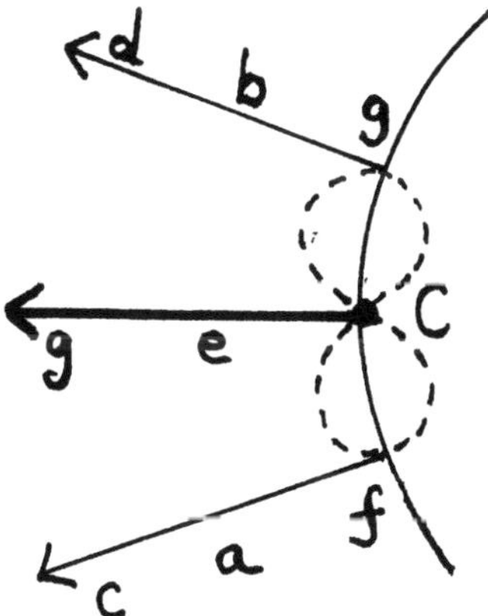

It also is of great significance that the new radial principle, which the third introduced into
the scale structure, is identical with the formative principle of the physical-acoustic overtone
series and undertone series. This makes it evident how, in experiencing the third, humanity
really enters musically into the laws of the Earth and at last is capable of discovering the overtone series there. Now we begin for the first time to make music as fully incarnate, earthly
beings and something lying at the heart of the earthly elements commences singing with us.
The chthonic, radial scales of antique times were simply preparatory exercises and anticipations of a state which mankind actually only achieved in the experience of the third. Tellurian
powers begin to make themselves felt in music as the third makes itself felt, whereas a Uranian
principle was fundamentally behind all the music of the past, namely the cyclic-spheric principle. Earlier music was divine music which resounded to humanity from out of the widths
of heaven.

The cosmic harmony of the spheres once was silenced by the heaviness of earthly material things. The formation of cyclic, centripetal systems is like an echo or a memory of this cosmic process. But now human beings, as musicians of the Earth, have the task of freeing the silent harmony of the spheres again—this harmony that has died into material things. It must be reenlivened and ensouled, and people must so penetrate their own earthly, incarnated spirit with it that it finds its way back to the spiritual cosmos. A tremendous realization will gradually dawn on anyone who has understood the connection between these things—that a real turning point in time was experienced musically when humanity began to achieve an experience of the third... not just one of the many turning points in cultural development, but *the* turning point in the development of humanity and of the Earth. From this vantage point one also looks with earnestness and deep shock upon what our age has made of experience of the third.

It is true that the historical events connected with Earth's turning point in time took place over one thousand years before third consciousness made its decisive entrance into the musical arena. Furthermore, we found that the musical prerequisites for modern third consciousness were already present in antique times: in the radial *aulos* scales of the Greek Dionysian mysteries. But it has not been until well into our own times that the full human impact of this turning point in time has been felt. The present and near future will show whether humanity can realize this decisive turning point within itself. For music this amounts to the question whether sufficient spiritual strength can be summoned to give new life and content to the third. The third must become truly radiant—that same third which humanity were able to receive, still living, from the stream of the past, but which inevitably became empty and insipid as it was reduced to merely earthly experience.

Rudolf Steiner described an event that was fundamentally bound up with the possibility of humanity's being able to grasp the third.[73] He tells how human thinking began to undergo a complete transformation in the last pre-Christian centuries. This process culminated in the fourth century B.C., but was only fully completed during the twelfth to the fourteenth centuries, i.e. at the time when the third decisively entered our culture. Prior to this transformation, thought was ruled from a spiritual sphere which affected people from without, through their senses. Therefore thoughts were experienced as flowing into consciousness along with perceptions of the outer world. A person did not formulate their own thoughts as belonging to themselves, but rather thoughts were discovered as cosmic thoughts living in or behind the things of the world. It was because regency over thought was given over to spiritual beings who work from within humanity that the subsequent transformation took place. Only since that time have people been able to speak of *their own* thoughts which they experience as originating in themselves and issuing from themselves. The breakthrough to the experience of the third—and, with it, to taking hold of radial powers—is nothing other than the musical expression of what went on in the depths of human souls as they experienced the transformation of the nature of thought.

If we turn once more to the Greek epoch we find in Socrates (470-399 B.C.) probably the most impressive personality to take an active part in this transformation of the life of thought. Indeed, he ushered in the change. He devoted his life to helping people give birth to thoughts from out of themselves. He called himself a midwife for this reason. Having become acquainted with inner human soul space as the realm of Dionysus, it will not surprise us that Socratic thinking had an effect on the Greeks that they experienced as unmistakably akin to the effect of Dionysian *aulos* music. The force of the *aulos* music, of course, originated in radial powers. In Plato's *Symposium* Alcibiades directly addresses Socrates as an *aulos* playing satyr, a Marsyas. For, on the one hand, Socrates was like a Satyr in a satyr play: he exposed the ignorance in the forms of handed down, unself-sufficient knowledge, which was based on capacities then on the wane. And, on the other hand, his conversations were like *aulos* music in the manner in which they drew forth the inner soul content of his listeners. The Socratic method was a truly Dionysian method for bringing to light the divinity hidden within humanity... as thought. A person's thought became truly their own, not a last remnant of the old clairvoyance working in through their perceptions, but something they for the first time are able to bring up out of the divine wisdom and truth residing deep in their own being. Socrates called this truth resident in us *daimonion*. It can only speak to us when "we know that we do not know anything," i.e., when we approach the world completely without presuppositions, without

110

the old clairvoyance or its remnants, and form our own thoughts about it.

We must understand how one side of Socrates' activity placed him in the chthonic-Dionysian stream. It is not insignificant that the Greeks saw him as a satyr or as the old Silenius who once had taught Dionysus the Younger. Nor is it insignificant that he named his profession, devoted to awakening thoughts in the individual, *maieia* (μαιεία) which means 'midwifery', or, literally, 'the work of the little old mother' (μαῖαι), for this profession, that of his own mother, belongs entirely in the chthonic-motherly realm. The significance of this lies in the connection Rudolf Steiner has shown to exist between thinking and the formative life forces: those divine forces which form, carry and maintain our bodily life in a motherly, natural way are the very same forces through which we give birth to thoughts. Since Socrates' time thought has been built *from out of* these forces. In pre-Socratic times, thought essentially was something that *attached itself to* these forces.

But, seen from the other side, namely from the side of further development, Socrates appears as the father of earthly understanding and of the scientific attitude of mind. No longer are sense impressions allowed to force ideas upon the mind. Instead, one forms one's own ideas about sense appearances, basing them on an inner, less fallible sense of truth. Thus we see how our earthly intellect is of Dionysian origin as regards its *substance* and the direction of its activity, even though its *form*, as centered and focused on single points, could only have come from Apollonian forces.

We must not be misled by the fact that today the intellect has become so abstract, so bloodless, so estranged from reality, that it has become destructive. For we know how everything that belongs to the Dionysian path of soul development must overcome the dangers of subjective illusion and destructive egotism. Thinking has undergone much the same trials the third has undergone. Musical experience of the third has become an insipid and empty thing, banal, and ultimately subhuman. In the realm of thought, the earthly intellect has become grey and spiritless, banal, and capable of engaging in quasi-scientific embroidering on every human or subhuman aberration.

The forces involved in third experience and those of earthly understanding stem from the same source in the depths of human soul and spirit. There thought and feeling still are united instead of being separated from one another. In its own domain, each of these has led humanity downward to the material, everyday, earthly world where a person is abandoned by God and by the spirit. But here is where we can become wholly free, self-responsible beings. Both forces are waiting for the human spirit to enliven and inspire them and so re-establish their spiritual nature. Then they can become forces for world transformation, radiating back into the world from out of the inner being of a humanity that has found its indwelling divine center and taken hold of its *daimonion* with the forces of the ego.

Now we have a vantage point from which we can throw further light on the problem of the physical overtone series, a problem we shall meet repeatedly. We called the overtones a last remnant of the harmony of the spheres that has died into matter. It was the earthly understanding of the natural scientist, a sibling of our modern third consciousness, which first discovered the marvel of the overtones in the vibration of matter. Certainly, as far as music is concerned, this is and remains a totally abstract and uninteresting discovery... at least for so long as our earthly intellect remains abstract. But the matter changes as soon as the intellect brings itself to life by rediscovering its Dionysian origins—which is something it can best do through music. Then overtone series also comes to life as a further revelation of the Dionysian principle which governs the intellect. Having lain buried in matter in a death-like sleep, the newly enlivened, ensouled and enspirited harmonies of the overtone series gradually open the way to a subterranean treasure trove containing immeasurable riches. Here are preserved the intervals that embody all the fundamemtal nuances of human soul as they were in primeval times and as they will be in the furthest future. Third consciousness, earthly consciousness, earth-bound understanding—these are the only treasure-seekers capable of penetrating to the 'middle of the earth'. When they do, what began with a true journey through the depths of hell—right down to the point of musical nullity—is transformed. Only when the null point has been reached can the sense of the Earth and the spirit of the Earth begin to reveal itself musically in a resurrection of earthly and cosmic music.

XXXIII. THE SYSTEM OF THIRDS: THE BATTLE OVER THE INNER SOUL-CONTENT OF THE THIRD

In the course of history there was one far-reaching attempt to thwart that transformation of human thought and musical experience that we just have been describing. This grandiose attempt occurred during the post-Grecian period and came from within the Persian and Arabic cultures. Up to the present day it has scarcely been noticed or identified by the historians and, if Rudolf Steiner had not so emphasized it in connection with the development of thinking, it might simply have remained hidden. In order to appreciate the full scope of this medieval Arabic-Persian movement in relation to musical development it is necessary to review the most significant spiritual and cultural events connected with the movement.[74]

When the Emperor Constantine (325) made Christianity the religion of the state, one result was the cessation of Rome's terrible persecution of the Christians. The youthful religion of the future was helped to a decisive, worldwide breakthrough. On the other hand, this marked the point at which Christianity began to become a religion of laws, prescriptions and dogmas—aspects more characteristic of the pre-Christian religions such as the Judaism of the Old Testament. The original spiritual life of the young religion was driven more and more into the background as the 'lawgivers' proceeded to rigidly specify what Christian belief was and what it was not. The comprehensiveness and profundity of a teaching became dependent on the comprehensiveness and profundity of its lawgivers.

The lawgivers of this Roman state-church could understand the human and historical significance of the outer events that had taken place in Palestine but they could not see through to the real spiritual background of these events. They were blind to the deep connections with certain earlier spiritual-cultural accomplishments, especially those of Greek culture. It was the accomplishment of Greek post-Socratic philosophy to have helped bring the divine Logos which lives in humanity to birth... from out of self-generated human thinking. By the time of classic Greek sculpture it had become possible to picture divinity through the beauty of the human form, whereas in earlier cultures divine representations always had had superhuman or animal attributes. In Greece, for the first time, the purely human came to be understood as an expression of the divine—just as, in Palestine, the purest humanity, the noblest human substance, became the vessel through which the divine Logos itself could walk upon the earth.

We are well aware that we are comparing two things that belong to widely divergent frames of reference. Greek philosophy and art arose out of human deeds whereas the appearance of the Christ was a divine deed. Nor does the realm of a Greek god, such as Apollo, begin to approach the spiritual heights from which the Christ comes. Yet both things belong to the same epoch of humanity and bear the same signature: the appearance of the divine in the human. Musically understood this is the signature of the *fourth*, which we always encounter as the intermediator between the human and the divine. The fourth mediates between interval experience in which a person still feels himself ecstatically drawn up into a divine-cosmic sphere, leaving his own humanness behind, and interval experience in which he feels the spark of divinity within himself and as a part of his own humanness.

The Roman spirit, which gradually took possession of exoteric Christianity, was incapable of comprehending that a true turning point in time had been passed—incapable of reading the signature of Greek culture. Greek culture was seen as a heathen product, useful as an aesthetic or educational luxury, but whose spirit had to be denied and weeded out. The consequence of this view was that Greek culture continued to find its way to educated Rome in the form of 'goods' such as marble imitations. Meanwhile, Greece's mystery centers and philosophical schools, which had been the spiritual focus of Greek culture, were forcibly closed by the state. Many teachers from these centers saw no alternative to exiling themselves to the neighbouring Persian kingdom. There they were received with open arms by the ruling Sassanid family which was intensely interested in learning. Thus did the true Greek spiritual achievements flow eastward into Persia: Aristotleanism, Neo-Platonism, Pythagoreanism, Gnosis and Alexandria's budding natural sciences.

In the period that immediately followed, these seeds bore rich fruits for Persian-Arabic civilization. The magnificent Persio-Arabic sciences developed. Especially in the medical sphere they would continue to outshine the collective wisdom of the west for the next thousand years. The spiritual center of this science was the Academy at Gondischapur.

The spiritual accomplishments of Greek culture—that new capacity for freely exercised, independent, earthly understanding which first had been cultivated in Greece—were transported into the ancient domain of Persia. There, the culture of the Magi. which was nourished by imaginations that possessed their possessors, still held sway although it had fallen into decadence. The transplantations from Greece set off a prodigious revival in the culture of the Magi. But it was a revival that was completely out of place. It did not belong in a culture that was a remnant from the second post-Atlantean epoch. Earlier, the still selfless humanity of the ancient Persian times with its old imaginative powers had had the task of building the human earthly body and earthly surroundings into a fitting habitation. This was in preparation for the spirit, which would enter the earthly sphere later accompanied by the human ego. Compared to the wisdom of ancient India, this wisdom was turned entirely earthwards, even though it still was based on supersensible experience. Zarathustra, the highest teacher of ancient Persia, took upon himself the task of preparing an earthly, bodily dwelling place for that high spiritual being whom he called the Aura of the Sun. His task was fulfilled when the divine Sun-being appeared in the body of Jesus. The only thing the ancient Persian wisdom could bring about by continuing to exercise its influence beyond its appointed time was to force humanity deeper into material culture. The use of ancient, supersensible, inspirational powers could not help humanity any further toward that which gives its life on earth its real meaning: the development of an individual personality with inwardness of soul and possession of free, self-sufficient powers of thought. For those old powers demanded that the human self be kept silent.

And this is precisely the influence which the new Persio-Arabic spiritual stream issuing out of Gondischapur actually had. It appropriated the philosophical and natural scientific knowledge that had arisen out of the newly awakened mode of rational thinking in Greece. With this as its basis, an extraordinarily ingenious science was developed, one which concerned itself exclusively with sense-perceptible, bodily, material things, even though it was largely based on old, supersensible abilities. What developed could be called a supersensible materialism, if the apparent paradox in the expression is properly understood.

Here we find an alliance between Persian culture which bore old, magical-inspirational powers and the Semitic-Arabic culture whose specially developed capacities gave it a particular aptness at reminting inspired ideas in the form of abstract-intellectual, brain-bound thoughts. Having first conquered Persia and then become its spiritual apprentices, the Arabs brought Persian culture what it lacked of the third post-Atlantean epoch, namely the trained senses and, above all, the abstract, brain-bound thinking founded on them. The imaginative thought-world discovered in their sense perceptions by the Hamitic Egyptians of the third epoch became an earthly world for the Semitic Chaldeans and, especially, for the Hebrews and the Arabs. For these latter, the old imaginative world was remoulded into a world of pictureless, abstract thoughts dependent on the physical brain.

Both the Hamitic and the Semitic modes of thinking were passive, submissive. They were completely at odds with the independent mode of thinking initiated by Socrates by means of which thoughts were born out of a person's own, Dionysian inner soul space. The Semitic-Arabic mode of thinking, one could say, is a superhuman, cosmic spirituality which has become earthly and chained to the physical brain. On the other hand, the Socratic mode of thinking originates in telluric powers. It is a purely human and earthly capacity of soul, but one which enables a person to evolve freely by means of his own activity, proceeding from a childlike lack of awareness to a more and more all-encompassing spirituality. But this latter sort of spirituality can only be born out of oneself through a process that involves much pain and error. As this spirituality grows our own spirituality grows, whereas the Arabic form of spirituality is absolutely unconnected with any individual soul center and, rather, uses the bodily organs of thought more or less as a tool.

In describing this contradiction we have exactly described a major conflict which ran through the Middle Ages, the conflict between the Christian spirituality of the west and the Arabic spirituality of the orient. In the west Europeans developed inwardness of soul. They had a childlike ignorance and trust and a pious respect for the spiritual authorities of ancient times. As history unfolded they had to endure terrible disputes, senseless religious persecutions, wars both internal and brought from without, plagues, and natural catastrophes. It was as though history had staged a century-long Dionysian tragedy in order to allow the fruits of an entirely inward bearing of soul to develop—Meister Eckhart's "small spark of the soul." During the same period, the impersonal, abstract, inspired science of Gondischapur grew like a radiant blossom in the east, proudly surpassing the Greek culture in which it had its beginning and finally encompassing all the wisdom and learning of the orient.

Had it not been attacked at the right time 'from behind'—from its own Semitic-Arabic quarter, by the Mohammedans—this science would have spiritually flooded the childlike west. It would have completely smothered the still-too-young seeds of its future, the seeds of inwardness of soul and spirit. As a strict continuation of the Old Testament religion of laws, Mohammedanism strongly opposed all forms of 'heathen' science, as did Rome. Through Mohammedanism's rapid spread, the Persian influence of Gondischapur was very much diluted. In this respect, Islam reveals itself as a secret protector of western Christianity even though it continues to this day to be a constant threat and scourge to it. In Arabism an ancient, spiritual, magically inspired power was pressing toward Europe. By transforming this into the outwardly warlike aggression of religious fanaticism, Islam reduced Arabism to a level at which the Christianity of the time was able to combat it—for example, through such a man as Karl Martell. Unprotected, the youthful west surely would have succumbed to the spiritual might of Persian inspired Arabism.

On the other hand, Islam promoted the spread of its weakened version of the impulse of Gondischapur. "What itself is created cannot create anything "—such a key statement from the revelation of Mohammed in the Koran still harmonizes with the spiritual background and the decisive impulses of Arabic culture. It clearly expresses the denial of the creative, Dionysian power of thought that Socrates embodied. It recognizes a selfless, passive reason and no more. Mohammed brought fantastically magnificent revelations of the hereafter which reach even into the seventh heaven. But, for all these, he had a blindness that was nothing less than demonic when it came to that divine creative principle through which humanity first became free and spiritually came of age—a principle born in the deepest recesses of the human soul—the Son of God, the Logos or, as the Bible names him, the Son of Man. Thus the spiritual stream of Gondischapur was able to develop further in Islam and, in the end, to unite with Islam. This came to pass particularly through the influence of personal physicians to those Caliphs who were negligent regarding the laws in the Koran that are unfriendly toward science. Nevertheless, through Islam the spiritual might of Arabism was sufficiently toned down to give the west time to develop a thinking that was strongly enough grounded in the individual soul for it to be able to arm itself and enter the field against Arabism. (According to the recent description in Schoeffler's *Die Akademie von Gondischapur*, even before the Islamic invasion there was an important confrontation between the new Persian stream and Nestorian Christianity, which was a Christian form of Aristotelianism.)

The spiritual influence of Arabism was able to penetrate to the heart of the Roman Church's dogma: in 869 the Council of Constantinople went so far as to disavow, dogmatically, that a person has an individual, creative spirit. It was only much later, in the thirteenth century, that Thomas Aquinas (1225-1274) was able to forge a decisive philosophical rejection of Arabism. In his struggle with the Arabic Aristotelianism of Averroes (1126-1198), Thomas wrestled with the question whether the individual person generates thoughts or whether the formation of thoughts takes place independently of the thinker. In other words, he wrestled with what we have discovered to be the basis of a musical experience of the third: do we form our thoughts independently out of ourselves and our own soul life (as Thomas asserts), or are our thoughts nothing more than the inspirations we passively receive from a non-human spirituality, an abstract cosmic rationality, (as Averroes says)? This implies the further question, whether we have something divine and immortal in us or whether we are just a mutable, selfless apparatus of thought played upon by universal cosmic reason.

In principle, the whole problem of modern Materialism is contained in this question. And, standing behind the philosophical thought of the Arabian, Averroes, looms the enormous force of the old, impersonal Persian spirituality transformed into a force that presses toward a spiritless materialism. It is amazing that the authority of Aristotle, himself the student of a student of Socrates and the first great systematizer of self-sufficient earthly understanding, was used to support the view that there is no such thing as self-sufficient understanding. But, according to what Arabism made of him in the translations of Averroes and others, this is what he is supposed to have taught! Thomas Aquinas had to look to Arabism to discover the spiritual ancestor of the West—one of the greatest paradoxes of cultural history! As by a single stroke of lightning, this issue reveals the nature of relationship between the Greek, Persio-Arabic and western cultures.

The art of the fourteenth and fifteenth centuries represented Thomas Aquinas' victory, which meant so much to the west, as a highly significant event. It pictured Averroes under the feet of Thomas, who bears a star or a radiant sun on his chest to show that, in contrast to Averroes he had established the authority of the divine, sunlike power dwelling within the soul. Sometimes the Madonna appears above him as a reminder of the feminine motherly nature of the soul which gives birth to the Logos.

We should be at pains to remind ourselve what battles, both spiritual and physical, the west has had to fight in order to win and retain that precious jewel that is revealed musically in the experience of the third: the divine spark that lives in the innermost depths of the human soul. Today the third has been subjected to widespread disdain and abuse and has been abandoned, yet it was the third that musically implanted this spark in the soul. It has taught us to feel the 'ground' tone of the scale, the prime. One day the prime will spiritually and musically illuminate an experience whose first dawning already can be discerned, an experience that reveals that "the center of the cosmos is within us." (Solzhenitsyn). The whole further development of humanity and of the earth depends on this spark whose first gleams are revealed by the third. It must kindle a fire that will radiate outwards so that the central point within us becomes a sun. Today this problem is a concrete reality.

Indeed, we live daily with the most frightful counterpicture of the radiance of soul and spirit that should issue from within the human being—the picture our technology gives us by rekindling the radiant power that resides in the nucleus of the atom, which is what today's materialism regards as the center of the cosmos. These, also, are chthonic powers through which the Earth can radiate into the cosmic periphery out of which it once was formed. But, unlike the divine, Dionysian powers, these telluric powers have never been transformed by passing through the inner human soul world. They are earthly forces that have been diverted from the chthonic-motherly, life-bearing realm of nature. They have degenerated into something subnatural instead of being raised up to the supernatural through the human feeling soul and the human thinking spirit. The divine, Dionysian powers bear the supersensible force of creative, unifying, cosmic love. Those other powers bear the sub-sensible forces of destructive, splintering cosmic hate.

Certain occult movements used Persian-inspired Arabism as their tool in order to introduce this cosmic hatred as an influence on the development of humanity. The opposition to these powers was sufficient to prevent their totally frustrating the great transformation of thinking that needed to take place in modern times. But they were nevertheless able to obscure this transformation to such a degree that people in general did not become aware of their own thinking—of their own creative, Dionysian spiritual center. Only in the cases of exceptional individual feats of consciousness was such an awareness realized. The whole of modern materialism, whose pivotal point is atomic theory, could only arise because people have begun to use their earthly understanding without becoming aware that their thoughts are the product of their own activity. Instead, thoughts are treated as if they simply flowed to a person out of their sense experience. Materialism lives on because of a permanent confusion between thinking and sense experience. And this confusion is the inheritance of Gondischapur.

The age of the natural sciences needed a modern Aquinas to fight for the freedom and self-sufficiency of human thought and for its divine spiritual nature: these were Rudolf Steiner's main themes in his *Philosophy of Freedom* (*Philosophie der Freiheit*). By sharply distinguishing the nature of perception, which comes from without, from the nature of thought, which comes from within, and by showing how these are related to one another, he was able to tear asunder the impenetrable veil that materialism had thrown over the inner, spiritual nucleus of the human soul. Up to now the significance of this renewed victory for the future of humanity has scarcely been noticed. But it shows a way—naturally with heightened inner efforts—by which people can discover themselves in their life of thought. Those who discover their own divine, spiritual nature will be able to have a radiant, spiritualizing influence on the world. Thus can the culture of the west begin to create a natural science and an art which remain conscious of humanity's divine, Dionysian origin. And such persons will begin to be able to take hold of a world that threatens to degenerate into the sub-natural because of materialism's blindness of soul and raise it to the supernatural.

Musically this signifies that we can overcome the crisis of third experience (see p. 57f.) which has brought present day music to the point of a total materialistic estrangement from its own inherent nature. It signifies that we can rediscover a spiritual continuity with the earlier great masters of the epoch of the third—but in such a way that the inwardness of the third, which for them came from the sphere of personal feeling, is transformed. Experience of the third can develop an objectivity in which the whole being of Earth appears illuminated by the nature of the One who, since the turning point of time, has taken up residence in the innermost depths of the human soul.

With the dawning of third experience comes the need for music to radiate from within the person. And, in so far as the music whose source is within must have an outer, perceivable embodiment in tones (in the sense we discussed in the first chapter), this embodiment has to be realized through a material that can be wholly imbued with inner, human soul life. This means that the physical sounds which clothe the musical tone must originate in a world to which the human soul has access via the senses—a world where the soul can feel itself at home, a world that can come to life when the soul and the senses work together. The transcendent cosmic musicality which earlier people still experienced in sound can only unite with what now radiates from within us in an ego-illumined, spiritual-musical experience if the sound is produced by instruments whose material comes from our perceptual world of wood and air and metal. The material furnishes the physical garment for the musical tone: a hidden alliance supporting the perceived tone which could be a 'sensible-supersensible' alliance.

The study of electricity gave us access to the sub-sensible realm which adjoins the world of the senses. This underworld is excluded from the realm of the senses. It cannot be reached by our senses alone. To be sure, the senses can perceive certain effects of electricity and magnetism in objects of the senses, but the forces themselves remain beyond the senses. There is no object whose electrical and magnetic tensions simply reveal themselves to the senses in the way, for example, the warmth of an oven can be perceived by our sense of warmth or in the way physical tension or compactness can be perceived by our sense of touch or by our sense of hearing.

If the sounds that clothe music are derived from this sub-sensible world, our musical self can only wear the resulting garment to the extent that sensible materials have helped to determine its quality. On the one hand this can be something such as the material-sensible quality of the membrane of a loudspeaker or of the speaker enclosure, or it can be the sound structure of some instrument (like a violin) whose character bears the qualitative imprint of physical material and which has been registered on a tape and, so to speak, has been electro-magnetically 'frozen solid'. But we cannot penetrate to those qualities that originate in the electro-magnetic processes themselves and thus bear the mark of the sub-sensible, electromagnetic, sub-natural world. Not with our inner musical sense. The musical sense rebounds as from a wall, for these qualities no longer offer it anything of a sensible-supersensible nature. Lacking this, there is nothing in which it can live, nothing through which it can radiate outwards.

Sounds that are produced purely electronically give one a chance to study this mostly half-conscious but extraordinarily long-lasting experience. The way my musical perception rebounds from this sub-sensible eletronic world gives me the impression that something superhuman and non-human, or else something cosmic, is streaming toward me. One has a direct impression that one is hearing the 'music of the spheres.' "This music is ensouled with cosmic charm," writes Fred Prieberg enthusiastically about electronic music, "for it is strictly speaking beyond the human sphere."[75] Along the same lines, H. H. Stuckenschmidt has commented, "This sort of music really does have a cosmic character. It is worlds removed from the realms of subjective

116

feeling. In its strange, new, often frightening forms, forces come to life which seem not only beyond the human, but also from realms beyond the earth."[76] We have called the achieving of third experience the great turning point in musical experience—after this point music can radiate out of humanity itself as an inward, purely human, individual experience. And with respect to precisely this achievement electronic music seems to represent a retrograde development. The human soul's radiant center seems to have been eliminated so that music breaks over us, resounding from out of the cosmic periphery as it did in ancient times. It is not difficult to recognize this as the work of that spiritual stream whose goal since the time of Arabism has been—and remains—to thwart the aforementioned transformation of human spirit and soul.

Electronic music's 'cosmic experience' is, of course, a great deception. It is not cosmic. It is our own inner musicality rebounding off the impenetrable wall of the sub-sensible. It imitates external cosmic experience by coming at us from without. That which naturally longs to radiate out of humanity into the cosmos is reflected back into humanity itself. It is just precisely when we have been walled up in ourselves in this way that we can believe that we are hearing the music of the spheres. Furthermore, we are thus exposed to radiation from out of the sub-sensible realms, although this aspect is not experienced musically. As a rule it remains unconscious, veiled by the virtually incestuous form of the musical experience. For the most part it is noticed only after the listening is over. There is a perceptible loss of vital strength and one feels as though one's soul had been hollowed out.

What has been said about purely electronic music is naturally also true of every sound that gains qualitative significance through the participation of sub-sensible electronic forces. This is the case with electronic pop music with its various typical electronic techniques such as feedback. In electronic pop and rock music the predominating sound of the popular rhythm guitar and the familiar, third-oriented harmony provide a more than ample basis for inner musical participation. So the listener enters much more intensively into the physical surface of the sound than is the case with purely electronic music. In contrast to the cool, intellectual constructions of electronic music, its whole mood is emotional and youthfully revolutionary, and is heated up by a corresponding rhythmic energy. This music is moved by a will to let world-transforming forces radiate from the youthful soul. But a ball rebounds further and more forcefully from a wall the more energetically it is thrown against it. Similarly, inner musicality breaks against the wall of the sub-sensible all the more forcefully in this music because of its great energy. And it rebounds all the more deeply into the inner realm of the soul. Flooded by a great profusion of sound which bears the imprint of the sub-sensible electronic world and breaks over them as if it came from more than human realms, people yield to the illusion that their emotions are some sort of cosmic inspiration.

Here, as in the preceeding chapter, we cannot be satisfied to merely sketch the past history of Arabism. The influence of what it once inaugurated must be traced into the immediate present. Thus it becomes ever clearer that one has hardly begun to do justice to what music calls the third when one has described the distance between, or the harmonic relationship between, two tones. Third consciousness involves much more than that. It involves a huge step in the development of human consciousness. True enough, previous centuries did make a start at taking this step, but its fulfillment still is a thing of the future.

XXXIV. THE SYSTEM OF THIRDS: THE ARABIC HYBRID-THIRD

The spiritual stance of the Persian-inspired Arabism characterized in the previous chapter was set hard against the development of an inner third awareness. What musical effects did this have on the structure of its scales?

In the chapter on Arabia in his book, *Lebendige Tonwelt*, Hermann Pfrogner points to an important aspect of the Arabic tone systems that has a direct bearing on the present question. He writes, "The history of Arabic music could well be called the history of the 'neutral third', the Arabs' favorite interval. It is a strangely obstinate interval that lies more or less halfway between a major third and a minor third. Up to the present day this interval has successfully resisted every attempt to fix it unambiguously."[77] Pfrogner describes how, looking in one direction, something approximating this interval already is to be found on the typically Arabic, pre-Islamic *tunbur* (or *pandore*), a two-stringed, long-necked lute that is fretted in quarter-tones. And, looking in another historical direction, one finds the Persian musician Mansur Zalzal (d. 791) reintroducing the neutral third into Arabic music in the eighth century at a time when the Pythagorean tuning inherited from the Greeks had become the standard model.

Among other things, this crossbreeding of Pythagorean scale structure with Zalzal's hybrid third produced the Arabic scale-form called *maquam rast* , "...which musicians today agree is the prototype of all Arabic melodic structures." (Pfrogner) The Persian word '*rast* ' means 'regular' or 'correct'.

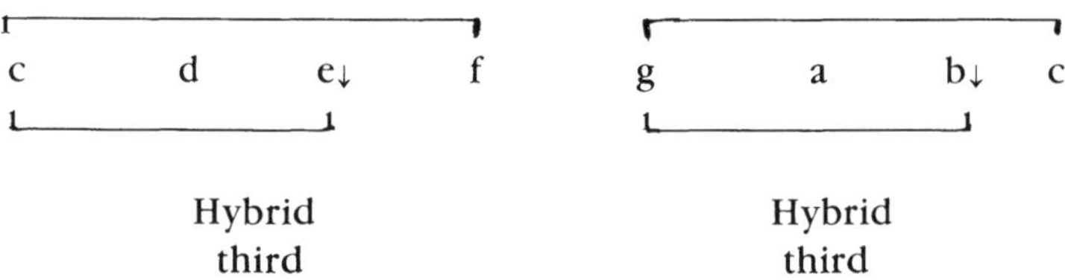

Husmann also agrees in calling *rast* "...the principle tonality of Arabic-Persian music" and he gives it in the following form [78]:

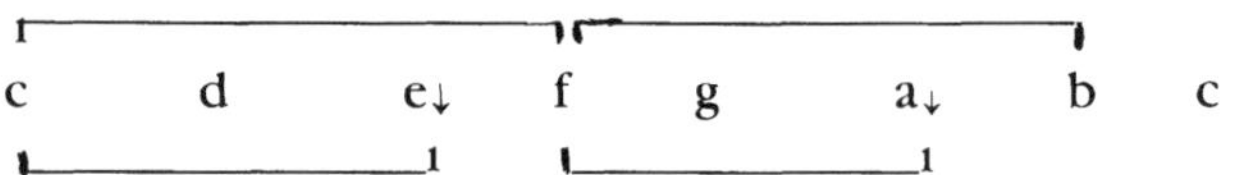

(Mch. 24-Div. or Pythag. Scale with e↓, b↓, a↓ from 24-Div.)

Three essential things are to be observed in scales with such a structure: 1) As in the western church modes, the Arabic scales strictly adopt the Greek, Pythagorean principle of employing the pure fourth as the framing interval. Here we encounter the power of the cyclic principle of fifths, but now it is turned inward. 2) As with the church modes, the descending direction of earlier, pre-Christian Greek scales now has been turned about to become ascending. All Arabic scales are cited in ascending form—as they are experienced. Thus far the Arabic development conforms to that in the west. 3) But there was a critical place in the scales where, during the Middle Ages, the radial principle of the future with its thirds and triads was able to gain a foothold in the church modes—especially in the Ionian and the Mixolydian modes. At this critical place, the Arabians' hybrid third bars the doors to the principle of the future. Precisely at the place where the pure third 5/4 should begin to open up the Dionysian inner realm and let it begin to radiate—just at that very place an interval appears that we can identify as the inversion of the hybrid sixth 13/8 of ancient Persia: the Arabian hybrid third 16/13.

118

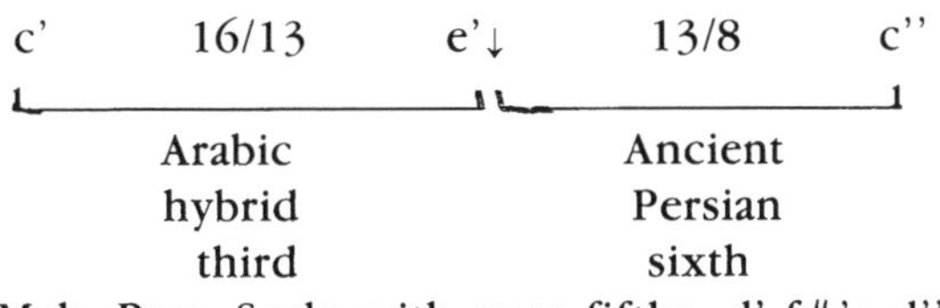

(Mch: Pers. Scale with pure fifths, d' f#'↓ d'')

In the version of *rast* given by Husmann the sixth also can appear as 13/8. Pythagoras once had built on the pure fourth 4/3, thereby reflecting the Apollonian, from-building, breathing power of the Egyptian fifth 3/2 into inner musical space. Later Zalzal did something similar by introducing the inversion of the ancient, ecstatic-inspirational, Persian sixth 13/8—namely the third 16/13—into the inner space of the fourth.

From the period of fourth consciousness up to the present time, the deed of Pythagoras has proven to be extraordinarily healing and clarifying, for he was the first to lead us across the boundary between outer world and inner world, between fifth and fourth. To accomplish this, the guidance of the Apollonian fifth was needed. Furthermore, we must realize that the advent of the primary interval of the *Kali Yuga* , the fifth, already had laid the groundwork for the radial stream of the future. The arithmetic series manifests itself in the overtone series. There the ray proceeds first through the octave, its primal, generative interval, then through *the fifth* , which is its first scale-building interval. And finally the radial principle announces itself in the third. (Compare p. 37ff)

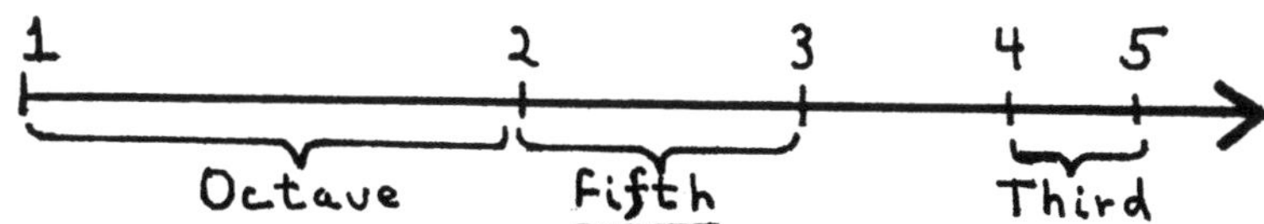

And, indeed, it was in the fifth that we found the first seed of self-discovery—of awareness of the "I". (See p. 51f)

No such accomplishments can be attributed to the Persian sixth. Being an ecstatic interval from an era prior to the *Kali Yuga* , it is so far removed from the self-unfolding, earthly principle of radiality that it gives only a ghostly illusion of the third when it is folded into the inner space within the fourth. In that space it remains like a stranger from an entirely other world. Here we can see the manifestation of the modern Persian impulse which Rudolf Steiner points to as "reintroducing the impulse of Zarathustra at a false time." [79] The Middle Ages was a false time because it was then that humanity needed to develop a real experience of the third and a real inner experience of the individual personality, both of which are contrary to the experience of the Persian sixth because it introduces an old, unfree, magical-inspirational consciousness into the personal sphere. The Persio-Arabic hybrid third blocked the path of development leading toward an experience of the real third.

The time will come when it is right for the Persian sixth to come to life again musically. That will be the time when the force of radiality reaches beyond the third and the triad which are its limit today. Then the radial principle will have become strong enough to affect the formation of seconds. The Greek *aulos* scale was an anticipation of this time, but in the minor (descending) radial form.

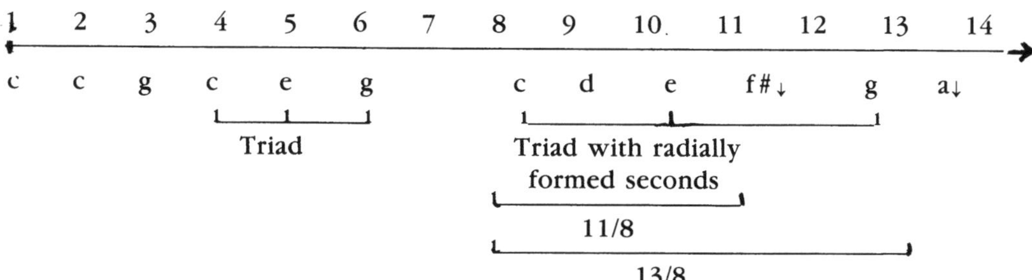

When this does happen, the first new interval to come to life out of the radially formed seconds will be the fourth 11/8, the interval that has become so exceptionally significant in the context of this book. (See p. 96f) Once we really have come to terms with the nature of the interval 11/8, the radial stream will lead us quite naturally over the threshold of the fifth to the sixth 13/8, which we then will be able to form from out of our own inner resources. (Later there will be a discussion of the divisions into 7 and 14.) When this time comes, the ancient Persian golden sixth will be born anew from out humanity's own inner soul world. But this is the very thing the modern Persian impulse wants to prevent by confusing our approach to the third. For the third, being the interval of the inner soul world itself, is the key to Dionysian radiality.

It seems that when the neutral third first appeared in the eighth century it was not tied down to a particular mathematical relationship. At that time, Mansur Zalzal introduced it into the Arabic system as his renowned 'third-finger-fret' on the lute. Only later does one find more exact string length relationships set down by the two great Arabic music theoreticians, al-Farabi (Abu n-Nasr Muhammed) and Avicenna (Ibn Sina Abu Ali-al-Husayn). And, surprisingly, it is in the earlier of these two, in al-Farabi (d. 950), that we encounter the most frequent hybrid thirds. He gives them numerical relationships involving the prime number 11.

Al-Farabi:

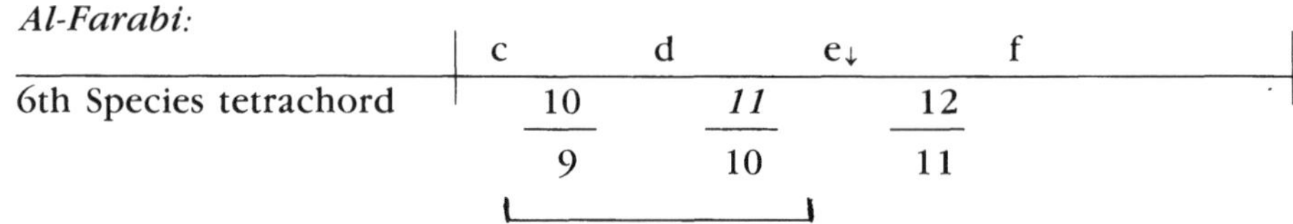

Third: 11/9 (3.474 ht)
(Inversion of Ptolemy's *diatonon homalon*)
(Mch: Arith. Series 9 10 11 12; transposed to d !)

Lute intonation   9   12   88
8   11   81

Third: 27/22 (3.546 ht)
(Mch: Pythag.d, e↓ = mark ♥ by f# on Pers. Scale w/ pure fifths, f = the same as 'g')

8th species tetrachord   9   11   320
8   10   297

Third: 99/80 (3.689 ht)

On one occassion he also uses the primary numbers 7 and 13 to form a neutral third:

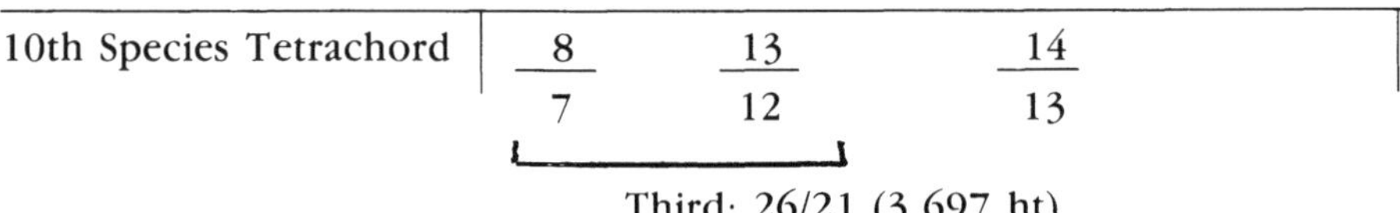

Third: 26/21 (3.697 ht)

On the other hand, Avicenna (d. 1037), who lived later, *always* employs the prime number 13 to form a neutral third. In this case, incidentally, the intonation 16/13 also appears—the exact complementary of the Persian sixth. (He was of Persian origin. Al-Farabi was Turkish.)

Avicenna:

	c	d	e ↓	f
4th Species tetrachord	8/7	14/13	13/12	

Third: 16/13 (3.595 ht)

(Mch: Harmon. Series   16   14   13   12   )

	c	d	e ↓	f
Lute intonation	9/8	13/12	128/127	

Third: 39/32 (3.425 ht)

(Mch: Pythag. d, e↓ = short mark by f# in Pers. scale w/pure fifths, f = the corresponding 'g')

	c	d	e ↓	f
8th species tetrachord	9/8	14/13	208/189	

Third: 63/52 (3.322 ht)

All the forms of tetrachord shown above were applied to the main tonality, *rast* . Only those with monochord indications are playable with the given divisions on our monochord; for the other forms, the appropriate divisions of the string must be calculated.

Here one can experience how the Persian impulse, which the Persian Zalzal first introduced into music, literally insinuated itself into Arabic music from below. To begin with, Arabic music had borrowed its elements from the Greeks. By the time of Avicenna, who also was a Persian, the Persian element had penetrated to the very numerical relationships employed in the Arabic tonal system.

It was from the Greeks, from Pythagoras, that Arabism first learned of the connection between number and tone. Thereby it became possible for the Arabians to begin to more and more minutely dissect that hidden numerical background by means of the intellect. Until the Greek era such knowledge had been the exclusive property of the temples and had been protected by the wise leadership of the mysteries. After Pythagoras these matter which had been restricted to the mysteries were laid in the hands of human rationality at large. From then on it became critical for people to develop self-sufficient human understanding... but to do so without being torn loose from all that had been cultivated in the realms of human feeling during the thousands of years of guidance under the mysteries. In the Christian era the only way the ancient mysteries' guidance could be continued was through awakening the realm of the individual human heart. In this way the ancient guidance continued, transformed. Its vehicle is nothing other than the manifestation of the Socratic *daimon* , the revelation of the Dionysian inner soul space. Lacking the guidance of the mysteries there is only one way that the newly awakened understanding can work positively, proceeding further in that direction of world and human development inaugurated in ancient times: it must remain deeply connected with the inner forces of the heart. This is all the more true when it is a matter of a rational treatment of musical laws, for these have their roots especially deep in the heart's home soil.

The Greek music theorists were particularly fond of using the principle of the supernumary series in their attempts to arrive at definite ratios for diatonic, chromatic and even for enharmonic intonation. This principle, which was pushed to the point of exhaustion, refers to the series of fractions, or proportions, whose numerators are larger by one than their denominators: 2/1, 3/2, 4/3, and so on. Ptolemy, for example, used elements from this series to construct the following tetrachord (*diatonon malakon*):

e	d	b	c
8/7	10/9	21/20	
2.312	1.824	0.845	ht

An intonation determined in this way always has an accidental, interpretive character. It never is enough to unequivocally clarify the real foundation, the fundamental form, and the cyclic origins of the wholetones and the halftones of a diatonic scale. All it can do is show ways of modifying the shape of a scale whose form already has been determined.

The supernumary series [80] is nothing other than the reciprocal of the harmonic or arithmetic series:

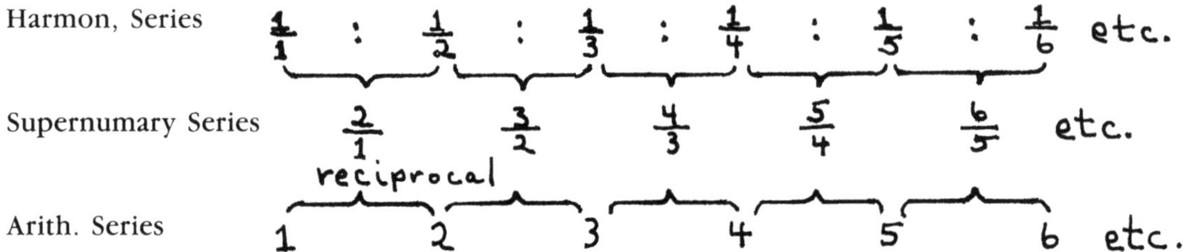

In other words, the series embodies precisely that radical principle we identified as the musical correlate of earthly understanding. The most consequent realization of this principle was the radial Greek *aulos* scale, for this scale arise directly out of the supernumary series instead of being just another one of those radial interpretations or restructurings of a pre-existing diatonic, chromatic or enharmonic form that one so often encounters in Greek music theory. But Greek music theory was unable to come to terms with the radiality of this very scale. Instead, Aristoxenos flatly denied the possibility of understanding it rationally because the intonation on the *aulos* is so variable.

Thus in Greek music we encounter a paradoxical situation. Radiality is the musical principle that corresponds to the newly awakening earthly understanding. The radial principle makes itself felt in aspects of Greek music to which it is by nature foreign. But then, precisely where radiality would most naturally have come to musical expression, our earthly understanding failed to grasp what was happening. Observe, for example, what feats of reckoning and reason Ptolemy performs with artificially pieced together elements of the supernumary series in an attempt to interpret the enharmonic tetrachord. And yet for all his efforts he is unable to come one bit nearer to the real nature of enharmonic:

e	c	c↓	b	
$\frac{5}{4}$.	$\frac{24}{23}$.	$\frac{46}{45}$		$= \frac{4}{3}$ (Fourth)
(3.867	0.737	0.381	ht)	

Ptolemy's mind is untouched, however, when he hears the prototype of the *aulos* scale, which embodies such a simple and clear supernumary, radial structure:

$$\frac{8}{7} \cdot \frac{9}{8} \cdot \frac{10}{9} \cdot \frac{11}{10} \cdot \frac{12}{11} \cdot \frac{13}{12} \cdot \frac{14}{13} = \frac{2}{1} \text{(Octave)}$$

(Mch: Harm. Series, 7—14)

Listening to the *aulos* scale reveals that particular element of Greek humanity which transcends the understanding, namely that "longing for the gods and their initiations" (see p. 100) which lies deep in the human heart.

This reveals the nature of what Rudolf Steiner has described as the 'intellectual-soul, or mind-soul.'[81] It is a stage in the development of the human soul when it fluctuated between two poles, a stage that was elaborated during the fourth post-Atlantean, Greek epoch. The intellectual-soul is restricted to processes of dissection in its coming to understand what has come into being. It must leave to its sister, the mind-soul, the apprehension of immediate, whole and undivided reality, but the mind-soul is not capable of understanding this reality. The ability to enter consciously into the powers of becoming and into the real process of becoming and of the formation of things is only attainable at the next stage of soul development, the stage of the 'consciousness-soul'. This is a stage at which we only now have begun to work during our present epoch, the modern, fifth epoch. During the Greek epoch this stage could only be anticipated in exceptional cases by going through an initiation. The consciousness-soul is capable of finally reuniting what was separated in the intellectual-soul and the mind-soul.

Now we can understand why Aristoxenos, a music theorist who drew on the powers of the intellectual-soul, strictly excluded the *aulos* and its tone systems from his music theory. The intellectual-soul can only understand what is clearly and unequivocally visible as string lengths on the monochord and what is determined ahead of time by the tuning of the strings of a string instrument. These things are grasped before an interval has actually sounded. Whoever wants to comprehend the laws of the *aulos* must actively participate in the birth of the actual tones and tonal relationships. In order to sense the laws behind this process one must enter into the process before it has come to an end, i.e. one must enter an arena where factors can cause deviations from the basic formative principles. For when a tone is played on an *aulos* it is not fully preformed, whereas the tone of a lyre or cithera has had its pitch already determined by a *past* process of tuning before it is actually played. The pitch of an *aulos* has to be maintained by the breath in an ongoing process of tone formation—the function of the spacing of the holes on the instrument is only to provide optimal circumstances for the production of one tone rather than others. Hence the discovery of the principles of the *aulos* was reserved to the age of the consciousness-soul.

As we said, people of the fourth epoch had to preserve some connection between intellectual understanding and immediate soul experience. It was crucial that these not be torn entirely asunder. The bond that secretly connected them had to be maintained, for in this bond resided the power of the consciousness-soul. And for the Greeks the consciousness-soul still was a thing of the future, sleeping in their unconscious. If this bond had been broken, the path to the consciousness-soul would have been blocked. Eventually the intellectually suppressed radiality of Greek music theory and the deeply seated realms of feeling touched by the radially based Greek *aulos* music have to be brought together. Only when this happens will the radiality inaugurated by the Dionysian mysteries have found fulfilment.

But so long as the tension between intellectual-soul and mind-soul ('heart', *'Gemüt')* persisted during the fourth post-Atlantean epoch, humanity was vulnerable to attack from the Arabistic impulse of Gondischapur. For it was a goal of Arabism to separate intellect and heart (mind, *'Gemüt'*) and to permanently destroy the bond between these two sisters so that the earthly understanding would once more entirely forget its source within the individual soul. The goal was to deny the earthly understanding any participation whatsoever in inner, personal, mind-soul experience; earthly understanding, lacking these other bonds and impulses, was to be led to being 'abstract'in the way Averroes had intended. It was to be restricted to being the mere instrument of a universal reason, capable only of passive reaction, divested of all inward, personal dimensions of awareness. This amounts to an attempt to supplant the approaching consciousness-soul which in the future, with the help of the intellectual-soul, needed to be able to develop gradually out of the Dionysian inner space of the heart (mind,

'Gemüt') It was an attempt to replace the newly ripening faculty of the consciousness-soul with a ghost from out of the past, a revised version of ancient, Persian-inspired consciousness, a totally self-unaware, uncentered consciousness which gave but the illusion of bearing a proud personality.

This conception of Arabism manifested itself in Arabic music and music theory as follows: the real musical principle of self-awareness, the principle of radiality, is so one-sidedly and totally subordinated to principles of abstract understanding that the self-aware, feeling, heart side of music is left empty-handed. Thus it was possible for the principle of the ancient Persian sixth, which really belonged to an age before the birth of selfhood, to occupy this empty space. It was appropriately 'camouflaged' during the Middle Ages by its being designated by the name of an apparently personal interval—it appeared in the guise of a third, the Arabian hybrid third. This interval has no supernumary foundations and does not really qualify as a consonance. It actually stands in opposition to the principle of radiality and, ultimately, it paradoxically eluded all attempts to calculate it by means of supernumary relationships.

In spite of all the Greeks' speculation with the supernumary series, actual musical experience continued to play such a strong role in their music theory that octave, fifth and fourth remained their sole and unquestioned models of consonance. They experienced all other intervals, whatever marvelous supernumary relationships they might embody, as non-consonant. The Greeks never allowed their own inner musical experience to be enslaved by their rationality.

Aristoxenos seems to have experienced to the full the misery created by the cleft between calculating reason and musical experience. He went so far as to leave the question whether an interval is consonant or not entirely to the discretion of inner musical experience without any regard for its mathematical credentials in the form of the supernumary series or anything else. The only place he was willing to give the calculating and dissecting understanding a say was in the purely spatial matter of pitch distances, i.e. where it was not a matter of having to decide what was consonant and what dissonant. The end results of inner musical-harmonic experience—e.g., the pure fifth—were simply measured to determine their spatial relationship. The Arabist, Avicenna, proceeded differently. He maintained that *all* supernumary proportions produced consonances. Also allowed as consonances were all their octave inversions and all other intervals of approximately the same span. [82] Thus where the Greek was typically careful to weigh intellect and heart against one another, taking pains that each should have its rightful say, the Arabist totally subjugated all matter of inner musically to the intellect.

The effect of Arabism was to make tonal relations inaccessible to a self-aware musicality founded on active personal involvement—this at a time when humanity stood at the gateway to the consciousness-soul and was seeking the path through the inner experiences of the heart into the outstreaming radiance of the third. The intellect already had misconstrued everything. With what? With its own, future-oriented principle, radiality, but a radiality which has bypassed the true third 5/4. This is the third we recognized as the pivot, the great musical turning point leading toward the future of the Earth, for in this musical interval we can grasp the earthly personality which also provides a home for the inner spark of our own personal, spiritual being. In bypassing the third—which he indeed considered a consonance, but one having no particular significance—Avicenna dragged radiality, the musical element of the future, into the music of his time. That music still awaited the dawning of third experience. He did this in such a way that the kind of musicality based on inwardness and self-awareness which was just trying to make a beginning could not connect with these radial elements. The only thing that could live in them was a passive musicality, the correlate in the field of tone experience to what Averroes called 'passive reason' in the field of thought. Such a passive musicality accepts everything—all the possible mathematical-harmonic relationships—in the world of tone. The selfhood that could have begun to manifest itself through inner activity of its own soul did not participate. The individuality slept while the musical self became nothing but an ear that was closed to all inward, personal soul experience. The musical self was reduced to being nothing but a mirror for the cosmic music rather than that living drop from out of the sea of creative, spiritual, cosmic music that we described earlier (p. 2f).

In al-Farabi's treatise on music theory, *Kitab al-musiqi al-kabir (Grand Book of Music)*, he writes, "In music theory one must proceed as do the researchers of those other sciences whose principles are mainly derived from *sense experience* ." Or, again, "In music theory,

124

by its nature, it is the elements derived from natural science, from physics, that stand in first place."[83]. Al-Farabi makes it clear that, for him, music is equivalent to an entirely passive sense experience that comes to the human soul from without. A mode of musical experience polar to this one—one whose source is within—is as good as nonexistent for him. Thus we also can understand why the fineness of sense perception required for the minute differentiations of pitch in Arabic music always has been far beyond anything encountered in western music. A quartertone system or even a system divided into sixths of a tone is not enough to satisfy this auditory epicureanism.

Consider by way of comparison the extraordinary simplicity and coarseness of the audible tonal material out of which Beethoven created his piano sonatas: only twelve tones in the octave, all the same halftone distance from one another, and no pure fifth or pure third! The contrast is clear: on the Arabic side we find the utmost refinement of tonal perception, but musical expression is always restricted to a non-individual, superhuman universality without its ever entering into anything really human. Thus this music shows little or no development over hundreds of years as against the grandiose unfolding of western music at the same time. And on the European side we find that the outward, perceptible differentiation of tones is decidedly coarse when compared with the Arabians' tonal subtlety. But there is the inner musical expressiveness that a Bach or a Beethoven could develop to such a peak of self-aware spirituality and self-aware ethos that it has become the globally experienced expression of what is truly human, freed from the fetters of racial and cultural traditions or boundaries.

By no means do we wish to suggest that the 'coarseness' of a tonal system is an ideal to be sought after. Later we shall see how a greater differentiation among the tones of our system is crucial for a further development of western music, what Rudolf Steiner pointed to as "a greater complication of the tones."[84] But while contemplating this proposed change it is important to remind oneself that inner, self-aware experience plays the decisive role in the development of western music. Within western culture, however, attempts at finer tonal differentiation that were restricted to the merely outward aspect of tonal difference always have remained theoretical, never having been taken up by composers of major stature. If an intonation allowing for finer nuances of the intervals does become necessary in the future, it will only be to allow the expression of new, inward, more self-aware experiences of soul, and not as a source of new, fascinating sense experiences. Such a development can only come about through an intensification, tempering and further spiritualization of the self-aware ethos already achieved by western music.

When we were investigating the interval 11/8, a fourth which requires a quartertone differentiation from our usual fourth (p. 96f.), we had an opportunity to catch a glimpse of what such an intensification and purification of musical experience might signify. Anyone who manages to awaken to the quality of this interval and find a place for it in their own inner world will clearly notice that they have only been able to come to the experience by working intimately but actively at transforming themselves from within. They will have the feeling that the experience that then unfolds lives in their own innermost nature. We saw that the Greek was not yet capable of experiencing the fourth 11/8. Therefore this interval remained extraordinarily well concealed behind the surface of Greek culture although it really was intimately bound up with it. Its function is only conceivable in the context of the mystery centers. People of the Middle Ages were equally unable to find their way to this transformed fourth, for first the "small spark of the soul" that is kindled by the third had to become a true inner light.

Now it becomes all the more deeply shocking to see how Arabism falsifies the nature and the force of the prime number 11, which should lead to a fundamental new interval, the spiritualized fourth. Instead of helping open the way to the future, Arabism uses the number 11 to smother the newly born third in its cradle, the third which later could lead to this new fourth. Instead of using 11 to build up an interval from a fundamental tone, namely the fourth 11/8, al-Farabi uses it to form the hybrid third 11/9, which is not based on any fundamental tone. Therefore this third 11/9 does not lead to the experience of a personal, inner center focused on a groundtone in the way the true third 5/4 does. The interval 11/9 is used to help rebuild the ancient Persian sixth and its inversion. Instead of leading into inner experience these intervals guide one into quite another realm.

Let us pause to test the quality of 11/9 on the monochord. It is indicated on the line, 'Persian scale with pure fifths', by the mark '7' below the 'f#↓':

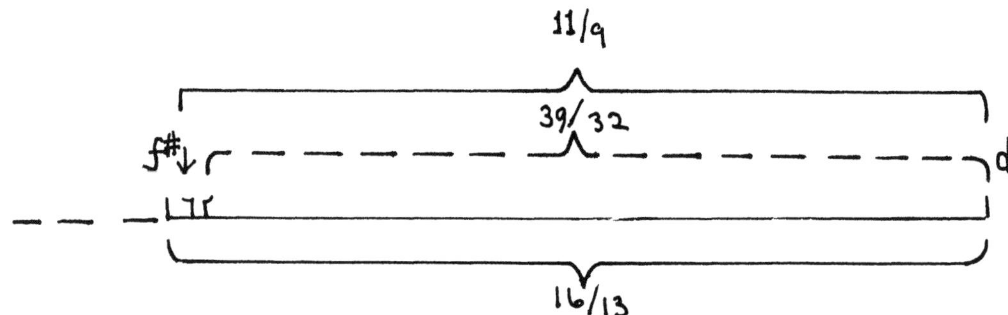

For the purposes of the exercise it is useful to hum the groundtone or to play it on another string instrument so that thirds can also be heard as chords.

If one has learned to enter inwardly into the quality of 11/8 then 11/9 will not be unpleasant either, although the lack of a ground tone gives it an unstable emotionalism as compared with the major third. Nevertheless, this third has a pronounced inwardness, a hidden radiance and uprightness that would be difficult to catch hold of without first having practiced the interval 11/8 (p. 96f). If we switch to the small third (e^b) the mood becomes introverted or sad as we sink into ourselves, whereas in 11/9 we are maintained as if by our own power in a mobile state of balance.

The next thing to listen for is the fine distinction (0.121 ht) between 11/9 and 16/13. If we make the small alteration needed to change from 11/9 to 16/13, the new third takes on a remarkably strident and cutting character as compared with 11/9; 16/13 takes on a thoroughly 'major' character by comparison with which 11/9 seems 'minor'. But a comparison with the major third 5/4 (Mch: Scale with pure triads) leads to the surprising discovery that we still are a long way from the real major. True major streams out from within the soul. 16/13 produces a kind of deceptive major. It gives our feelings access to a world of soul and spirit that is beyond humanity. It is not a world that flows up from out of the depths of our own soul but rather a world that strikes into us. Its radiance is definitely other-worldly, but it verges on the painful and it is blinding.

The difference between the pure third and the Pythagorean third is remotely comparable. (See Mch: 'Scale with pure triads', and 'Pythag. scale'.) But the relevant spheres of experience are entirely different, for here one is dealing with numbers belonging to the *senarius*, not with the qualities of number from what Hindemith liked to call the 'holy regions'. But here also the Pythagorean third, which is born of fifths, brings qualities of external soul life into the inner realm of the third whereas the pure third 5/4 is entirely at home in this inner realm. The Pythagorean third imports the bright outer light of the heavens into the third's inner space; the pure third radiates a mild inner light. Similarly, 11/9 can be experienced to be more appropriate to inner soul space than is 16/13.

In the *maquam rast* al-Farabi combines 11/9 with a framework of pure fourths and fifths. This leads us to a significant discovery.

al-Farabi: 6th species tetrachord:

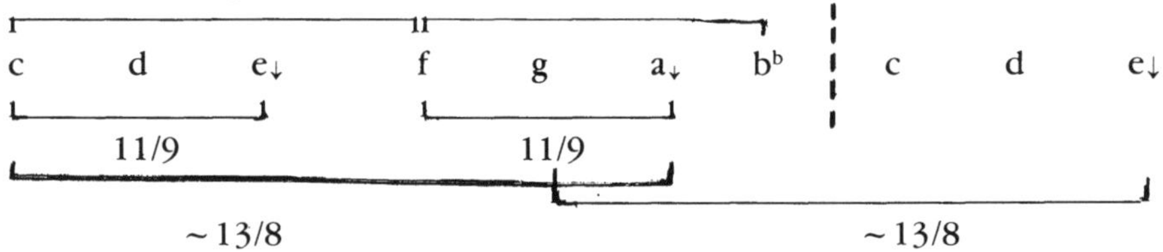

(Mch: Pers. scale with pure fifths, transposed to 'a': a b (= pyth.a) c # ↓ (꜒) d e (= pyth.d) f # ↓ (꜒) g a .)

The form of *rast* given by Husmann has an a↓ which diverges by only 0.049 ht from the sixth 13/8 (8.405 ht):

(c - f)		(f - a↓)	(c - a↓)
4.980 ht	+	3.474 ht	= 8.454 ht

The interval g-e↓ also yields this sixth. Avicenna achieves an intonation with an absolutely precise Persian sixth by a similar approach, employing the third 39/32.

Avicenna: Lute intonation:

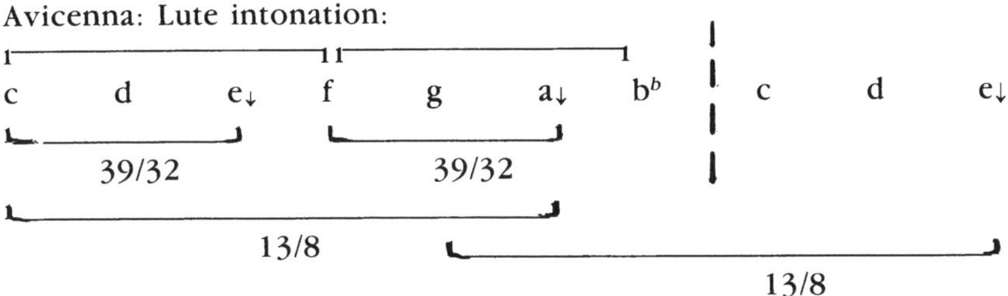

(Mch: Pers. scale with pure fifths, transposed to 'a' as previously. a b (= pyth.a) c # ↓(ㄱ) d e(= Pyth.d) f # ↓(ㄱ) g a .)

For:	(c - f)		(f - a↓)	(c - a↓)
	4.980 ht	+	3.425 ht	= 8.405 ht
Or:	4/3	•	39/32	= 13/8

Here we see how the principle 11 is combined with a framework of fourths and fifths and with the third 11/9 (which is not really connected with 11 at all) in order to slip back into the domain of 13. For 11/9 can be identified for all practical purposes with 39/32 from which it differs only by a minimal 0.049 ht (which is one third the amount a third is out of tune in today's piano intonation). Thus Arabism casts a spell over 11 so that it sinks into an enchanted sleep, unaware of its own true nature. Alas though, it is this very 11 whom the humanity of the Christian era must bring to life in order to be able to come to proper terms with 13 once more.

In both of these examples the principle of the fifth plays a key part. As was seen in the chapter on Egypt, the fifth is an interval that must be overcome in a particular way if the higher prime numbers are ever to regain musical significance. The two intonations of the hybrid third just examined are particularly significant. Both of them—al-Farabi's in connection with 11, Avicenna's in connection with 13—produce a pair which combines to form a fifth.

(11/9)		(27/22)		(3/2)
3.474 ht	+	3.546 ht	=	7.020 ht

(16/13)·		(39/32)		(3/2)
3.595 ht	+	3.425 ht	=	7.020 ht
7.069 ht		6.971 ht		
(~3/2)		(~3/2)		

Furthermore, the sum of the halftone values of 11/9 and 16/13, as well as those of 27/22 and 39/32, also yield what for practical purposes is a fifth (with only that small inaccuracy of 0.049 that we just encountered above.) The same error appears if the thirds that are in cross relationship to one another are compared: 11/9/ ³39/32; 16/13³27/22.

When *maquam rast* is built with 11/9 or with 39/22 it contains two ascending Persian sixths. And, as can easily be calculated, if *rast* is similarly built using 27/22 or 16/13, two descending 13/8 sixths appear. In addition to those already given, we can examine the form of *rast* given by Pfrogner.

Avicenna: 4th Species tetrachord, and al-Farabi: Lute intonation:

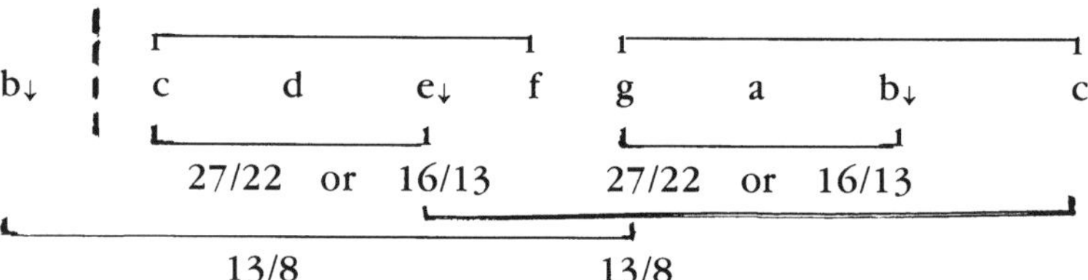

(Mch: Pers. scale with pure fifths: d   e (= pyth.d) f# ↓(ᵧ or ᵨ) g a b(= pyth.a) c# ↓(ᵧ or ᵨ) d .)

Here it is clear how the nature of 11 is entirely absorbed by that of 13, even though with a good will one can always read two 11/8-fourths into *rast*: e↓—a, and f—b↓. Indeed, in al-Farabi's version one of these fourths even receives a pure intonation! We are reminded how important the presence of two such 11/8-fourths was in the Greek enharmonic with its quartertones (see p. 105). The most important difference between this and *maquam rast* lies in the fact that the enharmonic scale's tone *mesopyknos* is derived solely from the fundamental interval 11/8 when it is given its quartertone intonation. Precisely that one interval crucial to *maquam rast* —the Persian sixth 13/8—was excluded from it (see p. 103). By contrast, 11/8 is an entirely subsidiary interval in *maquam rast* where the main intervals are established via 13/8 and its inversion. 13/8 determines the quartertone intonations of e↓ and b↓ and it is these which, starting from the framework of fourths, actually determine the scale's distinctive structure. We shall presently see how 13/8 takes over an even more dominating role in the formation of the Persio-Arabic scales and thereby eradicates all significance of the two possible 11/8 relationships, even as regards their intonation.

Our investigation has already uncovered the important role the fifth plays in al-Farabi's and Avicenna's manipulations: only with its help were they able to reinterpret the principle of 11 as the principle of 13. Just examine the pairs of thirds that complement one another to form fifths—the thirds that actually appear in various intonations of *rast*:

Al-Farabi's lute intonation:

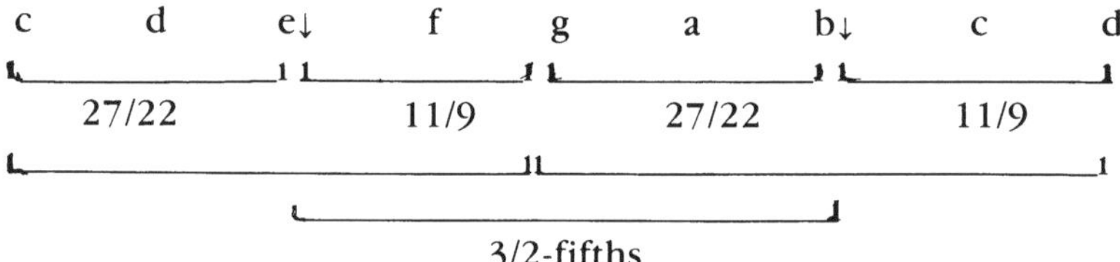

Avicenna's lute intonation:

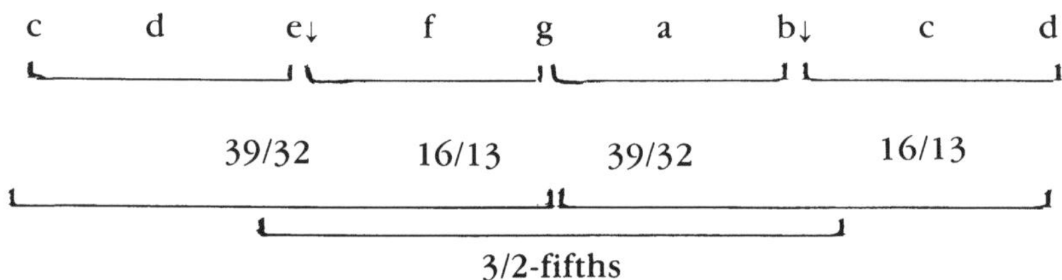

The fifth is the archetypal interval of the *Kali Yuga*. It also is the fundamental interval involved in the initial development of individual ego consciousness. The preceeding intonations of *rast* give the impression that the fifth is being manipulated so that it will produce the hybrid third (i.e. the ancient Persian sixth) instead of that third which finally did appear in the 14th century in the triad and which truly expresses inner consciousness.

It can be questioned whether al-Farabi and Avicenna introduced the principle of the hybrid third (the Persian sixth) into music consciously or whether—as seems more likely—they did

128

it instinctively, following an unconscious inspiration. In either case, the effect of ordering the intervals into such a scheme is clear. In the first place, the apparent progress of Arabic music from the system of fifths and fourths to the hybrid third is illusory. It is not a true and natural development. In the second place, and closely related to the first observation, the fact that there is an immensely important dividing line between the era of the Persian sixth and the era of the pure fifth is disguised. The line that is obscured is the one that divides the selfless clairvoyance of a pre-*Kali Yuga* era from the self-conscious awakening in the world of the senses which began in Egypt (see p. 74).

The Greeks' feeling for this decisive caesura in the development of consciousness almost certainly had its roots in the traditions of their mysteries. There, also, must be the source of the scrupulous fashion in which the Greek music theorists avoided the prime number 13 out of which the ancient Persian sixth is born. This traditional antipathy towards the number 13 has persisted into our own times, reduced to the status of a widespread superstition. On the other hand, Greek music theorists had no qualms about using 11 or 7. The power of 11, which manifests itself in the fourth 11/8 was, as we know, embedded in the very roots of Greek culture. The 7 generated the ancient Atlantean seventh experience. Perhaps for the Greeks it still carried something of that mythical memory, often referred to by Steiner, that connected them with old Atlantis. The world of the 7/4-seventh is too paradisically complete and rounded-out in itself to have been dangerous for the Greeks. At most, it brings a strong nature-bound mood into musical experience (see p. 97). But 13 and its interval carry the force that once split the ancient, wholly self-contained, clairvoyant consciousness of Atlantis and of ancient India, subjugating this consciousness to earthly conditions (see p. 72). That same power was capable of influencing the newly beginning self-consciousness attained through the fifth and the fourth so that it would dissolve again into a selfless perception of infinity and so would cut humanity off from its earthly tasks (see the exercise on p. 75f.).

It was a deception of genius on the grand scale and with a refinement bordering on the magical that managed not only to bring the hybrid third into relationship with the Pythagorean system of fourths and fifths, but actually went so far as to derive the hybrid third directly from that Pythagorean system. The genius in question was the Arab theorist, Safi al-Din (d. 1294). He took up the true interval of his epoch, the fourth. But he used the perfect fourth to build not a circle of twelve, but a circle of seventeen tones.

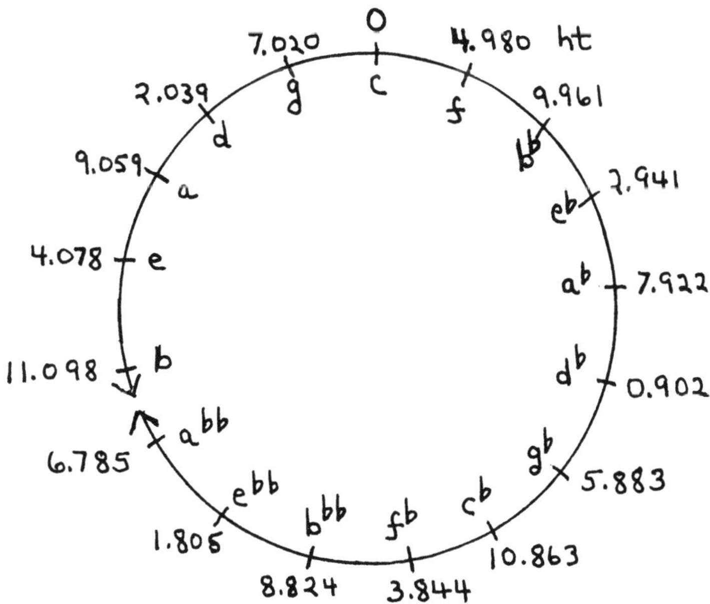

(Mch: Pyth scale, b♭—b♭♭ the short marks; e♭♭ and a♭♭ are omitted.)

For the sake of easier orientation we have used our familiar names for the tones on this circle, with c taken as o, and have given the halftone measurements for the tones as transposed to the octave lying above this c.

It is obvious that the circle cannot be closed if one holds to the true fourth. Between b^b and a^{bb} there appears a 'fourth' of 4.313 ht., which is one third of a tone (0.667 ht) too small. Furthermore, the circle of seventeen cannot produce equal sized seconds when it is projected into a single octave. Whether Safi al-Din did not recognize this or whether he deliberately failed to draw attention to it we cannot say. But in any event he asserted that the tonal steps were equal. "And, as a matter of fact, the entire Persio-Arabic practice is to treat this scale (i.e, the circle of 17) as if it were tempered." (Husmann)

One asks why Safi al-Din abandons the twelvefold system of fifths and fourths. Aristoxenos already had given it a clear, crystallized form.[85] Why is he willing to live with a fifth that is out of tune by +0.039 ht (at least, it is this far off if one takes the tempering of the circle of 17 seriously) whereas in the circle of 12 the fifth only has to be tempered by 0.020 ht? To be sure, in his day one was satisfied with the middle-tone tuning whose fifth was 0.054 ht too low (see p. 26f). But with the middle-tone tuning there was a stronger reason for hazarding this out-of-tune fifth, for here it was altered for the sake of an absolutely pure intonation of the third 5/4. As the harmonic embodiment of the dawning new interval experience, the third 5/4 needed to be distinguished clearly from the old Pythagorean third.

If the third 5/4 also had been the goal of Safi al-Din, then his system of seventeen fourths (but in its untempered form) could be understood as an intriguing transition from the old fifth to the pure third of the approaching age. Then the eighth link in the chain of pure fourths built up from c, the f^b (3.884 ht), would approach to within 0.019 ht of the pure third 5/4 (3.863 ht) of the triad c e g. This is seven times more accurate than the third in today's piano tuning. If one takes f^b as the intonation for e then, for practical purposes, the Pythagorean comma (0.234 ht) between e and f^b, and the syntonic comma (0.215 ht) which distinguishes the Pythagorean third from the pure third, cancel each other out. In other words, one can obtain an intonation of C major with nearly pure thirds from Safi al-Din's chain of 17 pure fourths, as well as similar intonations for B^b-, F-, G-, D-, and A-major (Compare p. 24f):

			4	:	5	:	6			
4	:	5	:	6			4	:	5	:	6
f		a		c	e		g		b		d
4.980		8.824		0	3.844		7.020		11.863		2.039 ht
		$(= b^{bb})$			$(= f^b)$				$(= c^b)$		

(Mch: Pythag. scale)

pure:	8.844	3.836	11.883	ht

(Mch: Scale with pure triads)

This amazing principle of using substitution to obtain a pure third—c^b = b, f^b = e, and so on —was used in some of the unequally tempered systems of the previous centuries. For example, the 'well tempered' ('wohltemperiert') tuning of J.S. Bach's student J.P. Kirnberger uses it. But Safi al-Din is silent about this possibility. Since his system is treated practically as if it consisted of seventeen equal steps, it provides a wonderful means for establishing the hybrid third, rather than the pure third, as the model third intonation. And it accomplishes this as if the hybrid third were a natural derivation from the circle of fourths. But with strictly accurate tempering, the path of fourths from c to f^b (= the pure third, e) takes the following course:

c	f	b^b	e^b	a^b	d^b	g^b	c^b	f^b
0	4.941	9.882	2.824	7.765	0.706	5.647	10.588	3.529ht

$$(16/13 = 3.595\text{ht})$$

(Mch: 17-division)

130

At the place—f^b—where pure fourths would result in an almost perfect intonation of the pure third 5/4, the hybrid third appears instead, in an intonation that only falls – 0.066 ht short of a perfect 16/13.

Husmann alleges that the tempered circle of 17 tones enables one to obtain a very good intonation of what he calls "the Persians' ideal scale".[86] We can set against this version our Persian scale with a framework of pure fourths and fifths (see p. 70):

Husmann's
"ideal Persian   :0   1.412 3.529 4.941 7.059 8.471 10.588 12   ht
scale"
(Mch: 17-div.)

Persian scale
with pure fifths :0   1.395 3.595 4.980 7.020 8.405 10.615 12   ht
(Mch: Pers. scale
with pure fifths d e^b↑ f#↓   g   a b^b↑ c#↓   d

                              16/13   39/32   16/13

What a staggering degree of agreement! For all practical purposes these minimal differences can be ignored, since the circle of 17 never was really determined in the exact equal tempered form pictured above. Instead it was left unclear, i.e. flexible. Within this flexible context not only was it possible to achieve an intonation of *maquam rast*, a somewhat elaborated form of the old Persian scale also could be recreated—a form with a framework of pure fourths. In the symmetrical form shown here it is called 'higaz' or, also 'awj'. Four other 'maquamat' were derived from it as modes. This scale contains four hybrid thirds of the 16/13 variety and two of the 39/32-thirds that complement these to form a fifth. In the equal tempered form intended by the circle of 17 these two kinds of third would be levelled to a single variety of 3.529 ht. Then the scale would have a seven-tone chain of identical hybrid thirds as its structural principle.

    Thirds →

$$e^b{↑} — g — b^b{↑} — d — f{\#}{↓} — a — c{\#}{↓}$$

                     ← Sixths

(Mch: 17-division)

Now the archetypal structure that is the background of the whole development of Arabic scales shines through in its entirety: the ancient Persian scale formed with a chain of 13/8-sixths within the cycle of ten. (See p. 68) The 13/8-sixth that a fundamental tone produces is sufficient in itself to produce the characteristic form of this scale. It is known as the gipsy scale today and it still conveys the musical essence of oriental magic. All that is missing is a pure intonation of the sixths for us to be back in ancient Persia with its ten-toned circle of sixths. The real inner principle of the Arabian hybrid third led it toward this as its ultimate goal: the ancient cycle, experienced as coming entirely from outside and as not yet harboring the principle of twelve which would have allied it with the human individuality. In order to steer toward this goal, Safi al-Din displaced twelvefoldness with his more complicated cycle of seventeen fourths. To be sure the goal was not absolutely achieved, but when we listen to *maquam 'awj* and compare it with the ancient Persian scale there is no mistaking the way the ancient Persian sixth shines through it.

The goal of the pure third 5/4 is the polar opposite. On the one hand, the inner, future-oriented, radial principle emerges from it, the very principle that the hybrid third dodges. On the other hand, the third 5/4 is essentially related to the twelve-fold principle of selfhood.

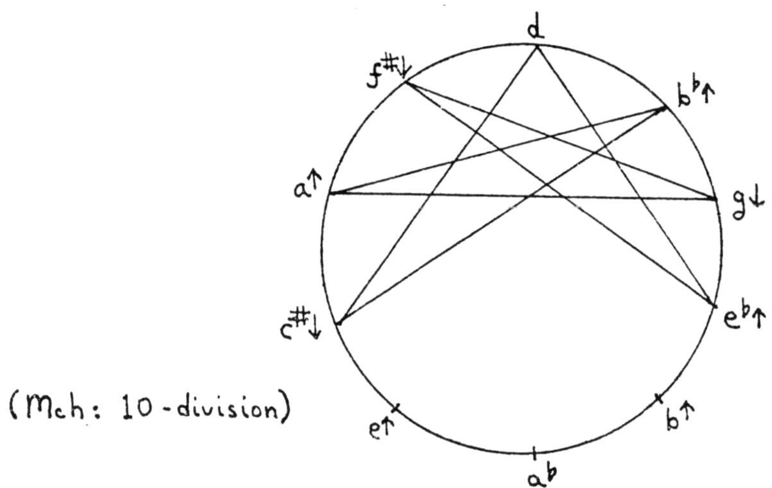

Because of the fact that the eighth fifth below c (f^b) gives a better intonation for the pure third e than the fourth fifth above c (Pythagorean e), the experience of the third inevitably leads to an identification of e with f^b, b with c^b, f with g^b, and so on. By encouraging this enharmonic interchangability, third experience exerts an influence on the chain of fifths, leading toward its becoming 'bent' into a real circle. In China, as the mythical account records, it was a cosmic, more-than-human spirit—the fabulous bird, the Phoenix[87]—that revealed the twelve *Liu*. When the third 5/4 is the guide, the closed twelvefold cycle is discovered and brought into being through earthly, human experience that kindles a new inner spark in the soul. Safi al-Din strives for just the opposite goal. Instead of uniting e and f^b in the twelvefold principle, his quasi-tempered circle of 17 drives them even further from one another than they are by nature thereby making of f^b a hybrid third.

Although later Arabic scales developed such a multiplicity of mixed forms and variants that an overview is virtually impossible, it nevertheless is possible to distinguish three stages within this development. Today the stages are found more or less coexisting:

Stage I: Greek diatonic, chromatic and enharmonic are adopted and inverted to form ascending scales. Chromatic and enharmonic remain theoretical. They do not enter into actual musical practice. The essential intonation for the diatonic scales is Pythagorean, But, coexisting with these, diatonic tetrachords embodying supernumary, radial elements are recognized in theory. One of these is the *diatonon* of Didymos, which is taken up by al-Farabi and which, in its ascending form, actually corresponds to a major scale with pure thirds. Another is the *diatonon syntonon* of Ptolemy. (See p. 84)

Stage II: The hybrid third is introduced into diatonic via Zalzal's 'middle finger fret' and the main Arabian tonality, *rast*, thereby comes into being. Although it still is possible to understand the tetrachord structure of *rast* as an inversion of Ptolemy's *diatonon homalon*, *rast* and its derivative modes are the first independent step in the development of post Grecian, Arabic music.

Stage III: The introduction of a second hybrid third which hangs downward from the fourth develops the structure of *rast* further in the direction of the ancient Persian scale. This further stage of development already is clearly evident in Avicenna's 7th Species tetrachord, which he says is "extremely popular":

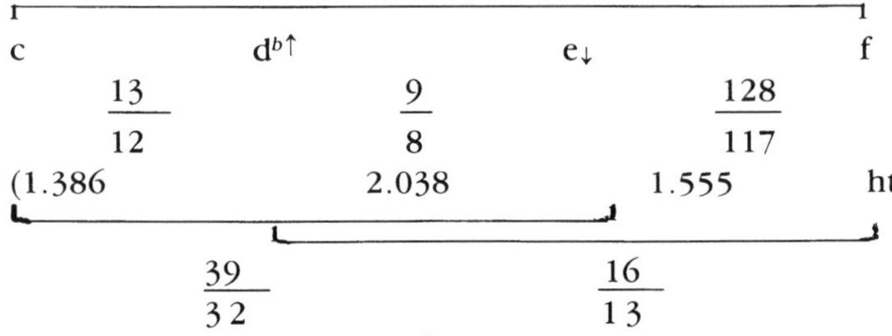

(Mch: Persian scale with pure fifths: d e♭↑ f # ↓ (r) g.)

The hybrid third 16/13 and the third that complements it to make up a fifth have been com-

132

pressed into the space of a fourth. This is made possible on the lute by an extra fret, which was given the characteristic name, 'Zalzal's first remedy'. A scale built of two of these tetrachords consisted in a continuous chain of alternating 16/13- and 39/32-thirds.

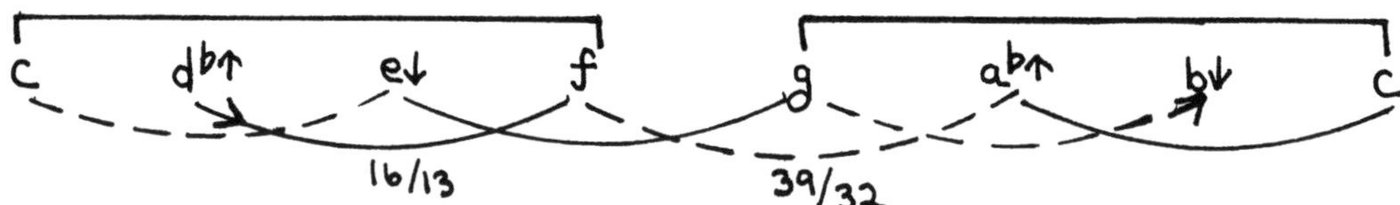

(Mch: Persian scale with pure fifths: d e♭↑ f#↓(ṛ) g a b♭↓(ṛ) d .)

Avicenna's 7th species tetrachord is a cardinal example for indicating how seriously we should take his and al-Farabi's consistently zealous use of supernumary formulations for steps of a second. We saw how Avicenna based his theory of consonance entirely on supernumary proportions such as those appearing here in the 7th species tetrachord: 13/12 and 9/8. He would also have accepted 128/117 as a 'consonance' because it is practically identical with the supernumary proportion 12/11. The scale derived from the 7th species tetrachord shows that Avicenna's supernumary theory of consonance is nothing but a swindle. This scale consists in nothing other than a wonderful chain of alternating hybrid thirds. There is not a trace in it of the genuine principle that underlies the supernumaries, i.e. radiality. Moreover the chain contains five perfect fifths.

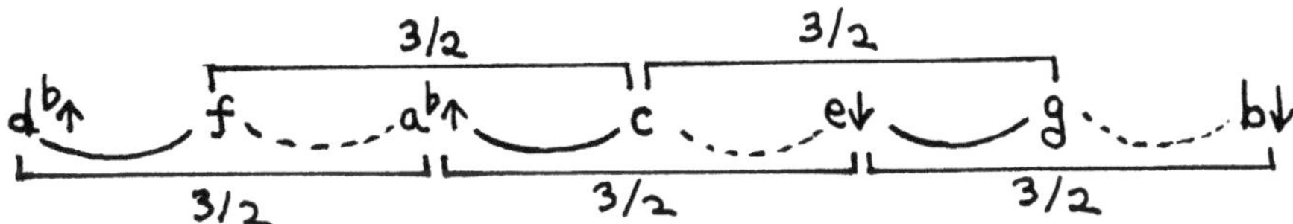

Safi al-Din's cycle of 17 also did away with the difference between the two sorts of hybrid third. It produced a scale which was based—cyclically—on a chain of equal hybrid thirds. And this is only one very small step removed from basing it directly on the ancient Persian sixth 13/8.

So we can say that a result of Persio-Arabic musical development was the artificial transformation of the third into a cyclic interval—the third being the very interval which, following the regular and natural course of development, needed to emerge during the Middle Ages as the first radial interval.

At the very beginning of the development of the Arabic scales, quartertones already appear. They occur on the ancient, pre-Islamic, long-necked lute, the Arabic *tunbur*. Its two strings are tuned to differ in pitch by one 20/19-halftone. Shorter string lengths are obtained with the help of five equidistant bands which are spaced one-fortieth of the length of the entire string from each other. These frets provide a stock of quartertones of various size within the compass of a narrow hybrid third (c—e♭↑).

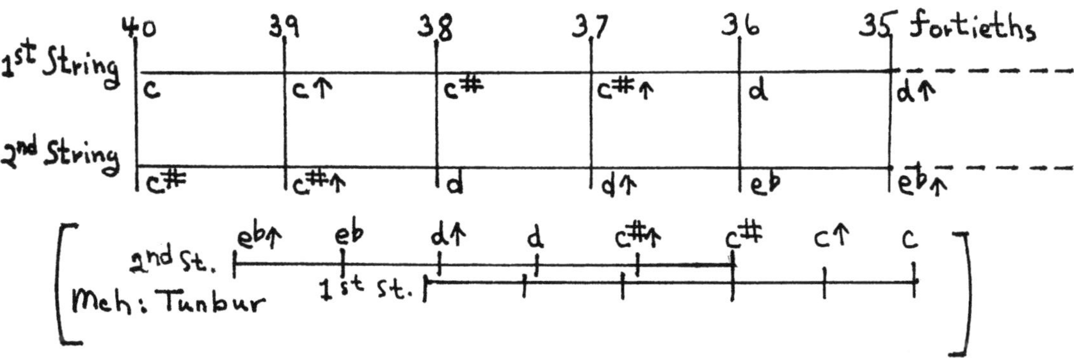

The succession of tones obtained from either string is a true supernumary sequence and its compass, or product (d—d$^\uparrow$ c#—e$^{b\uparrow}$), is also a supernumary ratio.

$$\frac{40}{39} \cdot \frac{39}{38} \cdot \frac{38}{37} \cdot \frac{37}{36} \cdot \frac{36}{35} = \frac{8}{7}$$

The quartertones of this sequence are intoned with very fine nuances in accordance with the harmonic (undertone) series. The distance between the tones becomes progressively smaller as one descends. (The series of seconds in Schlesinger's prototypal *aulos* mode is similarly intoned in accordance with the harmonic series.) The frequencies of c#$\uparrow$, d, and d$^\uparrow$ on the first string differ from the frequencies of c#$\uparrow$, d, and d$^\uparrow$ on the second string. This is because on the one string the tones are separated by intervals based on the proportions 38:37:36:35, while on the other string it is the proportions 40:39:38:37.—All of this was described by al-Farabi with extraordinary acuity.

But...radiality in a quartertone sequence? What a contrast to the *aulos* scale or the scale that radiates upward from a fundamental tone, where the principle of radiality guides one on a path through the qualities of the seven archetypal intervals to the octave! The latter is a path we can fully experience. It engages the whole range of our human faculties, leading us through the seven stages of an inner drama of the soul. The quartertones of the *tunbur*, on the other hand, can only be followed by extremely concentrated hearing. The listener must become a musical bloodhound. It is not just because this series of tones is unfamiliar. The radially formed scale that spans an octave is no less unfamiliar to today's westerner.

Tunbur's sequence of quartertones is a dwarf-like caricature of radiality, a caricature of its seven steps whose intervals culminate in the octave. Instead of the octave, the eighth and final tone of the *tunbur* is the hybrid third, e$^{b\uparrow}$. If radiality is the musical expression of earthly consciousness and earthly intelligence then what here comes to expression is that dwarf-like, abstract, earthly intellect that was a distinctive characteristic of the Semitic Arabs of that period.

This old Arabic tone system is like a negative form. It is the exact negative, or counter-picture, of the ancient Persian system of sixths. Just as the hybrid third (the complement of the Persian sixth) defines the compass of the seven quartertones and is their fulfillment so, earlier, was the hybrid sixth the initial step of a wide-spanning chain of sixths which only found its cyclic completion in the seventh octave. The ancient Persian cycle and this original Arabic radiality stand face to face, but this radiality is not even capable of filling the space of an octave—that archetypal and foremost interval of all radiality—let alone stream beyond the confines of the octave. Instead of really streaming outward, this radiality seems to be imprisoned in the ancient super-second 8/7. That had been the first second to appear, arriving on the scene as the ancient Indian cycle developed and began to contract. We should remind ourselves how the prototypal *aulos* scale sets out from this same interval and then reproduces it, seven times metamorphosed, in the incarnating, minor direction. (See p.88f.)

$$\frac{8}{7} \qquad \frac{9}{8} \qquad \frac{10}{9} \qquad \frac{11}{10} \qquad \frac{12}{11} \qquad \frac{13}{12} \qquad \frac{14}{13}$$

(Mch: Harmonic series 7—14)

After the time of the Christ's incarnation this metamorphosing extension of the super-second was turned around so that it flowed in the major direction (p.42). But something else happened in the old, proto-Arabic music. There nothing streamed outward from the old second. Instead, the second merely shrank into itself. In this case radiality seems to have developed a tendency which we met elsewhere as characteristic of cyclic systems: that of contraction and condensation. We can feel how it could come about, and must have come about, that a Persian impulse brought back to life in the wrong era became the ally of Arabism. It joined Arabism in its attempt to destroy radiality. Radiality was the principle of the future. It was a child of the Greeks' Dionysian culture.

The instrument that assisted in this effort to bend the course of history was the lute.[88] It is an instrument not to be found anywhere in old Greek culture although the long-necked lute

134

had long since been known in Egypt. Lutes can be seen as a kind of combination of the principle of the flute or *aulos* with that of the lyre or harp. Although it is a string instrument, its frets or bindings tend to be equidistant like the holes of the *aulos*. In other words, the lute introduces the radial principle of the *aulos* into the domain of the (typically cyclic) string instruments. Lutes with several strings also manifest the cyclic principle in that their strings are tuned in successive fourths, which has been the most usual tuning since the lute first was developed in Arabia. Thus the lute, the favorite instrument of Arabia, unites two principles that the Greeks fastidiously separated in two distinct instrument groups: the Apollonian string instruments and the Dionysian *auloi*. Because of the way it bound these two principles together the lute was ideally suited to adulterate and confuse the polar relationship between cyclic and radial systems. So in Arabia it was possible for the ancient cyclic principle to reabsorb the radial principle, that future-bearing, Dionysian principle which had made itself so strongly felt in Greece.

The bowed string instruments that developed out of the lute unite the natures of the harp-type and the flute-type instruments to a still greater degree. In these instruments the tone is not only determined—as on the lute—by the way the string is gripped. The tone is actively formed from beginning to end by the bowing, just as the breath builds the tone of a wind instrument. It is thanks to medieval Arabic culture that western culture has its lute and its bowed instruments. Nevertheless, it was the destiny of western culture to develop the first true musical marriage of the cyclic and radial principles embodied separately in lyre and *aulos* respectively. The true marriage is in the classical cadence and that is why the highest flowering of the bowed instruments had to wait for the seventeenth and eighteenth centuries, which saw the development of the classical cadence. For it is the marriage and intensification of these two polar principles that is the secret of the inward nature of the string instruments.

Thus, in our view, a task confronts our present western culture. Arabic music assimilated the prime number relationships up to thirteen far in advance of western culture. But this anticipation of the future turned out to be more like a disguised return to the past. We believe it to be the task of western music to take up these prime-number relationships in a fully human and self-aware fashion so that they can lead into the future. Seen positively, this aspect of Arabic development is an unavoidable challenge, the challenge that we open up once more the door to that holy domain of the intervals built on seven, eleven and thirteen, now that the *Kali Yuga* has ended. Radiality gives us the key to this door if we grasp it with real, inner qualities of soul. Those qualities began to develop in the inward experience of the third, but this interval still is awaiting its fulfillment.

Arabic music, with its unbounded magical mood and its moon-like mysteriousness, is itself a veritable 'Thousand and One Nights.' In the future this music must be led out of its seductive, egoless realm of illusions into the daylight realms of a self-aware, suffering and loving humanity. It must be transformed by the sun-like spirituality that has dwelt in the inner human being since the turning point of time.

The Thousand and One Nights is the quintessence of Arabia's oriental, fairytale magic. One does not have to be a kabbalist to uncover the sources of this remarkable and mysterious number's qualities.

$$7 \quad \cdot \quad 11 \quad \cdot \quad 13 \quad = \quad 1001$$

The qualities of the three prime numbers of the holy domain unite in 1001, which is their product. For the person restricted to earthly senses they are numbers that belong to the 'realm of night'. In other words they belong to the realm of the supersensible, beyond the limits of the *senarius*. (See p. 74)

XXXV. THE SYSTEM OF THIRDS: THE DEVELOPMENT OF WESTERN THIRD CONSCIOUSNESS AND ITS CRISIS

As Rudolf Steiner once said, the music of our age stands at "one of the high points of its whole historical development." (See p. ix) It has freed itself from the art of poetry, to which it previously had almost always been attached, and has become a self-sufficient art. Earlier, the literal contents of speech had almost always connected music with the external world. But now it has become a wholly inward art, an art which itself is capable of enriching other arts from within. The literature of our time contains ample praises and descriptions of the music that has developed since the beginning of third consciousness. It is a wonder in the history of the earth and of humanity. It is a spiritual gift of inexhaustible richness and stands in inconceivably stark contrast to the materialistic development of reason which came about at the same time.

The main theme of the unfolding of modern western music is the blossoming of the radial principle. The interval of the third is intimately involved in this, but more than anything else, the real marriage of the radial principle with the cyclic principle is the decisive step. Without this marriage, which involves a genuine Goethean intensification of two opposites,[89] such a "high point in the history of the world" never could have been attained. Volume after volume could be filled if one wanted to describe exactly how the two polar forces, the radial and the cyclic, are united in ever new and characteristic ways in each style, in each school and, indeed, in the work of practically every composer. Here we will restrict ourselves to the most pronounced stages of development, well aware, however, that much of importance must remain unmentioned. Our present goal is not so much to produce a complete music history but rather to achieve a living picture of the interplay of these forces and the way they influence music so that this picture can throw light on our contemporary artistic task of achieving a truly modern music. Then we will be able to look at the 20th century and see where the stream carrying these forces has been weakened and was bound to die out because the field of tension between the two poles had been lost, and where the stream still lives and is capable of further development.

The earlier polyphony of the Middle Ages, which was founded exclusively on fourth and fifth consciousness, was a prelude to the development of the modern age. This first polyphony, furthermore, is not restricted to the West, but also is found in various non-European countries. Its seeds are to be sought as far back as ancient Greece, even if we exclude from the picture the still more ancient heterophony and the singing in parallel fifths which, like octave parallelism, are not yet true polyphony. Early polyphony is always associated with the intervals of the fourth and the fifth, in contrast to the polyphony of thirds that has been radiating out of Europe into other lands since the 18th and 19th centuries. The birth of polyphony is not an exclusively western event. But the consequent development of polyphony so that it was penetrated and worked through by third consciousness is specifically western.

In the art of counterpoint cultivated in the Middle Ages it became possible for melodic experience to divide itself between countervoices. The fact that it could do so is obviously connected with the situation of musical consciousness as the age of the fourth ran toward its conclusion and people stood before the gateway of approaching era of the third. Musical experience was moving into the inner realms of the soul, and things developed for music much as they often develop for a young person when their own personal soul life first begins to announce itself: their previously cohesive experience of the world splits into experience of the external world and experience of the inner world, and these two begin to weave a 'counterpoint of life' with one another. And so it also is in this very first era of inner musical consciousness: melodic experience splits into separate voices, the one voice which I myself sing, and the other voices which sound forth from my surroundings, sometimes agreeing with my voice, sometimes against it, sometimes in consonance with it, sometimes in dissonance with it. Polyphony, above all when it is experienced in singing, is musical self-discovery and musical self-realization, for it requires me to hold my voice over and against all the others. At the same

136

time it embodies the experience of discovering 'the Other' as I experience how my voice accompanies or supports other voices, how it is taken up by the others or clashes with them. And, finally, I experience how it is not my voice alone, but all the voices together, that bring the music into being. Earlier, the musical-harmonic laws were fulfilled by one single, unified, melodic-rhythmic experience, or movement. But as the era of the fourth drew to a close, musical harmony was sought particularly in the bringing together of several distinctive, individual voices. We can see polyphony as providing just what is necessary to balance the subjectivization and individualization introduced by the fourth and the third. For in bringing order into the simultaneous working of several subjective, rhythmically and melodically individualized, experiences or movements, music again achieves the objectivity it must have if it is to continue to reflect the great, universal World Harmony.

As we have mentioned, the earliest counterpoint sprang entirely from the soil of the old fifth and fourth consciousness.

(French descant, Kyrie Trope)

In this 11th century example, the two-part harmonies are restricted to the intervals of the unison, fifth, and fourth (or eleventh). Although the cantus and the distant still are rhythmically united, their melodic movements strictly maintain their own individuality. Melodically, the composition has been written so as to separate the voices and make them self-sufficient. Even at the point where there is a momentary parallel motion, the musical effect still is more that of two separate voices than of two unified ones. This is because of the quality of the fourth, which is an interval of delimitation and of self-assertion. This medieval feeling for the fourth also led to those motets in which each voice not only has its own rhythmic and melodic movement, but also its own text and its own distinctive instrumental accompaniment whose tone color sharply contrasted with that of the other voices (medieval 'split coloration').

Listening to the following example from Josquin des Pres (1450-1521) we can clearly hear how the nature of the third has begun to influence the counterpoint.

On the one hand, the two voices move entirely freely and independently of one another. This is the work of the old counterpoint with its source in the devisive, individualizing fourth consciousness. On the other hand, the way the independently moving voices often stand in third relationship to each other (here mostly in inverted thirds, i.e. in sixths) gives them an affinity for one another, a brotherliness, which is entirely foreign to counterpoint based on fourths and fifths like that of the previous example. We feel the outward-radiating, connecting power of the interval of the third. What the pure fourth, which is primarily a cyclic, Apollonian interval, has separated and individualized to an extreme degree, finds its way beyond individualization into a new interconnectedness by virtue of the radial, Dionysian power of the third. Without the joining together of these two powers, the unique flowering of the so-called Netherlands, or Franco-Flemish, School to which Josquin belonged, never could have happened. Ultimately, the roots of J.S.Bach's counterpoint lead back to this school.

In the mid 16th century (1558), Zarlino was able to formulate exactly the force that held several voices together—namely the force of the triad: either the major triad which is born out of the 'arithmetic series,' or the minor triad, which is born out of the 'harmonic series.' Because Zarlino expressed matters in terms of string length rather than in terms of frequencies, he called major the 'harmonic' proportion and minor the 'arithmetic'. (String length is reciprocally related to frequency.) The moment when Zarlino discovered his formulation marks the point where the earthly, human understanding, which was just entering into the modern situation of the consciousness soul, achieved a new awareness. It is the point in musical development where human understanding was first able to recognize in music the presence of its own archetypal principle, radiality. It grasped it in such a way that radiality was not made *antipathetic* to the impulses of the heart (or of the mind-soul) as it had been when it was encountered in the Greek Arabic periods (see p. 123f). Rather it was grasped in such a way that this rational knowledge was fully *substantiated* by a purely heart-felt, musical experience and even developed under the influence of such experience.

Shortly after Zarlino's time, in the age of the figured bass (ca. 1600—1750), the relationships between the voices were experienced and dealt with as follows: every main tone of the bass voice was seen as a source from which a radial column flowed upward, creating either a major or a minor triad. The other voices found their place as octave, fifth or third in this column, or, one could also say, the bass distributed its octave, fifth, and third among the other voices. The radial triadic principle, which earlier had been born out of the polyphonic meeting of voices, now had itself become, to a certain degree, the very source of the polyphony.

Our example is from Monteverdi's opera, *Arianna* (1608). Here, triadic columns, some of them not belonging to the key (those distinguished by accidentals), appear over all seven degrees of the d mode. These were what the right hand of the figured bass player sought out at the keyboard to accompany the bass line. Above the sixth degree, b♭ or b, and above the delayed g♯ the triad appears in the form of a sixth chord (i.e. in its first inversion, with the third in the bass.) The first inversion of a diminished triad also appears, but only over an unaccented e. Monteverdi also composed a polyphonic choral version of the "Lasciate". It was based on the same chordal structure, with the triadic columns of the figured bass being 'distributed' among the voices—naturally with the addition of highly expressive dissonances resulting from temporal alterations in individual voices (suspensions and anticipations), as well as melodic passing tones and changing tones.

138

Although Monteverdi here builds triads on all degrees of the scale, the predominating triads of the cadence of the approaching classical period already announce their presence in his principal close, "mi morire" in bars 5-6. These appear in their usual classical order: the triad on the first degree being followed by, in that order, triads on the fourth degree, g (subdominant), the fifth degree, a (dominant), and again on the first degree, d (tonic).

The circle of fifths with seven tones of the chain of fifths removed to form a scale gives us a picture of musical development up to this point in time. The picture encompasses polyphony based on fourths and fifths as well as the Medieval-Pythagorean monody of the church modes.

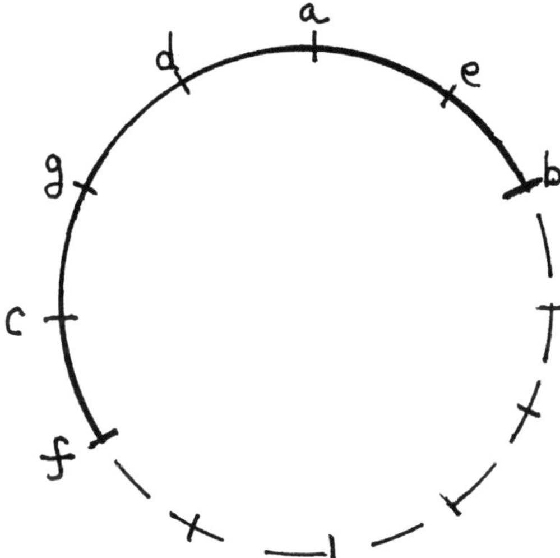

In Medieval polyphony, the consonances of fifths and fourths serve to underline all the more the fact that the scales' source is in the fifth. Here it is exclusively cyclic forces that are at work. By no means does it follow from the nature of the cyclic principle, as we have characterized it, that a closed, tempered circle of fifths already is presupposed. The assumed tuning here is the Pythagorean.

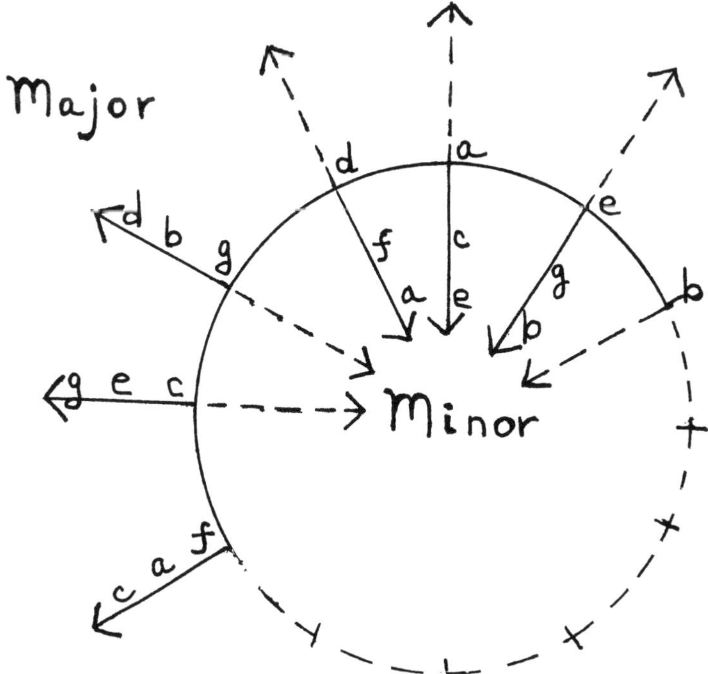

At the stage of the Netherlands, or Franco-Flemish, School we can see how it is precisely in the polyphonic music that third relationships arise between the tones—radial forces are woven into the contrapuntal fabric of the voices. Then, with the advent of the figured bass, it becomes clear that a triad radiates from out of each tone of the scale. In the case of the c scale, for example, the rays from f, c and g are major, the rays from d, a and e are minor.

Monteverdi's "Lasciate" shows how accidentals—or 'accidents', as they were then called—were used to allow both major and minor triads to appear on the same scale degrees. In this phase of development, the fundamental framework for the seven degrees of a scale continued to be cyclic, based on fifths. The radial life of the triad sprang forth from each of the seven scale degrees with a youthful color and freedom, and with scintillating changes between major and minor. Since the laws of the fifth and the laws of the third here have equal voice, this system necessitates tempering. The natural tuning—and the most used—at this stage is *middle-tone tuning*.

The classical cadence is characteristic of the following stage, although it already began to crystallize out during the era of the general bass. At this next stage, the participation of the cyclic chain of fifths is reduced from six steps of a fifth to two steps, or to the three corresponding tones. In C major, for example, it is reduced to the tonic tone c, with its dominant and subdominant, g and f. No longer do the seven tones of the scale have their genesis in the chain of fifths. Rather they originate in three triads that are a fifth apart from one another.

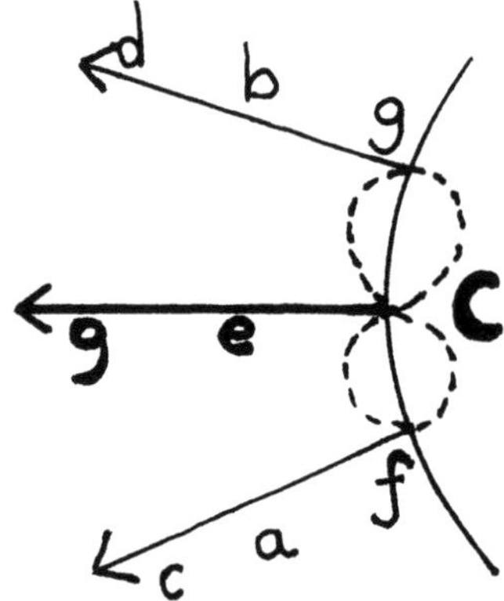

This reduction of the cyclic aspect brings a clear order into the radial aspect: only major triads remain on the three degrees of the cadence. The pure major cadence, or major tonality, has been distinguished from the minor.

To begin with, the natural minor cadence analogously contained only minor triads: in a—minor, for example, the tonic was a c e, the subdominant, d f a, and the dominant, e g b. Because of this division into pure major and pure minor, the only one among all the various church modes that could become major was the Ionian, the c-mode, for it was the only mode with large thirds on its first, fourth and fifth degrees.

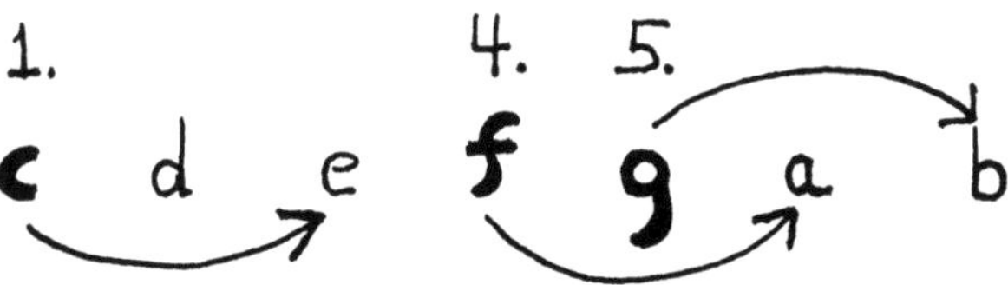

Only the Aeolian, the a-mode, could become natural minor, since it was the only mode with small thirds on these degrees.

140

In the 17th century, major and minor had not yet been so strictly differentiated from one another. In earlier works of J.S.Bach, for example, one still encounters key signatures for a minor that is built on the Dorian mode. But from the 18th century on, the signatures for major and minor were restricted to the 'Ionian' and 'Aeolian', respectively.

Furthermore, we know that the natural, or Aeolian, minor was ever and again thwarted by another principle. During the course of development of third-consciousness and triad-consciousness, the sense for the groundtone had more and more firmly established itself, and this sense expected an ascending leadingtone to the tonic and its octaves. Older music theory had called this the '*subsemitonium modi*' (the halftone beneath the tonic-tone of the mode). Under this influence, a-minor acquired the large seventh, g#, which does not actually belong to the key and which transforms the dominant triad into the major triad, e g# b. In order to avoid the augmented second, f—g#, f ultimately was raised to f# in the ascending half of the so-called 'melodic' minor scale. This means that the only thing left to distinguish a-minor from a-major was a single small third.

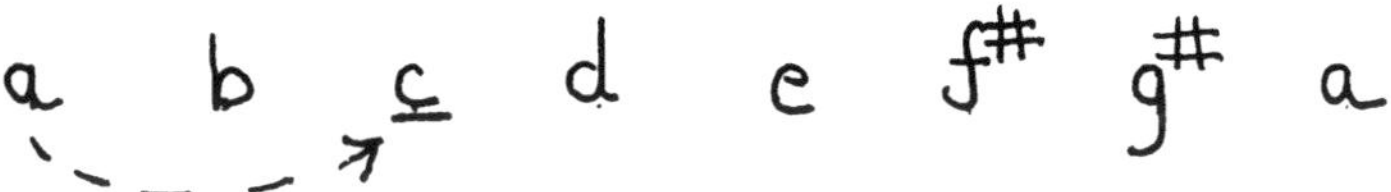

We can see that it is the third alone which determines the tonality in the era of the third. Furthermore, the minor principle (as we already noted on p.40f.) has fallen very much under the influence of the major principle, which is the predominating principle of our age. But this should not stand in the way of our recognizing minor as itself being a self-sufficient principle that is the polar opposite of major.

It has been described how the three chords of their respective cadences distinguish major and minor from one another. But this approach seems to break down when confronted with the use of what harmonic theory calls the 'relative minors' to the major tonic and its dominant. But this is a case in which the exception does prove the rule : every musician will experience how they slide back into the 17th century, or earlier, when they make frequent use of these parallels:

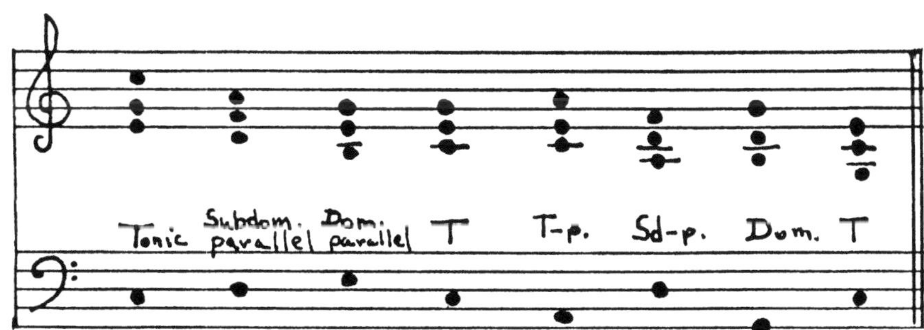

Such regressions were deliberately introduced into music in the 19th century, when there was a tendency toward a romantically retrospective style. These functional parallels are beautiful relics of an earlier time. They are ideally suited for softening once more the hard, crystal-clear logic of the classical cadence and for bringing a quasi-medieval oscillation between major and minor within the scope of the more refined harmony of the later romantic ear. On the other hand, for someone with a classical harmonic sense (of ca. 1750—1820), the relative minors set up a strong tendency to actually modulate into the parallel minor tonality, and the major functional parallels gravitate similarly toward the parallel major tonality. During the period in which the three-chord cadence flourished there was definitely more a tendency to distinguish major and minor from one another than to mix them together.

By restricting the influence of the cyclic principle, the classical cadence brought an order and clarity into the functioning of the radial pole. At the same time it very noticeably strengthened the effect of the radial principle of the triad. Whereas the triad had previously been essentially a principle governing the harmonious sounding together of several voices, in the 18th century it became a principle out of which melodies were formed—melodies of leading voices as well as accompanying ones.

In this example from Joseph Haydn there no longer are any contrapuntal countervoices. Triadic pillars, strictly changing with each new bar, unroll as broken chords... in slow figures in the leading voice and as rapidly repeated figures in the accompaniment. Such a style of composition is not merely typical of the classical piano style. With appropriate changes it appears in orchestral and chamber music as well. Often, triadic plateaus are built up in this fashion, plateaus that do nothing but pulsate rhythmically and melodically in themselves for bars at a time. The first movement of Beethoven's *Pastoral Symphony* is one example. Another, a uniquely expansive one, is Wagner's prelude to *Rheingold*, where an E^b plateau extends over more than one hundred bars: here, the radial principle wins absolute sovereignty for a while— the only exception being a few subsidiary tones that appear as mere 'passing tones' between the tones of the triad. They are the only surviving reminders of the cyclic principle.

The immobile, triadic plateau, pulsating in itself, became a characteristic of Classical and Romantic music. Although it played an important role in musical development at that time, it had long since been a familiar feature in European folk music: on wind instruments such as the alphorn, the lur[90)] and the trumpet, and also in alpine yodeling. This triadic technique already appears in Baroque and Renaissance hunting pieces where it is an explicit imitation of the natural horn as played among the folk. Thus does that old stream of nature-bound, radial music reveal itself, an issue from the springs of antique, chthonic-Dionysian culture that has made its way into the national—especially the rural—music of the Christian era (compare p. 42ff., p. 45f. , p. 51f., p. 90f.). Naturally, the old radiality originally went beyond the *senarius* as far as the quasi-quartertone intervals based on 7, 11 and 13—intervals one still finds in the alphorn playing of today. But, thanks to the triad that is inherent in radiality, radial elements were able to play an increasingly active part in the development of musical culture from the beginning of the era of third experience and on into the Classical period (in spite of this music's being limited to the bounds of the *senarius*). The result was a fertilization and enrichment of music. The Vienna classics are unthinkable without this mother soil of alpine-like music-making, and so are the counterpoint of the Netherlands' and Italy's monodic *cantilena*. All of these were nourished on this same soil.

Both of the characteristics of the Classical style that we have described (the restriction of cyclic forces through the role of the cadence and the extension of radial forces through the use of triadic plateaus) led to a concentration of tonal experience around the center of the tonal field, the tonic tone and its (tonic) triad. Through this centering it first became possible to really awaken a sense for the distinctive character of each key, for only the tonic triad bears in itself the character of one particular place in the circle of keys, whereas the dominant and subdominant triads always swing over to the next-darker or the next-brighter place in the circle. It is no accident that Richard Wagner, whose prelude to *Rheingold* developed one-sided restriction to the tonic to its most colossal dimensions, was able to use the qualities of the different tonalities in his work with the greatest imaginable aritistic consciousness and pregnancy. This has been described by Hermann Beckh (in *Die Sprache der Tonart*). Only someone who has been able to penetrate to the very heart of the spiritual region embodied in a tonality, e.g. in E^b major, would be able to shape something artistically that is as one-

142

sided as the prelude to *Rheingold*. On the other hand, we can also say that there is scarcely another passage in music literature where the nature of E^b major has been more strongly revealed.

The centering of tonal experience around the mid-point of the tonic had yet another significant consequence for the development of music. People thereby acquired a sharper sense for the characteristics of the twelve regions of the circle of tonalities, each represented by its triad. This led to a tendency to change tonality, i.e. to modulate, whenever music moved from one place in the circle to another. In other words, one actively sought to experience the immediate musical location in the circle as a new tonic in its own right. This is shown in the increasing use of the so-called secondary dominants, beginning about 1700. Before then, the movement between tonic, dominant, subdominant and their relative minors was experienced more as a breath-like swinging *within* the boundaries of a single tonality, for, during the age of the figured bass, all seven regions of the circle from f to b, each with its own triad, belonged in the domain of C major. But then there developed a need to concentrate tonal experience still further, so that this feeling for the individual quality of each region of the circle could be awakened immediately without having to rely on the relationship of dominant to tonic. Thus arose the harmonic striving towards especially distant tonalities. The extreme changes helped to express the experience of going from one region of feeling to an entirely different region. This is how modulation—especially distant modulation, which had previously been an exceptional event—became an important and inwardly necessary feature of music.

This development finally manifested itself as a universal tendency of Romantic music. But it also leads us back to a specific type of music cultivated in the figured bass era: the operatic recitative, in which quick affective changes led to dramatic confrontations between contrary qualities of experience. The rigorous modulatory style of the recitative first entered instrumental music in the form of imitations of vocal recitative, such as Kuhnau's *Biblical Histories* and J.S.Bach's *Chromatic Fantasy*. But only when we come to the development section of a Beethoven sonata or symphony movement can we feel that distant modulation definitely has become a musical reality so that we actually do penetrate into powerfully expressed, highly differentiated regions of experience. By contrast, the modulations of Baroque recitative are more external, originating in the language and in the dramatic event rather than in the purely musical events. Only in the tonally unified aria which follows the recitative does inner musical experience come to full and independent expression. Furthermore, the free use of accidentals without regard for tonality, which we observed in Monteverdi and which is not yet genuine modulation, still plays a role in the modulation techniques of Baroque recitative.

The roaming, modulatory character of a sonata development section took over more and more of all Romantic compositions. Often an entire piece has the character of a development section. The music moves freely through the various tonalities and often only finds its way back to its own tonality at the close of the piece. Max Reger's works represent a kind of a high point of this aspect of Romanticism; his modulatory rambling through the whole circle of tonalities in the compass of a single piece can be downright relentless.

Such a development was made possible by the closed, tempered circle of twelve fifths. Superficially viewed, Andreas Werkmeister's creation of the closed cycle of twelve and its coming into general use since J.S.Bach's Well-Tempered Clavichord looks like a victory of the cyclic principle over the radial principle. But the role the closed circle had to play in Western music was different from its role in the ancient Chinese circle of twelve (see p. 79). It did not enter Western music so that the cycle could dominate, but rather on behalf of radial experience. The radial nature of the triad had led to an ever stronger, more concentrated, individualized tonic consciousness, so that tonic experience could be given free reign over the whole house of the twelve, ruling and directing there according to its will. In other words, this circle of twelve did not establish the sovereignty of the cycle, but rather the sovereignty of radiality. This absolute sovereignty over all the tonalities is evident in Richard Wagner. It is already present in Beethoven. But when one gets as far as Max Reger there is the uneasy feeling that the prince no longer lives in his castle—that he has begun to wander around in it like a lost person and that the castle has begun to rule over its inhabitants. Here, we already are noticing signs of the situation at the beginning of the 20th century.

The house of the twelve is becoming a mausoleum or, more accurately expressed in the light of the spiritual implications of this world event, it is becoming an 'Egyptian house of the dead.'

* * *

But before we turn to the deep and urgent problems of our own musical present, we must follow one last Ariadne's thread through the maze of musical development. It will lead us to the very heart of the problem. It will show how the cyclic principle attached itself more and more to the service of the radial nature of the third, to which it itself had given birth in the polyphony of the Netherlands School at the dawning of the modern age. This process divested the cyclic principle of its original, cosmic, super-human, universal nature and subjected it to a total transformation.

For the sake of grasping what this means, let us put before ourselves the two forms in which the cycle of twelve has appeared musically: as the circle of twelve fifths and as the circle of twelve halftones. If we listen to the successive fifths

e^b b^b f   c   g   d   a   e   b   f#   c#   g#

we feel that the musical force of this structure extends much further than our capacity for musical experience can follow. Our musical sense can only accompany one fifth-movement fully, as it ascends or descends from a given tone, e.g.

f←c→g

If more fifths follow, the individual fifths lose their intensity. The whole thing expands to an ever more powerful tonal structure whose lawlike order, it is true, can be dimly sensed, but whose fifths come in potencies that increasingly elude the musical grasp. For earthly man, these rigidify into a form occupying tonal space. Only a cosmic being—such as the musical humanity of primeval times—would have the capacity to really accompany this expanded movement of fifths with a living musicality.

If the successive fifths are drawn together into the space of a single octave, however, it is another matter, e.g. if 'f c g d a e d' are drawn together as 'c d e f g a b (c).' Now it is possible to experience the power of breath and movement inherent in all these fifths in a living way, for the cosmos of fifths has accommodated itself to the octave boundaries of our human, earthly sphere of experience. But, surprisingly, this approach is not possible with the complete cycle of fifths, but only when at least five of its tones are omitted—in the case of our example, f# c# g#, e^b and b^b. If these five tones are included, the result is a twelve-step sequence of halftones within one octave:

c   c#   d e^b f   f#   g   g#   a b^b b   (c)

Anyone who is musically awake will feel that it is a mistake when our music theory calls this chromatic sequence of tones a 'scale,' which it often nevertheless does. For, in contrast to a scale like 'c d e f g a b c,' it is not a path to the octave and has no inherent field of forces of its own. In the chromatic sequence the living impulses of movement natural to the ascending and descending fifth relationships have died out. No longer can one experience the tone f as carrying the dark, contracted quality of the interval of the fourth as one experiences it in the c-scale, and g has lost the quality of the opening-out, brightening fifth which leads us out into the widths of space. A chromatic succession of tones leads the melodic, musical sense smoothly past these degrees of the scale just as it slips past all the others, as if they were undifferentiated milestones offering it no orientation or sense of purpose. Unless a person has an absolute sense of pitch and thus does not have to depend solely on his own inner musical experience, he will discover that when he practices singing the chromatic sequence he will instinctively orient himself by the framework of the seven-toned scale, introducing the extra chromatic tones into it. It is almost impossible to achieve a musical grasp of the halftone

144

sequence as such unless, perhaps, one goes in a slow tempo, experiencing each step as the leading-tone to the next step. But then all sense of exact intonation goes by the board because the leading-tone cannot be experienced in itself. On its own it eludes harmonic or intervalic experience.

When it is nothing more than a leading-tone, the halftone brings us to the border of musical experience. It merely glides in musical space without any harmonic or intervalic foundation. It is interesting that an excessive proliferation of leading-tone type halftones, such as the chromatic sequence (the 'chromatic scale'), is experienced as a musical 'wailing.' What such a description expresses is the feeling that the musical experience no longer is pure (in the sense of our first chapter), but is more like a soulful outburst. This is a highly significant discovery that should not be lost sight of: the circle of halftones marks a border where inwardly grounded, musical experience runs up against sound experience which comes merely from without...where sound is experienced as utterance or as physical sound.

Precisely the effect of falling out of a musical context is an aspect of the chromatic sequence that musicians have played upon ever since the Classical period. If we listen to the chromatic run in Mozart's *Fantasy in D Minor* (K 397), or to one of the many other similar passages in the Classical literature, we will notice how our inner musical sense temporarily abandons us during the course of rapid halftone steps, leaving us to slide through external musical space without any support or means of orientation. At last, with the final tone of the chromatic run, we suddenly regain our 'inner musical feet' and again experience the music as having its source in inner experience. At that moment the musical experience is all the more intense, like the feeling of a child once more in its mother's arms after it has wandered from her and been lost for a while.

Thus the wide-spanning chain of fifths confronts us, on the one hand, with musical powers that are beyond our reach, given the way we are musically constituted, and, on the other hand, with powers that we experience as having died out when they are fully contracted into the circle of halftones. Ever since the advent of fifth-consciousness we have used a musical scale derived from fifths, and the fifth still stands behind our major and minor scales, notwithstanding their triadic aspect. This scale that is born of fifths exists in the middle ground between the two poles we have described: although it is contracted to the span of one octave, it does not contain the full circle of twelve. As a heptatonic scale it only swings twice to the side of the 'death pole': with the two halftones, e—f and b—c. Just this encounter with the 'death pole' gives a heptatonic scale its sharper contour and greater awakeness as compared with a pentatonic scale. A pentatonic scale avoids all halftones and thus can particularly well express the cosmic life of the wide-spanned chain of fifths.

Pentatonic and heptatonic based on fifths contrast with one another in the way a plant contrasts with a human being or an animal: the plant is just a living being, whereas a person or an animal has consciousness, or soul, in addition to life. Rudolf Steiner described how the potential for consciousness, or 'life of soul' ("astrality"), exists only in beings in whom the developing life forces and the destructive death processes comprise the two sides of a polarity and so mutually intensify one another. Just this sort of 'polarity between life forces and death forces' is to be found musically in the scale of seven tones with its two halftones. If the part of the scale in which the death forces make themselves felt is omitted, namely the two halftones, the result is the scale which is the most natural expression of the primal human being, or of the young child not yet conscious of its own soul: a pentatonic scale containing no halftones. Mysteriously, it is when we take seven consecutive tones produced by a series of fifths that we first obtain a scale that has these 'soul-evoking' halftones in it. In another context (p. 77), we already have encountered seven as the number connected with the nature of the soul. (This last comment refers to the *quantity* of tones in the scale and in the circle of fifths; seven expresses something else when it governs the inner *harmonic relationship* between tone—as, for example, 7/4.)

If I increase the number of tones in one octave of my scale by drawing more than seven tones from the circle of fifths, e.g.

b♭   f   c   g   d   a   e   b   f# ,

then I increase the number of halftones:

c   d   e—f—f#—g   a—b♭—b—c .

145

In this way I can heighten awareness of those places around which the halftones are concentrated, but only so long as the scale, as in our example, is such that the feeling for a sevenfold structure is not obscured. Since the time of the 16th century Italian madrigal, modern chromaticism has served the expression of increased self-awareness and astral contraction that verges on the experience of pain (but always in the context of a sevenfold scale.) The early culmination of chromaticism in the Italian madrigal is an exception. Essentially it arose out of that period's typical freedom with accidentals, major and minor not yet having clearly separated themselves from one another. Otherwise, modern chromaticism developed in stages exactly parallel to those in which radial powers came to the fore. Indeed, as we shall see, chromaticism can be seen as a consequence or a counterpart of radiality.

Let us look again at the two diatonic halftones that naturally arise in the scale of seven degrees: e—f and b—c. The following idiom is often found in 15th and 16th century polyphonic compositions: The first inversion, d f d b, of the diminished triad on the seventh scale degree, b d f, leads to the tonic. Here, as the b *subsemitonum modi* ascends as a matter of course to c, the octave of the tonic. This is demanded by the feeling for the tonic that has been establishing itself since the Middle Ages. This b is the original leading-tone.. It preceeds the tonic like a herald and announces him unmistakably as the ruling king. Beginning approximately in the 17th century, this idiom underwent a significant change:

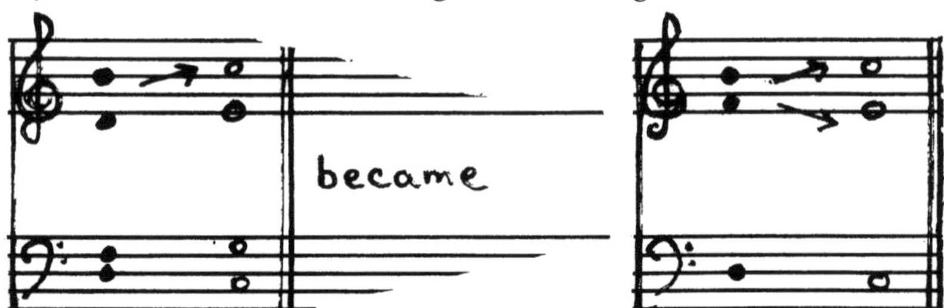

The f (in the 14th century the tone was f#) which previously had ascended to g, the fifth above the tonic, now descends as a leading-tone to the third, e. We can hear at once how the new leading-tone reinforces the feeling for the third in the tonic chord. Such voice-leading for the diminished triad, b d f, points altogether more emphatically toward the tonic, because yet another 'herald'(the f) for the tonic has appeared on the scene. The highest and the lowest tones of the seven-toned chain of fifths out of which the scale is built are b and f. Taken together as a tritone, b and f are wholly representatives of the cyclic principle—the tritone forms the diameter of the circle of fifths and, as such, is *the* cyclic interval *par excellence*. Now the two, b and f, have descended from their cosmic heights to sacrifice themselves on the 'funeral pyre of the leading-tone' and to 'hold the stirrup' for the earthly, radial principle of the tonic and the third, c—e.

In spite of its structure consisting of two small thirds, the triad on the seventh degree is a thoroughly cyclic structure. Because of its false, dissonant fifth, it always had been the black sheep among the pure, radial triads formed on the degrees of the scales. With its sequence of small thirds, it manifests the principle of the geometric series (compare p. 44).

	b		d		f
	5	:	6		
			5	:	6
=	25	:	30	:	36

By the 18th century, the addition of another small third had expanded this structure to a diminished seventh chord. Not only does this new structure encompass the limits of a seven-toned chain of fifths, it also encompasses the entire cycle of twelve. Its tones mark the quadrants of the cycle of twelve. With its double tritone relationships it forms a cross in the circle of twelve.

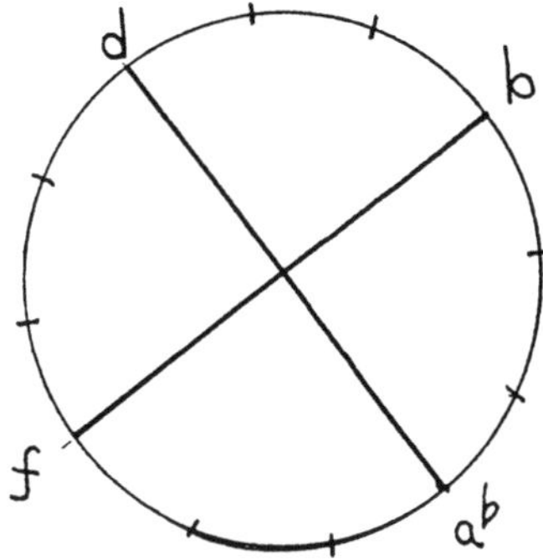

This chord no longer owes allegiance to any diatonic group of seven tones. Rather it is a representative of the forces of the entire cycle confined within the space of a single octave. There is no doubting that this chord contributed to the decisive closing of the twelve into a circle in the 18th century. If a further third, a^b—c^b , is added to it, the diminished seventh chord closes on itself, but this requires a tempered circle of fifths so that the enharmonic relationship, c^b = b, is possible. By means of enharmonic changes this single chord can appear in four different forms, each of which is oriented toward one of four places in the circle of keys that are related as quadrants of the circle.

1)		b	d	f	a^b	→	C major or minor
2)		c^b	d	f	a^b	→	E^b major or minor
3)	Enharmonic	c^b	e^{bb}	f	a^b	→	G^b major or minor
	equivalents	b	d	e#	g#	→	F major or minor
4)		b	d	f	g#	→	A major or minor

Such an event must be viewed as having deepest significance for the development of music: this extraordinary tonal structure that encompasses the entire cycle offers itself on 'the altar of the leading-tone' in order to merely 'hold the stirrup' for earthly, human, radial inwardness of soul.

The diminished seventh chord provides each of the three tones of the major triad with its own 'leading-tone herald'.

This tonal structure plays such a central role in the works of J.S.Bach that it could be called *the* Bach chord. It is no accident that when this great musical mystic seeks to present the crucifixion on Golgotha musically in his two passions, his deepest and most individual works, he repeatedly employs the chord that forms the cross in the cyclic system. For example, the following passage is to be found in the *Saint John's Passion*:

Singnificantly, after Bach's time the diminished seventh chord ceased being used to express a self-sacrificing cosmic being. It became more the expression of the forces which led this cosmic being into death. Thus in Weber's *Freischutz* the diminished seventh chord appears as the satanic 'Samiel's chord.'

Approaching the 18th century, as the three functions of the Classical cadence became ever more prominent, the triad on the seventh degree, as well as its extension, the diminished seventh chord, took on a dominant function in the cadence. And the chord, b d f, acquired the dominant tone, g, as its root, thus forming a chord that has been much loved ever since, the dominant seventh chord:

This chord weds the radial dominant triad to a cyclic, leading-tone structure. Its striving toward the tonic is stronger than that of the diminished triad, b d f, on the one hand, or that of the pure dominant triad, on the other. With the dominant seventh, the decisive fall of the bass tone g to the tonic c works together with the twofold leading-tone impulse of the tritone b—f. In the former, one pole of the cyclic force manifests itself, namely that represented in the chain of fifths; in the latter, the pole represented in the compressed series of halftones is manifest.

Music theorists have made various attempts to explain the dominant seventh chord as a purely radial structure based on the overtone relationships, 4 : 5 : 6 : 7—in other words, as a triad with an added natural seventh, 7/4. Theoretically, this explanation is extraordinarily attractive because of the simplicity and clarity of the numerical relationships. In the 18th century, musical experiments using the natural seventh as a substitute for the dominant seventh were made by G. Tartini, J. Ph. Kirnberger and K. Chr. K. Fasch.[91] Tartini did not go further than theoretical speculation, but Kirnberger and Fasch did, especially the later, who really struggled with this problem in his compositions. The work of these two showed that the natural seventh is not a possible substitute for the dominant seventh. In the last analysis it is only usable, and only really beautiful, as an augmented sixth, c—a #, which reveals that the whole concern with the natural seventh is only a mirror trick, since an a # in middle intonation is identical for practical purposes with the natural seventh (they only differ by 0.030 ht). Therefore this tone, b^b or a #, was not really being experienced as the true natural seventh 7/4. If it had been, it would have been conveying a direct, self-sufficient relationship with c as the root of the interval, just as the third 5/4 had done to link c and e since the beginning of the modern period. But the contrary was the result: c—a # was experienced as a dissonance resulting from alteration. It had the dynamic force of a leading-tone whose function was to lead the listener beyond it to some other tone.

If we compare the dominant seventh chord c e g b^b (Mch: pure triadic scale, middle tone tempering or 12-division) with the tonal sequence 4 : 5 : 6 : 7 (ideally these tones should be heard as chords), then it can be clearly heard how the dominant seventh chord demands a resolution in the tonic towards which it is striving, whereas the chord with the natural seventh is at rest within itself, free of tension and without any impulse in some further direction. In any case, such tension as one can experience in the natural seventh is in no way resolved by its being treated as a leading-tone. On the contrary, a leading-tone progression to F major is extremely unpleasant in this case. The small difference of 1/6 of a tone between the natural seventh and the dominant seventh results in a radical alteration of the musical expression of the chord: the chord with the natural seventh is wholly and exclusively the expression of nature-bound, Dionysian radiality, whereas the dominant seventh carries a strong cyclic component which has been dedicated to the service of the radial tonic-regent, providing it with its 'leading-tone heralds.' (The situation is different again with Debussy's chords with small sevenths. These no longer have a dominant function and they even appear in parallel voicing. It is easy enough

148

to imagine that the number 7 could be influencing a seventh chord in his music, since one now and again finds clear examples of his forming halftone approximations of relationships based on 7, 11 and 13—see p. 158f.)

The theory that the tone f in the dominant seventh chord extends the dominant sphere over into the sphere of the subdominant is much more in accord with the musically experienced reality. Within a given tonality, the dominant sphere represents the ascending, opening stream of fifths, the subdominant sphere represents the descending, closing stream. The former (in the key of C) contains the tone b, the summit of the seven-toned chain of fifths; the latter contains its deepest tone, f. In the 15th and 16th centuries, the upper and lower poles already had begun to approach one another in the diminished triad on the seventh degree of the scale (see(1) in the illustration below). The result was a chord that strove toward the ruling tonic with redoubled leading-tone intensity, rather than some sort of ambiguous hybrid. The same tendency is embodied in the dominant seventh chord (2), as well as the seventh chord on the seventh degree which, with its a^b yields the 'chord of the cross' (3), and also, finally, the dominant chord with seventh and ninth (4). All of these 'added dissonances' to the dominant chord introduce the tritone b—f and bring together the qualities of the dominant and subdominant spheres.

There also are two chords that reach over from the sphere of the subdominant, chords with added dissonances based on the fundamental subdominant tone f: the subdominant sixth chord (5) and the 6-5 chord (6). Both reach over into the field of the dominant via the aded tone d. Significantly, the subdominant cannot appropriate the highest tone of the chain of fifths, the b, without sacrificing its own subdominant nature.

All the chords with added dissonances thus far described have been in the context of C major. If we alter the a to a^b, obtaining the corresponding chords for c minor, we then have before us the entire spectrum of diatonic (i.e those not involving chromatic alterations) dominant and subdominant chords with added dissonances that are dealt with in harmonic theory. What they have in common is that they all cross the border between the tones d and f in the diatonic circle of thirds—upward-bound in the one case, downward-bound in the other. (See diagram.) This is the same border between dominant and subdominant spheres that we noted earlier on p 22. It is that critical place in an harmonically pure C major where tempering becomes necessary. Thus we are getting signals that all these chords have something essential to do with the cyclic pole, for the necessity of tempering only arises in connection with a cycle (see p. 44). The seven-tone circle of thirds of a given tonality also can only arise through the helping influence of the cyclic chain of fifths.

Dominant and subdominant represent the cyclic force of series of ascending and descending fifths. The preceeding diagram shows clearly how there has been a many-sided intermingling of the two since the 17th century. Together they build a protective circle around their king, guaranteeing the authority of the ruling tonic so that it can provide a stable point of reference through the increasingly more dramatic modulatory storms of the 18th and 19th centuries. The more firmly modulation established itself in music, the more the added dissonances were used.

Beginning in the Classical Period, but above all during the later Romantaic Period, the supplementary chords were altered more and more frequently. They were chromatacized in order to form leading-tone relationships with the tonic, for example:

What does this signify? The cyclic forces have closed lovingly and protectively around their 'royal child', the radial tonic-triad. In them, the heights and depths of the cyclic stream of fifths—the dominant and subdominant streams—are joined together. Now these cyclic powers, for the sake of the radial tonic, proceed to give up more and more of their original, superhuman, cosmic, objective being and totally sacrifice themselves in a 'leading-tone death.'

Musical experience verifies the unbelievable transformation that has been undergone by these cyclic powers that have become chromatic. Music that contains many of theses altered dominants is experienced as having a strikingly close correspondence to our subjective, wholly personal experience. All of music's cosmic elevation is lost and the listener is thrown back upon his own feelings, sentiments and passions. The great Late Romantics like Bruckner still were able to imbue this sphere of personal feeling with an objective, spiritual fire and even able to unite it with its counterpole, the cosmic power of the fifth. Thus their music achieves an unprededented intensity. When it ceased to be possible to maintain some spiritual intensity within this harmony of alterations, music fell into the limbo of the salon, or of the 20th century 'music hall' with its' commercial dance music, show music and background music. We do not want to say that all this music is aesthetically worthless and should automatically be condemned. The music hall has its pretty corners. But one characteristic of such music is the lack of that deeply-felt suffering, that genuine pathos, which distinguished the music of the great Late Romantics, who had a feeling for the 'death' of cyclic music in the harmony of alterations that was based on leading-tones. When that feeling goes, all that remains is a subjective, hedonistic enjoyment of the alterations, and a music that expresses a feeling for life that is satisfied by ignoring its spiritual background and merely pursuing whatever brings personal enjoyment. In consequence, all the cyclic forces—both those 'dying out' in the harmony of alterations and those that still are very much 'alive' in the cadence—degenerate into spiritless slang, an empty facade: neither are experienced with any artistic spirit. (Incidentally, something entirely different happened around 1960 when beat and pop music appeared on the scene. The use of leading-tones and the harmony of alterations disappears at the same time as electrified sound, which is essential to this music, appears. Music *seems* to have become objective and superpersonal again—compare p. 116f.! This is a significant symptom, worthy of a study in its own right!)

The most astonishing thing in the development of Late Romantic chromaticism (the harmony of alterations) is the way the cyclic forces harbored in the altered dominant chords were wholly given over to subjective, indeed, to all-too-subjective, expression, whereas the radial triad now appeared as the bearer of a clearly-expressed cosmic principle. Earlier in this study we became acquainted with cyclic forces as trans-human, cosmic and objective...as in pentatonic music or in the medieval experience of the fifth and the fourth. Specifically human, subjective, inner experience was first introduced into music by the radial forces at play in the major and minor triads with their thirds. What clearly seems to have happened is that the cyclic forces took on essential characteristics of the third and of the nature of radiality when the harmony of alterations made them totally dependent on the triad. At the same time they imparted some of their own objective nature to the radial components. The early 20th century saw the significant reversal of a musical polarity that had been established during the Greek period: that between the Apollonian, cyclic experience of objective, cosmic law and the Dionysian, radial experience of one's own inner being. In the 20th century what had been Dionysian came to express objective, cosmic law, and what had been Apollonian came to express subjective, inner experience. Here we touch on a central aspect of our modern development, a secret whose unraveling appears to me to be the true musical-artistic task of the future. For this reversal is directly connected with the 20th century's musical crisis.

Since the second half of the 19th century, the spiritual climate of the West has been anything but suitable for permitting the Dionysian streams, carrying the inward life of the human soul, to flow into the realm of objective, cosmic law. And yet the reversal just described in the sphere of music indicates a predisposition towards such a confluence. Only Goethe was able to achieve it, somewhat earlier, in his work in the natural sciences. Otherwise, science remained materialistic. The progressively more materialistic view of life born of this science had brought things to such a pass by the 19th century that the inner soul-experience of the Romantic artists was increasingly more divorced from the merely materialistically conceived world and from cosmic laws. Instead, these artists sought out a non-earthly, inner universe—a tendency that the aging Goethe viewed with the greatest concern. Whoever sees the interconnections between these things will see how, at the end of the 19th century and the beginning of the 20th, the radial musical principles bound up with the earth were more and more deprived of the spiritual air which gives them life. Ultimately, the radial triad came to be experienced as a musical falsehood, for people no longer were capable of understanding what it expressed: "The earth is a spiritual being and bears within herself the laws of your own, innermost being." (Compare p.111)

While he was composing *Tristan and Isolde*, Richard Wagner underwent the Romantics' escapist crisis in a particularly dramatic fashion. The way the prelude to *Tristan* employs chromatic harmonic alterations that no longer resolve in a (radial) triad is symptomatic: three times the prelude finds its way to a dominant seventh chord and then stops there without going on to its tonic triad. The cyclic forces no longer find their way to the triad, that radial, earthly principle to which their leading-tone existence had once bound them. Now they wander over the earth, lost in an in-between, twilight world, having lost their connection with the earth and with the widths of the objective cosmos. The chromaticism of *Tristan* paved the way for early 20th century atonality, in which music's triadic radial orientation finally disappears. This brought with itself the break-up of the seven-fold order of the major and minor scales, as well as the dissolution of the order of the circle of keys, for both of these were founded upon the simultaneous working of the radial and the cyclic poles: the loss of the radial pole meant their death as well. Early atonal music, in which wandering cyclic powers still weave, expresses intimate stirrings of the soul. Works of Schoenberg's middle period were called "seismographs of the soul",an expression that makes it clear that the inversion described above really has taken place: the cyclic powers really have implanted themselves in the inner recesses

of the soul and become the vehicle of expression for that inward soul-world. But this is a soul-scape of deep isolation, estranged from the cosmos out of which the cyclic powers were born and also from the being of the earth.

Arnold Schoenberg and Josef Matthias Hauer decisively transformed atonality by inscribing the law of the cosmos into it, the absolute twelvefoldness of cosmic, spherical space: the Twelvetone Principle. Until they had done this, atonality floated in a netherworld of the soul, truly abandoned by God and by the world. In his book, *Die Zwölfordnung der Töne* (*The Twelvefold Ordering of the Tones,* not translated), Hermann Pfrogner gives a unique description of the spiritual background of their deed, so I will not go into the finer details here. The ordering principle of the circle of fifths always had been twelvefold, but the powers of the cycle were split up into a multiplicity of values—*b, bb,* # and x—because of the tones' functioning as leadingtones to the radial triad. The Twelvetone Principle abolishes this fracturing and gives each tone of the cycle of twelve its own absolute individuality. So, whether one writes *b* or # becomes a matter of indifference, since each of the twelve tones has its own unchangeable value. In this way the law of the enduring, cosmic, spherical space became the law of tonality. Ever since the flourishing of Egyptian and Chaldean cultures, this space has been pictured as the circle of fixed stars in the Zodiac. In ancient China, music came to be governed by the inspired, cosmic, superhuman principle of the twelve *Liu* (see p. 78f). In the music of the West, the twelve had always remained in the background, a principle of order supporting the tonal system and the circle of keys. But now it has entered directly into music, unmediated by any connection with the principles of the pentatonic or heptatonic scales.

(from Anton Webern, Op. 27; "very slow"!)

For the first time in the history of humanity's musical development since the time of the Atlantean/Ancient Indian (Eastern) cycle of sevenths, an entire cycle appears again, embodied in music. (see p. 67) The circle of tones, which had been broken apart into endlessly ascending and descending progressions in Ancient Persia, is once more closed and whole. Once more the two paths, the path inward (*b*) and the path outward (#), meet as they met in that original cycle of the Atlanteans. Thus, humanity seems to have achieved one of its ultimate musical goals. At any rate, this seemed certain to J.M.Hauer when he wrote (*Zwoelftonspiel Manifest*, 1952) that humanity had once more found its way to the divine, cosmic, archetypal principles of music.[92]

But what has become of the Earth and her own musical principle? Looking back to the time of that great reversal at the end of the 19th century when radial, Dionysian inner awareness and cyclic, Apollonian cosmic awareness exchanged roles, we can imagine the radial triad speaking to the truly musical listener of today, reminding him that "the laws of your own innermost being are contained in the spiritual being of the Earth." This is one aspect of the reversal—it calls for a recognition and an artistic awareness of the inner soul-world that is approachable through the laws of nature and the cosmos. Goethe's views of nature and the cosmos were the first artistic, spiritual realization of such an approach. And when we learn, for example, to hear the musical, excarnating gesture of major in listening inwardly to an exemplar of that external law of nature called the overtone series, or to hear the incarnating gesture of minor in the external phenomenon of the undertone series (see p. 51f.), we are thoroughly justified in feeling ourselves to be Goetheanists. Goethe's sentence (out of *Epirrhema*) applies exactly: "Nothing is inside, nothing is outside: for what is within is also without."

The other aspect of the reversal, which transformed the cosmic, Apollonian cyclic realm into an inward domain of the soul, would have to be expressed in such words as: "your own

152

soul bears the laws of the cosmos within itself''—a statement that becomes a musical reality in the twelvetone compositions of Hauer and Schoenberg, but even more so in the work of Schoenberg's student, Anton Webern. Such music is only possible when the earth-bound side of the human soul had died musically. A musical sensibility based on the inner musical nature of the earth finds in twelvetone music a powerful death experience. It is no wonder, then, that the places where this music is most pure and most convincing are the places where it most separates itself from sound as such, i.e. from the earthly, acoustic laws of the overtone series such as in those pianississimo passages so characteristic of Webern, where he often has added such indications as ''scarcely audible.'' The more twelvetone music gets involved with the physical texture of sound, or even with metrical rhythm, the more unfortunate the musical result. Both of these elements are appropriated from music that is built on triadic harmony. But twelvetone music is a music whose inner nature is threatened by every sound that becomes earthly. So it is evident why the majority of people necessarily experience twelvetone music as sounding ''false'' or unpleasant, since most people of today only have access to a music founded on earthly experience. It is equally evident that such music entails very great risks, for, by its very nature, it is divorced from the processes that make sound audible. Such music lacks the field of resistance provided by the laws governing earthly sounds. After Webern's death it mostly became a ghostly apparition of thought processes, either music not meant to be heard, or music all the better composed the more unpleasant it was to hear—at which point musical composition and artistic activity parted company. Once a composer no longer had to penetrate into the elemental world of sensible sound (into its inner musical structure, which entails more than just composing with external tonal color), it then was possible for this music to deviate still further into the subsensible, electronic realms.

Here we should remind ourselves that, in any case, musical experience never is exclusively a matter of the senses (compare p. 1f.). Nevertheless, there is a musical listening which spiritually and musically experiences the supersensible, spiritual laws of number that underlie physical, perceived sound; these laws are embodied in the overtone and undertone series. Such experience is inscribed in the musical sensibility of the present day: in the experience of the third, especially of the third and the triad in the major mode. While examining the principles of major and minor we observed, speaking of the major triad (p. 40), that being related to it, it entirely penetrates the world of physical sound. When major rings out it is as though an awakener enters into the enchanted elemental world of sound imprisoned in matter and calls it by its own true name. Rudolf Steiner said that earth-bound humanity first became a musician when we began to feel the third. In the music based on experience of the fourth or fifth, it was the super-earthly being that was the musician, and this was even more markedly the case in music based on sixths or sevenths.

During the 5000 years of the *Kali Yuga*, the 'Dark Age,' humanity was abandoned, restricted to live on Earth and to live in its own inner world. A feeling for the third, which enables music to become entirely earthly and inward, is the fruit of the *Kali Yuga*. The end of the 19th century is also the end of the *Kali Yuga*. With the beginning of the 20th century, a 'Light Age' begins, in which humanity again can turn toward the spiritual cosmos, but now with a newly-won inwardness. This immense upheaval reveals itself with utmost clarity in the development of music: in the reversal just described, which led to the establishment of inward, Apollonian-cosmic feeling for the cyclic realm and of an outer, Dionysian-earthly feeling for the radial realm. Twelvetone music showed us one side of this reversal: the penetration by cosmic law and cosmic forces of cyclic experience that has become inward. But this is only one side. Although the power of the third, which embodies the radial, earthly principle, really is the active force behind all this, the third seems to have entirely vanished from the scene if one is looking at the development of twelvetone music. At the beginning of the Light Age, twelvetone music bursts on the scene, bringing a powerful spiritualizing impulse into music and bringing also a cosmic universality. Its flames consume all that remains of the now past Dark Age, including the third. The development of twelvetone music must be seen in the same light as the massive, catastrophic wars of the 20th century—as a spiritualizing fire that sweeps over human culture, destroying everything that remains of the *Kali Yuga*, and as summoning all the powers, good and evil, that have a role to play in the future of humanity.

Thus, along with many other things, the primal, ecstatic, rhythmic-magical forces that essentially belong to periods before the advent of the *Kali Yuga*, break through the burning, crumbling crust of the Dark Age. Having slumbered for thousands of years in Africa's primeval forests, these forces well up in the development of jazz and its derivatives and sweep in huge waves over Europe and the West. In no other age have diverse and conflicting musical powers out of the past and out of the future collided as they do in our age. To describe them all within the compass of a single book is impossible. It is as if everything from out of the entire musical development of humanity were being pressed together in order to make it possible to achieve a decisive breakthrough on the path toward its ultimate goals.

XXXVI. THE SYSTEM OF THIRDS:
THE TRANSFORMATION OF THIRD CONSCIOUSNESS.
EXTENSION OF OUR TONE SYSTEM.

Transforming musical consciousness? Expanding our tone system? Working in our day and age, can such goals play a part in shaping our artistic vision? They must play a part if we are ever to find a way out of the present chaos. (As we have seen, the chaos has arisen out of a certain historical necessity.) Once more it is Rudolf Steiner who has given us a key to the musical future. Beginning in 1915, he described a form of musical consciousness that would arise in the future, a musical consciousness that would result in a single tone's being experienced in a way comparable to the way an entire melody is experienced today. In 1920 he said that the 'expressionistic' music of that time already foreshadows this future experience of the single tone—that in this music there is "...without a doubt the beginning of something that will come to have very great significance."[93]

A "melodic experience" of the single tone, of the prime? Surprising and challenging expressions for a musician of today! But if we examine our musical experience of a sensitively performed composition of Anton Webern, we will ascertain that, in this case, single tones have much greater significance and inner intensity than they have, for example, in a turbulent, Romantic piano concerto or, for that matter, in a two-voiced minuet of J.S.Bach. In both cases, one tone has as much or as little significance as a single spot of color in Raphael's *Sistine Madonna*, or as a single word in Dante's *Divine Comedy*. In both minuet and piano concerto, the single tone is absorbed into the total melodic-harmonic-rhythmic flow of the music. But with Webern one can experience intimations of great depths in a single tone and such an experience opens up a realm that has no relationship to what is externally hearable. To be sure, this experience is extraordinarily delicate. An inadequate interpretation throws us all too easily back to the painful awareness of empty, twelvetone shards of sound which no longer reveal anything of their spiritual-musical origin. In their atonal unrelatedness they are then little more than dead noise.

But why does twelvetone atonality destroy the harmonic relationships *between* the tones? For the very reason that it wants to force the musical awareness *into* the single tone. Admittedly, no composer has put it in quite these terms, so far as we know. They tend to speak more of wanting to achieve a weightless suspension, an independence of the tones from one another, i.e. they speak more about what happens *in between* the tones. But in twelvetone music it is just this 'in-between' that has become a musical-harmonic vacuum. Listening to a strict, twelvetone composition, for example, one should (according to composer-theorist Eimert) never experience the fifth as an harmonic relationship, but merely as the pure spatial distance of seven halftones. What seems to be going on in this music is that something is trying to happen *within* the tone itself—that each individual tone wants to be experienced as a 'root tone' whose melodic and harmonic ramifications remain unheard and transcendent.

Rudolf Steiner believed that a yet to be developed feeling for the prime and for the single tone would even make it possible to enter into the musically and harmonically non-related, composite components of a noise and experience something musical in them.[94] In the same context Steiner contrasts the perception of the 'tonal spirit' immanent in a single tone with the perception of its outer surface. The new prime experience of our era seems to be a post-*Kali Yuga* revival of an ancient form of musical experience, a transmuted form of the primal experience of noise that we described earlier (see p. 7). The ancient music composed of noises was founded on a feeling for the transcendent tonal spirits in sounds. This revival surfaces most obviously in contemporary attempts to equate music with noise and physical sound, although the required artistic consciousness is lacking. The creative musician has to do more than just submit the listener to untransformed outer sounds. The hearable tones have to be shaped musically so that the resulting form reveals the unhearable reality that exists at the heart of the single tones. And, up to now, it has only been possible to express the unhearable aspect of music through a minimum of two tones—through intervalic relationships.

We can observe how resolute impulses to spiritually intensify music arose with the dawning of the Light Age in the 20th century. But materialism has worked its way so deeply into our very modes of perception over the course of centuries that these new impulses are misunderstood time and time again and the misunderstandings have led to their being twisted into directly opposite impulses. Twelvetone music carries one of these impulses to spiritualize music, an especially strong one. Nowadays it is usually viewed as a detour that music already has lived through, but the significance of twelvetone music for the future has not yet even been recognized. This music ushers the Light Age into the arena. It is a music that makes a giant leap towards a future when musical consciousness will be based on experience of the prime. In it, the cosmic, cyclic principles take up their abode in the inner chambers of the human soul.

The problem of the third, which carries earthly, radial forces, is one of the still unsolved problems of our modern music. Did the dawning of the Light Age really terminate the epoch of the third, a mere five or six hundred years after it had begun? Notwithstanding the frequency with which this view has been propounded in colleges of music and in musical congresses, the musical realities decisively contradict it: for people today, the roots of musical experience are in the experience of the third, whether the person in question is musically 'educated' or musically 'untrained'. The third is, and remains, the interval of our age. I have tried to show how today's consciousness of the third still is like a green fruit, one that needs a long time yet to ripen.

Glancing back at the schema on p. 59, which shows the relation of the seven intervals to the seven post-Atlantean cultural epochs, we can draw comfort from the thought that the third belongs to the entirety of our fifth post-Altlantean epoch, which extends to the middle of the fourth Christian millenium. Projecting ourselves into the era following this one, we can vaguely picture an age of the second, which finally is followed by an age of the prime. What the schema cannot show, though, is something that is always occurring, namely the persistence of the older, superceded stages of development alongside of anticipations of impulses that still belong to the future. This is especially true of the way things are developing in our age, when all the stages of historical development seem to be thrown together and active at the same time. Twelvetone music, anticipating the distant future, introduces elements from the age of the prime into the music of the age of the third. Such an anticipation is both necessary and dangerous. It is *necessary* in order to help 20th century music over the barrier of materialism. The third never could accomplish this on its own, for it is too earthy and too 'subjectivizing.' But the anticipation is also *dangerous* because such an incursion from the future undermines the present stage of development so that the real tasks of the present can too easily be forgotten. The task of the present lies in the third—in its spiritualization and its further development. Until this task has been fulfilled no other real future is possible.

Nevertheless, the quest for a rebirth of third-consciousness requires us to take up twelvetone music's spiritualizing impulse with its anticipation of the prime experience of the future and this must be done with a sense of deep inner commitment and affirmation. When, starting out from our present day third consciousness, we really feel our way into twelvetone music, it leads us to an experience of death. This death is the 'needle's eye' we have to pass through to attain the music of the future. It is the spiritual region through which the musicians of the future and of the present must find their way, the inner region of mystic transformation and recasting. According to Chinese legend, it was a mythical bird, the Phoenix, that brought the ancient inspiration which established the cycle of the twelve absolute *Liu* as a cosmic-spiritual principle of their music. (Pfrogner calls these the twelve 'tone-locations'; German, '*Tonorte*'. See *Lebendige Tonwelt*.) Ancient legends also recount how the Phoenix is consumed by fire only to be born anew out of its own ashes. Wolfram von Eschenbach takes up the image of the Phoenix (Chinese, 'fong') to characterize the Holy Grail's power to transform and renew.[95]

We have seen how the powers of the cycle of twelve were drawn in from the cosmic, superhuman widths of the circle of fifths and compressed into the narrow confines of a single octave. They sacrificed themselves out of love for earthly radiality and were consumed in the fires of leading-tone harmony. At last only ashes remained—the series of twelve halftones

156

which furnishes the starting point for atonal, twelvetone music: twelve "dead, tempered tones on a keyboard" (Pfrogner), tones whose power to transform themselves into the most varied 'tonal values' (c, b #, d^{bb}, etc.) has died out. These twelve are the slag thrown off by the musical life of the *Kali Yuga*, which had been built on the principle of the twelve. Twelvetone music begins with the death of the old, but it also creates the possibility of a new spiritual birth by introducing the prime consciousness of the future into music. On the one hand, musical life has died out in the realm of the senses; the "dead tones of the keyboard" are all that is left to be heard. On the other hand, the restrictions of that dead, spatial world which is the world of the senses and whose natural law is the law of twelvefoldness, have been overcome and the creative, cosmic archetype of the twelve can begin to illuminate the inner world of the human soul.

Twelvetone music tests us by dismembering us. It involves us in a sundering of spirit and soul, which is a test otherwise only experienced after death, as the 'weighing of the soul.' It makes it mercilessly clear how much our soul still is a captive of the senses and to what extent it already is spiritually self-sustaining. Everything that is dependent on the senses is condemned to death and nothingness. Everything spiritual is released from the sensory bonds that lame it. It seems inevitable that people of the future will distinguish music that has gone through twelvetone music's process of "dying and becoming " (and the prime experience) from music that has remained untransformed and still is music in the old sense. By no means does this imply that all music of the future must be twelvetone music. The future will surely produce a music more beautiful and more spiritually alive than twelvetone music. But a precondition of this music to come is a real inner passage through the trials of twelvetone music. So the third consciousness of our age also must submit to the twelvetone death and resurrection in order that the third can become not only the most human and earthly interval, but also the first spiritually alive interval of the Light Age.

One of the most significant twelvetone, atonal works is Alban Berg's violin concerto (1936). It accompanies the suffering of the radial, earthly, soulful third in its passage through death, and it sustains and shapes that suffering artistically. The destiny of this concerto is bound up with that of a dying young woman. As it still was being composed, it became her requiem. This is indicative of the essential nature of the work. For, as the modern age began, the archetypally feminine, earthly, radial forces began to blossom in the consciousness of the third. But before they can become fruitful and give birth to the true music of the Light Age, music embodying an objective, spiritual, earthly consciousness, even the most beautiful of these blossoms must endure death. In the "Allegretto" of Berg's requiem violin concerto, he plaits an Alpine yodeling tune into the twelvetone texture which itself has chromatic, or polytonal, strands with many fifths and thirds. The yodeling tune is typical of those of the 18th and 19th centuries in its dependence on cadential functions and on dominant seventh chords with their cyclic leading-tones, but, in the last analysis, such a melody originates in the chthonic, radial stream of humanity, the stream of the shepherds (see p. 42f.). The score contains the direction *"come una pastorale"* for this passage:

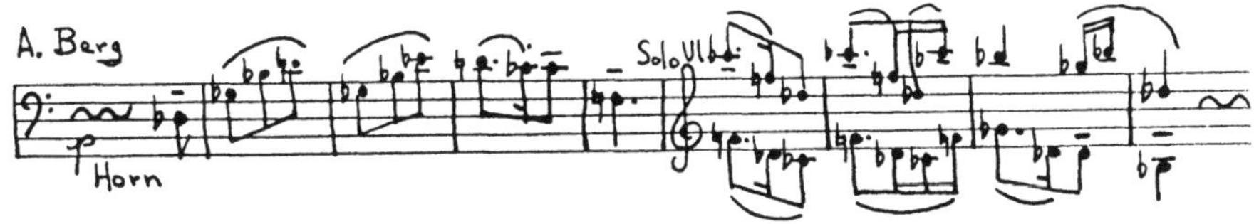

Deeply moved, we feel in Berg's work how the third, with its earthly inwardness of soul, is led to its twelvetone death. In the following "Allegro", music itself seems to have died. The atonally developed chorale of the final section has trombone passages which sound as if they speak from beyond the threshold of death.

Stravinsky characterized Webern's music as "cut diamonds." The 'crystalline heavens' already have become an inner reality of the soul in his music, a reality that corresponds to an advanced

stage of the experiences following death. The archetypal experience conveyed by Alban Berg's
works is a different one. It is the shattering of all that is earthly, the loss of earthly orientation
and the feeling of being a 'solid citizen,' the loss of the bonds of nature, the bonds of blood
and the bonds of love. Both he and Webern were students of Schoenberg. Berg, however,
is a composer of the *third*, albeit of a third which has to undergo death, whereas Webern is
a composer of the *prime*. Both are servants of the dawning Light Age, the one more from
the aspect of the present, the other more from the aspect of the future.

We have to thank another composer of the early 20th century, Béla Bartók, for carrying an
entirely different but equally important impulse for the future into our music. If we search
his work for an underlying tendency and also follow him on his path as an artist. we find
that, at least in part, he is a composer of the *second*. As regards the outline of musical development, second experience precedes that of the prime and thus is closer to our time. It is the
interval of a consciousness typical of the coming cultural epoch, the sixth post-Atlantean epoch,
which Rudolf Steiner describes as being carried particularly by the Slavic peoples. Thus Bartók
was drawing from a musical impulse that lies deep at the roots of the Slavic and Magyar folk.

The text of Bartók's *Cantata Profana* (1930) is based on a fairy tale from Siebenburgen,
"The Enchanted Stags." He called this work his "most personal declaration of faith". It is
a quintessence of the side of his artistic development that draws upon these Slavic sources.[96]

Immediately following the prelude, the entrance of a double choir of tenors and basses makes
it clear that one is entering the mysterious world of the second. (The currently stylish, catch-
all term 'tone cluster' does not convey very much of what is going on in this passage.) An
old man elicits the fairy tale from out of this tone-world of whispering seconds (compare
p. 53). His sons, he reveals, once went hunting. They wandered deeper and deeper into the
forest, until at last they crossed over a bridge and went completely astray and were transformed
into stags. Remember how the feeling of the second has been characterized as a kind of 'forest'
— it is an interval which submerges one in the life forces, dimming consciousness to the state
of deep dream (p. 61). The father has been searching for his sons and found them transformed
into stags. But he cannot bring them home with him because they have been wholly absorbed
into the realm of nature. The 'good mother' waits alone, at home, sitting by the table she has
laid for them, but their antlers are too large to pass through the door of the house. This is
the incipient tragedy of the second, the tragedy of wanting and needing to submerge oneself
in the natural realm ruled by Pan, the realm of the life forces. Formerly, these forces belonged
to the realm of the 'good mother,' but they no longer are what they used to be. (The inherent
threat leading to this tragedy is to be set against the dangers inherent in twelvetone music,
whose anticipation of prime experience threatens music either with death or with a flight into
the cosmos that would remove it from everything that is connected with Earth and with nature.)
Ever since music passed its great turning point and entered the realm of the third, the 'good
mother' has been living as a force within the individual soul. She waits, '*in* the house of the
father,' mourning her sons. They have lost their humanity and their egohood for the sake of
a natural existence beside the 'clear stream ' where they can live a sorrowless life, free from
the weight of destiny and the weight of error:

158

In this passage, Bartók uses the scale he discovered as the scale of the Maramuresian bagpipes. It is the same scale that we discovered at the roots of our earthly musical development (p. 59f.), the ancient, nature-related, Dionysian scale with its series of seconds that are shaped in systematic accord with the radial, arithmetic series. The same scale appears in the last movement of Bartók's *Music for Strings, Percussion and Celeste* (1936), when the transformed chromatic fugue theme makes its triumphant entry. It is also to be found in *Microcosmos*, as well as in Debussy's *Isle Joyeuse*, which was written long before Bartók's time. There it conveys a joyful sense of natural existence. As Pfrogner has shown, the mirrored form of this scale, which is minor in mood and which corresponds to the ancient *aulos* scale, also plays a significant role in the *Cantata Profana*, as well as in other of Bartók's works.

One must add, however, that neither Bartók nor Debussy employed these scales in their pure intonation, which would have involved them in more-or-less quartertone divergences from our usual tonal system. As Pfrogner aptly expresses it, the scale appears in a form that has been "frozen" into the tempered system of twelve halftones.

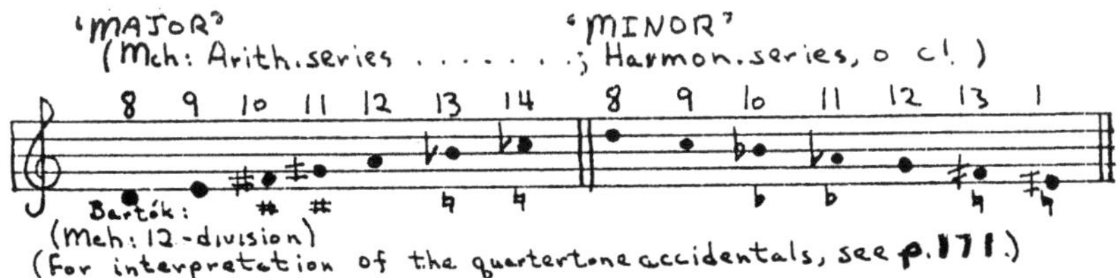

The twelvefold order of halftones forms a protective, limiting skin, making possible an individualized, objective consciousness of space and of objects. It is as though Debussy and Bartók were not yet willing to undergo the fate of Marsyas and have their skins torn from them. That would have been the only way they could have really entered fully into that world of the second alluded to in their music, the Dionysian, nature-bound realm of the life-forces. Consequently their relationship to the realm of the second still is burdened by the weight of the *Kali Yuga* and by the old twelve that have not yet been through the tempering fires of twelvetone atonality.

The foregoing by no means implies an artistic fault in the music of Debussy or Bartók. On the contrary, the only possibility of entering this Dionysian world of the second while still leaving the listener free was to proceed indirectly. For this world of divine, life-bearing forces also has the power to bewitch, as was well known in the old mysteries (compare p. 89f). An indirect approach was the only artistic option. The radial powers of the second had to be approached as Perseus approached Medusa: by catching their reflection in one's shield, i.e. by reflecting them in the Apollonian system of twelve halftones which protects the individual's self-awareness. Schiller would have called this sort of an artistic relationship with the world 'sentimentalistic' (not 'sentimental'!).[97] As a representative of the sphere of Roman influence, Debussy conveys more of the Classical world's longing for beauty. He enjoyed contemplating the magically vibrant world of colors that is reflected on the surface of this mirror. But Bartók hails from the East European world of the Slav and Magyar peoples. His choice of text for his "declaration of faith" shows that, for all his longing for nature, his soul is profoundly aware of the bewitching might and the dark, unredeemed forces that are encountered in the natural realms of Pan.

It would be one-sided to present Bartók's and Debussy's musical worlds exclusively from the point of view of how they employ the scale of seconds. The scale only occurs in particularly distinctive passages in Bartók; in Debussy, the composition just mentioned is the only example known to me. It has already been mentioned how the confluence of all the history of music is typical of the dawning of the Light Age and one finds this far-flung meeting of musical past and musical future in both of these composers' work. For both of them, a pentatonic that is free of all halftones is a major structural element —and Wagner had already used it in the "Waldweben" scene of *Siegfried*. Debussy was particularly influenced by an encounter with the Slendro music of an Indonesian orchestra at the World Fairs of 1889 and 1900[98]; Bartók was especially influenced by his research into the music of the Hungarian peasants. Intimations of the Persian scale of sixths reach Debussy through Spain, where the Moors had injected it into the culture; Bartók found the 'gypsy scale' in the folk music of southern Europe, which had been influenced directly from the East. In the music of both composers one finds the Greek and Medieval ('church') modes playing a large role; the inevitable third and the triad are important, as well; one also finds the scale of seconds just mentioned, along with a strong feel for the experience of the second in general; and, finally, there are elements of prime experience which give their music an affinity with twelve-tone atonality—a subject which surely could be developed in greater detail for both composers.[99] With different points of emphasis, the works of Debussy and Bartók actually contain the whole of human musical development.

One must emphasize the fact that this marvelous panorama of musical development only appears to the extent that it can be mirrored in the twelve tempered halftones; Debussy does not really enter the realm of the Slendro seventh, even though he had encountered it directly, nor does Bartok employ the over-sized seconds of the 'gypsy scale' or the real scale of seconds, even though his research into folk music had made him well acquainted with both. We spoke of a 'sentimentalistic' relationship to the natural forces at play in the scale of seconds, which is the Dionysian scale that harbors forces essential to the future of post-*Kali Yuga* humanity. The same sentimentalistic relationship was necessary with regard to the musical-spiritual spheres embodied in other pre-*Kali Yuga* scales: the Slendro scale and the 'gypsy' scale.

Schiller uses the term 'sentimentalistic' to characterize the situation of the artist who no longer simply stands in the midst of the realities of life and nature, participating in their immediacy and creating directly as an extension of this participation. Instead, sentimentalistic artistic creation is the result of 'reflection'. Its source is in the individual artists and in the ideal pictures of nature and life that they have had to create for themselves because their age puts them in a natural and spiritual surrounding that has nothing more to give them. For Schiller, Greek culture marks the end of 'naive' art. Thereafter, art ceased to be born out of a natural harmony between art and life—with the exception of a few artists whom Schiller calls 'late-born strangers,' who 'run amok in their own age.' [100]

As regards music, the beginning of the 'sentimentalistic' age can be set at that point where feeling for the third begins, in other words at what we have called the point of the great turning in musical consciousness. From this time on the starting point of all artistic activity and intellectual activity lies in the inner world of the active human being. Musical experience would be 'naive', in Schiller's sense of the word, if seventh-consciousness or sixth-consciousness were conjured up in order to draw people wholly out of themselves and transport them directly into the spiritual region that lies behind outwardly perceived nature and, as well, at the source of their own soul-life. Formerly, people only were able to sing when they were able to establish an intimate union with this spirituality — it breathed through them, so to speak. Their singing was wholly 'naive'. When, at the beginning of the *Kali Yuga*, people began to acquire fifth-consciousness and find an inner footing, music still continued to transport them to regions outside of themselves. In the following periods, during which fourth-consciousness and third-consciousness developed, there was increasing isolation from the outer world and its inherent spirituality, and people were increasingly exiled to their own inner world. Experience of the outer world can only be sentimentalistic in Schiller's sense when third-consciousness develops; when people begin to experience themselves exclusively within the bounds of their own personal, inner soul-world. Someone whose capacity for awareness has developed this far has attained the goal of the *Kali Yuga*.

Meanwhile, a naive artistic approach has been preserved in the old stream of the shepherds' and peasants' music, which is a Dionysian, radial stream. The force impelling this music continued to be a pagan bond with the spirit of a nature—a bond undisturbed by individual self-awareness and free from all artistic 'reflection.' It is known that as a child Bartók did not feel any special connection with the folk music that was around him. As a modern artist, however, he bore the burden of reflection and individual loneliness, the burden of the *Kali Yuga*, and he longed for the naiveté of this music and for the spiritual reality he could sense at work in it. There was a widespread outbreak of such longing at the end of the 19th century and it increased as the 20th century began to unfold: the longing for the naive musical awareness that had been preserved in folk music. Even though this longing did not always lead to such palpable results as in the case of Bartók, the impulse, nevertheless, is clearly attributable to the dawning of the Light Age. It is the impulse to break out of the confines of artistic activity that is based on merely personal, inner reflection, and to find once more a direct path to a spiritual reality. This is a search for 'naive' experience in a *new* sense—the folk music movement only seems to be preoccupied with the past.

Schoenberg's goal was fundamentally the same, only he sought direct musical access to spiritual experience along an entirely different path. He was unwilling to constemplate the past—at least not the tone-experience and interval-experience of the past. Thereby he let the future-bearing impulses of Dionysian, radial life slip by him, for these had already been active in the past. The result was that he was obliged to force music into the sphere of death in order to lead it to a concrete spiritual reality. Bartók wanted to find musical access to spiritual reality by drawing from the stream of naive musical experience he had discovered, still living, in the folk music around him. But to a certain degree Bartók had to deaden this life and bind it in the fetters of the tempered, cyclic order of halftones. Otherwise the inwardness and Apollonian, clear self-awareness attained during the *Kali Yuga* would have been loosened and swept away on the tides of an overwhelmingly direct musical experience. In other words, Bartók had to bide his time. He could not separate himself entirely from the sentimentalistic attitude of the *Kali Yuga*.

There are a few passages in Bartók's works where he shifts to a quartertone intonation in an attempt to break through the rigid framework of tempered halftones. But the relationship of these passages to the scale of seconds is unclear—or perhaps not yet clarified. The same is true of similar passages in the work of that foremost among quartertone and sixth-tone composers, Alois Hába. Certainly both composers were led to such intonations through the inspiration of South European folk music. But over the course of centuries the most diverse and contrary impulses have met and combined in the music of these peoples: halftone pentatonic with oversized seconds (see the Transdanubian death lament, p. 71); the 'gypsy' scale, which also has oversized seconds in it (see p. 69f), as well as other structures of clearly Arabic origin; and, alongside of these cyclic, oriental influences, the radial scale of seconds, whose Dionysian sources are to be sought in Greece. It should not surprise us that the quartertone and sixth-tone intonations one sometimes finds in this music are not always easy to trace back to clear and unequivocal musical relationships. For one must reckon with the fact that the confusing, enchanted mist from Arabia had swept over Southeast Europe long enough to blur all contrast between musical forces of the future and those of the past. Furthermore, Hába sometimes even used elements borrowed from atonality in his quartertone compositions, even though there is no greater contradiction imaginable than that between atonality in Schoenberg's sense and the quasi-quartertone, radial intonation required for the intervals based on 7, 11 and 13. To demonstrate this is a principal aim of the present study. (On the other hand, Hába very much felt that his technique of composition was confirmed by Schlesinger's discoveries—probably more because of the *aulos* scales' quartertone and sixthtone divergences from the halftone system than because of their tonality based on seconds.)

In what follows I want to appeal to the listener by way of a concrete musical example in order to clarify the contradiction between the principle by which tones are ordered in halftones, and the quasi-quartertone intonation of the purely intoned scale of seconds. This will shed light on the comtemporary problem of the so-called 'irrational' intonations and the problem of expanding our tone system. It would be best to use the monochord to retune a piano or spinet to the arithmetically intoned 'major' scale of seconds so that the f-key is tuned to tone 11, the a^b-key to tone 13, and the b-key so that it plays 14. For tones 9, 10 and 12, the tempered tones d, e, and g can remain as they are without their causing any problems. Thus prepared, one can play the following bagpipe tune at a reasonable tempo (ca.d = 120) more easily than on the monochord.

161

Afterwards, one should play the same melody with the normal half-tone intonation, using the usual, unaltered tones, f#, a and b^b, for 11, 13 and 14—in other words, modifying the scale of seconds in the way that Bartók modified it.

It is clearly discernable how the first version leads our feelings into a natural realm. Listening to it, we can almost catch the very scent of earth and sheep. (Nor is this merely a matter of association—how many Westerners like ourselves have ever heard a bagpipe play in this intonation?!) This music is not particularly beautiful, but it has a strong, masterful life of its own, and a lack of inhibition that begins to feel compulsive once the newness has worn off. After a while one feels a threat to one's own inner freedom. Every commitment and every kindness feels beside the point; whatever confronts us confronts us straight on. without any regard for our personal feeling. Consequently there is neither the sense of self-conscious—or even shameless—audacity, nor is there the contrary feeling of embarrassment or shame. Even when played more slowly, the melody leaves no time for reflection or passive contemplation; nor is there the feeling of active joy typical of rhythmically accentuated major melodies. On the other hand, we can feel unimagined depths being uncovered in our own inner world, even though we are not experiencing ourselves as masters of this realm. In order to harmonize with such a world either we have to regress to the state of being immersed in nature or else we have to expand and purify our individuality to such a degree that it can encompass the absoluteness and the necessity of nature without our losing our own moral freedom or our supernatural being. Either we must become a faun or else we must become wise—wise, not with the knowledge the head yields but with a wisdom that springs from a perfection of the heart and from a capacity for action.

The tempered version of the melody sounds fundamentally more cultivated, more 'polite', as compared with the rude profanity of the first version. It is better formed and expresses a brighter consciousness. It keeps itself at a certain distance from us so that it can be observed and enjoyed more from without, from a safe distance. Its tones stand in clearly defined, spatial relationship to one another rather than flowing into one another as in the first version. Especially interesting is the way the unaltered tones, c, d, e, g, which fit within the framework of tempered halftones, completely accommodate themselves to both versions: in one case they have neatly defined boundaries, in the other they flow into one another. In the first version the tone 11 (f↑) draws them into the radial stream of seconds, 8 : 9 : 10 : 11 : 12, thus leading us to experience the *relationship* of all the seconds between each pair of tones. In the second version the halftone g—f# immediately shatters these connections, forcing the tones to stand *separately*, side by side, rather than interweaving with one another. The second, tempered version speaks more to the side of experience that is conscious, individualized and influenced by analytical understanding, and less to the darker world of the emotions with its deep forebodings.

The contrast between these two differently intoned versions of a little bagpipe melody also expresses the contrast between the clear daylight of head-centered consciousness and half-conscious to totally unconscious dream states with which we submerge in the life-forces. In *The Archetypes of the Collective Unconscious* we find that modern discoverer and explorer of the subconscious, C.G.Jung, saying, ''The unconscious is the psyche that reaches down from the daylight of mentally and morally lucid consciousness into the nervous system that for ages has been known as the 'sympathetic.' This does not govern perception and muscular activity

162

like the cerebrospinal system and thus control the environment; but, through functioning without sense organs, it maintains the balance of life and, through the mysterious paths of sympathetic excitation, not only gives us knowledge of the innermost life of other beings but also has an inner effect upon them. In this sense it is an extremely collective system, the operative basis of all *participation mystique*, whereas the cerebrospinal function reaches its high point in separating off the specific qualities of the ego and only apprehends surfaces and externals—always through the medium of space. It experiences everything as an outside, whereas the sympathetic system experiences everything as an inside.'[101]

Especially as regards artistic experience, it would be more helpful to speak of the contrast between *super*consciousness and *sub*consciousness, rather than of consciousness and unconsciousness as Jung does. Jung's own description makes it clear that the 'unconscious' is a form of consciousness, albeit a more muted and night-like form than our normal day-consciousness. Furthermore, we know that it interpenetrates our day-consciousness in such a way that the health of our soul-life wholly depends on it—on the sort of foundation our superconscious has in our subconscious. Like a ship, our superconscious floats on the sea of our subconscious and it is constantly influenced by that sea. Our really creative ideas always flow to us from the subconscious. Without them, our superconscious could only move automatically, revolving within itself in closed, logical circles.

Artistic activity always involves the reconciliation and the inward union of these two levels of consciousness—and this is especially true of music. Herein lies the source of the real hygienic and therapeutic power of art. And so, once more we confront what Goethe called the intensification of a polarity which makes possible the existence of something higher—that higher thing being, in the present case, the true central point of the human soul, the self. For the self is not to be found either in the daylight of superconsciousness or in the dark waves of the subconscious.

When Jung speaks of the superconscious as "separating off the specific qualities of the ego," he is referring to the specific *form* of the individuality, which is experienced as strictly marked-off from everything that is 'not-I.' This is the work of the cosmic, centripetal, Apollonian forces (see p. 86f.), whose physiological expression is the cerebro-spinal nervous system. As Rudolf Steiner often mentioned, the ancients referred to this system as 'The Lyre of Apollo.' But the creative *fullness* of the self has to be sought elsewhere. The capacity of the self to radiate outward, to break through the boundaries of selfhood into 'the Other' and unite with the Other—this has to be sought in the subconscious, in the telluric, centrifugal, Dionysian powers whose physiological expression is the streaming, pulsating blood system. Jung is pointing to this same distinction, but as it is expressed again in the nervous system itself as the polarity between the sympathetic and cerebro-spinal systems. Expressed in the whole human form, it is the contrast between nerve and blood.

Since art, and music in particular, always involves the marriage of the two levels of consciousness, it never can originate in merely one of them, nor can it be at home if it is restricted to merely one level. Art can never be exclusively logic and self-assured clarity, never exclusively *participation mystique* But, drawing on a middle, intensified state, it can lean more to one side or the other. Thus the intonation of the first version of our example tilts it noticeably toward the subconscious side of musical experience: the delimiting, self-aware side of superconsciousness retreats so that we can enter more intensively into the tones, experiencing their inner aspect and inner qualities. All is focused on their interconnections; each tone reveals its inner nature, its particular coloration and plenitude in the way it interweaves with the other tones... 'through the mysterious paths of sympathy' one could well say, borrowing Jung's phrase.

This mysterious agency is based on nothing other than a musical experience of the simple, direct, numerical relations between the tones. For example, if I hear c—b♭↓ as a natural seventh 7/4, the c also is filled with the musical quality of 7; the 7 is not conveyed by the b♭↓ merely on its own. If my starting point is the harmonic relationship rather than the arithmetic, then it would be possible for the b♭↓ to carry the character of 4, and the c that of 7. When they interweave each reveals its inner quality by way of the other—through sympathy. The numerical relationships embodied in the scale of seconds lead us to experience this inward, qualitative mutual revelation between tone and tone. In the presence of such an intense,colorful inner life, the outer, spatial ordering of the tones is almost entirely forgotten.

With the second version of our example the situation is different, for now we are hearing an intonation based on halftones. To be sure, our impulse still is to enter 'inwardly' into the tones. But the numerical-harmonic leveling brought about by tempering also camouflaged the tones or, perhaps better said, 'imprisoned' them. Because they all originate in the circle of fifths, the only thing that weaves between them, other than the octave relationship, is the prime number three and its powers. Thus, all the tones seem to have more or less the same inner quality. Even though a consciousness that is sensitive to thirds will be aware of qualities originating in five intermingied with those of the prime number three, there is no five relationship in the system of twelve that is not diluted by potencies of three—all the more so when the twelve are tempered. To be sure, when two tones, say c and b^b, are compared with regard to their respective places in the chain of fifths, c turns out to have a brighter, higher quality, and b^b to have a darker and deeper quality. But this can not be compared with the contrasting inner qualities we have just been discussing, qualities reflecting direct, simple numerical relationships. The characterization of the experiences as 'bright-high' and 'dark-low' already indicates that the qualities originate in the comparative positions in the chain of fifths, not in the inner nature of the tones themselves or in the way they interweave. Naturally, there still is a living relationship between tones of the chain of fifths when seven of them form a tonality, as in Bartók's scale. If, instead of these tones, we were to compare the individual tones of an atonal, twelve-tone melody (as found, for example, in the passage from Webern. p. 152) with the scale of seconds, we would find a markedly greater isolation and spatial definition. A twelvetone row is the polar opposite of the scale of seconds: the one has a maximum individuation and isolation of tones, the other. a maximum interconnectedness from second to second; tonal relationships are extinct in the one, in the other there is the greatest possible life in the tonal relationships.

Two things are particularly important for our contemporary musical situation: the first challenge is to find a way that leads beyond our system of twelve tones which is so predominantly a creation of a head-centered, daytime consciousness. This system and the musical awareness it embodies are a product of the human development that took place during the *Kali Yuga*. During the course of this development people became more and more exclusively head-oriented and more and more isolated from spiritual reality. We will remain captives of the *Kali Yuga* until the tyranny of the system of twelve has been overcome. The numerical relationships of this system are restricted to the *senarius;* since ancient times, earthbound consciousness has been associated with these numbers—no further comment should be necessary for anyone who has followed the exposition this far. When Hindemith, in *The Craft of Musical Composition*, makes the observation—one I have often referred to—to the effect that there is a 'holy domain' of 'mystical' numerical relationships that lies beyond the limits of the *senarius*, he is intuitively pointing to a truth that is deeper than he himself is able to measure. He believes that this realm is "inaccessible to tonal experience." I maintain, however, that it is a demand of the Light Age that we enter this holy region and master it artistically. Everything about us today points toward the necessity of our freeing ourselves from the limitations of a consciousness that is merely head-oriented reflection, and toward the necessity of our achieving direct perception of spiritual reality. Otherwise we will remain bound to the now decadent—and decaying—forces of the *Kali Yuga*. The discovery of the subconscious by Depth Psychology is only a head-oriented gesture in the right direction. A modern, scientific head does not know how to deal seriously with this spiritual reality. In our post-*Kali Yuga* period, anything that has to do exclusively with the forces of the head turns into a materialistically interpreted, illusionary structure, be it ever so spiritually real.

The second important challenge of our age is to find or build a bridge leading from the daytime consciousness of the *Kali Yuga* to a newly realized 'subconscious.' But to naively submerge the Apollonian gifts of clear individuation, logic and moral consciousness in the ocean of mystic, unconscious 'participation' would be a one-sided regression to those very states of human development that were overcome during the *Kali Yuga*. Musically, this would involve an exclusive concentration on experiencing the interweaving of tones in the scale of seconds, so that the 'mystic' intervals based on 7, 11 and 13 would throw us, excarnated, far beyond the limits of our individual, earthly consciousness. Appealing as that might seem at first glance, our example already has shown us how such a musical experience ultimately leads into something compulsive and unfree and, for the humanity of today, inartistic. Every step by which we transcend our normal, daytime consciousness must originate in the clarity and freedom of an individualized superconsciousness. To be sure, it is clear that this consciousness must be transformed before it can enter the realms of the subconscious, and also that the result should not be a confused mixture of the two levels of consciousness. Rudolf Steiner built such a bridge—it is another example of the Goethean-style intensification of a polarity. He did so in his unique exploration of what he called the Anthroposophical path to knowledge and spiritual experience. The corresponding bridge has not yet been built for an artistic-musical consciousness or for our tone system. In the case of music one also must set out from the clear, individualized consciousness that is supported by the system of twelve halftones. Shortly, I will discuss the few pointers that Steiner gave regarding the need to expand our tone system.

We have recognized a full-fledged polar opposition between the two sorts of interval experience that flow into our present-day music from the future: the experience of the prime and of the second. When we are able to come to really deep experience of the prime in atonal, twelvetone music, we will be completely drawn into ourselves. If we were inwardly capable of following this experience to its ultimate completion—something that is hardly possible yet— we would experience the center of the cosmos within us. (compare p. 62). Everything contrary to the integrity of selfhood, everything not centered on our own innermost, spiritual nucleus, would be consumed in the fire of such an experience and would fall away. Second experience is entirely different. The scale of seconds leads us to a deepened second experience that would surround us with an ocean of life in which we would feel ourselves expanded and woven into the endlessly rich fabric of nature with all its mysterious harmonies. Whereas the prime leads us to a death experience, to a crystallization in our innermost core, the second expands and dissolves us in the unbounded life and ceaseless growth of the periphery.

People as they are at the beginning of the Light Age, earth-bound inheritors of third consciousness, cannot yet maintain themselves in either of these spheres of experience. The one requires that they become naked spirit divested of all earthly garment and belonging nowhere on earth; the other requires them to abandon their own cosmic inner center, the crystal sphere of their cosmic self, and dissolve into the life-stream of nature (which, to be sure, also is of cosmic origin in the last analysis). The only solution possible lies in uniting the centering, systolic death-forces of the prime with the unfolding, diastolic life-forces of the second, thus creating a musical breathing process. The two can be united in a breathing in which prime forces determine the systole and rhythmically alternate with a dyastole determined by forces of the second: just as we concentrate our consciousness and enter more into the daylight of the head-sphere when we breathe in and then relax when we breathe out, sinking into more dreamlike, dimly-lit widths.

Thus today's music must find a new way of uniting the cyclic and radial principles. What ultimately stands behind twelvetone atonality's prime experience is the centering, cyclic principle—modern twelvetone music is its youngest child. The centrifugal, radial principle comes to purest expression in the scale of seconds. We should recall that it was the third that brought about the first true musical marriage of radial and cyclic powers. So in binding these principles to each other again we are reviving the task of the third, which meanwhile has fallen victim to the 20th century conflagration of the dawning Light Age—not, however, by restoring the third to its previous state, but in an entirely new way that leads toward the future. For the earlier, classical marriage was accomplished by the cadence, in which both the old, cyclic system based on fifths and fourths, and the radial system of thirds or triads, played a part. In their new union, the cyclic forces rule the twelvetone system of primes while the radial forces rule the seven-membered scale of seconds. It will become so apparent that the original founder and inaugurator of the cosmic-telluric unification of cyclic and radial forces, namely the third, still has such an affinity for its work that it will become the unquestionable ruler of this new dwelling that is built out of the forces of the future. The third is *the* bridge between the world of halftones, whose order is primarily cyclically determined, and the world of quasi-quartertone intonation that is required by the purely radial principle of seconds. So it turns out that our contemporary, third-oriented consciousness is just the right soil for a fruitful development of the two contrasting forces of the future that are embodied in the prime and second. And here they can develop side by side, in harmony.

Because of Rudolf Steiner's premature death, plans for a music conference on the theme of the experience of the single tone and expansion of our tone system never were realized. But the few, brief comments he did make on this theme all point in the direction I have been suggesting. Thus, on September 29, 1920, in answering a question that was put to him he said that an expansion of the tone system only makes sense in conjunction with a concrete experience of the single tone.[102] He elaborated this comment on the following days, clearly implying that the 'melody' which one should learn to hear in the single tone is experienced independent of the element of time.

Thus it is a pure, inner experience that Steiner is talking about, an experience that does not involve anything that is outwardly audible except for the one tone. In other words, the 'melody' in question is not very much like a usual melody. Steiner also says that if we "expand" this time-free, quasi-melodic experience "in time," then "we will be able to capture this melody, but only if we have a different tone system." Speaking of the same process, he said, somewhat earlier, "...here one encounters tones that are not to be found in today's tone system. And I believe that in this way we will come to see the necessity of expanding our tone system." In a later discussion on January 5, 1922, Steiner said, further, "...when we have come to that point of experiencing a melody in what today is experienced as a single tone, then it will be necessary to make certain modifications in our scale for the simple reason that the intervals will need to be filled out in varied ways, in more varied ways than one has assumed up to now. They will be filled out more concretely. And then—so I believe—we will once more be able to find a connection with certain elements of what I would call 'primal music' [German 'Urmusik'], important aspects of which I believe can be found in the modes discovered by Miss Schlesinger."[103] We have seen that the *aulos* scales discovered by Kathleen Schlesinger are one form—the 'minor' form—of a scale that is systematically built on the radial principle of seconds. On pages 52 and 60 I tried to indicate why Steiner would have viewed them as elements of a primal music.

Taken together, these comments from Steiner lead to the following conclusions: the melody that can be experienced in the single tone is inaudible and is not bound up with time. This is what we have described as the real experience of the prime (the systole), through which one tone comes to embody a transcendent musical nature that either has passed through the threshold of death or else is not yet born. Subsequently this inaudible 'melody' is expanded in time (the dyastole), and in so far as it thus is incarnate in audible music (or in the musical imagination), the melody seeks out tones belonging to the living stream of seconds. In this stream it becomes musically immanent. Thus, second experience helps the inaudible, spiritual experience to which the prime leads to be reborn in the realm of audible sound. Prime experience is the real musical *agens* of future, a 'father principle' of generation out of the spirit; second experience is a more serving, 'motherly-receptive', nourishing and life-giving, mediating principle of realization. Without her it would be impossible for inner richness and spiritual beauty to unfold in an artistic work.

* * *

This brings us to the limits of the present book's discussion of musical problems. This is where the real artistic work of today's musician begins, work that will furnish the substance for future discussions. Now that a certain overview of musical development up to the present has been presented, I would like at least to sketch some practical ways of working musically with the sort of expanded tone system that I have been describing—ways of musical practice and of composition.

What follows is based on the personal, artistic experiences of the author. These go back to 1959, in Paris, where Jean Louis Gaensburger first played Schlesinger's *aulos* scales for me on a monochord. That first encounter with the 'Schlesinger scales' eventually precipitated all that has been described in this book. But, I would like to emphasize, the artistic results that came of it were not primarily a product of the discoveries that have been discussed here—the purely musical discoveries generally preceeded the intellectual ones.

166

The following example is from some songs I composed in 1972 to texts by Hoelderlin. It should be mentioned that when I found myself led to the method of composition employed in these pieces I had as yet no idea that it was connected with the matters discussed in this book. Only gradually, in the course of the following years, did the significance of the aforementioned statements of Rudolf Steiner become clear to me. I do not care to have my way of composing understood as *the* way of composing that is in accordance with Steiner's indications. This would simply be putting obstacles in the way of those future composers who will be—and must be—much more capable of composing from out of experience of the prime. Those who have had some experience with Rudolf Steiner's statements know how they can provide the inspiration for the most varied forms of individual development: they point to what is most essential but, as a rule, they leave one free to choose how to work. Thus the following example is only meant as a stimulus and as a suggestion as to how someone might proceed in a direction that Steiner pointed out. The most important thing is the question, 'Where might I be led by this musical constellation formed of twelvetone elements and the scale of seconds?' Only pure musical hearing and musical experience can decide whether these two elements can work together, whether they belong together, or whether they must go separate ways—whether these two polar elements mutually intensify each other or whether they interfere with one another and necessarily break apart.

The pastoral mood of the text led to an extreme, diastolic broadening of the head of the twelvetone row (f♯ d e) in D Major. With the mention of "the fallow wheatfields" ("*wenn im falben Kornfeld*"), the remainder of the row appears in its naked, twelvetone form (systole), once more gathering together what has begun to dissolve into nature. Meanwhile, at "the growth rustles" ("*das Wachstum rauscht*"), the accompanying instrumental voices broaden out the last three tones of the row in F Major. In the passage cited, the A♭ Major section marks the place of the greatest relative musical concentration. In other songs in the Hoelderlin cycle (eg. "The Eagle"), the twelvetone row appears in its strict, contracted, atonal form as a sequence of primes, and then at other times it broadens out, metamorphosed by the influence of seconds. Naturally, these two possibilities have to be implanted in the row, or else the composer has to discover them.

(Text: "And sweet lime trees scent the air beside the beeches at midday when in the fallow wheatfield the growth rustles." For interpretation of the unusual accidentals, see p.171.)

The 'major' scales of seconds on d, b, a^b, and f have been worked into the twelvetone row contained in the vocal line: f# e d d# c# b c a^b b^b g a f:

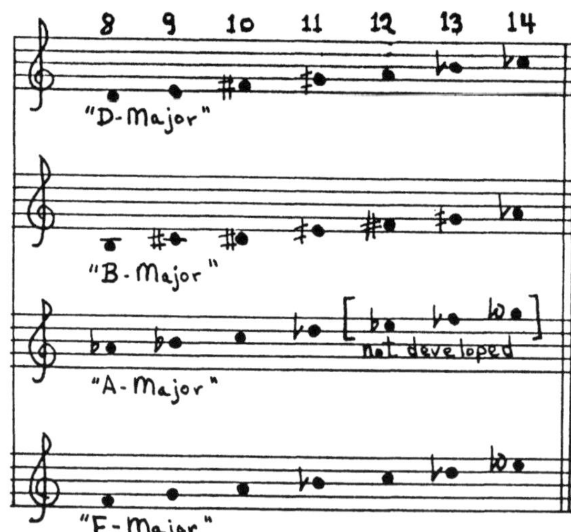

Perhaps my example shows already what other passages in the Hoelderlin cycle make even more clear—namely that this music has a natural affinity with experience of the third and the triad. Thus the D Major triad, d f# a, unmistakably underlies the first three tones that are sung: f# e d a. The triad tones emerge from the second-influenced D Major tonality of the instrumental introduction. Similarly, the descending B Major triad, f# d# b, is clearly heard and experienced when the voice sings the words, "*Mittags, wenn im*" ("at midday, when..."). Furthermore, the four different, second-based tonalities are separated from one another by small thirds.

It might be objected that, on the one hand, it is nothing new to bring tonal interpretation into twelvetone music (Alban Berg, for example, did this in the violin concerto mentioned earlier). And, on the other hand, from the very beginning, Schoenberg refused to discuss the question—raised by Webern, of all people!—whether his twelvetone method might be tonally interpreted.[104] One could plausibly argue that a tonal interpretation of a twelvetone row does nothing but water it down and compromise its real, atonal, twelvetone principle. I believe that Schoenberg was right to remove himself from this discussion. Although he does not speak it out in so many words, his purpose in finding the twelvetone principle was to dissolve the principle of tonality and clear the way for an absolute prime experience, not to find some way of putting together the old, established tonalities. In the case of Berg's work, the very dissolution of tonality into twelvefoldness is itself at the heart of the artistic expression. Those who do not follow Berg's example are, indeed, watering down prime experience when they introduce the old, triadic tonality into twelvetone music.

But tonalities based on seconds and the triads they generate are another matter altogether. Immediate artistic experience teaches one the difference. The scale of seconds has entirely different principles from those of the old tonality, which is half cyclic and is related to a chromatic tonal order. Standing behind the scale of seconds are radiality as regards tone production and a quartertone system as regards the distance relation of its tones. These are entirely different principles from those that order the twelve, so neither is in danger of being watered down by the other. In contrast to the old tonality which, from this point of view, is too closely related to the order of the twelve, the pure, radial scale of seven seconds stands in polar opposition to a pure, cyclic atonality with its twelve primes. Each is so strong, so indissoluble in the other, that both poles can remain active, even when their fields of force cross in a single tone. On the basis of my own experience I would even go so far as to claim that twelvetone atonality will never be able to reveal and fulfill itself until it enters into a 'breathing' encounter with the tonality of seconds which is its polar opposite. The much-discussed 'impossibility' of atonal hearing will be turned into a possibility when we have learned to swing back and

168

forth between a full-blooded, tonal dyastole and an atonal systole. So long as atonal music lacks this polarity its listeners will continue to search unconsciously for tonal connections— no matter how much care is spent in avoiding tonal allusions (and, artistically, this is a vexing problem in itself). These assertions, I realize, can only claim to be suggestions for those practicing musicians who want to work with this problem. Certainly the example I have given (which shows more the second-oriented side of the matter, anyhow) is no proof.

Along the path I have sketched, Schoenberg's twelvetone serial principle[105] can and will be progressively transformed until it finally will seem superfluous because the feeling for the absolute prime quality of the single tone has become so strongly established that it is enough in itself to support a sense of the process of 'dying and becoming' as it fluctuates between atonal contractions and tonal expansions. I believe that the only way to overcome the twelvetone principle and, ultimately, to discard it, is for it to be thoroughly assimilated into our art. Simply following the antipathy aroused by its nearness to death and to the lone intellect is no solution, nor is it any help to declare unilaterally that the twelvetone principle is no longer a live musical issue.

Practical experience has shown that the following exercise gives string players and singers an easy and natural way to acquaint themselves with the intonation of the scale of seconds. It develops the sequence of radial seconds out of a triad.

The exercise should first be taken in a rhythm which allows 9, 11, 14 and 13 to appear as short, unaccented 'passing tones':

A sense for the intonation of the new tones from the scale of seconds is most easily awakened in this gliding between the tones of a triad. One should try to free oneself from the help of the monochord as soon as possible. Then, when one feels more certain, one can try to approach the new intonations more directly and to sustain them:

It is a great help if the root tone c is sounding in the bass as one practices the exercise in the 'major' direction, and if a high c is sounding as one practices in the 'minor' direction, so that the tones can be heard together. Usually a sense for the correct 'place' of these tones develops more quickly than one had expected. After all, as the old European peasants' and shepherds' scales demonstrate, these intonations do slumber in the musical dispositions of Europeans. They are only waiting to be awakened and ushered out of the depths of our souls where they have been preserving for us a source of deep musical experience.

169

The scale of seconds developed out of an f minor triad has here been called 'f minor', since that is how it is felt when one starts out from the experience of the triad. In other words, it is not named according to its tone of origin, 8 = c, but according to the root tone of the triad. The problem of the minor tonic already has been discussed in the chapters, "Major and minor triads" and "Monistic and dualistic conceptions of minor" (p. 37ff; p. 39ff.).

As we have seen, the scale of seconds develops twelvetone music and brings it to life. Thus the qualities of major and minor and the key centers with their twelve different qualities—which otherwise are lost in twelvetone music—are restored, but in a new way. Whether the characters of these keys will remain as I have tried to describe for Classical and Romantic music is something one cannot predict. (See p.31ff.) That is a question that the musical life of the future will have to decide.

There is only one way to unite twelvetone atonality with the principle inherent in the second: that is by expanding the halftone system of twelve tones to a quartertone system of twenty-four. Just as the root intervals within the *senarius* —i.e. intervals up to, but not beyond, the fifth overtone produced by a fundamental, root tone—all are integrated within the system of twelve halftones, the new system of quartertones accomodates three further intervals from beyond the limits of the *senarius*, the intervals corresponding to 7, 11 and 13.

	Numerical relation	pure	Size in ht tempered	Divergence due to tempering (ht.)
Octave	2/1	12	12	0
Fifth	3/4	7.020	7	− 0.020
Large third	5/4	3.863	4	+ 0.137
Root-seventh	7/4	9.688	9.5	− 0.188
Root-fourth	11/8	5.513	5.5	− 0.013
Root-sixth	13/8	8.405	8.5	+ 0.095

A glance at the table makes it clear which interval is most at home in the quartertone system: the root fourth 11/8. Earlier we discovered that this interval generates the cycle of twenty-four tones (for the exact account, see p. 94). And it only requires two-thirds as much tempering as the fifth requires when it is used as the generating interval of the cycle of twelve. The interval 13/8 is more nearly in tune in the tempered quartertone system than is the pure third 5/4 in the tempered halftone system. The interval most severely affected by tempering is the natural seventh, but practical experience has shown that it can be thoroughly integrated. It is simply a matter of interpreting the quartertone system as a structure of flexible 'tone locations,' rather than as a group of rigidly established pitches. These 'tone locations' can undergo slight variations of intonation according to the 'tone value' (Pfrogner's terms) that they assume, i.e. depending on whether the tone in question appears as 7/4, 11/8 or 13/8.

The ideal intonation of Classical and Romantic music comes about in a similar fashion. All the 'guests' that can reside at a given tone location (b♯, c, d♭♭, b×, c♯, d♭, etc.) are not bound tyranically to its abstract, logarithmic intonation. We can bend our hearing to the necessities of an instrument like the piano, but such instruments serve our 'sentimentalistic' fantasy much better than they serve direct musical perception. Unless a string quartet is playing strict twelvetone music, such an intonation would be musically unreal. When a string quartet plays Classical or Romantic music, each 'innkeeper tone' adjusts itself naturally to the value of the 'guest tone' that is lodging with it without thereby infringing on. or confusing the twelvetone order or the characteristic 'tone location' in the twelve. Whenever there are modulations or enharmonic changes, the tonal location asserts its total sovereignty, for then its complete lack of ambiguity of tonal place is the only support that can prevent the harmonic structure from wobbling—or, one could say, the 'abstract' tone location functions as the fireproof smelting vessel in which the tone value can be recast.

One must have a similar command over the quartertone system so that in practice one can summon either a living flexibility for the tonal dyastole of a scale of seconds or a precise, crystal-clear and sovereign embodiment of cyclic order. The system must allow situations where several radial tone values converge on a single tone location, as well as situations that involve a completely atonal systole. The latter circumstances only apply to the halftone system that is contained within the quartertone system. Quartertone atonality is not a viable musical entity. Although it is easy enough to formulate such a thing in theory, there is not a genuine possibility of working with twenty-four-tone rows in a way analogous to twelvetone rows. The sole function of the quartertones is to enliven this world and to give access to the stream of 'subconsciousness ' so that the two regions can interpenetrate one another. The quartertones, therefore, must be able to remain more flexible than the halftones—which means, in effect, that instruments with fixed pitch are not well adapted to the quartertone system. I have found a clavichord with quartertone stops to be an ideal instrument for composition, since it allows me to alter pitch by altering the pressure on the key and so allows for a continuous modification of intonation.

For purposes of notation, I use the accidental signs that were introduced by Tartini (Tartini's Hook ⌐ , ⌐♭) and by Fokker and Badings (≠ , #). The tone-names used by Fokker (which originally were thought of in the context of a division of the wholetone into fifths) can be adapted neatly to current German usage. [As to English usage, alas, matters are not so straightforward. Here there is clearly scope for some linguistic creativity.—Trans.] In this way one arrives at a natural extension of current (German) usage regarding accidentals.

	✕ 2/2	cisis	disis	eisis	fisis	gisis	aisis	hisis
tone	3/4	cisi	disi	eisi	fisi	gisi	aisi	hisi
raised	1/2	cis	dis	eis	fis	gis	ais	his
by	1/4	ci	di	ei	fi	gi	ai	hi
		c	d	e	f	g	a	h
	1/4	cē	dē	eē	fē	gē	aē	hē (Spoken 'seh', etc.)
tone	1/2	ces	des	es	fes	ges	as	b
lowered	3/4	cese	dese	ese	fese	gese	ase	hese
by	2/2	ceses	deses	eses	feses	geses	asas	heses

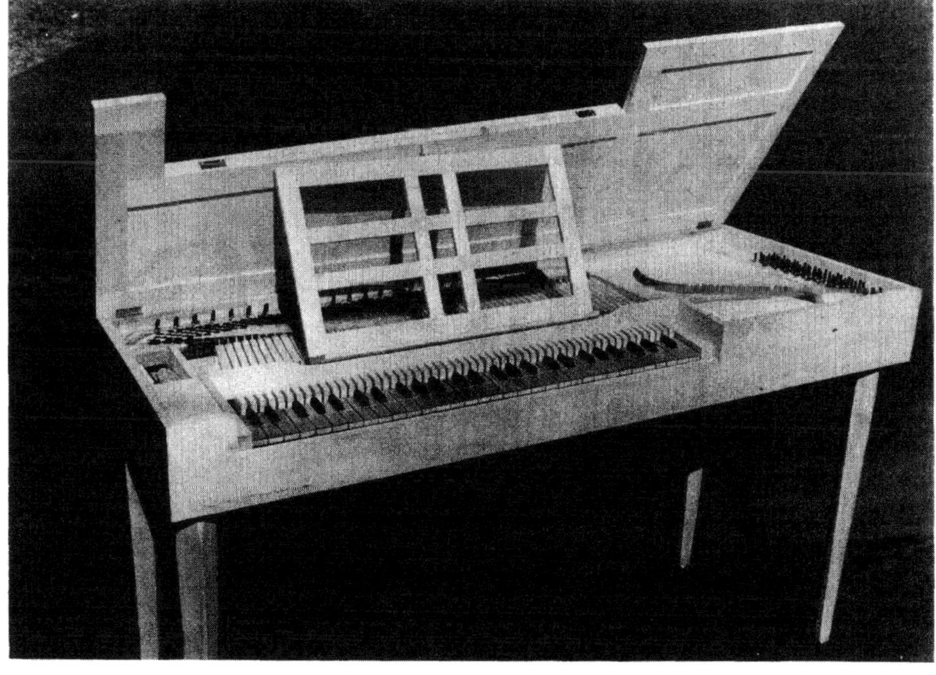

(A twentyfour-tone clavichord built by P. Kraul and G. Joli, Schwendener Orgelbau, D-7796 Schwende, Germany. The manner in which the tangent stops the string of a clavichord and so helps to determine the pitch of the tone obtained, makes it possible to obtain the quartertones from the same strings used for the halftones. Twelve extra tangents are all that is required to produce 12 extra quartertones.)

171

As I already have mentioned, the quartertone alterations usually do not indicate tempered tones. When a singer or a string player comes to the '*fi*', f ≠ (11) in the exercise for the major scale of seconds on root c (p. 169), for example, their sense for the second-oriented tonal relationships soon will tell them that the quartertone intonation scarcely needs any modification in this case. But when they come to '*hese*', b⌄(14), they will hear that the b should not be lowered three full quartertones—and thus with a little practice, a musical feeling for the natural seventh can take charge. With a⌄ (13), on the other hand, one must go somewhat lower than a quartertone below a, so that the interval b⌄-a⌄ is noticeably larger than a tempered halftone. This can be practised with the monochord by comparing the tempered, twenty-four-fold division with that of the arithmetic series. One soon discovers that the actual practice is easier than a theoretical description would lead one to think. Once there is a thorough enough acquaintance with 11/8, 13/8 and 7/4, the natural musical sense that we all potentially have for these intervals takes over so that the scale of seconds can be transposed to other tones with the help of the quartertone system. The twelve halftones are the only tones I use as root tones, never the quartertones—otherwise the circle of twelve is undermined, and the twelve are what keep the earthly, head-centered part of us oriented so that we do not lose our bearing in the twenty-four-tone system. Similarly, if 7, 11 and 13 are allowed to coincide on a single tone location in the way that tones of the *senarius* can do, the river of the sub-conscious entirely swallows up clear 'over-consciousness,' so I have learned to be fastidious about keeping these distinct from one another in handling tonal relationships.

Practising the minor scale of seconds, the same relationships are encountered in the intonation as were encountered in the major scale—only they are upside down: in f minor, d⌖ (14) must be lowered more than a quartertone and e⌄(13) must be raised somewhat more than a quartertone. In both cases, the main goal is to develop such an intense and direct sense for the new intervals based on 7, 11 and 13 that each is known by its own particular inner quality, like a characteristic scent or taste, so that their external location on the grid of quartertones no longer has to be considered. The quartertone system is like a map. It indicates where everything is and shows us how to get there. But in order to really experience the forests, mountains and lakes of the musical landscape one has to be able to pack away the map and forget about it. Nevertheless, the procedure of starting from a clear picture showing where the tones are in tonal space and then progressing toward a really artistic experience of their musical qualities is a procedure than can be recommended. It is a practical method of proceeding, a path that is well adapted to our modern consciousness. Otherwise there is scarcely any chance of our finding a successful way of getting from our modern tone consciousness to the intervals of this holy domain. The quartertone system is the bridge we need. It spans the gulf between the musical consciousness that developed during the *Kali Yuga*, which was restricted to the *senarius*, and the newly sought-for consciousness of the Light Age, which must once more find access to the 'mystic' intervals.

* * *

Kathleen Schlesinger (see p. 88f) sought the planetary qualities[105a)] of the scale of seconds in modes. But this avenue of approach is closed to musicians of today, for modes have ceased to be a living musical reality. Modal consciousness has been excluded by the way musical consciousness has developed. Looking at aspects of the course of musical development that I have been at pains to describe, one sees how radial forces have entered into our music, leading to the development of a consciousness of musical root tones. Modal music belongs to an earlier form of consciousness, one which could not yet experience a tonic tone. The earlier consciousness rightly ended in modern times with the advent of tonic-based, triadic, major and minor tonalities. The relation of major and minor to one another is not modal. They are polar opposites. But both the major and the minor scale of seconds embody the planetary qualities mentioned by Schlesinger: they can be rediscovered in the individual tones, in their numerical-harmonic relation to their root tone and to the other tones in the scale of seconds.

Entering into the numerical-harmonic quality of 14 and it root interval 7/4 without regard for absolute pitch, one can sense its mooklike character: mysterous, dreaming, dark violet, and yet saturated with natural life-forces, like some sweet-smelling flower of the night. By

172

contrast, 13 (root interval 13/8) drives one restlessly into uncanny deep regions of the soul. It is more bitter, sharper, harsher, and it has a restless, vibrating, Mercurial character. In 12 (root interval 12/8 = 3/2), with its total clarity, beauty and naive devotion, one finds the protective and yet chastely unapproachable love of Venus. In 11 one can sense what we already have tried to express in discussing its root interval 11/8 (p. 95f.): the all-encompassing, all-redeeming spiritual being of the Sun, a being of loving earnestness and self-sacrificing radiance. And in 10, although it is accompanied by the inwardness of the pure third, one finds that the root interval 5/4 (10/8) expresses a most self-occupied, individualistically creative character: Mars. (Although I would hasten to add that I believe that the real Mars quality of the third will only come into its own when third experience has been transformed and filled out from within by the growth of an awareness for the prime. At present the third obviously remains a 'pampered child' of Venus (3/2), who gave birth to it five hundred years ago. Or, one could say, that thus far the third is the earthly Venus who is in love with Mars and who is to be contrasted with the heavenly, archetypal Venus 3/2. In this regard, one should consider the old symbolism of the lily and the rose (see p. 21)! The third will only be able to convey its true Mars character after prime consciousness has freed it from the guardianship of Venus' cyclic fifth and given it its own, wholly radial, creative, courageous radiance.)

Those who devote themselves to an intimate study of these things will discover that there is a distinction between the character of a particular interval in a scale and the character which results from the numerical-harmonic quality of a tone. Thus the lunar quality of 7/4 is not necessarily connected with the character of the seventh. With the intervals of a scale one has to look elsewhere for the planetary qualities — as Steiner's indications for tone eurythmy show.[106] And the planetary characters appear in yet another form when related to the seven basic tones of the Classical major scale. These latter have a character that is based more on the outer position of the tones in the whole force-field of the tonality, like the ancient, traditional order of the planets.[107] The numerical-harmonic aspect of a tone gives it its own particular, individual character from within; its location or its absolute pitch are not of any importance to a tone's character in this sense.

Thus the numerical-harmonic quality of 9 and its root interval 9/8, the dreamlike, murmuring second, introduce something entirely new and distinctive: the wise clarity and loftiness of Jupiter. This character distinguishes both the *tonos* of the Greek Pythagoreans as well as the wholetone as it is found, for example, in the modal Gregorian Chant. It is significant that the root interval 9/8, which determines the quality of the root-based second, is the only numerical relationship we will meet that belongs both to the radial, arithmetic-harmonic order—

$$...7 \quad \mathbf{8} \quad \mathbf{9} \quad 10...$$

as well as to the cyclic-geometric order of the circle of fifths. For the second fifth of the cycle

$$(3/2)^2 = 9/4$$

also produces the wholetone 9/8 by means of the process of contraction into the space of one octave, which is a process typical of cyclic systems. Other root intervals—7/4, 13/9, 3/2, 11/8—*build* cycles; 9/8 *embodies* both cyclic and radial qualities. In the ancient myths, Jupiter-Zeus is the father of men and of gods, the ruler of heaven and of earth. Thus he has both an older aspect as a Pan-like, chthonic god and an Olympian aspect as the cosmic hurler of thunderbolts.

To be sure, Saturn-Chronos, the son of Uranus and Gaia, also has a double, cosmic-telluric nature. His darkly serious, universal depths that encompass both the heavens and the earth are manifest in the numerical quality of the root interval of the prime, 8/8 / 1/1. Here, in the sounding of one and the same tone, one meets the first emergence of time as well as the determination to hold back time and prevent it from unfolding. Emerging temporal development is kept in its first, primal phase, or else it is continually returning to this phase: in the mythical picture, Saturn-Chronos immediately devours his offspring as soon as they are born, until, at last, his son, Jupiter-Zeus, forces him to yield up what he has devoured and to allow it to develop. And in the musical sphere something similar happens: the quality 9/8 prevails over the quality 8/8—the second prevails over the prime—and provokes it into a temporal movement and development that reveals what it bears within itself, which is nothing less than the whole sevenfold scale.

It is also important to notice that prime 1/1 (Saturn), second 9/8 (Jupiter) and third 5/4 (Mars) represent the outer planets, the planets which have been associated with the forces of the human head since ancient times. Although none of the three is of itself capable of generating a cycle (what was said on p. 109 about the cycle-building possibilities of 5/4, also applies to 9/8), these three nevertheless belong to the cyclic, twelvetone realm of head-oriented consciousness by virtue of their musical-harmonic qualities. It is the inner planets, those associated with the limbs and the metabolic system, that have the power to produce a cycle: the Moon, 7/4, produces the cycle of sevenths; Mercury, 13/8, the cycle of sixths; and Venus, 3/2, the outermost of the inner planets, finally produces the cycle of fifths which lovingly encompasses the entire head of the human being (8/8, 9/8, 10/8). It is the inner planets, which Steiner calls the "determiners of destiny," whose musical-harmonic qualities can create enclosing circumference. In contrast, the outer planets are the ones with the powers that can free humanity,[108] and these are the planets whose power generates the radial energy that streams out of our own inner soul-world. As we saw when considering the development of experience of the single tone, Saturn's interval, the prime, has this power to an especially high degree when it is stimulated by the power of the second.

But if the Sun interval 11/8 were not there to divert the flow of seconds into a new course, the development of radiality would not be able to get any further than today's half-cyclic, triad-based major: although the major scale begins 8 : 9 : 10, it never could develop a place for 13 and 14 without the critical transition over the Sun interval, 11/8. Furthermore, the different planetary qualities could not be united in a single cycle if 11/8 were not capable of generating the cycle of twenty-four. Thus we can recognize the Sun in 11/8 the principle of the middle, marvelously encompassing and uniting the radial and the cyclic powers.

I would like to state with the greatest possible emphasis that these observations regarding planetary qualities should not lead to some sort of mysticism —nor should they be interpreted as mysticism. It is easy enough to show that this is not the case: all the direct references to the planets can be removed from the schema above so that one can simply immerse oneself in the interweaving of the principles mentioned, in and for themselves. What eventually will emerge is the Classical order of the seven planets, whether one knows it by name or not.

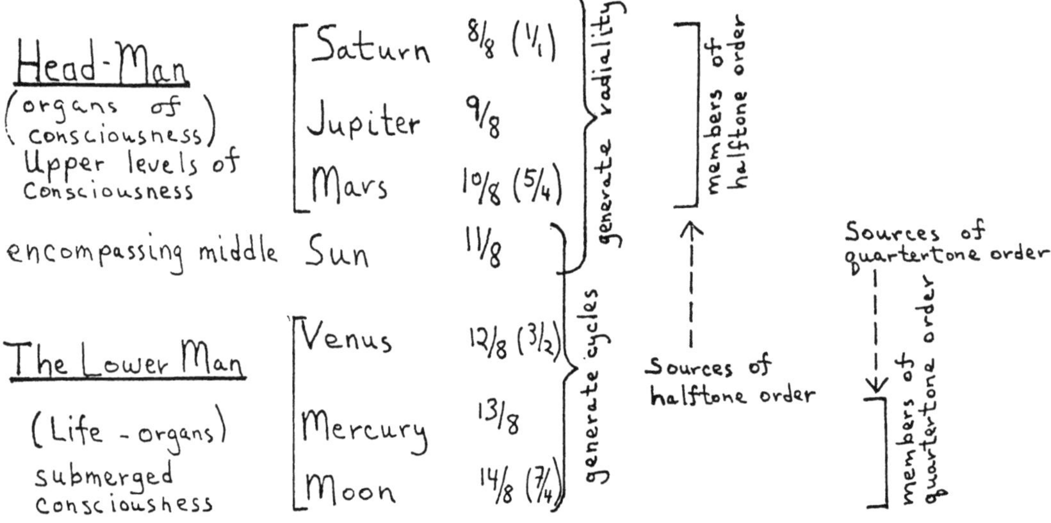

The Moon quality 7/4 encloses itself in a circle of sevenths without assuming any other quality—except for that of the octave. It produces the only example of a cycle so complete in itself that the totality of the cosmic circumference is reflected in a single scale (the *slendro* scale). Steiner spoke of the closed-off, cosmic 'Moon fortress' in which the whole cosmos is reflected.[109] The very different Mercurial quality is combinatory and it interconnects. When the Mercurial quality unites with the 7/4 quality, as in halftone pentatonic, it springs open the gates of 7/4's Moon-fortress and leads over, by way of immense and manifold tensions, to the realm of Venus 3/2 (see p. 70ff.). Ultimately, it leads over into the realm of 11/8, and so leads to all the other qualitative regions, as well.

> "...And Mercury quickly enacts your marriage"

is the way it is expressed in the old alchemists' verse of Basilius Valentinus (15th century),[110] which then continues:

> "...Though all in vain, lacking Venus' patronage.
> As chosen man Mars shows his face
> Sustained for you is Jupiter's grace..."

Venus (3/2) produces the circle of fifths, without which music never could have 'come to earth.' She unyieldingly rejects the old connections with 7, 13, and, also 11, all of which involve a cosmic, supersensible awareness. Instead, she devotes herself entirely to the musical consciousness appropriate for the earth-bound humanity of the *Kali Yuga*. Thus, within the confines of the system of twelve, she unites with the Mars quality 5/4 to produce the triad.

The "grace" of Jupiter is preserved in the triadic scale just as it had been preserved for the Greeks both in the Pythagorean scale and in its polar opposite, the *aulos* system, which was pregnant with the future. This grace consisted in keeping cyclic and radial aspects—heaven and earth—from being totally separated from one another. Through 9/8 something of the radial life-stream of seconds flows into the comparatively 'abstract' Pythagorean scale based on fifths and fourths (see p. 82). On the other hand, the dream-haunted 9/8-seconds that are so full of natural life are penetrated with cosmic-cyclic wisdom and clarity. And, finally, as I mentioned earlier, the quality inherent in 9/8 has the power to arouse the Saturn quality of 8/8 so that it develops what it bears hidden within itself:

> "...That thereby Saturn, old and gray
> Himself in many colors doth array."

is how the verse continues. The development of 8/8 = 1/1, i.e. of the single tone as experienced by an inward, but cosmically awakened, musical faculty, is the goal of musical development. When it has been achieved, musical experience will have acquired the "many colors" referred to in the verse. These are, indeed, all of the many colors that have clothed the music that has rung out during the course of humanity's musical development.

One of the sublimest visions of Saint John's *Apocalypse* pictures a man who holds in his hands the powers, or qualities, of the seven planets. The picture of the enthroned Christ of the Apocalypse is a theme that was ever and again taken up by the artists of the past. Today this is a picture we should try to comprehend musically. Then, as a matter of course, our artistic work will begin to yield us premonitions of what Rudolf Steiner saw as a goal of the music of the future: "that picture so wonderfully represented in Renaissance and pre-Renaissance painting—the approach of the living, spiritually alive, form of the Christ—is a highpoint in the development of humanity. But *in the future, this picture must be discovered musically*...And thus it can come about—whether or not lies in human hands—that music will also achieve an external revelation of the Christ-Impulse in its true form."[111]

In Saint John's vision "the Son of Man" is holding seven stars in his right hand and is surrounded by seven golden candlesticks which represent the seven churches of Asia Minor. According to Steiner, the essence of the seven post-Atlantean cultural epochs is the reality that stands behind these seven churches—and, I would like to add, also the seven musical intervals with their planetary qualities. The self-sacrificing Christ appears as the Lamb with seven horns and seven eyes. The Lamb is "as though it has been slaughtered " and it alone is able to open the book with the seven seals. Christ is surrounded by the four quadrants of the Zodiac, the cross of the Zodiac: the Lion, the Bull, the Angel-man (Waterman) and the Eagle (which is the archetypal imagination of what later became the Scorpion). These four, each with three pairs of wings, represent the whole twelvefold order. Medieval artists, like those who created the Kings' Portal at Chartres Cathedral, represent these four as being accompanied by twelve angelic beings.

Inner musical life depends on the Seven, which are embodied in the sevenfold tones and intervals of a tonality. Since the advent of the *Kali Yuga* these have been surrounded by the primal circle of twelve in which the cross is engraved. Eventually, for humanity, the Twelve were reduced to nothing more than the circle of the twelve senses and the head-oriented thinking connected with the senses. The Seven underwent death on the cross of the head-oriented world of the senses—their inner life was sacrificed, musically, to the twelve "dead, tempered tones of the keyboard." The power of the Seven can open the seven seals on the book of cosmic wisdom and cosmic future, but only the Seven as embodied in the "sacrificial lamb" on the cross. When this happens, the twenty-four kingly, crowned, string-playing 'presbyters' (= priests, elders) will break into a song of praise. Their all-encompassing circle, which surrounds the Seven and the Twelve, will resound with it. Musically, this circle of twenty-four is engendered by the Sun-quality of 11/8, whose nature can be characterized as being like that of Him who sits enthroned in the midst of the Seven and the Twelve and whose countenance is "radiant as the Sun in all its might."

176

Appendix I: Rudolf Steiner on the twelve senses [112]

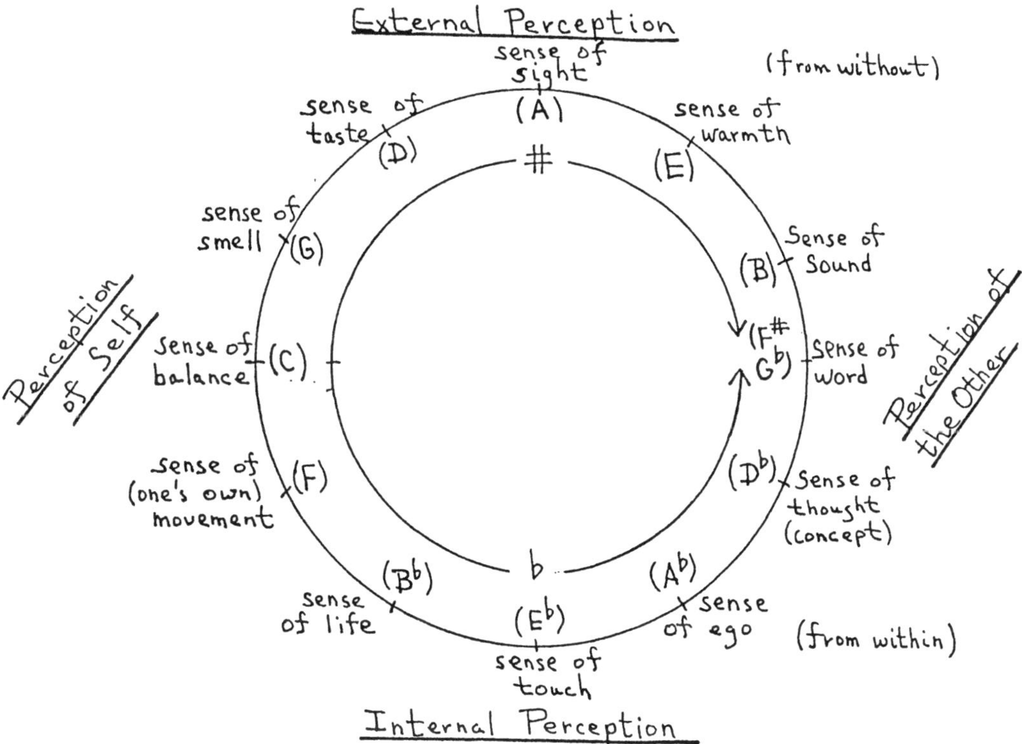

By means of our sense of balance we perceive the relationship of our bodily, inner world to the external world. There is a balance between awareness directed inward and awareness directed outward. (In C Major we find the corresponding attitude in artistic-musical form.)

The sense of smell is the first of the senses to be turned toward the outer world, although the outer world is taken in passively, with the breath, without its as yet undergoing any active transformation in the process. (G major)

The sense of taste is more active in the way it takes hold of the outer world. It penetrates further into the world and is more bound up with our own enjoyment than is the sense of smell. (D Major)

In seeing, we are transported into the outer world to such a degree that visual experience overshadows personal, bodily consciousness. This is by no means the case with the senses of smell and taste—both of these other modes of experience contain a strong, explicit references to our bodily nature. The only thing that speaks to us through our sight is the light of the of the external world. (A Major)

The sense of warmth gives us, on the one hand, a still deeper access to the outer world. In seeing we only perceive its outer surface, whereas with the sense of warmth it is more a matter of feeling our way into an inner condition of outer things: their inner warmth. On the other hand, the whole experience does not remain so objectively outside of us as with seeing; the perception of warmth penetrates further into our own soul-world. (E Major)

This is even more the case when we are involved with the sense of sound (B Major) and

177

the sense of word (F # Major). In hearing there is communication between our own inner being and that of an external object; with the sense of word, our inner nature communicates with the innermost soul nature of some other ensouled being.

There is a progressively greater going out of ourselves as we proceed from the sense of balance—through the sense of smell, taste, sight, warmth and sound—to the sense of word. This series of senses opens out more and more into the external world (the series of ascending fifths of the sharp keys !) At the same time, beginning with the sense of warmth, this outer world comes more and more into contact with our own inner world (increasing inwardness beginning with E Major !)

When we proceed in the other direction around the circle from the sense of balance, we find in the sense of movement a mode of experience that is more embedded in our own body (F Major). The sense of movement brings us as far into our own body as the sense of smell leads us out of it.

The experience of our own bodily condition becomes even more prominent, as a sense of well-being or of illness, through the life-sense (B^b Major). In its more original form, before it was so strongly attached to bodily consciousness, this sense "... was intended to allow our astral body [i.e. our inner, star-like feeling nature] to experience itself in our life-organism."[113]) (Hermann Beckh's "key of the stars" is B^b major!)

Finally, through the sense of touch the outer world is encountered inside of ourselves (E^b Major). Steiner characterizes this sense as containing a hidden sense of our own ego. It is polar opposite to the sense of sight: with that sense we press so far into the outer world that we forget ourselves whereas with the sense of touch the counter-pressure of the outer world leads us to experience ourselves.

The next sense is called 'the sense of ego'—by which is meant the sense for another ego, not for our own. Just as, by comparison with the sense of sight the sense of warmth both penetrates further into the outer world and yet also brings the outer world more deeply into the perceiver, so, also, does the sense of ego work more deeply into the perceiver's own inner world than does the sense of touch (or:'sense of our *own* ego'). Through the sense of self we discover the nature of our own innermost being, our own spiritual kernel,—but outside of ourselves in another being. (A Major)

The sense of thought, or concept, leads still further inward, into the inner realm of other, embodied spiritual beings. But it does so in an entirely inward, spiritual fashion that draws us still further out of ourselves. This sense allows us to participate—almost intuitively—in a purely spiritual activity, the formation of thoughts by another human self. (D^b Major)

Finally, this inward-turning progression that begins with the sense of balance, leads to a new encounter with the outer world through the sense of word, or sense of the sounds of speech. (G^b Major = F # Major) The progression leads us by way of the sense of (our own) movement, to the sense of life, to the sense to touch, and so on, following the series of descending fifths of the flat keys. With the sense of word we reencounter the upper stream of the outward-oriented sense (the sharp keys!) : in a speech-sound something perceived in the outer world conveys the inner world of another ensouled being into the space of our own inner world; similarly, the perceived word conveys the spirit-penetrated soul-world of another being to us.

As we noted on p. 1ff, a musically experienced tone also announces the presence of another spiritual being—but this only applies to genuinely artistic musical experience, experience which is more than just sense-activity. Understood as a pure sense-activity, hearing never can lead to perception of an immanent soul-being or spiritual-being unless the sense of word and the sense of concept participate in the activity. In this respect, the sense of word or speech-sound (corresponding to F # Major and G^b Major) reveals itself as the enharmonic bridge between external perception (hearing) and inner perception (conception, 'inner grasp.') When listening to a song, however, the perceptions of the sound-elements of speech and the perceptions of words and concepts do not form an inherent part of the musical experience. These only touch the outer garment of the musical tone. Disregarding all these and looking exclusively at the purely musical side of the experience we see that the participation of the senses of word (and speech-sound), of concept, and of ego disappear when hearing becomes musical. With music the world of soul and the world of spirit are perceived in a 'spiritual' manner in the truest sense of the word: we by-pass those senses which otherwise give us access to the immanent worlds of sound and spirit.

The preceding observations should make it perfectly clear that the musical experience of a tonality does not imply a special connection with a particular sense modality. For example, D Major is not tasted, nor is A Major seen! In order to grasp the connection of the senses of taste and sight with the keys of D Major and A Major, respectively, these senses first have to be understood as the expression, in bodily organs, of supersensible qualities of soul and spirit—indeed, of those very qualities of soul and spirit which are the hallmarks of the musical experience of D Major and A Major.

Appendix II: Eratosthenes and the Prime Number Thirteen

Eratosthenes (3rd century B.C.) developed an intonation of the enharmonic tetrachord which is the only known example of the use of the prime number 13 in Greek music theory:

$$e \qquad c \qquad c_\downarrow \qquad b$$
$$19/15 \qquad 39/38 \qquad 40/39$$

But, on closer scrutiny, it turns out that 39 (3x13) is not intended as a numerical-harmonic quality. Because he would only accept a diatonic tetrachord with a strict Pythagorean intonation—

$$e \qquad d \qquad c \qquad b$$
$$9/8 \qquad 9/8 \qquad 256/243$$

Eratosthenes, in contrast to all the other antique theorists (compare p. 93f), tried to preserve the pure Pythagorean third 9/8 x 9/8 = 81/64 (4.078 ht) in his *Enharmonion* . To do so , he replaces it with the mathematically more simple relationship, 19/15 (4.092 ht), which is, however, a very close approximation. This procedure resulted in the *lemma* between c and b which can be expressed by the relation 20/19 (0.888 ht), and which is very nearly the same size as the Pythagorean *lemma* 256/243 (0.902 ht). Clearly, the reason for transforming 256/243 into the superparticular relation 20/19 lay in Eratosthenes' which wish to 'insert' (compare p. 93f.) the enharmonic tone c↓ (*mesopyknos*)as a quartertone into the real Pythagorean *lemma*. The Greeks could not determine the square root of 256/243, but Eratosthenes *could* expand 20/19 to 40/38, which then, with the help of the arithmetic midpoint, 39, could be divided into 39/38 and 40/39. Thus one is led to use 39 without its numerical-harmonic quality's ever being taken into consideration. Although the resulting quartertones are not equal, they are obtained by using a superparticular series to divide the interval in question which was the usual method in Eratosthenes' time. Here we have an eloquent example of how the feeling for a living quality in numbers is already on the wane. The radial superparticular series—and with it, numbers in general—already is becoming a mere rational, abstract instrument for measuring and counting (compare p. 121ff.).

Appendix III: Tempering in Jakob Boehme, Franz von Baader and Andreas Werckmeister

The following passage is to be found in Kurt Poppe's article, "Franz von Baader's doctrines contrasting supernature, nature and subnature with non-nature":

> Baader's conception of the coming-into-being and the persistence of "eternal nature in God" involved the profound mystery of the "manifestation of the Divine" as a "threefold spirit that is free from nature, but not lacking nature." There are three moments to be distinguished in this mystery. The first moment issues "out of the unrevealed unity," where multiciplicity still is absorbed in the undifferentiated unity, *which is what Jakob*

Boehme called tempering; the second moment is indicated by "the appearance of variety in and through nature;" and the third moment marks the "new termination of variety, whereby it becomes possible for the members to experience the unity."[114]

Even though what we have here is Boehme's concept of tempering at third hand, the connection with the preceeding musical studies is so interesting and so significant that it should not be ignored. We must ask, on the one hand, the students of Boehme, and, on the other hand, the musicologists, whether Boehme's mystical-philosophical concept is not the godfather of the musical concept of tempering that was developed by Werckmeister. Even if this turns out not to be the case historically, there still is an astonishing agreement between the two concepts. Both are directed at the same facts—the one, philosophically, the other, musically.

In this book, *Zwoelfordnung der Toene* (*The Twelvefold Tonal Order*, not translated), Hermann Pfrogner shows how a generalizing, integrating principle lies behind the impulse to temper the circle of twelve. Unlike the principle embodied in our seven-toned scales, this principle does not unfold itself musically in time. Instead, it reveals itself in the timeless realm of duration. The 'tonal values,' e.g., f# and g^b, are still undifferentiated at the single 'tonal location,' f#—g^b, in this timeless, integrated, spatial order. One particular 'tonal value' only takes precedence when a tonality is developed. Thus the aforementioned tonal location takes on the value f# when it belongs to G Major, D Major, etc., or takes on the value g^b when it belongs to b^b minor. The tones f# and g^b are united at a higher level by that which is the spiritual-musical source of tempering, thereby reintroducing the power of the "unrevealed unity" where multiplicity still is absorbed by the undifferentiated oneness. The unity of f$^#$ and g^b can be said to be "unrevealed", because it is musically inconceivable. Nevertheless, every musical enharmonic transformation testifies to its reality—as Pfrogner has repeatedly emphasized (see *Zwoelfordnung* ...,p.27).

Pfrogner once made some discerning observations concerning Baader's three 'moments'. He wrote, "Actually, our tempering would have to be associated with the third 'moment', 'the termination of variety whereby it becomes possible for the participators to experience the unity.' The first 'moment', the 'unrevealed unity where multiplicity still is absorbed in the oneness,' has more to do with the twelve *Liu*, of the Chinese."[115] Pfrogner is referring to a subject I discussed on p. 79f: at the very beginning of the *Kali Yuga* , China anticipated future development by adopting the principle of the twelve holy *Liu* , a cosmic, spatial principle of duration; whereas the regular post-Atlantean development only found its way to the fully realized circle of twelve at the end of the *Kali Yuga* in the work of Werckmeister, J.S. Bach and, finally, in twelvetone atonality. In Aristoxenos, Greece had witnessed a tentative prelude to this development.

To be sure, the archetype of a closed cycle is the Atlantean/ancient-Indian system of sevenths, in which multiplicity really was "absorbed in the undiffereniated oneness." There the twelve transpositions of the pentatonic scale do not yet exist since one, single pentatonic scale already contains the entire cycle. There no musical 'upward and downward' exist—no successions of opening or closing fifths—for the intervals have not yet separated out into the succession of intervals that enables them to convey the quality of establishing pathways, not yet separated into prime, second, third, fourth, fifth, sixth, seventh. This qualitative differentiation does already exist, however, in the intervals out of which the five Chinese pentatonic modes are built, although not in the structure of the scale itself. (In China, the tones were generated by pure fifths.) But in *Slendro* the second and the small third still are united in a single interval, and so are the fifth and the small sixth, the large sixth and the seventh (see p. 64). The heterogeneous intervals that are allowed to coincide in modern enharmonic music—for example the augmented second and the small third—do not yet exist as distinct entities for the musical consciousness that corresponds to *Slendro* .

In China the premature adoption of the closed circle of twelve that is appropriate for the stage of fifth-consciousness was a method of imitating and prolonging the "first moment" in the development of tone systems. In the regular course of post-Atlantean development the first moment was followed by the second as sixth-consciousness and fifth-consciousness developed. A musical "multiplicity" arose as the tone system was split into two endless streams

180

of sixths or fifths, one 'major', one 'minor' (see p. 35f and p. 72). The split into two endless streams, one leading inward, one leading outward, was healed when the two streams were reunited, joined together in a single stream by the modern closed circle of twelve, a circle which we discovered (p. 131) to be intimately connected with third-consciousness. Thus the third of the three moments did come. But it only came after the variegated experiences of the second moment were established so they could enrich the new unity with a new manifoldness that could in no way be attributed to the archetypal oneness of the first moment: one experiences the tones of the circle of sevenths as being somehow not self-sufficient; by contrast, each tone of the modern circle of twelve embodies an individuality. Each of these latter has the capacity of entering the b-stream (say as g^b) and developing itself there, or of entering the #—stream (as f# or even as e^x), or of existing enharmonically in a tonally ambivalent or atonal, in-between, state. In the latter circumstances, the primal condition of the "first moment" ("tempering"), the moment of the "still undifferentiated oneness", shines through once more in the "third moment." Only in this context can one understand how a person with the spiritual penetration of J.M.Hauer could flatly assert that twelvetone atonality is the primal music of the original, divine unity, the external representative of the "divine speech of the Father." (See *Zwoelfordnung* , p.231.)

That our tone system has developed—as the cosmos and humanity also developed—from an original oneness into a multiplicity, and that the tone system somehow strives, or must strive, to regain that oneness, were ideas that were very much alive for Andreas Werckmeister. "*Omnia ab Uno, omnia ad Unum* " ("Everything from One, everything toward the One") is the key statement in his profound observations concerning 'spritual tempering.'[116] The chain of fifths does not of itself arrive at an octave and so close itself into a completed form. On the contrary, if it is not tempered it spins itself out in a never-ending multiplicity. For Werckmeister this musical fact was connected with the fall of Lucifer, which led to the fall of humanity. For him 'spiritual tempering' is associated with the deed of Christ, which guided what Lucifer had led to stray into a infinite nothingness back to unity in its original source in the Father, back to its home in the octave.

Werckmeister's thoughts about the divergence between the sequence of fifths and the corresponding octave

$$\left(\frac{3}{2}\right)^7 \neq 2^7$$

do not seem like such a mystical digression if we think about intonation problems musically, and not just mathematically or technically. Musically the soul strives outward in the 'dominant' (#)stream of fifths and inward in the 'subdominant' (*b*) stream of fifths (see p. 102f.). An ever-widening abyss opens out between the two streams as they strive toward their goals. It is clear that Werckmeister's ideas about tempering fifths to form a closed circle of twelve (it is known that he envisaged this as an equal tempering, although he himself did not realize his goal) belong to the sphere of 17th century, mystic-pietistic philosophy which was influenced by Boehme.[117] Therefore it is all the more reasonable to assume that Boehme's conception of tempering directly or indirectly influenced Werckmeister's thinking.

BOOKS AND ARTICLES REFERRED TO IN THE TEXT

Beckh, Hermann, *Die Sprache der Tonart*. Verlag Urachhaus, Stuttgart:1977. (First published in 1937.)

Bindel, Ernst, *Die Zahlengrundlagen der Musik*, I-III. Verlag Freiesgeisteleben, Stuttgart: 1950—53. Reprinted in one volume by the same press in 1986.

Von Gleich, Sigismund, *Geisteswissenchaftliche Entwicklungslinien im Hinblick auf den Impuls von Gondi-Schapur*. J.Ch. Mellinger Verlag. Stuttgart: 1966. (Also in the periodical, *Blaetter fuer Anthroposophie*, 1963, Vol XV, numbers 1-6.)

Handschin, Jacques, *Der Toncharakter*, Zurich: 1948.

Hindemith, Paul, *Unterweisung im Tonsatz*, I. Mainz:1940. (*The Craft of Musical Composition*, Vol. I. Associated Music Publisher, Inc. New York: 1942.)

Husmann, Heinrich, *Grundlagen der antiken and orientalischen Musikkultur*, Berlin: 1961.

Jung, Carl Gustav, *Bewusstes und Unbewusstes* . Fisher-Bucherei. Frankfurt a.M./ Namburg:1970. (*See The Archetypes and the Collective Unconscious*, Vol I. Pantheon Books, Inc. U.S.A.: 1959.)

Kodály, Zoltan, *Die ungarishe Volksmusik*, Budapest: 1956, (Published in English as *Folkmusic of Hungary*, Barrie and Rockcliff. London: 1960)

Lauer, Hans Erhard, *Die Entwicklung der Musik im Wandel der Tonsysteme*. Basel: 1976.

Pfrogner, Hermann, *Die Zwölfordnung der Töne*. Amalthea-Verlag. Vienna: 1953.

Pfrogner, Hermann, *Musik, Geschichte ihrer Deutung*. Verlag Karl Alber. Freiburg-Munich: 1954.

Pfrogner, Hermann, ''Hat Diatonik Zukunft?'' Published in the periodical, *Musica*, Vol. XVII, 1963/4.

Pfrogner, Hermann, ''All-Konsonanz und Ich-Konsonanz.'' Published in the periodical, *Blaetter fuer Anthroposophie*, Vol. XVI, 1964/2.

Pfrogner, Hermann, *Lebendige Tonwelt: Zur Phaenomen Musik*, Langen Muller, Munich and Vienna: 1976.

Plato, *Opera omnia*, Edited by G. Stallbaum. Leipzig: 1899.

Poppe, Kurt, ''Franz von Baaders Lehre zur Uebernatur—Natur—Unternatur und zur Unnatur.'' Published in the German periodical, *Die Drei*, XXXI, 1961/3.

Prieberg, Fred K., *Musik unterm Strich*. Freiburg/Munich: 1956.

Ruland, Heiner, ''Zur Tonalitaet einer Indianermelodie.'' Published in the *Jahrbuch fuer musikalische Volks-und Voelkerkunde* Vol. IV. Berlin: 1968.

Ruland, Heiner, ''Zur Genealogie der Zigeunerskala und Halbtonpentatonik.'' (Not published.)

Sachs, Kurt, *Vergleichende Musikwissenschaft, Musik der Fremdkulturen*. Heidelberg: 1959.

Schiller, Friedrich, *Ueber naive und sentimentalische Dichtung*. (Included among his theorectical works.)

Schlesinger, Kathleen, *The Greek Aulos*. London: 1939.

Schoeffler, H.H., *Die Akadamie von Gondischapur*. Verlag Freiesgeisteleben. Stuttgart:1979.

Schulz, Joachim, ''33-jaehrige Rhythmen und deren Abbild im Jahreslauf.'' Published in the annual *Sternkalender* for 1960-61, issued by the Mathematical and Astronomical Section at the Goetheanum in Dornach, Switzerland.

Steiner, Rudolf (The 'GA' numbers refer to the bibliography number in the Swiss edition of the collected works currently being issued.)

GA4 *Die Philosophie der Freiheit*. Stuttgart:1955. (*The Philosophy of Freedom*. Rudolf Steiner Press. London:1970. Also published under the title, *The Philosophy of Spiritual Activity* .)

GA6 *Goethes Weltanschaung* . Verlag der Rudolf Steiner-Nachlassverwaltung. Dornach, Switzerland: 1963. (*Goethe's World View* . Mercury Press. Spring Valley, New York: 1985.)

GA13 *Die Geheimwissenschaft im Unriss* . R.S.-Nachlassverwaltung. Dornach, Switzerland: 1962. (*Occult Science—An Outline* . Rudolf Steiner Press. London:1963.)

GA45 *Anthroposophie. Ein Fragment* . R.S.-Nachlassverwaltung. Dornach, Switzerland: 1980. (Not yet published in English.)

GA113 *Der Orient im Lichte des Okzidents* . R.S.-Nachlassverwaltung. Dornach, Switzerland: 1960. (*The East in the Light of the West* . Rudolf Steiner Publishing Co. London:1940.)

GA170 *Das Raetsel des Menschen* . R.S.-Nachlassverwaltung. Dornach, Switzerland: 1964. (*The Riddle of Humanity*. Rudolf Steiner Press. London: 1990.)

GA184(b) *Der Entwicklungsgang der Menschheit*. R.S.-Nachlassverwaltung. Dornach, Switzerland: 1963. Lecture of December 16, 1918: ''Wie finde ich den Christus?''(Some of these lectures are published as *Three Streams in Human Evolution*. R.S. Press, London: 1965.)

GA228 *Initiationswissenschaft und Sternenerkenntnis*. R.S.-Nachlassverwaltung. Dornach, Switzerland:1964. (Not yet published in English, but the lecture referred to has been printed in the English periodical, *The Golden Blade*, 1961-issue as ''The Spiritual Individualities of the Planets.'')

GA231 *Der Übersinnliche Mensch, Anthroposophisch Erfaßt*. Dornach 1962.

GA243 *Das Initiatenbewusstsein* . R.S.-Nachlassverwaltung. Dornach, Switzerland:1960. (*True and False Paths in Spiritual Investigation* . R.S.Press. London:1985.)
GA275 *Kunst im Lichte der Mysterienweisheit.* R.S.-Nachlassverwaltung. Dornach, Switzerland:1966. (*Art as seen in the Light of Mystery Wisdom* . R.S. Press. London: 1984.)
GA277 *Eurythmie. Die Offenbarung der Sprecheden Seele.* R.S.-Nachlassverwaltung. Dornach, Switzerland: 1980. (Some of the lectures included in this volume have been published in English as *An Introduction to Eurythmy*. Anthroposophic Press Spring Valley, New York: 1984. One single lecture also has been published separately as "A Lecture on Eurythmy." R.S. Press. London:1977.)
GA283 *Das Wesen des Musikalischen und das Tonerlebnis im Menschen.* R.S.-Nachlassverwaltung. Dornach, Switzerland: 1969. (*The Inner Nature of Music and the Experience of Tone.* Anthroposophic Press. Spring Valley, New York: 1983.)
GA303 *Die gesunde Entwickelung des Leiblich-Physischen als Grundlage der freien Entfaltung des Seelisch-Geistigen.* R.S Nachlassverwaltung. Dornach, Switzerland: 1969. (*Lectures to Teachers.* R.S. Press. London: .)
Stuckenschmidt, Hans Heinz, Quoted in the periodical, *Die Reihe*, Vol. I, 1955, p. 19. Vienna; 1955. (*Die Reihe* was published in English at Bryn Mawr, Pennsylvania: 1958- 68.)
Vogel, Martin, *Die Zahl Sieben in der spekulativen Musiktheorie.* Bonn: 1955.
Vogel, Martin, *Die Enharmonik der Griechen*, Vol. II. Duesseldorf: 1963.
Wiora, Walter, *Europaeischer Volksgesang*, in Vol. IV of *Das Musikwerk*. Cologne.
Wustmann, Rudolf, "Tonarten zu Bachs Zeit," in the *Bach-Jahrbuch* for 1911.

NOTES

1. R. Steiner, G.A. 283, 7 March, 1923, p. 107ff. (See *The Inner Nature of Music...*, p. 146ff.)
2. G.A. 283, p. 125. (*The Inner Nature of Music...*, p. 68f.)
3. Ideophones are the family of instrument whose body is the sound-producing element. Lithophones are composed of a series of resonant stone slabs, hung up and played by striking with a hammer or mallet. (Translator's note)
4. C. Sachs, *Vergleichende Musikwissenschaft*, p. 12.
5. C. Sachs, *Vergleichende Musikwissenschaft*, p. 13.
6. Z. Kodály, *Das ungaricshe Volksmusik*, p.125.
7. This carol is not so well known in the English-speaking world as in Germany. But it is included in *The Oxford Book Of Carols* by Dearmer, Vaughan Williams and Shaw (Oxford University Press), number 90, page 193. (Translator's note.)
8. The Greeks described their modes in the *descending* order of the tones. But these descriptions were interpreted *upwards* in the Middle Ages so the names of the Greek modes were inadvertently given to quite different sequences of notes. The result: was analogous to what would happen if someone interpreted our usual (upward-bound) description of C major in the wrong direction. It begins on c with two whole-steps, we say. So our wrongheaded interpreter would begin with the tones c, b^b, a^b. (Translator's note)
9. The connection between the lily family and the quality of the number 3, and the rose family and the number 5, was a discovery of Johannes Kepler! See Ernst Bindel, *Zahlengrundlagen der Musik im Wandel der Zeiten*, Vol. I, p.998.
10. Readers daunted by the mathematics in this section are encouraged to skip over it and read on, taking heart from the observation, two paragraphs on, that these *spatial* measurements are just a way of comparing the size of intervals. The numbers involved do not reveal inherent musical values.(Translator's note.)
11. See p.79ff. (Translator's note.)
12. The date of Aristoxenos' death is not known. He was a student of the Pythagoreans and, later,of Aristotle. He wrote numerous books on music and other subjects, only parts of which have survived. (Translator's note.)
13. 'Beat' refers to the pulsation which occurs when two tones not exactly tuned to one another sound at the same time. It is the result of interference. When the two tones are very out of tune, the pulsation is very rapid; the nearer one comes to the pure intonation, the slower the pulsation becomes.
14. See R. Wustmann, 'Tonartensymbolik zu Bachs Zeit' ('The symbolism of keys in Bach's time').
15. Herman Beckh, *Die Sprache der "Tonart"* (The Language of Tonality. Not translated.)
16. The arithmetic and harmonic series are discussed later. See especially chapters XIX to XXII. (Translator's note.)
17. P. Hindemith, *Unterweisung in Tonsatz*,I. (*The Craft of Musical Composition*, Vol. I, pp22-24)
18. See chapters XX-XXII, where the arithmetic and harmonic series are discussed. (Translator's note).
19. When two tones of different frequency sound together, they produce a third tone—a 'difference tone '—whose frequency is the difference between the frequencies of the first two tones. (Translator's note)
20. *Unterweisung in Tonsatz*, I, p.57. *The Craft of Musical Composition*, I, p.37-38.
21. The Sea of Marmora separates Asiatic from European Turkey. (Translator's note.)
22. Swabia was one of the original Germaan dukedoms. Geographically it roughly corresponds to S.Baden, Wuertenburg and Bavaria. (Translator's note.)
23. Pfrogner, *Lebendige Tonwelt*, p.478 ff.
24. W.Wiora, *Europ. Volksgesang*, p.14. The indications in brackets have been added by the present writer. (Appenzel is a canton of Switzerland. Translators note.)
25. Istria is an area now included mainly in NW Yugoslavia. (Translator's note.)
26. See Pfrogner's "Hat Diatonik Zukunft?" in *Musika*, 1963/4, p.148.
27. Kathleen Schlesinger (1862-1953) was an Irish musical scholar who devoted much careful research to the ancient Greek pipe instruments, the results of which first were published in 1939 in her book, *The Greek Aulos*. (Translator's note)
28. H.Pfrogner, *Lebendige Tonwelt*. p.121 ff.

29. Also see p.9f.
30. See E.Bindel, *Zahlengrundlage der Musik*, I, p.42.
31. *Politics*, 399 d.
32. The string vibrates in parts, as well as as a whole—in precise halves, thirds, fourths, and so on. The points on the string that mark the divisions between these parts are nodes. (Translator's note.)
33. G.A. 303, p.349. (Rudolf Steiner, *Lectures to Teachers*).
34. See J.Handschin, *Der Toncharakter*
35. Rudolf Steiner, G.A. 283, p. 108. (*The Inner Nature of Music...*, p. 55 ff.)
36. The arrows, '↑' and '↓', following the name of a tone, indicate that the tone referred to is higher or lower in pitch than the tone normally so named. 'A^b↑' refers to a tone somewhat higher than our normal, tempered A^b. (Translator's note)
37. See Rudolf Steiner, *An Outline of Occult Science* (Rudolf Steiner Press, London: numerous editions) and other writings and lectures. (Translator's note.)
38. See the discussion of Bartók in the final chapter of this book. (Translator's note.)
39. GA275, p.104f. (Rudolf Steiner. *Art as seen in the Light of Mystery Wisdom*. Rudolf Steiner Press. London: 1984. But the passage cited comes in a transcribed discussion that has not been included in the English version. (Translator's note.)
40. See H.Husmann, *Grundlagen* ..., p. 188 ff.
41. G.A. 283, p. 108. (R. Steiner, *The Inner Nature of Music* , p. 55 ff.)
42. Walter Wiora (b. 1907 in Poland) is a German musicologist and author of numerous books and articles. Some of his work was in the field of folk music and folk song. (Translator's note.)
43. See H. Ruland, "Zur Tonalität einer Indianermelodie", p. 106 ff.
44. See, e.g., Ch.XXXI on the Greek enharmonic system. (Translator's note.)
45. See Appendix III, p.179
46. One does frequently encounter the tendency to expand two of the seconds into small thirds, producing an analog to the pentatonic based on fifths. This occurs, naturally enough, where loss of a sense for the natural seventh has undermined the basis of Slendro and put it on the path toward becoming a pentatonic of pure fifths.
47. Jaap Kunst (1891-1960), a Dutch ethnomusicologist and musician, was one of the founders of modern ethmomusicology. Early in his career he lived in Java where he became interested in the Javanese gamelan and in Indonesian music in general. (Translator's note.)
48. Husmann, *Grundlagen*, p. 158.
49. Ruland, "Zur Genealogie..." (See Foreword!)
50. Compare Husmann on the "persische Idealleiter", p. 119 of *Grundlagen*.
51. Ruland, "Zur Genealogie..."
52. Refer to the figures on p.69: the mode with the most tones in the chain of sixths above its starting tone would start on c#♦ ; the mode with the most tones below, on e^b↑. Use Mch (10-Div.). (Translator's note.)
53. Steiner, G.A. 113. Lecture of August 30, 1909. (Rudolf Steiner. *The East in the Light of the West. P. 173 ff.*)
54. P.Hindemith, *Unterweisung in Tonsatz*, I, p.57. (*The Craft of Musical Composition*), I, pp.37-38.
55. Erich M. von Hornbostel (1877-1935) was an Austrian scholar of wide-ranging interests which included comparative musicology, ethno musicology, and the psychology of musicaltone perception. (Translator's note.)
56. See Appendix I.
57. See Herman Beckh, *Die Sprache der Tonart*.
58. After Pfrogner, *Musik: Die Geschichte ihrer Deutung* , p. 28.
59. 'Anthroposophy' is Rudolf Steiner's name for the spirit which inspired his approach to understanding humanity, nature and the cosmos. One aspect of Anthroposophy is that it seeks through a path of inner development to extend the range and intensity of our perception, to give us access to areas that, to start with, are 'occult,' i.e hidden from us. Another aspect is that it seeks to embody our modern scientific ideals of truth and objectivity in the manner in which that inner path is followed. Hence the term 'spiritual science'. (Translator's note.)
60. H.Progner, *Zwoelfordnung* ... , p. 82.
61. J. Handschin, *Der Toncharakter* , p.71.
62. Plato, *Republic* , 399 d.
63. Plutarch speaks of splitting the halftones. So does Aristides Quintilianus. (See M. Vogel. *Enharmonik* II, p. 106.) See also Appendix II , p.179)
64. P.Hindemith, *Unterweisung* ...I, p.57. *The Craft of Musical Composition*, Vol. I.pp.37-38.
65. See J. Schulz in *Sternkalendar* 1961/62, p. 60.
66. GA 303, p.349. (Rudolf Steiner. *Lectures to Teachers*.)

67. See M. Vogel, *Der Zahl Sieben...*, p.6.
68. But note that the scale is not diatonic in our usual sense. Each second in this 'diatonic' scale is different from every other second—is larger or smaller. (Translator's note.)
69. See Martin Vogel, *Enharmonik*. Vogel (b. 1923) is a German musicalogist who has concerned himself with questions having to do with tone systems and tuning in ancient and modern music. These interests have led him to develop new instruments such as 'enharmonic' trumpets, horns and tubas. (Translator's note.)
70. See Appendix II, p.179
71. Greek text in Vogel, *Enharmonik* II, p.125.
72. Abraham Z. Idelsohn (1882-1938) was of Latin Jewish origins. Originally trained as a cantor, he was active as a musicologist, teacher and composer. His works on the history and liturgy of Jewish music includes a monumental 10 volume thesarus of Herbrew-Oriental melodies. He was one of the first to study oral tradition seriously and to record it. His works demonstrated previously unrecognized relationships between early eastern and western music—such as Hebrew liturgical chant and Gregorian chart. (Translator's note.)
73. G.A.283. *Das Tonerlebnis im Menschen*, lecture 3. (Rudolf Steiner. *The Inner Nature of Music...*, p.77 ff.
74. Also see S. von Gleich, *Geisteswissenschaftliche Entwicklungslinien im Hinblick auf den Impuls von Gondi-Schapur*. (Also see H. H. Schoeffler, *Die Akadamie von Gondischapur*. Translator's note.)
75. F. Prieberg, *Musik unterm Strich*, p.14.
76. *Die Reihe*, Vol.I, Vienna, 1955, p.19. (Also published in English. See bibliography.)
77. H. Pfrogner, *Lebendige Tonwelt*, p.140.
78. Husmann, *Grundlagen*, p.130.
79. Lecture of October 16, 1918. In G.A. 184(b), p.44. (*see Three Streams in Human Evolution*, pp.84-90, for a related passage, Translator's note.)
80. The supernumary series is the series of fractions whose numerator exceeds the denominator by one. (Translator's note.)
81. See *An Outline of Occult Science*, Ch. II, 'The nature of humanity.' German text: See 'Verstandes- und Gemütsseele.' (The translation above conforms to the usage in the translation of George and Mary Adams.)
82. See Pfrogner, *Lebendige Tonwelt*, p.175 f.
83. Cited in Pfrogner, *Lebendige Tonwelt*, p.150 f.
84. In answer to a question on January 5, 1922. See G.A. 303, p.349. The original German phrase was 'einer grossere Komplikation der Töne.' (Rudolf Steiner. *Lectures to Teachers*.)
85. Compare Pfrogner's discussion of these issues, *Zwölfordnung*, p.89 ff.
86. Husmann, *Grundlagen...*, p.119. In three cases the halftone values have been carried further.
87. See Pfrogner, *Lebendige Tonwelt*, p.61.
88. See Chapter III.
89. For a discussion of Gothe's concepts of polarity and intensification see Rudolf Steiner, *Goethe's World View*, p.58 ff. (Translator's note.)
90. The lur is an instrument that has been traced back as far as the Nordic Bronze Age. It is a lip-vibrated instrument—like our brass instruments—consisting of a conical tube two to three meter in length, twisted into a contorted S-shape with a disk instead of a bell at the speaking end. Some include hanging metal plates that rattle. (Translator's note.)
91. See M. Vogel, *Die Zahl Sieben*, p.193 ff.
92. See Pfrogner, *Zwölfordung...*, p.230 f. Also, see Appendix III.
93. G.A. 283. Lecture of September 29, 1920, p.52. (Rudolf Steiner, *The Inner Nature of Music*. The passage cited comes from a transcript of a discussion not included in the translation.)
94. G.A. 283, *loc. cit.*
95. *Parzifal*, 469, 8.
96. In "Hat Diatonik Zukunft?" ("Does diatonic music have a future?") Pfrogner has examined the example given here and also the significance of this composition in the whole of Bartók's work. See p. 147 f.
97. See p.160f.
98. See J.Handschin, *Der Toncharakter*, p.75.
99. See Pfrogner, *Lebendige Tonwelt*, p.370 ff.
100. Friedrich von Schiller, *Über naive und sentimentalische Dichtung*.
101. See C.G. Jung, *The Archetypes and the Collective Unconscious*, p.19 f.
102. G.A. 283, p.48 ff. (Rudolf Steiner. *The Inner Nature of Music*. The passsage cited is from a discussion not included in this translation.)
103. G.A. 303, p.349. (Rudolf Steiner, *Lectures to Teachers*.)

104. See the report on the Schoenberg Week in Moedling, in *Musica*, 1975/6, p.571.
105. 'Serial' methods of musical composition first appeared around 1911. The order in which tones sound was treated serially. As Schoenberg's follower, Anton Webern, expressed it, the twelvetone (serial) principle is the law that "until all twelve notes have occurred, none of them may occur again." Later, the serial principle was applied to other elements of a piece, such as dynamics, time value of a note, timbre. (Translator's note.)
105a. G.A. 231, p.108 ff.
106. Eurythmy is an art of movement, inagurated by Steiner, in which the processes that lead to speech and song become the source of movements of the whole body in space—rather than the source of speaking or singing. See Rudolf Steiner: *An Introduction to Eurythmy* and "A Lecture on Eurythmy." (Translator's note.)
107. See Pfrogner's extensive treatment of this problem in *Lebendige Tonwelt*, p.133 ff. and p.643 f.
108. G.A. 228, p.14. (For the lecture cited, see the English journal, *The Golden Blade*, 1966, "The Spiritual Individualities of the Planets.")
109. G.A. 228, p.10 ff. (See preceeding footnote.)
110. After Steiner, G.A. 170, p.260.   The entire verse runs as follows:

Oh Sun, of this world thou king
All thy race fair Luna doth sustain
And Mercury quickly binds you in marriage
Though all in vain lacking Venus' patronage.
As chosen man Mars sets his face
Sustained for you is Jupiter's grace
That thereby Saturn old and gray
Himself in many colors doth array.

According to the editor of G.A. 170, Steiner follows the text of *Basilius Valentinus: Chymische Schriften*, Hamburg, 1717, p.144:

O Sonn', ein Koenig dieser Welt
Die Luna dein Geschlecht erhaelt
Merkur kopuliert euch fix
Ohn' Venus' Gunst erreicht ihr alls nicht
Welch Marten sich als Mann erkoren
Jovis G'nad ist euch unverloren
Damit Saturnus, alt und greis
In vielen Farben sich erweis.

111. G.A. 243, p.251 ff. (Rudolf Steiner, *True and False Paths in Spiritual Investigation*, p.219 ff.)
112. G.A. 45, p.29 ff; G.A. 170, lectures 7 and 14.
113. G.A. 170, p. 251. (See preceeding footnote.)
114. *Die Drei*, XXXI, 1961/3, p.152. The passages cited by Poppe are from V.F. Hoffmann's edition of Baader's works, Leipzig 1851-1860, Vol XIII, p.77 ff.
115. Letter to the author, July 17, 1979.
116. *Musicalische Paradoxal-Discourse oder Ungemeine Vorstellungen, wie die Musica einen hohen und goettlichen Ursprung habe*, Quedlinburg, 1707, Ch. XXIII. Relevant passages are cited by Pfrogner in *Zwoelfordnung...*, p. 271.
117. See *Zwoelfordnung...*, p.158